D0991976

COMMUNICATION LAW

The Supreme Court and the First Amendment

Joseph J. Hemmer, Jr.

Austin & Winfield, Publishers
Lanham • New York • Oxford

Copyright © 2000 by
Austin & Winfield, Publishers

4720 Boston Way
Lanham, Maryland 20706

12 Hid's Copse Rd.
Cumnor Hill, Oxford OX2 9JJ

Library of Congress Cataloging-in-Publication Data

Hemmer, Joseph J.
Communication law : the Supreme Court and
The First Amendment / Joseph J. Hemmer, Jr.
p.   cm.
Includes index.
1.   Mass media—Law and legislation—United States. 2. Press law—United
States. 3. Freedom of speech—United States. 4. Constitutional law—United States.
I. Title.
KF2750.H46   2000   342.73'0853—dc21   00—044339 CIP

ISBN 1-57292-151-X (cloth: alk. ppr.)
ISBN 1-57292-150-1 (pbk: alk. ppr.)

⊖™The paper used in this publication meets the minimum
requirements of American National Standard for Information
Sciences—Permanence of Paper for Printed Library Materials,
ANSI Z39.48—1984

To my students:
thanks for making work enjoyable

ABOUT THE AUTHOR

JOSEPH J HEMMER JR., is Professor and Chairperson of the Communication Department at Carroll College, Waukesha, Wisconsin.

Dr. Hemmer has previously published four volumes on the subject of communication law — Communication Under Law: Free Speech (Scarecrow, 1979), Communication Under Law: Journalistic Expression (Scarecrow, 1980), The Supreme Court and the First Amendment (Praeger, 1986), and Communication Law: Judicial Interpretation of the First Amendment (Burgess-Alpha, 1992). He has published periodically in the field of communication studies: his articles have appeared in the Quarterly Journal of Speech, Central States Speech Journal, Southern Speech Journal, Speaker and Gavel, Journal of the Wisconsin Communication Association, Communications and the Law, The Howard Journal of Communications, and Free Speech Yearbook.

Dr. Hemmer has served as Editor of the Journal of the Wisconsin Communication Association, and as Guest Editor for an issue of The Howard Journal of Communications. He has also served as President of the Wisconsin Communication Association and as President of the Carroll College Faculty. In 1982, he received the Andrew T. Weaver Award, presented annually by the WCA to the outstanding communication professor in the state of Wisconsin. In 1996, Dr. Hemmer received the Benjamin F. Richason Jr., Faculty Award For Excellence in Teaching, Research, and Educational Innovation from Carroll College. He currently holds the Cordelia Pierce Endowed Chair in Communication at Carroll College.

Dr. Hemmer holds a B.S. from Wisconsin State College (Oshkosh), an M.A. from Bradley University, and a Ph.D. from the University of Wisconsin.

TABLE OF CONTENTS

PREFACE

Communication law and judicial interpretation of the First Amendment — the subject matter of this book — influences our lives on a daily basis. Many First Amendment questions beg for answers. To what extent can dissatisfied citizens protest against the foreign and domestic policies of government? In what ways can municipalities restrict the assembly and petition rights of socially-conscious groups? Can school boards or parent groups ban books from school libraries? Should obscenity and pornography guidelines apply differently for children than for adults? When may a person refuse to be communicated with? Are celebrities entitled to control their own publicity? How can celebrities protect themselves from defamatory remarks of their critics? Do courts adequately balance the rights of criminals with the rights of a free press? Under what conditions may the government refuse to release information to the news media? Are the air waves sufficiently regulated? How can society protect itself from deceptive advertising? Should the flow of communication through cyberspace be controlled? These questions, and many others, are the focus of this book. Clearly, an understanding of how legislatures and courts have grappled with these First Amendment issues is a vital concern for students and, in fact, for all citizens.

This work deals with First Amendment issues that affect the general public, academic institutions, business enterprises, journalistic professionals, government agencies, and the broadcast industry. Accordingly, the book contains chapters entitled Dissent, Association, Academic Freedom, Obscenity, Silence, Defamation, Privacy, Copyright, News, Fair Trial, Electronic Media, and Advertising.

The book is designed as an introductory textbook for communication-law courses in journalism, communication, and political science departments. The book can also serve the needs of journalists and various business communicators as an encyclopedia of First Amendment case law. It is not intended as a substitute for in-depth research. Readers are encouraged to consult the complete case accounts found in <u>Supreme Court Reporter</u>. The book is intended as a brief description and analysis of communication law decisions. The work considers Supreme Court cases relevant to a variety of free-speech and free-press issues. The focus is on recent and precedent-setting cases. Some important lower-court cases are considered as well. The methodology involves a description of the communication act under challenge, analysis of the issue facing the Court justices, and explanation of reasons behind the opinion. Some concern is given to the impact of the decision on case law and societal behavior. The cut-off date for the material discussed is the Supreme Court's decisions through March, 2000.

My gratitude is extended to the individuals who provided valuable assistance in the preparation of <u>Communication Law: The Supreme Court and the First Amendment</u>. In particular, I am thankful to Sharon Hart, Bob

Beitz, Keri Brezgel, Susan Klingberg, Kristy Wisniewski, and Leah Michaelson who researched cases and edited sections of the manuscript. My appreciation also goes to Vicki Buinowski, Jane Mikolajczak, Beth Binder, Jennifer Kohlbeck, and Stephanie Book, who typed various sections of the manuscript. I am indebted to Terry Serio, who provided valuable technical assistance in establishing format guidelines for the manuscript. Finally, I want to thank my wife for putting up with me while I was engrossed in this work. To Joy goes my heartfelt thanks.

Joseph J. Hemmer Jr.
Carroll College
Waukesha, Wisconsin
April 1, 2000

CHAPTER 1

FOUNDATIONS OF COMMUNICATION LAW

Freedom of expression has been encouraged in the United States since the foundation of the country. Yet, within a climate favorable to free expression, legislators and jurists have debated about which freedoms should be guaranteed, and which restraints should be imposed on expression in a democratic society. This debate has existed since the inception of the government, and continues to the present time.

SOURCES OF FREE EXPRESSION

Delegates to the Constitutional Convention in 1787 adopted the Constitution of the United States. While the Constitution delineated such governmental powers as the right to collect taxes, declare war, and regulate trade, it provided few personal guarantees. Accordingly, the first congress penned the Bill of Rights — ten amendments to the Constitution. In so doing, the framers of the government responded to the influence of John Locke, John Milton, Thomas Jefferson, Thomas Paine, and James Madison, and acknowledged that citizens possess certain inborn rights that the federal government may not violate.

Since December 15, 1791, the day the bill went into effect, the First Amendment has been the basic safeguard of freedom of expression. In part, the First Amendment provides that "Congress shall make no law...abridging the freedom of speech, or the press, or the right of the people peaceably to assemble and to petition the government for a redress of grievances." While the language of the amendment seems clear, the purpose, scope, and function of its meaning have been subject to dispute. Throughout the nineteenth century, individual states guaranteed freedom of expression when they adopted their constitutions. Yet, the states disagreed among themselves regarding what constituted an abuse of free expression. In 1868, in an effort to eliminate such discrepancies, Congress passed the Fourteenth Amendment, which declares that no state shall "deprive any person of life, liberty, or property, without due process of law." For several decades, however, states continued to apply their own divergent concepts of free expression. Finally, in <u>Gitlow v. New York</u>, 45 S.Ct. 625 (1925), the Supreme Court cited the Fourteenth Amendment in declaring that freedom of expression was protected from abuse by the states.

> Freedom of speech and the press — which are protected by the First Amendment from abridgement by Congress — are among the fundamental personal rights and "liberties" protected by the due process clause of the Fourteenth Amendment from impairment by the States.

As affirmed in <u>Gitlow</u>, the First and Fourteenth Amendments provide a "national" legal basis for the freedoms associated with expression.

In addition, communication rights are guaranteed by other amendments contained in the Bill of Rights. The initial words of the Fourth Amendment state: "The right of the people to be secure in their persons, houses, papers, and effects, against unreasonable searches and seizures, shall not be violated...." This amendment provides the basis for the right of privacy. The Fifth Amendment is also relevant to freedom of expression. It provides that "No person...shall be compelled in any criminal case to be a witness against himself, nor be deprived of life, liberty, or property, without due process of law." The former part of the Fifth Amendment provides for a right to remain silent while the latter section provides for procedural safeguards against unwarranted usurpations of personal liberty. The Sixth Amendment concerns the right of the accused to a fair trial. It guarantees that "in all criminal prosecutions the accused shall enjoy the right to a speedy and public trial" and "to be confronted with the witnesses against him [or her]." All of these amendments have an impact on the public's communication rights.

PURPOSES OF FREE EXPRESSION

Why did the founding fathers establish freedom of expression? What purposes of free expression did they envision for a democratic society? Four specific benefits can be identified: freedom of expression facilitates self government, provides for social change, fosters a search for the truth, and enables individuals to achieve human dignity.

SELF GOVERNMENT

Without unimpaired discussion and dissemination of ideas, self government is but a hollow fantasy. Democracy requires that all views be heard and analyzed in the "marketplace of ideas." A principal function of the First Amendment is to guarantee ample opportunity for citizens to determine, debate, and resolve public issues. Free expression is the tool by which democracy is exercised.

SOCIAL CHANGE

Free expression provides a mechanism for social change by allowing those not in power to criticize weaknesses within the system. Such criticism prevents established authority from becoming isolated from the people. Free expression, by its very nature, produces an atmosphere where new ideas constantly challenge older ones. Free expression combats the inherent tendency of those in power to maintain the status quo.

SEARCH FOR TRUTH

Only through the clash of the widest diversity of ideas via legitimate forums of communication can the "truth" be discerned. The history of the United States, in fact, of civilization, emphasizes that one person's truth is another's falsehood. Ideas which once held sway as official "truth" have been displaced by beliefs which in turn have yielded to other "truths." The freedom to search for truth ought not to be fettered, no matter which orthodoxy may be challenged. Liberty of thought soon shrivels without liberty of expression.

HUMAN DIGNITY

Freedom of expression grants to each citizen the dignity of individual thought. People can speak their innermost thoughts without fear or shame. Each individual is thus able to develop his or her potential to the fullest, and to take his or her place in society as a productive citizen — a unique human being secure in his or her "natural rights." An individual may *feel* free in any society, no matter how autocratic, if he or she accepts the rules of that society, but he or she can only *be* free in a society that is willing to allow those rules to be questioned.

THE LEGAL SYSTEM

The United States is a nation of laws. In other words, in America human behavior is regulated by specific rules of conduct which are accompanied by appropriate sanctions for enforcement. Law originates in a variety of ways — common law, equity law, statutory law, constitutional law, administrative rule, and executive order. Each type contributes to the body of law that governs this nation. Several laws were developed with the expressed intention of regulating communication behavior. The remainder of Chapter 1 describes and illustrates how laws are established by the legal system and interpreted by the judicial system.

COMMON LAW

During the 200 years following the Norman conquest in the 11th century, a system of law worked out by judges came to replace the collection of religious customs that had characterized Anglo-Saxon society. The common law, which represented the thinking of justices rather than the customs of the people, served as a sharp contrast to the ecclesiastical (church) law prevalent at the time. This body of law constituted a great legacy handed down to the American colonists by Great Britain. The system worked well in colonial America, a new land of developing problems, because the common law functioned inductively (rule established after consideration of the case) rather than deductively (rule expounded and then strictly applied to the case). A historical example of common law, brought to America by the colonists, involved a strong sentiment against prior restraints. Colonial courts rejected such practices. A modern example of common law, established during the 20th century, concerned the right of privacy. As mass media became pervasive throughout society, courts in several states allowed individuals to sue those persons who invaded their privacy. The decisions established precedents for other courts to follow. Eventually, a right to privacy became embedded throughout the legal system.

Fundamental to common law, or case law, is the concept of *stare decisis* (let the decision stand); judges should consider previous decisions and apply established precedents. This practice has occurred frequently in the development of communication law. For example, in determining the specific obligations of the plaintiff in libel suits, courts turn to precedents established by the Supreme Court in such cases as New York Times Company v. Sullivan, 84 S.Ct. 710 (1964), Gertz v. Welch, 94 S.Ct. 2997 (1974), and Wolston v. Reader's Digest

Association, 99 S.Ct. 2701 (1979). Sometimes, the Court will establish and then overturn its own precedent. For example, in Valentine v. Chrestensen, 62 S.Ct. 920 (1942), the Court determined that commercial advertising did not qualify as protected expression, but reversed its stand in Virginia State Board of Pharmacy v. Virginia Citizens Consumer Council, 96 S.Ct. 1817 (1976).

The cases decided by a specific court are gathered in a case reporter for that particular court. The cases are collected chronologically; each has its own separate citation. For example, Miller v. California, 93 S.Ct. 2607 (1973) is the citation for a precedent setting obscenity decision. The case can be located on page 2607 of volume 93 in the Supreme Court Reporter. For another example, United States v. Dickinson, 465 F.2d 496 (1972), a federal appeals court case that dealt with gag orders, can be found on page 496 in volume 465 of the Federal Reporter.

LAW OF EQUITY

Equity law is another judge-influenced contribution to the legal system. Equity law developed at the same general time as the common law. During the 14th and 15th centuries the English courts became rigid and narrow in deciding cases, but disappointed litigants were able to take their complaints to the king for resolution. An aggrieved individual had to establish that there was no adequate remedy under the common law and that a special judicial hearing was needed. Decisions in such instances were made on the basis of fairness or "equity." To this day, the procedures under equity are more flexible than those under common law. Equity cases are not heard by juries; rulings come from judicial decree. Although precedents are considered, judges remain free to act according to what their conscience thinks is fair. There are some contemporary circumstances in which faithfully applying the law simply does not result in a fair decision. For example, a judge hearing a case which involves a public demonstration (a First Amendment right) that disrupts public peace and safety can order preventative measures such as an injunction or restraining order (an equitable ruling). The distinction today between equity law and common law has blurred; the cases are heard by the same judges and they take place in the same court rooms. There is no clear distinction as in earlier historical periods.

STATUTORY LAW

Legislative bodies at the federal, state, county, and local levels pass statutes which deal with problems affecting groups of people or society as a whole. This contrasts with common law, which usually deals with individual instances. Statutory law can anticipate problems; a statute may prohibit a specific behavior. Contemporary criminal laws are statutory laws. Passage of a law, however, is rarely the final word on the subject. The judicial system becomes involved in the process of interpreting what the statute means. At the city and county levels, these legislative enactments are called ordinances. Statutes and ordinances are systematically arranged by subject, numbered, indexed, and printed in bound volumes. These formal compilations, which are updated frequently, are called codes. Federal statutes are published in United States Codes, abbreviated as "U.S.C." An example of statutory communication law consists of the various shield laws passed in several states to protect a news reporter's use of confidential sources.

CONSTITUTIONAL LAW

The United States is governed by constitutions at the federal, state, county, and local levels. These documents organize the government, outline the duties and responsibilities of the three branches, and guarantee basic rights to the people. The U. S. Constitution is the supreme law of the land. No law that conflicts with the Constitution is valid. Constitutional law includes not only the language of the document itself, but also the meaning as interpreted by the court system. It is difficult to change constitutional law. In order to change the federal constitution, an amendment must be proposed by a vote of two-thirds of the members of congress and ratified by a three-fourths vote of the states. The First Amendment to the Constitution is especially vital to communication law because it established the basic freedoms of expression. State and local constitutions also contain free speech guarantees that roughly approximate the wording of the First Amendment. State and local constitutions may not restrict personal freedoms to a degree greater than the federal constitution, but they may provide greater liberty. For example, a state may protect expression in a privately owned shopping center, contrary to the U. S. Supreme Court's interpretation of the First Amendment. That was the Court's determination in PruneYard Shopping Center v. Robins, 100 S.Ct. 2035 (1980).

ADMINISTRATIVE RULE

During the 19th and 20th centuries, the task of governing America became increasingly complex. Many issues facing the nation required specialized knowledge and expertise. Numerous federal agencies, boards, and commissions were created to deal with these issues. For example, the Federal Communications Commission is the administrative agency with regulatory power over network and cable broadcasting. The Federal Trade Commission has regulatory power over the advertising industry. Persons dissatisfied with a ruling by an agency may seek reversal by appealing to a court. A ruling may be overturned if the agency exceeds its authority or lacks evidentiary basis to support its rule.

EXECUTIVE ORDER

In some instances, an executive officer — President, Governor, Mayor — has the power to make law. For example, after the Japanese attack on Pearl Harbor, President Franklin Delano Roosevelt issued an executive order which declared that the successful prosecution of World War II required that the government take "every possible protection against...sabotage to national-defense material." Subsequently, Americans of Japanese ancestry were forced to move away from the Pacific coast. This executive law was upheld by the Supreme Court in Korematsu v. United States, 65 S.Ct. 193 (1944).

THE JUDICIAL SYSTEM

Trial and appellate courts are common to the judicial system. Trial courts, also known as courts of original jurisdiction, have a fact-finding function, such as determining the guilt or innocence of the accused. Appellate courts have an evaluative function; they study the record of a lower court to ensure that proper procedures were used and that the law was applied correctly. Only trial courts employ juries. All courts have the power of judicial review, that is, the right to declare a law invalid because it violates a constitutional provision. The judicial system consists of federal and state courts.

FEDERAL COURTS

The federal system includes the Supreme Court, district courts, and circuit courts. The Supreme Court of the United States is the oldest court, having been in operation since 1789. It is comprised of the chief justice and eight associate justices. The Supreme Court exercises both original (limited to a few specific instances) and appellate jurisdictions. Its primary task is to hear appeals of cases already decided by lower federal courts and state courts of last resort. Out of more than 5000 petitions, the Supreme Court accepts only a few hundred cases annually for a full hearing, and issues about 140 formal opinions each year. The fact that the Supreme Court declines to review a lower court case establishes no precedent; in such cases the lower court decision stands. There are occasions when the Supreme Court agrees to decide a case and then merely affirms the opinion of the lower court rather than issuing its own opinion.

A case may come before the Supreme Court through a direct appeal or via a request for a *writ of certiorari*, a discretionary order issued by the Court when it feels an important legal issue has been raised by a petitioner who has exhausted all other legal remedies. Once a case is accepted, both sides are expected to submit legal briefs which are studied by the justices. Then, each side has a limited amount of time to present oral arguments. In important cases, "friends of the court" (*amici curae*) are allowed to present briefs and offer oral arguments. After a period of discussion, the Court prepares its opinion(s). One of the justices voting in the majority prepares the court's opinion. A justice who agrees with the decision but has different reasons than the majority may prepare a concurring opinion. Justices who disagree with the majority may prepare a dissenting opinion. A justice may concur in part and dissent in part of the opinion. The Court can offer a *per curiam* opinion, that is, an unsigned opinion drafted by one or more members of the majority. The high court can prepare a memorandum order, that is, announce the decision but offer no opinion. If the case ends in a tie vote, the decision of the lower court is affirmed and no opinion is written. If none of the opinions attract the five votes necessary for a majority, the view with the most support becomes the plurality opinion. Supreme Court opinions are published in <u>Supreme Court Reporter</u>, <u>United States Reports</u>, and <u>United States Supreme Court Reports, Lawyer's Edition</u>.

Congress created district courts in the Federal Judiciary Act of 1789. There is at least one district court in each of the 50 states and the District of Columbia. The primary duty of these courts is to serve as trial courts for a variety of criminal and civil matters. All federal judges are appointed by the President and must be confirmed by the Senate. Appointment is for life. The only way a federal judge can be removed is by impeachment. Political affiliation plays a major role in the appointment of federal judges. District court decisions are published in the <u>Federal Supplement</u>.

There are 13 circuits of the Court of Appeals, also created by the Federal Judiciary Act of 1789. Twelve "circuit" courts serve a specific geographic area, the thirteenth has nationwide jurisdiction over certain kinds of cases, such as patent and customs appeals. The nation is divided into circuits, each of which is served by one court. Typically, a panel of three judges hears a case. In such instances, two judges constitute a majority and may issue a majority opinion. Sometimes, a case is considered so important that all justices serving a particular circuit will decide the case. This is known as hearing a case *en banc*. Appellate cases are decided by judges alone, unassisted by jurors. Federal appeals court decisions are not binding outside their jurisdiction but are often influential. For example, the court serving the District of Columbia is highly influential on federal regulatory matters including decisions of the Federal Communications Commission and the Federal Trade Commission. If an appellate court discovers that a trial court made an error, the case may be remanded (sent back) to a lower court for a new trial or for action consistent with the court's opinion. At times, courts from various circuits rule differently regarding the same legal issue. In these instances, the U.S. Supreme Court often intervenes, establishing a uniform precedent applicable to the entire country. Opinions of the courts of appeals (circuits) appear in the Federal Reporter.

STATE COURTS

The state court system duplicates the federal structure at several levels. State courts have jurisdiction within their borders over matters of law not designated by the U.S. Constitution as the domain of the federal government. At the lowest level are courts of limited jurisdiction, for example traffic court. Also at the lower level are county and state trial courts that hear jury cases. There is usually an appeals court at the intermediate level and every state has a supreme court, although some states do not call it that. The state supreme court reviews only the most important cases. Most state judges are elected in a nonpartisan process, though in some states judges are appointed. State court opinions are published in the National Reporter System, which includes such volumes as Atlantic Reporter, North Eastern Reporter, North Western Reporter, Southern Reporter, South Eastern Reporter, South Western Reporter, and Pacific Reporter.

TYPES OF LAWSUITS

There are two kinds of lawsuits. Some cases are civil matters. One party claims another party caused injury, without necessarily doing something that could be considered a crime. Almost any time one party injures another, the resulting lawsuit is a tort action (any civil wrong that creates a right for a victim to sue the perpetrator). The party who commences the action is the plaintiff; the person against whom the suit is brought is the defendant. A judge may grant a summary judgment to either the plaintiff or defendant if the judge believes that one party should win as a matter of law. A summary judgment terminates the suit in its early stages, saving attorney's fees and avoiding unpredictable jury verdicts. A successful civil suit usually results in the awarding of money damages. If either party is unhappy with the decision, an appeal can be lodged. The person seeking the appeal is the appellant. The other party is the appellee or respondent. The burden of proof in a civil case is described as "a preponderance of the evidence."

A criminal suit involves the machinery of the county or state prosecutor who brings charges against an individual who is thought to have committed a crime. In the federal system a suspect must be indicted by a grand jury, a panel of 21 citizens. After being charged, the defendant is arraigned, at which time a formal reading of the charge occurs. The defendant may either plead guilty and be sentenced by the judge or he or she may plead not guilty, in which case a trial is scheduled. It is not uncommon that pretrial hearings precede the trial. The burden of proof is much tougher in a criminal case; the prosecutor must show guilt "beyond a reasonable doubt."

JUDICIAL TESTS

Even though the Supreme Court has generally upheld the free and unimpaired dissemination of information and ideas, various justices have held divergent views regarding the nature and scope of the First Amendment. Accordingly, the justices have established competing ways of interpreting the First Amendment: clear and present danger, bad tendency, balancing, preferred position, no protection, and absolutism. These judicial tests, as illustrated in the chart below, can be classified by the amount of freedom or control they grant to expression.

Freedom_____Control

absolutism	preferred position	clear and present danger	balancing	bad tendency	no protection

CLEAR AND PRESENT DANGER

Justice Oliver Wendell Holmes introduced the "clear and present danger" test in Schenck v. United States, 39 S.Ct. 247 (1919).

> The most stringent protection of free speech would not protect a man in falsely shouting fire in a theatre and causing a panic.... The question in every case is whether the words used are in such a nature as to create a clear and present danger that they will bring about the substantive evils that Congress has the right to prevent.

In Abrams v. United States 40 S.Ct. 17 (1919), Holmes clarified the test: The government may punish expression "that produces or is intending to produce a clear and imminent danger that it will bring about forthwith certain substantive evils." Holmes emphasized that "the power is greater in time of war than in time of peace because war opens dangers that do not exist at other times." Eight years later, in Whitney v. California, 47 S.Ct. 641 (1927), Justice Louis Brandeis elaborated on the doctrine:

> To justify suppression of free speech there must be reasonable ground to fear that serious evil will result if free speech is practiced. There must be reasonable ground to believe that the danger apprehended is imminent. There must be reasonable ground to believe that the evil to be prevented is a serious one.... In order to support a finding of clear and present danger it must be shown either that immediate serious violence was to be expected or was advocated, or that the past conduct furnished reason to believe that such advocacy was then contemplated.

In Bridges v. California, 62 S.Ct. 190 (1941), the Court stressed three elements that had to exist in order to find a "clear and present danger": 1) the circumstances must involve a "substantial evil," 2) the anticipated result must be "extremely serious," and 3) the "degree of imminence" of the danger must be extremely high.

The "clear and present danger" test provided guidance in a variety of cases throughout the next couple of decades. It was used to decide the constitutionality of convictions under espionage acts in Schenck v. United States, 39 S.Ct. 247 (1919) and Abrams v. United States, 40 S.Ct. 17 (1919), under criminal syndicalism statutes in Gitlow v. New York, 45 S.Ct. 625 (1925) and Whitney v. California, 47 S.Ct. 641 (1927), under an anti-insurrection act in Herndon v. Lowry, 57 S.Ct. 732 (1937), under an antipicketing law in Thornhill v. Alabama, 60 S.Ct. 736 (1940), and under breach-of-the-peace ordinances in Cantwell v. Connecticut, 60 S.Ct. 900 (1940) and Terminiello v. Chicago, 69 S.Ct. 894 (1949). In the 1950s, the Court generally stopped applying the "clear and present danger" test. Still, the test has had some durability, appearing in such cases as Cox v. Louisiana, 85 S.Ct. 476 (1965), and Brandenburg v. Ohio, 89 S.Ct. 1827 (1969).

BAD TENDENCY

In Gitlow v. New York, 45 S.Ct. 625 (1925), Justice Edward Sanford espoused the "bad tendency" test — a standard that conferred low priority to freedom of expression. A legislature, Sanford argued, was entitled to "extinguish the spark without waiting until it has enkindled the flame or blazed into a conflagration."

It cannot reasonably be required to defer the adoption of measures for its own peace and safety until the revolutionary utterances lead to actual disturbances of the public peace or imminent and immediate danger of its own destruction; but it may, in the exercise of its judgement, suppress the threatened danger in its incipiency.

According to this test, any expression that had a tendency to lead to substantial evil could be banned. Under the "bad tendency" test, questionable expression was effectively "nipped in the bud."

More than a decade later, in Herndon v. Lowry, 57 S.Ct. 732 (1937) and Bridges v. California, 625 S.Ct. 190 (1941), the Supreme Court rejected the "bad tendency" doctrine. In Herndon, Justice Owen Roberts argued: "The power of a State to abridge freedom of expression and of assembly is the exception rather that the rule, and the penalizing even of utterances of a defined character must find its justification in a reasonable apprehension of danger to organized government." In Bridges, Justice Hugo Black wrote: "In accordance with what we have said on the 'clear and present danger' cases, neither 'inherent tendency' nor 'reasonable tendency' is enough to justify a restriction of free expression." In Herndon and Bridges, the Court returned to the "clear and present danger" test and set aside the notion that speech could be banned if it engendered a "bad tendency."

BALANCING

The "balancing" test recognizes that when other rights conflict with the First Amendment — for example, the right to fair trial, right to privacy, right to peace and order — the competing rights are balanced to determine which has priority. Chief Justice Fred Vinson fashioned the "balancing" test in American Communications Association, C.I.O. v. Douds, 70 S.Ct. 674 (1950).

When particular conduct is regulated in the interest of public order, and the regulation results in an indirect, conditional, partial abridgement of speech, the duty of the Courts is to determine which of these two conflicting interests demands the greater protection under the particular circumstances presented.

The "balancing" test appeared again in Justice Felix Frankfurter's opinion in Dennis v. United States, 71 S.Ct. 857 (1951): "The demands of free speech in a democratic society, as well as the interest in national security, are better served by candid and informed weighing of the competing interests, within the confines of the judicial process."

In Barenblatt v. United States, 79 S.Ct. 1081 (1959), Justice John Harlan employed the test; he noted that when First Amendment rights are asserted to prevent governmental inquiry, "resolution of the issues always involves a balancing by the courts of the competing private and public interests at stake in the particular circumstances shown." In

Konigsberg v. State Bar of California, 81 S.Ct. 997 (1961), Harlan claimed that when constitutional protections conflict with the exercise of valid governmental power, "a reconciliation must be effected, and that perforce requires an appropriate weighing of the respective interests involved." In United States v. Robel, 88 S.Ct. 419 (1967), Chief Justice Earl Warren acknowledged the "delicate and difficult task" facing the Court when "Congress' exercise of one of its enumerated powers clashes with those individual liberties protected by the Bill of Rights." In such instances, a balancing of interests must be undertaken.

A limitation of the balancing test should be noted — the judicial opinions offer little guideline for future cases because they apply only to the specifics of the particular case. Nonetheless, the test has been used extensively by the Court.

PREFERRED POSITION

The "preferred position" test resembles "balancing," except that the test is balanced in favor of the First Amendment. In Murdock v. Pennsylvania, 63 S.Ct. 870 (1943), Justice William Douglas noted that "freedom of press, freedom of speech...are in a preferred position." Justice Wiley Rutledge strengthened the test in Thomas v. Collins, 65 S.Ct. 315 (1945).

> The case confronts us again with the duty our system places on this Court to say where the individual's freedom ends and the State's power begins. Choice on that border, now as always delicate, is perhaps more so where the usual presumption supporting legislation is balanced by the preferred place given in our scheme to the great, the indispensable freedoms secured by the First Amendment. That priority gives these liberties a sanctity and a sanction not permitting dubious intrusions.

In Marsh v. Alabama, 66 S.Ct. 276 (1946), Justice Hugo Black noted that in balancing the rights of property owners against the rights of the people to enjoy freedom of expression, the Court must "remain mindful of the fact that the latter occupy a preferred position."

A few years later, in Kovacs v. Cooper, 69 S.Ct. 448 (1949), Justices Felix Frankfurter and Stanley Reed reassessed the "preferred position" doctrine. Frankfurter considered it "a mischievous phrase, if it carries the thought, which it may subtly imply, that any law touching communication is infected with presumptive validity." He suggested that "various forms of modern so-called 'mass communications' raise issues that were not implied in the means of communication known or contemplated by Franklin and Jefferson and Madison." In Kovacs, Frankfurter upheld the regulation of communication emanating from sound trucks: "Only a disregard of vital differences between natural speech...and the noise of sound trucks would give sound trucks the constitutional rights accorded to the unaided human voice." Justice Reed also supported the regulation: "The preferred position of freedom of speech in a society that cherishes liberty for all does not require legislators to be insensible to claims by citizens to comfort and convenience. To enforce freedom of speech in disregard of the rights of others would be harsh and arbitrary in itself." According to Reed, even though expression enjoys a preferred position, it is not immune from regulation.

NO PROTECTION

In <u>Konigsberg v. State Bar of California</u>, 81 S.Ct. 997 (1961), the Supreme Court acknowledged that "certain forms of speech, or speech in certain contexts, has been considered outside the scope of constitutional protection." In <u>Chaplinsky v. New Hampshire</u>, 62 S.Ct. 766 (1942), Justice Frank Murphy offered specific examples:

> There are certain well-defined and narrowly limited classes of speech, the prevention and punishment of which has never been thought to raise any Constitutional problem. These include the lewd and obscene, the profane, the libelous, and the insulting or "fighting words" — those which by their very utterance inflict injury or tend to incite an immediate breach of the peace.

In <u>Roth v. United States</u>, 77 S.Ct. 1304 (1957), Justice William Brennan affirmed that libel and obscenity fall "outside the protection intended for speech and press." In <u>Valentine v. Chrestensen</u>, 62 S. Ct. 920 (1942), Justice Owen Roberts limited the protection awarded to "commercial speech."

> This court has unequivocally held that the streets are proper places for the exercise of the freedom of communicating information and disseminating opinion and that [government]...may not unduly burden or proscribe its employment in these public thoroughfares. We are equally clear that the Constitution imposes no such restraint on government as respects purely commercial advertising.

Clearly, expression which falls within certain categories (obscenity, defamation, fighting words, commercial speech) has been judged to violate the right to personal dignity. Such expression is entitled to no protection.

ABSOLUTISM

During the 1950s, Justices Black and Douglas argued that the First Amendment denied the government any power to abridge expression;

in their opinion, any law that restricted free speech and press was unconstitutional. The "absolutist" test was designed to enlarge the scope of expression protected by the Constitution. The position was described in Black's dissenting opinion in <u>Konigsberg v. State Bar of California</u>, 81 S.Ct. 997 (1961): "I believe that the First Amendment's unequivocal command that there shall be no abridgement of the rights of free speech and assembly shows that the men who drafted our Bill of Rights did all the "balancing" that was to be done in this field." Black reiterated his belief in "absolutism" in <u>Ginzburg v. United States</u>, 86 S.Ct. 942 (1966): "I believe the Federal Government is without any power whatever under the Constitution to put any type of burden on speech and expression of ideas of any kind." Black again stressed "absolutism" in <u>New York Times Company v. United States</u>, 91 S.Ct. 2140 (1971), when he discussed the test from a historical perspective.

> The Bill of Rights changed the original Constitution into a new charter under which no branch of government could abridge the people's freedoms of press, speech, religion, and assembly. Yet the Solicitor General argues and some members of the Court appear to agree that the general powers of the Government adopted in the original Constitution should be interpreted to limit and restrict the specific and emphatic guarantees of the Bill of Rights adopted later. I can imagine no greater perversion of history. Madison and the other Framers of the First Amendment, able men that they were, wrote in language they earnestly believed could never be misunderstood: "Congress shall make no law...abridging the freedom...of the press...." Both the history and language of the First Amendment support the view that the press must be left free to publish news, whatever the source, without censorship, injunctions, or prior restraints.

The "absolutist" test received support from Justice Douglas, who, in <u>Ginzburg</u>, claimed that "the First Amendment allows all ideas to be expressed whether orthodox, popular, offbeat, or repulsive." He did not think it was permissible for the Court "to draw lines between the 'good' and the 'bad' and be true to the constitutional mandate to let all ideas alone." Under the U.S. Constitution, "all regulation of control of expression is barred."

The "absolutist" test has found few proponents. In fact, the "absolutist" view never received support from a majority of Supreme Court justices.

CONCLUSION

Throughout history, Supreme Court justices have applied a variety of tests while interpreting First Amendment freedoms. Application of the specific tests has varied with the issue facing the Court, the historical climate of the times, and the predispositions of individual justices. This book examines significant and recent First Amendment cases in terms of how Supreme Court reasoning has shaped communication law.

RECOMMENDED READING

Anderson, David A., "The Origins of the Press Clause," UCLA Law Review 30 (1983), 455-541.

Bernstein, J. M., "Was Warren Burger Antipress?" Communications and the Law 10 (1988), 19-30.

Blasi, Vincent, "The Checking Value in First Amendment Theory," American Bar Foundation Research Journal (1977), 521-649.

Bloustein, Edward J., "The First Amendment 'Bad Tendency' of Speech Doctrine," Rutgers Law Review 43 (1991) 507-538.

Cline, Rebecca, and Timothy R. Cline, "The Opinions of William O. Douglas: Defining and Defending Freedom of Speech," Free Speech Yearbook 20 (1981), 78-98.

Farber, D. A., and J. E. Nowak, "Justice Harlan and the First Amendment," Constitution Commentary 2 (Summer 1985), 425-462.

Galloway, Russell W., "Basic Free Speech Analysis," Santa Clara Law Review 31 (1991), 883-995.

Gard, Stephen W., "The Absoluteness of the First Amendment," Nebraska Law Review 58 (1979), 1053-86.

Haiman, Franklyn S., "Justice Brennan and the First Amendment, 1956-1984," Free Speech Yearbook 22 1983), 33-42.

Hasian, Jr., Marouf, "The Rhetorical Turn in First Amendment Scholarship: A case Study of Holmes and the 'Marketplace of Ideas'," Free Speech Yearbook 31 (1993), 42-65.

Hentoff, Tom, "Speech, Harm, and Self Government: Understanding the Ambit of the Clear and Present Danger Test," Columbia Law Review 91 (October, 1991), 1453-94.

Higdon, Philip R., "The Burger Court and the Media: A Ten-Year Perspective," Western New England Law Review 2 (Spring, 1980), 593-680.

Hill, Alfred, "The Puzzling First Amendment Overbreadth Doctrine," Hofstra Law Review 25 (1997), 1063-89.

Hopkins, W. Wat, "Reconsidering the 'Clear and Present Danger' Test: Whence the 'Marketplace of Ideas'?" Free Speech Yearbook 33 (1995), 78-98.

Huffman, John L., Carol Mills, and Denise M. Trauth, "Vanishing Constitutional Standards: The Rehnquist Court and Symbolic Speech," Free Speech Yearbook 32 (1994), 73-85.

Lahav, Nina. "Holmes and Brandeis: Libertarian and Republican Justifications for Free Speech," The Journal of Law and Politics 4 (1988), 451-82.

Lewis, Anthony, "Justice Black and the First Amendment," Alabama Law Review 38 (1987), 289-306.

Nelson, William E., "Justice Byron R. White: A Modern Federalist and a New Deal Liberal," Brigham Young University Law Review (1994), 313-348.

Napoli, Philip M., "The Marketplace of Ideas Metaphor in Communications Regulation," Journal of Communication 49 (1999), 151-182.

Osborn, Chrysta, "Constitutional Scrutiny and Speech: Eroding the Bedrock Principles of the First Amendment," Southwestern Law Journal 44 (1990), 1013-1044.

Rodgers, Raymond S., "Absolutism and Natural Law Argument: William O. Douglas on Freedom of Expression," Southern Speech Communication Journal 48 (Fall, 1982), 22-37.

Schauer, Frederick, "The First Amendment As Ideology," William and Mary Law Review 33 (1992), 853-869.

Stone, Geoffrey R., "Justice Brennan and the Freedom of Speech: A First Amendment Odyssey," University of Pennsylvania Law Review 139 (1991), 1333-1355.

Stone, Geoffrey R., "The Burger Court and the Political Process: Whose First Amendment?" Harvard Journal of Law and Public Policy 10 (Winter 1987), 46-118.

Stonecipher, Harry W., "Safeguarding Speech and Press Guarantees: Preferred Position Postulate Reexamined," in The First Amendment Reconsidered: New Perspectives on the Meaning of Freedom of Speech and Press, Bill F. Chamberlin and Charlene J. Brown, (eds.), New York: Longman, 1982, 89-128.

Strong, Frank R., "Fifty Years of 'Clear and Present Danger': From Schenck to Brandenburg — and beyond," The Supreme Court Review (1969), 41-80.

Strossen, Nadine, "The Free Speech Jurisprudence of the Rehnquist Court," Free Speech Yearbook 29 (1991), 83-95.

Torke, James W., "Some Notes on the Uses of the Clear and Present Danger Test," Bringham Young University Law Review (1978), 1-37.

Yassky, David, "Eras of the First Amendment," Columbia Law Review 91 (November, 1991), 1699-1755.

CHAPTER 2

DISSENT

Contradictory tendencies permeate the history of dissent in the United States. During certain periods, a strong zest for dissent characterized citizen behavior. For example, when the country was established, colonial patriots voiced opposition to an oppressive English monarchy. Prior to the Civil War, abolitionists expressed dissatisfaction with the institution of slavery. In the early 1900s, women waged hunger strikes to call attention to a government which restricted the right to vote on the basis of gender. During the 1960s and 1970s, student activists protested against U.S. involvement in the Vietnam War. Throughout the 1980s and 1990s, pro life advocates marched against abortion doctors and clinics. At times, in an effort to promote stability, the government has punished extremism in dissent. Especially during times of war and national crisis, the government has restricted forms of dissent that might disturb public order or which might endanger national security. The clash of these conflicting standards — the zeal for dissent versus the maintenance of security and order — presents a significant area of study for students interested in freedom of expression.

FORMS OF DISSENT

The U.S. Supreme Court has established guidelines which regulate various forms of dissent. In so doing, the Court weighed the right to free expression against the public interest in protecting national security and maintaining order.

ADVOCATING OVERTHROW

During the twentieth century, laws have been directed at dissenters who obstruct the military operations of the country or who advocate the overthrow of the government by force or violence. The constitutionality of such laws has been a concern of the Supreme Court. In 1917, shortly after declaring war against Germany, Congress enacted the Selective Service Act in order to raise an army. Another law, the Espionage Act of 1917, prohibited anyone from interfering with the military effort of the United States. The Supreme Court considered the constitutionality of such laws in Schenck v. United States, 39 S.Ct. 247 (1919). Charles Schenck was convicted of distributing leaflets which criticized the military draft and which urged draftees to decline to serve. Supreme Court Justice Oliver Wendell Holmes acknowledged that in ordinary times Schenck would have been within his constitutional rights, but expression designed to obstruct recruiting when the country was at war constituted a "clear and present danger." The Schenck case established that dissent was not absolutely guaranteed, but rather depended upon the circumstances of the case.

During 1919, the Supreme Court upheld three similar convictions. It upheld the conviction of Jacob Frohwerk for publishing newspaper articles designed to cause the refusal to serve in the military. The Court affirmed the conviction of Eugene Debs, who had expressed opposition to U.S. entry into World War I and had approved the behavior of individuals who obstructed military recruitment. Even though Debs had not urged his audience to resist the draft, he was convicted of attempting to obstruct the draft and was sentenced to ten years in prison. The Court also upheld the conviction of Jacob Abrams and five associates who had published and distributed circulars that called for a general strike of munitions workers. Even though there was no evidence that any person actually stopped any kind of war work or that the leaflets actually reached a single munitions worker, the defendants were convicted and sentenced to 20 years in prison. In Abrams v. United States, 40 S.Ct. 17 (1919), Frohwerk v. United States, 39 S.Ct. 249 (1919) and Debs v. United States, 39 S.Ct. 252 (1919), the Supreme Court supported the Schenck decision by affirming that, during wartime, certain forms of advocacy were not protected by the First Amendment.

Shortly after the assassination of President William McKinley, New York passed the Anarchy Act of 1902. This statute forbade the publication or distribution of material advocating the overthrow of the government by force or violence. The Supreme Court decided the constitutionality of this act in Gitlow v. New York, 45 S.Ct. 625

(1925). Benjamin Gitlow and three other members of the left wing of the Socialist Party were indicted for publishing a radical "manifesto" which predicted and urged "mass strikes" by the working classes. The trial court convicted Gitlow and his colleagues and sentenced them to five to ten years of hard labor. The Supreme Court affirmed the convictions. Justice Edward Sanford, writing for the majority, concluded that words that advocate the overthrow of the government may be punished, regardless of whether there is any imminent danger. The Court upheld the convictions on the ground of "bad tendency."

> Such utterances, by their very nature, involve danger to the public peace and to the security of the State. They threaten breaches of the peace and ultimate revolution. And the immediate danger is none the less real and substantial, because the effect of a given utterance cannot be accurately foreseen.

Two years later, the Court heard a case involving the constitutionality of the California Criminal Syndicalism Act. This statute was not directed against the practice of criminal activity, but rather at the preaching of it, and especially at association with persons who advocate it. In the five years following the enactment of the law, 504 persons were arrested and 264 were brought to trial. Anita Whitney, a woman nearing 60 years of age, had attended a convention that established the Communist Labor Party of California. She was convicted on the grounds that the Party was set up to teach criminal syndicalism, and by becoming a member, she had committed a crime. In Whitney v. California, 47 S.Ct. 641 (1927), Justice Sanford affirmed that California could punish utterances "tending" to produce crime or disturb the peace. Furthermore, concerted action involved a more significant threat than isolated words or acts of individuals. Assembling a political party designed to advocate revolution by mass action at some future date was outside constitutional protection. The Court upheld Whitney's conviction because of the "bad tendency" of her act.

In 1937, the Court heard a case involving a similar state law, but this time the justices arrived at a different conclusion. The case involved Dirk DeJonge, who was convicted under the Oregon Criminal Syndicalism Law for participating at a meeting of the Communist Party. The Supreme Court found the statute unconstitutional. Oregon could not cite mere participation in a peaceable assembly as the basis for a criminal charge. Whatever the objectives of the Communist Party, DeJonge was "entitled to discuss the public issues of the day, and in a lawful manner without incitement to violence or crime, to seek redress of alleged grievances. That was the essence of his guaranteed personal liberty." In DeJonge v. Oregon, 57 S.Ct. 255 (1937), the

Court required more than a mere "tendency" toward criminal action as the basis for punishing advocacy. The DeJonge case marked the end of the Court's practice of punishing dissent simply because it had a "bad tendency."

In 1940, Congress passed the Alien Registration Act, which made it a crime to advocate the violent overthrow of the government or to organize or belong to a group advocating it. This act, known as the Smith Act, was designed to control subversive groups. During the 1950s, the Dennis and Yates cases tested the conspiracy provisions of the Smith Act; in 1961, the Scales and Noto cases tested convictions under the membership clause of the act.

Eugene Dennis, Secretary of the Communist Party, was convicted of violating the conspiracy provisions of the Smith Act. The prosecution charged Dennis with knowingly conspiring to organize the Communist Party as a group that advocated the overthrow of the government by violence. Dennis appealed, arguing that he had merely expressed his belief that violence was necessary to attain a Communist form of government in an existing democracy where the ruling class would not permit the transformation to occur peacefully. The Supreme Court held that the government must act when a group dedicated to its overthrow urged its members to strike when the circumstances permitted. Dennis had been "properly and constitutionally convicted for violation of the Smith Act." In Dennis v. United States, 71 S.Ct. 857 (1951), conspiracy to overthrow the government, rather than overthrow itself, was considered adequate to justify suppression of dissent. In all, 29 persons served prison terms under the conspiracy provisions of the Smith Act.

In Yates v. United States, 77 S.Ct. 1064 (1957), the Court provided a different interpretation of the conspiracy section of the Smith Act. Oleta Yates was convicted for conspiring to organize the Communist Party for the purpose of overthrowing the government as soon as circumstances could permit. The Supreme Court reversed the decision. Justice John Harlan claimed that advocacy of forcible overthrow as mere abstract doctrine was within the free-speech protection of the First Amendment. Harlan stressed that "those to whom the advocacy is addressed must be urged to do something, now or in the future, rather than merely to believe in something." In Yates, the Supreme Court distinguished between "advocacy of abstract doctrine," which was permissible, and "advocacy of action," which was not.

The Court further developed the distinction between advocacy of ideas and advocacy of action in Scales v. United States, 81 S.Ct. 1469 (1961). Janius Scales, was convicted under the membership clause of the Smith Act for holding membership in an organization that advocated the overthrow of the government. Scales was sentenced to six years in prison. The Court confirmed Scales' conviction because evidence supported a finding of advocacy of action rather than advocacy of ideas.

> Since the evidence amply showed that [Communist] Party leaders were continually preaching...the inevitability of eventual forcible overthrow, the first and basic question is a narrow one: whether the jury could permissibly infer that such preaching, in whole or in part, was aimed at building up a seditious group and maintaining it in readiness for action at a propitious time,...the kind of indoctrination preparatory to action which was condemned in Dennis.... On this score, we think that the jury, under instructions which fully satisfied the requirements of Yates, was entitled to infer...that advocacy of action was engaged in.

A companion case, Noto v. United States, 81 S.Ct. 1517 (1961), also tested the membership clause. The key point in John Noto's case was insufficiency of evidence. The Supreme Court noted that much of the evidence reflected the Communist Party's teaching, through abstract doctrine, that revolution was inevitable to achieve communism in a capitalist society, but testimony that suggested advocacy of action to accomplish that goal was sparse. In Noto, the evidence was insufficient to show that the Communist Party advocated the forcible overthrow of the government. Following Noto's reversal, the government discontinued pending prosecutions. As a result, Janius Scales was the only person to serve a prison sentence under the membership provision of the Smith Act.

In 1969, the Supreme Court further defined its position on acceptable advocacy. The case involved Clarence Brandenburg, a leader of the Ohio Ku Klux Klan. Brandenburg invited a Cincinnati television newsman to attend a rally. The event was filmed and portions were later broadcast on local and national television. The film showed 12 hooded figures, some of whom carried firearms, gathered around a large wooden cross, uttering derogatory statements about blacks and Jews. One of the scenes showed Brandenburg, in Klan regalia, deliver the following statement: "If our President, our Congress, our Supreme Court, continues to suppress the white, Caucasian race, it's possible that there might have to be some revenge taken." Brandenburg was convicted under the Ohio criminal syndicalism statute; he was fined $1,000 and sentenced to one to ten years' imprisonment. The Supreme Court overturned the conviction, noting that the guarantee of free expression does not allow a state to forbid advocacy "except where such advocacy is directed to inciting or producing imminent lawless action and is likely to incite or produce such action." The statute was unconstitutional because it punished mere advocacy, and assembly with individuals who advocated action. In <u>Brandenburg v. Ohio</u>, 89 S.Ct. 1827 (1969), the Court held that advocacy which does not call for illegal action is protected under the First Amendment.

> More important, speech which calls for illegal action but does not seek immediate action is protected. In addition, speech which calls for immediate illegal action but where there is reason to believe that the audience will not commit the action is also protected.

When compared with the <u>Schenck</u>, <u>Gitlow</u>, and <u>Dennis</u> decisions, it seems clear that the <u>Brandenburg</u> test of advocative incitement allows considerable latitude to dissenters who advocate the overthrow of the government.

PROVOCATIVE WORDS

A situation that is perplexing for police officers occurs when a speaker expresses ideas which cause an audience to become unruly and unmanageable. What is the police officer's duty? Should the speaker be instructed to stop speaking because the unruly crowd represents a threat to public order? Should the speaker's right to communicate be protected by police officers who attempt to manage the unruly crowd? The Supreme Court considered these questions in <u>Terminiello v. Chicago</u>, 69 S.Ct. 894 (1949). Father Arthur Terminiello, a Catholic priest, delivered a speech in a Chicago auditorium that was filled to capacity; more than 800 persons attended. The meeting was called to consider the issue, "Christian Nationalism or World Communism." Outside, a crowd of 1,000 protested the meeting. Policemen were present to maintain order, but they were unable to prevent disturbances because the large crowd was turbulent. The crowd interfered with access to the front door. Members of the crowd called Terminiello and his followers "God-damned Fascists," "Hitlers," and "Nazis." Bottles, stink bombs, and bricks were tossed inside, breaking about 30 windows. The crowd broke the front door partially open. At the outset of his speech, Terminiello, realizing that some of the protesters had broken inside, claimed: "...nothing I could say tonight could begin to express the contempt I have for the slimy scum that got in by mistake." In the body of the speech, Terminiello referred to some of the elements that were "going to destroy America by revolution." He stated that "we have fifty-seven varieties of pinks and reds and pastel shades in this country." He specifically attacked the "communist Zionistic Jew.... We don't want them here; we want them to go back where they came from." The speech provoked vehement responses from some members of the audience inside the auditorium: "Send the Jews back to Russia," "Kill the Jews," "Dirty kikes." Terminiello was convicted of "breach of peace" and fined $100. Terminiello appealed. The Supreme Court held that Terminiello had been improperly convicted for delivering a speech that stirred the public to anger, invited dispute, and brought about a condition of unrest. Justice William Douglas, writing for the Court, noted that a purpose of free speech, perhaps its highest function, was to invite dispute, induce a situation of unrest, create dissatisfaction with undesirable conditions, or even stir people to anger. For this kind of public speech, Terminiello could not be punished.

Two years later, the Court examined the remarks of a college student, Irving Feiner, who addressed a crowd of about 80 persons on a street corner in Syracuse, New York. Feiner stood on a large wooden box on the sidewalk and spoke through a loudspeaker system. The primary purpose of his speech was to urge audience members to attend a meeting, sponsored by the Young Progressives, to be held that evening in the Syracuse Hotel. Feiner made derogatory remarks about President Truman, the American Legion, the Mayor of Syracuse, and other local political officials. The Young Progressives had been given a permit to meet in a public school auditorium, but the permit had been canceled; so the meeting was shifted to the Hotel Syracuse. The change in meeting plans sparked Feiner's remarks against city officials. Police officers arrived at the scene; they noticed that the crowd was restless and that traffic was congested. When Feiner urged that blacks in the audience "should rise up in arms and fight for their rights," a white person told the policemen that if they did not get that "son of a bitch" off the soapbox, he would. The police officers feared that a fight would begin so they told Feiner to stop speaking, but he continued. The crowd became more restless. Feiner was arrested for disorderly conduct, convicted, and sentenced to 30 days in jail. He appealed. The Supreme Court decided that the police were not acting to stifle Feiner's views, but were attempting to preserve order. Feiner had not been arrested because of the content of his message, but rather for the reaction to it that Feiner's own behavior had provoked. In Feiner v. New York, 71 S.Ct. 303 (1951), Chief Justice Fred Vinson claimed:

> We are well aware that the ordinary murmurings and objections of a hostile audience cannot be allowed to silence a speaker, and are also mindful of the possible danger of giving overzealous police officials complete discretion to break up otherwise lawful public meetings.... But we are not faced here with such a situation. It is one thing to say that the police cannot be used as an instrument for the suppression of unpopular views, and another to say that, when as

here the speaker passes the bounds of argument or persuasion and undertakes incitement to riot, they are powerless to prevent a breach of peace.

Certain factors differentiate the situations in Feiner and Terminiello. Terminiello addressed an audience in a hired hall, thereby having no "captive audience" as did Feiner, whose speech was conveyed through an amplifying system to people walking down the street, who unavoidably heard the remarks. Terminiello was not convicted of creating any danger to public disorder; Feiner was. The key distinction was that in Feiner, the speaker contributed significantly to the public disorder, while in Terminiello, the audience, rather than the speaker, contributed substantially to the chaos. When the speaker provoked disorder, the expression was not protected, but when the audience was primarily responsible, the speech fell within First Amendment guarantees.

FIGHTING WORDS

An utterance that stirs another to anger but has little if any social utility may be considered "fighting words." This doctrine was outlined by the courts in Chaplinsky v. New Hampshire, 62 S.Ct. 766 (1942). Walter Chaplinsky, a Jehovah's Witness, was passing out literature in Rochester, New Hampshire, when citizens complained to the Police Chief that Chaplinsky was denouncing all religion as a "racket." The Chief warned Chaplinsky that the crowd was getting unruly. Chaplinsky then said to the Chief: "You are a God-damned racketeer" and "a damned Fascist." Chaplinsky was convicted for violating a law that banned "addressing any offensive, derisive or annoying word to any other person." When the case reached the New Hampshire Supreme Court, the justices created the "fighting words" doctrine. In their opinion,

> ...the test is what men of common intelligence could understand to be words likely to cause an average addressee to fight.... The English language has a number of words and expressions which by general consent are "fighting words" when said without a disarming smile.... Such words, as ordinary men know, are likely to cause a fight.

The United States Supreme Court agreed. The words used by Chaplinsky "are epithets likely to provoke the average person to retaliation and thereby cause a breach of the peace." Furthermore, the words possess low social usefulness; "such utterances are no essential part of any exposition of ideas, and are of such slight social value as a step to truth that any benefit that may be derived from them is clearly outweighed by social interest in order and morality." The words did not warrant First Amendment protection.

Since Chaplinsky, the Court has heard other cases involving allegations of "fighting words." Gooding v. Wilson, 92 S.Ct. 1103 (1972) involved the alleged "fighting words" of Johnny Wilson, who said to a police officer, "I'll kill you," "You son-of-a-bitch, I'll choke you to death," and "You son-of-a-bitch, if you ever put your hands on me again, I'll cut you all to pieces." Wilson was convicted under a Georgia statute for using opprobrious words and abusive language. The Supreme Court did not rule on the alleged "fighting words," but instead ruled that the law was vague and overbroad; no meaningful attempt had been made to define the terms. Dictionary definitions of "opprobrious" and "abusive" give them greater reach than "fighting words." Such definitions cover incidents in which words convey disgrace or insult, but fall short of "fighting words."

In Lewis v. New Orleans, 94 S.Ct. 970 (1974), the Supreme Court heard another test of "fighting words." Mrs. Mallie Lewis, while her son was being arrested, allegedly called the police officers "god-damn, mother-fucking police." Mrs. Lewis was convicted for violating a Louisiana ordinance making it unlawful "to curse or revile or to use obscene or opprobrious language toward or with reference" to a police officer in the performance of his duties. The Supreme Court declared the ordinance to be overbroad; it was equally applicable "to speech, although vulgar or offensive, that is protected" by the Constitution as it is applicable to speech that is not protected. Justice Lewis Powell noted:

> Quite apart from the ambiguity inherent in the term "opprobrious," words may or may not be "fighting words" depending upon the circumstances of their utterance. It is unlikely, for example, that the words said to have been used here would have precipitated a physical confrontation between the middle-aged woman who spoke them and the police officer in whose presence they were uttered. The words may well have conveyed anger and frustration without provoking a violent reaction from the officer.

In Chaplinsky, the Court established that "fighting words" were outside the scope of First Amendment protection. In Wilson and Lewis, the Court threw out instances of alleged "fighting words" because the statutes were vague and overbroad. In Lewis, the Court acknowledged that "fighting words" are determined by "the circumstances of their utterance."

HATE-SPEECH

The latter half of the 1980s witnessed an increase in discriminatory harassing behavior on college campuses throughout the United States.

In response, several institutions adopted restrictions on hate-speech. The University of Michigan adopted a policy which prohibited persons from "stigmatizing," "victimizing," "threatening," or "interfering with" individuals or groups on the basis of race, ethnicity, religion, gender, sex-orientation, creed, national origin, ancestry, age, marital status, handicap, or veteran status. In Doe v. University of Michigan, 721 F. Supp 852 (1989), the court determined that the policy was unconstitutional for two reasons. First, it was vague; the words "stigmatize" and "victimize" are general terms that "elude precise definitions," and the words "threaten" and "interfere" were not clarified as to how they would impact on a student's academic efforts. Second, the policy was overbroad; it "swept within its scope" a significant amount of "verbal conduct" that was protected by the First Amendment.

The University of Wisconsin adopted a narrower policy which disciplined "racist or discriminatory comments, epithets, or other expressive behavior" directed at an individual(s). The behavior had to occur "intentionally" and had to "create an intimidating, hostile, or demeaning environment for education." In UW-M Post v. Board of Regents of the University of Wisconsin, 774 F. Supp 1163 (1991), the court overturned the policy. First, it was overbroad. Using the "fighting words" test, the court held that prohibited speech must not only break decorum, it must also have the potential to bring the parties to fisticuffs. The UW Rule punished words which were merely offensive. Second, the rule was vague; the term "intentionally" posed problems for implementation. The rule failed to specify whether the hateful expression must actually demean the listener and create a hostile educational environment, or whether the speaker must merely intend to do so.

Efforts by colleges and universities to restrict hate-speech were dealt another damaging blow in R.A.V. v. St. Paul, Minnesota, 112 S.Ct. 2538 (1992). The case arose when a young man who burned a cross on a black family's lawn was charged under an ordinance which prohibits the display of a symbol which "arouses anger, alarm, or resentment in others on the basis of race, color, creed, religion, or gender." The Supreme Court, per Justice Antonin Scalia, found the law to be unconstitutionally content-based "since an ordinance not limited to the favored topics would have precisely the same beneficial effect." Scalia concluded: "Let there be no mistake about our belief that burning a cross in someone's front yard is reprehensible. But St. Paul has sufficient means at its disposal to prevent such behavior without adding the First Amendment to the fire."

A related case involved a challenge to a Wisconsin statute which provided for sentence enhancement whenever a criminal intentionally selected a victim on the basis of race. Todd Mitchell was among a group of young black men who, after viewing a film that depicted a white man beating a black boy, sought out a white youth and beat him severely. The boy was rendered unconscious and remained in a coma for four days. After a jury trial, Mitchell was convicted of aggravated battery, an offense that ordinarily carried a maximum sentence of two years imprisonment, but in this instance the penalty was increased to seven years. Mitchell challenged the penalty enhancement on First Amendment grounds. He noted that the statute punished bigoted thought and not conduct. Writing for the Court, Chief Justice William Rehnquist observed:

> While it is...true that a sentencing judge may not take into consideration a defendant's abstract beliefs, however obnoxious to most people, the Constitution does not erect a *per se* barrier to the admission of evidence concerning one's beliefs and associations at sentencing simply because they are protected by the First Amendment.

Rehnquist compared R.A.V., in which the ordinance at issue was "explicitly directed at speech" and the statute in Wisconsin v. Mitchell, 113 S.Ct. 2194 (1993), which was aimed at conduct unprotected by the First Amendment." According to Rehnquist, a state was entitled to redress the individual and societal harm caused by bias-inspired conduct. In Mitchell, the Court upheld the sentence-enhancing statute. A criminal act based on hate may be punished with a more severe sentence than the same crime that lacks the hate motive.

INTERRUPTIVE SPEECH

One day, Raymond Hill observed a friend who was stopping automobiles on a busy street, evidently to enable a vehicle to enter traffic. Two police officers approached the friend and questioned him. Shortly thereafter, Hill shouted at the officers "in an admitted attempt to divert...attention." When an officer asked, "Are you interrupting me in my official capacity as a Houston police officer?" Hill shouted, "Yes, why don't you pick on somebody my size?" Hill was arrested under an ordinance for "interrupting a city policeman...by verbal challenge during an investigation." Following his acquittal, Hill brought suit seeking judicial judgment that the law was unconstitutional. The Supreme Court overturned the law because it dealt with protected speech; the law made it unlawful to "oppose, molest, abuse, or interrupt any policeman," and thereby prohibited "verbal interruptions." The First Amendment protects a significant amount of verbal criticism directed at police officers.

It [the law] is not limited to fighting words nor even to obscene or opprobrious language, but prohibits speech that "in any manner... interrupts" an officer. The Constitution does not allow such speech to be made a crime. The freedom of individuals verbally to oppose or challenge police action without thereby risking arrest is one of the principal characteristics by which we distinguish a free nation from a police state.

In Houston v. Hill, 107 S.Ct. 2502 (1987), the Court concluded that the ordinance was overbroad and declared it to be invalid. An individual enjoys the right to "interruptive speech."

THREATENING WORDS

A 1917 law made it a crime to threaten to take the life of the President of the United States. A violator can be fined up to $1,000 and/or imprisoned for not more than five years. The Supreme Court heard a case involving this form of "threatening words" in Watts v. United States, 89 S.Ct. 1399 (1969). On August 27, 1966, at a public rally on the Washington Monument grounds, 18-year-old Robert Watts participated in a small group discussion. At one point, Watts announced that he had received a 1-A draft classification and had to report for a physical exam. Then Watts said: "I am not going. If they ever make me carry a rifle the first man I want to get in my sights is L.B.J." Watts was convicted of threatening President Lyndon Baines Johnson. He appealed. The Supreme Court noted that Watts made the statement in the heat of political debate, his statement was made under pressure of induction into the armed forces, the remark would never become reality, and the crowd laughed along with Watts after the statement. The Court also noted that "the language of the political arena...is often vituperative, abusive, and inexact." Watts' statement had to be examined in context; the remark was "a kind of very crude offensive method of stating political opposition to the President." Watts' words were entitled to First Amendment protection because, taken in context, the words were "political hyperbole" rather than a threat upon President Lyndon Johnson's life.

Another case, Kelner v. United States, 534 F.2d 1020 (1976), involved an instance of "threatening speech." The Jewish Defense League held a press conference to protest the appearance of Yasir Arafat, leader of the Palestine Liberation Organization, at the United Nations. During the interview, Russell Kelner announced that the League was planning to assassinate Arafat. A television station broadcast Kelner's statement on an evening news program. At his trial, Kelner argued that his statement was "political hyperbole," and not a threat. The court rejected this argument and convicted Kelner because he apparently intended to inflict injury. On appeal, the court concluded that Kelner could be convicted without a showing that he intended to harm Arafat, so long as he clearly stated that intention. The United States Supreme Court denied certiorari. In Watts, the Court protected words that apparently intended to threaten President Johnson because no actual intent to injure was shown. In Kelner, however, the Court punished words that apparently intended to threaten Yasir Arafat even though no actual intent to injure was demonstrated. The Court's position on "threatening words" is unclear.

OFFENSIVE WORDS

In the early 1970s, the Supreme Court heard two cases that involved potentially "offensive words." Both cases concerned protests against the Vietnam War. On April 26, 1968, Paul Cohen appeared in the corridor of the Los Angeles County Courthouse wearing a jacket bearing the words, "Fuck the Draft." When arrested by police officers, Cohen said that he wore the jacket as a means of informing the public of his feelings against the Vietnam War and the draft. Cohen was convicted for disturbing the peace "by tumultuous or offensive conduct." The trial court believed that Cohen's behavior had a tendency to provoke others to acts of violence. Observers might become angered and attempt to remove Cohen's jacket. Cohen was sentenced to 30 days' imprisonment. In Cohen v. California, 91 S.Ct. 1780 (1971), the Supreme Court overturned the conviction. According to Justice Harlan, offended persons could avoid contact with the crude message simply by turning their eyes away from the jacket. Harlan pointed out that words are not perceived in the same way by all people; a word that is vulgar to one person may have an acceptable meaning for another. Harlan also noted that the Supreme Court cannot "forbid particular words without running a substantial risk of suppressing ideas in the process." Government officials might censor a particular word as a convenient method of banning the expression of unpopular views.

The second case, Hess v. Indiana, 94 S.Ct. 326 (1973), involved an antiwar demonstration on the campus of Indiana University. When a police officer heard Gregory Hess say in a loud voice, "We'll take the fucking street later," he arrested Hess on a disorderly conduct charge. Witnesses claimed that Hess's remark was not addressed to any particular individual or group, and that his tone, although loud, was no louder than that of the other people in the area. Nevertheless, Hess was convicted. Upon appeal, the Supreme Court ruled that Hess's words did not fall into any of the classes of words that were denied First

Amendment protection. Hess's remark could not be punished as obscene or offensive under the ruling in Cohen. Any suggestion that Hess's speech amounted to "fighting words" could not withstand scrutiny. The remark could not be regarded as a personal insult because the statement was not directed at any specific person. Since Hess's remark was not aimed at any particular person, it could not be claimed that he was advocating any action. And, without evidence that his words were intended and likely to produce imminent disorder, Hess could not be punished for using words that had a "tendency to lead to violence." The conviction was overturned. In Hess, as in Cohen, the Court refused to punish "offensive words."

POLITICAL PROPAGANDA

The Foreign Agents Registration Act requires any person who engages in "political propaganda" to register as a foreign agent, label all relevant materials as "political propaganda," and identify locations where the materials will be displayed. Barry Keene, a member of the California State Senate, wished to show films identified by the Department of Justice as "political propaganda," but did not want to be publicly regarded as a disseminator of such materials. The films were documentaries about the holocaust and acid rain. Keene brought suit in an attempt to prevent the application of the term "political propaganda" to the films. The Supreme Court determined that use of the term "political propaganda" is a constitutional form of classification; it is used to identify "any communication intended to influence the foreign policy of the United States." The term is not discriminatory; it not only includes slanted, misleading advocacy in the popular, pejorative sense, but also encompasses materials that are completely accurate and merit the highest respect. The term does not constitute prior restraint; the Act neither inhibits an individual's access to the films nor prohibits, edits, or bars the distribution of materials classified as "political propaganda." It places no burden on protected expression. In Meese v. Keene, 107 S.Ct. 1862 (1987), the Court held that in compelling citizens to label material as "political propaganda," the government was not expressing disapproval, but merely identifying a category of speech.

WRITE-IN VOTING

Alan Burdick, a registered Honolulu voter, filed suit claiming that Hawaii's prohibition on write-in voting violated his First Amendment rights of expression and association. The Supreme Court disagreed. In Burdick v. Takushi, 112 S.Ct. 2059 (1992), the Court held that the ban, when "considered as part of an electoral scheme that provides constitutionally sufficient ballot access," does not unreasonably infringe upon the rights of citizens. Writing for the majority, Justice Byron White argued:

> In such situations, the objection to the specific ban on write-in voting amounts to nothing more than the insistence that the State record, count, and punish individual protests against the election system or the choices presented on the ballot through the efforts of those who actively participated in the system. There are other means available, however, to voice such generalized dissension from the electoral process; and we discern no adequate basis for our requiring the State to provide and to finance a place on the ballot for recording protests against its constitutionally valid election laws.

The Court recognized that while the right to vote is precious in a free society, participation in the electoral process is necessarily structured in order to maintain integrity in the democratic system.

SYMBOLIC SPEECH

Dissenters rely heavily on the use of "symbolic speech" even though, in most instances, the meaning is less obvious than with pure speech. In several cases, the Supreme Court considered whether "symbolic speech" rests under the umbrella of First Amendment protection. The cases fall into two categories: symbol desecration and symbol display.

SYMBOL DESECRATION

The Vietnam War divided the United States as much as any event of the preceding century. Many citizens had to choose between loyalty to government policy and dedication to the soldiers who were fighting in support of that policy, or loyalty to their own personal belief that the policy was immoral and likely to fail. Some outspoken opponents of the war recorded their opposition by burning their draft cards. Others chose to alter or destroy the U.S. flag. These forms of symbolic communication, through desecration of a symbol, posed a significant question for the Supreme Court — was "symbolic speech" subject to First Amendment protection, and if so, to what extent?

Draft card

The Universal Military Training and Service Act stipulated that men, upon reaching 18 years of age, had to register with a local draft board and be issued a registration certificate. In 1965, Congress made it a crime to mutilate the certificate. On March 31, 1966, David O'Brien burned his draft card on the steps of the South Boston Courthouse. A crowd, including several FBI agents, witnessed the event. At his trial, O'Brien said that he burned his certificate publicly in an effort to influence others to adopt his antiwar beliefs. He was convicted. Before the Supreme Court, O'Brien argued that the act of burning his draft card was protected "symbolic speech" within the First Amendment. The Court disagreed; the justices rejected the notion that a limitless variety of conduct could be labeled "speech" whenever a person intended to express an idea. In United States v. O'Brien, 88 S.Ct. 1673 (1968), the Court established a four-part test to determine the acceptability of the government's draft card policy: 1) was the policy within the government's constitutional power? 2) did the policy further a substantial governmental interest? 3) was the interest related to the suppression of free speech? and 4) was any incidental restriction on First Amendment freedoms greater than was essential to further that interest? In O'Brien, the Court decided that the power of Congress to classify and conscript manpower for military service was an important governmental interest "beyond question." It was essential for the United States to have a system for raising armies that functioned with maximum efficiency. The requirement that each registrant have access to his card furthered the smooth functioning of the system. The justices noted that even if a communication element in O'Brien's action justified the application of the First Amendment, it did not necessarily follow that the destruction of a draft card was constitutionally protected. When "speech" and "nonspeech" elements were combined in the same conduct, important governmental interest in regulating the "nonspeech" element justified incidental limitations on First Amendment "speech" freedoms. In O'Brien, the Supreme Court ruled that Congress could establish a system of registration, and could require individuals to cooperate in the system.

During the next few years, the Court heard other cases involving the destruction of draft cards. A nationwide draft card turn-in was held on October 16, 1967. Thousands of persons attended a rally on the Boston Common, followed by a march to the Arlington Street Church, where more than 300 young men either burned their draft cards at the altar candle or deposited them in the collection plate. Among these men was a divinity student named James Oestereich. Meanwhile, in the midwest, 20 protestors turned in their cards to the authorities in Minneapolis; when the U.S. Marshal refused to accept them, the protesters dropped the cards at his feet. One of the 20 was an activist named David Gutknecht. One month later, 40 young men participated in a turn-in sponsored by the Boston Resistance at the Old West

Methodist Church. Among them was an undergraduate music student named Timothy Breen. As a result of their actions, Oestereich, Gutknecht, and Breen were either reclassified or moved up in the draft call list by their local draft boards. All sued on the grounds that their freedom of speech had been violated and that the punitive use of the draft was unconstitutional. In Oestereich v. Selective Service Board No. 11, 89 S.Ct. 414 (1968), the Supreme Court, in the opinion written by Justice William Douglas, decided: "Once a person registers and qualifies for a statutory exemption we find no legislative authority to deprive him of that exemption because of conduct or activities unrelated to the merits of granting or continuing that exemption." In this case, the "conduct of a local board...is basically lawless." The local draft board rulings in Gutknecht v. United States, 90 S.Ct. 506 (1970) and Breen v. Selective Service Local Board No. 16, 90 S.Ct. 661 (1970) were likewise vacated.

It should be noted that the Court did not absolve draft resisters. Possession of both the registration certificate and the notice of classification remained responsibilities required by the Selective Service regulations, and failure to comply with those responsibilities remained punishable under the Universal Training Act. In 1973, however, following extensive protest against the draft during the previous decade and succeeding the signing of a cease-fire agreement terminating involvement in Vietnam, the United States adopted a system of all-volunteer military forces. The registration policy was temporarily curtailed.

A 1980 Presidential Proclamation reinstated the policy, directing all 18-year-old male citizens to register with the Selective Service System. An eligible young man, David Wayte, wrote letters to government officials, including the President, stating that he had not registered and did not intend to do so. These letters were placed in a file along with similar letters. Subsequently, the Selective Service adopted a policy of passive enforcement under which it prosecuted only the nonregistration cases contained in the file. Prior to prosecution, however, pursuant to the government's "beg" policy, Wayte received a letter urging him to register, or face prosecution. Wayte failed to respond. Accordingly, he was convicted for failing to register. Wayte appealed, arguing that he had been the victim of selective prosecution — only vocal opponents to the registration policy were subject to prosecution. The Supreme Court, per Justice Lewis Powell, applied the test originated in the O'Brien case and held that the government's passive enforcement and "beg" policies were within the government's constitutional power, and furthered a substantial government interest without unduly suppressing free speech. In Wayte v. United States, 105 S.Ct. 1524 (1985), the

Court sided with the government and punished Wayte's refusal to register.

U.S. flag

On June 6, 1966, upon hearing that civil rights leader James Meredith had been shot by a sniper, Sidney Street burned a U.S. flag on a street corner. A police officer heard Street say, "We don't need no damn flag," and when the officer asked Street if he burned the flag, Street replied, "Yes, that is my flag; I burned it. If they let that happen to Meredith, we don't need an American flag." Street was convicted for violating a New York statute that prohibited the defiling of a U.S. flag by either words or action. When the case reached the Supreme Court, a majority of the justices felt that Street might have been punished for his words rather than the act of burning the flag. According to the opinion written by Justice John Harlan, Street's words offered no justification for a conviction. First, Street was not inciting the public to commit unlawful acts. Street simply recommended that the country should, at least temporarily, abandon one of its national symbols. Second, Street's words were not so inflammatory as to provoke others to retaliate physically against him. Even though the words might excite some people, they are not "fighting words." Third, Street's words were not offensive; they did not necessitate protecting the sensibilities of passersby. Any shock effect of the expression stemmed from the ideas and not the words. The Constitution forbids outlawing "the ideas themselves," even if they may be offensive to their hearers. Fourth, Street's speech was within the constitutionally protected freedom to disagree with the existing order. His remarks about the flag were not punishable for showing improper respect for the national emblem. In Street v. New York, 89 S.Ct. 1354 (1969), the majority refused to uphold the conviction because it could have been based upon speech which, even though distasteful, was guaranteed by the Constitution. The minority justices decided the case on a different basis. In their view, Street was convicted for his act of burning the flag, not for his words. Chief Justice Earl Warren said: "I believe that the States and the Federal government do have the power to protect the flag from acts of desecration and disgrace." Justice Abe Fortas wrote:

> One may not justify the burning of a house, even if it is his own, on the ground, however sincere, that he does so as a protest. One may not justify breaking the windows of a government building on that basis. Protest does not exonerate lawlessness. And the prohibition against flag burning on the public thoroughfare being valid, the misdemeanor is not excused merely because it is an act of flamboyant protest.

In Street, the minority viewed the act for which Street was convicted —
burning the flag — as not protected by the First Amendment. The
majority, however, held that the conviction may have been based on
Street's words, which were protected. The majority did not consider
whether the act of flag burning deserved First Amendment protection.

A year after Street, the courts considered another instance of flag
desecration. Stephen Radich, the proprietor of an art gallery, offered for
sale several pieces of sculpture that expressed opposition to the
Vietnam War. The sculptures prominently displayed the U.S. flag in
the form of the male sexual organ, erect and protruding from the upright
portion of a cross, and in the form of a human body hanging from a
noose. Radich called the sculpture "protest art." He was convicted of
violating the New York flag-desecration statute. The trial court ruled
that the sculptures cast the flag into dishonor. The court compared
Radich's treatment of the flag with that in Street.

> Here, the expression, if less dramatic, was given far wider circulation
> and, in consequence, perhaps, a measurable enhancement of the
> likelihood of incitement to disorder, by the placement of one of the
> constructions in a street display window of defendant's gallery on
> Madison Avenue in the City of New York, and the exhibition and
> exposure for sale of the companion pieces in the public gallery and
> mercantile establishment within. Implicit in the invitation to view
> was the opportunity thereby afforded to join in the protest, or in
> counter-protest, with the consequent potential of public disorder.

The court concluded that the public interest was threatened by Radich's
"protest art." His conviction was upheld. The U.S. Supreme Court
denied a petition to hear Ross v. Radich, 459 F.2d 745 (1972), and
thereby let the conviction stand.

Two years later, the Court further developed its position regarding
flag desecration. Valorie Goguen wore a small flag sewn on the seat of
his blue jeans. He was convicted of violating the Massachusetts flag-
misuse statute. In Smith v. Goguen, 94 S.Ct. 1242 (1974), the
Supreme Court acknowledged that "flag wearing in a day of relaxed
clothing styles may be simply for adornment or a ploy to attract
attention." The Court found the law to be vague and overbroad because
it failed "to draw reasonably clear lines between the kinds of
unceremonial treatment that are criminal and those that are not." The
Court allowed Goguen's unusual use of the flag.

In another case, Harold Spence displayed a U.S. flag from his
apartment window in Seattle. A large peace symbol was attached to
both sides of the flag with removable tape. Spence was arrested under a
Washington law that prohibited improper display of the flag. Spence
admitted that he displayed the flag as a protest against the invasion of

Cambodia and the Kent State University killings. He intended to associate the flag with peace rather than war. He was convicted. In Spence v. Washington, 94 S.Ct. 2727 (1974), the Supreme Court reversed the conviction. The flag was owned privately, displayed on private property, and displayed without breach of the peace. The majority concluded that "given the protected character of his [Spence's] expression and in light of the fact that no interest the State may have in preserving the physical integrity of the privately owned flag was significantly impaired..., the conviction must be invalidated." Justice Rehnquist's dissent stressed that the First Amendment allows a State to restrict expression in order to further an important interest. In this case, the interest was preserving the "physical integrity of the flag" and "preserving the flag as an important symbol of nationhood and unity." Rehnquist acknowledged the presence of "symbolic speech" but denied such activity First Amendment protection.

The Texas v. Johnson, 109 S.Ct. 2533 (1989), decision continued the Supreme Court's position in which a majority of justices protected free expression while a solid minority supported the national symbol. The case began on August 22, 1984, when Gregory Johnson was arrested during the Republican National Convention in Dallas for setting fire to an American flag. He was convicted for violating a Texas statute which prohibited "desecration" of a national flag. When the case reached the Supreme Court, the deeply divided justices applied the O'Brien test to evaluate Texas' two interests in justifying Johnson's conviction. According to the majority, the first interest, preventing breaches of the peace, was not relevant because "no disturbance of the peace actually occurred or threatened to occur because of Johnson's burning of the flag." The second, preserving the flag as a symbol of national unity, was not defendable because "the Government may not prohibit the expression of an idea simply because society finds the idea itself offensive or disagreeable." Writing for the majority, Justice William Brennan concluded: "We do not consecrate the flag by punishing its desecration for in doing so we dilute the freedom that this cherished emblem represents." Chief Justice Rehnquist disagreed. Writing for the minority, he observed:

> The flag is not simply another "idea" or "point of view" competing for recognition in the marketplace of ideas. Millions and millions of Americans regard it with an almost mystical reverence regardless of what sort of social, political, or philosophical beliefs they may have. I cannot agree that the First Amendment invalidates the Act of Congress, and the laws of 48 of the 50 states, which make criminal the public burning of the flag.

Public outrage over the Johnson decision was considerable. Within a few months, Congress passed the Flag Protection Act of 1989. The constitutionality of the Act was challenged in United States v. Eichman, 110 S.Ct. 2404 (1990). The government argued that the Act was constitutional because, unlike the statute at stake in Johnson, this Act "did not target expressive conduct on the basis of the content of its message." Instead, the Act protected "the physical integrity of the flag under all circumstances" in order to safeguard a "unique and unalloyed symbol of the Nation." The Court majority, per Justice Brennan, found the Act to be unconstitutional because it was "related to the suppression of free expression."

> The Act criminalizes the conduct of anyone who "knowingly mutilates, defaces, physically defiles, burns, maintains on the floor or ground, or tramples upon any flag." Each of the specified terms — with the possible exception of "burns" — unmistakably connotes disrespectful treatment of the flag and suggests a focus on those acts likely to damage the flag's symbolic value.

The Court held that even though the Act was cast in broader terms than the statute at issue in Johnson, it "still suffers from the same fundamental flaw: it suppresses expression out of concern for its likely communicative impact." Brennan acknowledged that "desecration of the flag is deeply offensive to many"; nonetheless, he reiterated a point made in Johnson — "punishing desecration of the flag dilutes the very freedom that makes this emblem so revered, and worth revering." The majority in Eichman, as in Johnson, decided that burning a national flag is protected expression under the First Amendment.

DISPLAY SYMBOLS

Dissent can involve displaying a "symbol" in some prominent location, thereby calling attention to the point of the protest. A red flag, arm bands, uniforms, and a license plate have been among the "symbols" of dissent used to protest various causes. The Supreme Court has defined regulations that control the display of such symbols.

In 1931, the Supreme Court decided that California could not ban a group from flying a red flag as a symbol of opposition to organized government. Yetta Stromberg, a 19-year-old member of the Young Communist League, supervised a summer camp for children in the San Bernadino Mountains. She directed a daily ritual that involved raising a red flag and pledging allegiance "to the worker's red flag, and the cause for which it stands; one aim throughout our lives, freedom for the working class." A library at the camp contained Communist literature that urged incitement to violence and armed uprising, though Stromberg claimed that none of the material was brought to the attention of the children and that no word of violence, anarchism, or sedition was used in her teaching. Stromberg was convicted under a California law which cited three conditions for banning the display of a flag in a public place: as a symbol of opposition to organized government, as an invitation to anarchistic action, or as an aid to propaganda of a seditious character. At trial, the judge indicated that Stromberg should be convicted if the flag were displayed for any of the three reasons. The Supreme Court reversed the conviction in Stromberg v. California, 51 S.Ct. 532 (1931), because it was unclear which of the reasons had been the basis for conviction. If Stromberg had been convicted for flying the flag as a symbol of opposition to organized government, her First Amendment freedom of speech had been violated.

Thirty-eight years later, in Tinker v. Des Moines Independent Community School District, 89 S.Ct. 733 (1969), the Court decided a case involving the display of armbands by students. Some children of the Des Moines school district, encouraged by their parents, wore black armbands to school to protest U.S. involvement in Vietnam. School administrators announced that any student wearing armbands would be suspended. The fathers of the students brought suit and the case reached the Supreme Court. The justices decided that wearing an armband to express views is an act of symbolic communication which is protected by the First Amendment. According to Justice Abe Fortas, a school administration cannot ban expression simply because it might cause discomfort or unpleasantness. Fortas claimed that the wearing of armbands had not contributed to any disruptive behavior.

> Their [students] deviation consisted only in wearing on their sleeve a band of black cloth, not more than two inches wide. They wore it to exhibit their disapproval of the Vietnam hostilities and their advocacy of a truce, to make their views known, and, by their example, to influence others to adopt them. They neither interrupted school activities nor sought to intrude in the school affairs or the lives of others. They caused discussion outside of the classrooms, but no interference with work and no disorder.

According to Fortas, the school administration sought to punish a few students for passive expression of their opposition to the war. Fortas noted that no other symbols were excluded; students were allowed to wear political buttons. School officials prohibited only one symbol, and without any indication that it was necessary to avoid disruption of school activities. Such a ban was not constitutionally permissible.

In Schacht v. United States, 90 S.Ct. 1555 (1970), the Court continued its liberal interpretation of symbol display. Daniel Schacht and his colleagues participated in a skit as part of a peaceful antiwar demonstration at the Houston Armed Forces Induction Center. The skit was designed to show undesirable aspects of U.S. presence in

Vietnam. Schacht and another person were dressed in military uniforms. A third person was outfitted in Viet Cong apparel. The first two men carried water pistols. They would yell, "Be an able American," and then they would shoot the Viet Cong. The pistols expelled a liquid which, when it hit the victim, gave the impression that the person was bleeding. Once the victim fell down, the other two walked up and exclaimed, "My God, this is a pregnant woman." Schacht was indicted for wearing the uniform of the armed forces without authority. Schacht claimed that he was authorized to wear the uniform under a law which provides that "while portraying a member of the Army, Navy, Air Force, or Marine Corps, an actor in a theatrical or motion picture production may wear the uniform of that armed force if the portrayal does not tend to discredit that armed force." Schacht argued that he wore the army uniform as an actor in a theatrical production. Nevertheless, he was convicted. He appealed. In a unanimous decision, the Supreme Court held that the part of the law stipulating that dramatic portrayal is lawful only if it "does not tend to discredit that armed force" was an unconstitutional abridgement of freedom of speech. The Court overturned Schacht's conviction. Three justices, however, in a concurring opinion pointed out that a "theatrical production" in which a military uniform is permitted must be restricted to a setting where viewers realize that they are "watching a make-believe performance." If this thinking had been supported by the majority, Schacht would not have been engaged in a "theatrical production" and could have been found guilty.

Wooley v. Maynard, 97 S.Ct. 1428 (1977), presented a unique form of display. Rather than dissenting through the act of showing a symbol, George Maynard dissented by partially covering his automobile license plate. Maynard covered the portion of his plate stamped with the New Hampshire state motto, "Live Free, or Die." He found the motto repugnant to his moral and religious beliefs as a Jehovah's Witness. Maynard was convicted for obscuring the license plate. The Supreme Court sided with Maynard. First, the Court noted that First Amendment protection includes the right to speak freely as well as the right to refrain from speaking at all.

> A system which secures the right to proselytize religious, political, and ideological causes must also guarantee the concomitant right to decline to foster such concepts. The right to speak and the right to refrain from speaking are complementary components of the broader concept of "individual freedom of mind."

Second, the Court considered the interests claimed by New Hampshire in requiring people to display the motto. New Hampshire claimed that display of the motto facilitated the identification of passenger vehicles.

The Court decided that license plates contain "a specific configuration of letters and numbers, which makes them readily distinguishable from other types of plates, even without reference to state motto." New Hampshire also argued that requiring the display of the motto promoted appreciation of history and state pride. The Court reasoned that a State's interest in disseminating an ideology "cannot outweigh an individual's First Amendment right to avoid becoming the courier for such messages." New Hampshire could not require Maynard to display the motto upon his license plate.

The lesson of Maynard, Schacht, Tinker, and Stromberg is that "display" is a form of "symbolic speech" which is entitled to First Amendment protection. O'Brien, Street, and Radich suggest that the level of protection given to "desecration" as a form of "symbolic speech" remains limited. The Supreme Court has recognized the right to "display" symbols of dissent while, at times, being reluctant to award "desecration" the same status. Furthermore, the Court has granted greater First Amendment protection to "pure speech" than to "symbolic speech."

CONCLUSION

The following principles regulate communication law regarding DISSENT:

1. Advocating the overthrow of the government through abstract doctrine is protected under the Constitution, while advocacy of action is not. However:
   a. advocacy which does not call for illegal action is protected,
   b. advocacy which calls for illegal action but does not seek immediate action is protected,
   c. advocacy which calls for immediate illegal action when it is unlikely that the audience will commit the action is protected.

2. In cases involving advocating the overthrow of the government, the Court tends to extend First Amendment protection to peacetime dissent but limits protection in times of war.

3. Specific forms of dissent — advocating overthrow, provocative words, fighting words, threatening words — have been punished under certain conditions. Interruptive speech and offensive words have been protected by the Court.

4. The Court has recognized the right to "display" symbols of dissent

while, at times, refusing to award "desecration" of symbols the same status.

5. First Amendment protection is greater for "pure speech" than for "symbolic speech."

KEY DECISIONS

1919 — <u>SCHENCK</u> — established "clear and present danger" test of First Amendment

1925 — <u>GITLOW</u> — established "bad tendency" test

1942 — <u>CHAPLINSKY</u> — established "fighting words" doctrine

1949 — <u>TERMINIELLO</u> — when audience provokes public disorder, speaker's words are protected

1951 — <u>FEINER</u> — when speaker provokes public disorder, speaker's words are not protected

1968 — <u>O'BRIEN</u> — suggests that the Supreme Court is more willing to protect "pure speech" than "symbolic speech"

1969 — <u>TINKER</u> — indicates that Supreme Court is more willing to protect symbolic speech of "display" than that of "desecration"

1969 — <u>WATTS</u> — "threatening words" are punishable, while "political hyperbole" is permissible

1969 — <u>BRANDENBURG</u> — advocative incitement which does not call for illegal action is protected

1989 — <u>JOHNSON</u> — burning the national flag is protected expression

1992 — <u>R.A.V.</u> — content-based statute designed to punish hateful expression is unconstitutional

RECOMMENDED READING

Goodman, Richard J., and William I. Gordon, "The Rhetoric of Desecration," Quarterly Journal of Speech 57 (February, 1971), 23-31.

Haiman, Franklyn S., "Speech Acts" and the First Amendment Carbondale: Southern Illinois Press, 1993.

Haiman, Franklyn S., Speech and Law In A Free Society Chicago: University of Chicago Press, 1981, pp. 245-283.

Hemmer, Joseph J. Jr., "Hate Speech Codes: The Constitutionality Issues," Communications and the Law 18 (1996), 23-41.

Hemmer, Joseph J. Jr., "Hate Speech — The Egalitarian/Libertarian Dilemma," Howard Journal of Communications 5 (1995), 307-317.

Herbeck, Dale A., "Limits to Political Expression: The Rise and Fall of the Smith Act," Free Speech Yearbook 25 (1986), 67-89.

Konvitz, Milton R., Expanding Liberties: Freedom's Gains in Postwar America. New York: Viking Press, 1966.

McBride, James, "'Is Nothing Sacred?': Flag Desecration, the Constitution and the Establishment of Religion," St. John's Law Review 65 (1991), 297-324.

Nahmad, Sheldon H., "The Sacred Flag and the First Amendment," Indiana Law Journal 66 (1991), 511-548.

Siegel, Paul, "Protecting Political Speech: Brandenburg v. Ohio Updated," Quarterly Journal of Speech 67 (February, 1981), 69-80.

Smith, James M., Freedom's Fetters. Ithaca, N.Y.: Cornell University Press, 1956.

Stevens, John D., Shaping the First Amendment: The Development of Free Expression. Beverly Hills, CA.: Sage, 1982.

Suffet, Stephen L., "The Resistance and the Court: the Punitive Draft Cases," Free Speech Yearbook (1971), 50-63.

Waldman, Joshua, "Symbolic Speech and Social Meaning," Columbia Law Review (1997), 1844-1894.

CHAPTER 3

ASSOCIATION

The United States is a nation of joiners. Everywhere, people gather together to achieve political, religious, social, and economic goals. Contemporary Americans view associational rights as necessary for achieving objectives which they are unable to accomplish when acting alone. The specific tenets of associational protection developed over several years, and the Supreme Court played an influential role.

FORMS OF ASSOCIATION

The right to associate is not mentioned in the Bill of Rights because the founders of the government viewed associations as potentially harmful to the country's well-being. The framers did, however, recognize the more specific rights of assembly and petition. From the inception of the country, these rights acknowledged that citizens can gather peaceably (assembly) and make grievances known to others (petition). The specific forms of association — picketing, boycotting, demonstration — were guaranteed by the Supreme Court during the latter half of the twentieth century.

FREEDOM TO ASSOCIATE

In 1958, the Supreme Court recognized association as a constitutional freedom. The case involved the National Association for the Advancement of Colored People, which, during the 1950s, had achieved several accomplishments on behalf of the civil rights of black citizens. In response, southern politicians developed strategies designed to cripple the NAACP. They required corporations to file a charter prior to conducting business in their states. The Alabama

NAACP never complied with the requirement because it considered itself exempt. In 1956, the Attorney General initiated court proceedings, during which the NAACP was ordered to produce records, including the names and addresses of the members of the association. The NAACP produced the records, but refused to release the membership lists. Subsequently, the organization was held in contempt and fined $100,000. The NAACP appealed. The Supreme Court unanimously ruled that the NAACP had the right to protect the lists on behalf of the private interests of its members. According to Justice John Harlan,

> Petitioner [NAACP] has made an uncontroverted showing that on past occasions revelation of the identity of its rank-and-file members has exposed these members to economic reprisal, loss of employment, threat of physical coercion, and other manifestations of public hostility. Under these circumstances, we think it apparent that compelled disclosure of petitioner's Alabama membership is likely to...induce members to withdraw from the Association and dissuade others from joining it because of fear of exposure of their beliefs shown through their associations and of the consequences of this exposure.

In NAACP v. Alabama, 78 S.Ct. 1163 (1958), the Court ruled that compelled disclosure of membership lists would hamper the Association in pursuing its lawful goals. It constituted a restraint on freedom of association.

A few years later, the Court reaffirmed the right of association. Bates v. Little Rock, 80 S.Ct. 412 (1960), involved the Little Rock occupation-license-tax ordinance which stipulated that, upon request, any organization had to produce its official records, including the names of members and contributors. Upon such request, Daisy Bates, custodian of records of the Little Rock NAACP, supplied some of the required information. She refused, however, to divulge the names of the organization's members and contributors. She claimed that because of anti-NAACP sentiment, disclosure of the names would lead to harassment and perhaps even bodily harm. Bates was convicted for refusing to provide the list of names. Upon appeal, the Supreme Court agreed with Bates. Furthermore, the Court unanimously ruled that "it is now beyond dispute that freedom of association for the purpose of advancing ideas and airing grievances is protected."

A similar case, Gibson v. Florida Legislative Investigation Committee, 83 S.Ct. 889 (1963), further strengthened the right to associate. In 1956, a subpoena was issued to obtain the membership list of the NAACP's Miami branch. When Reverend Theodore Gibson refused to produce the list, he was sentenced to six months in prison and fined $1,200. He appealed. The Supreme Court, per Justice

Arthur Goldberg, argued that groups that "are neither engaged in subversive or other illegal or improper activities, nor demonstrated to have any substantial connections with such activities, are to be protected in their rights of free and private association." He viewed such protection as especially vital in this instance.

> While, of course, all legitimate organizations are the beneficiaries of these protections, they are all the more essential here, where the challenged privacy is that of persons espousing beliefs already unpopular with their neighbors and the deterrent and "chilling" effect on the free exercise of constitutionally enshrined rights of free speech, expression, and association is consequently the more immediate and substantial.

In Gibson, as in NAACP and Bates, the Court protected the NAACP and upheld the right of association.

RIGHT TO SOLICIT MEMBERS

The right to solicit members is essential to the freedom of association. Yet, unrestrained solicitation can lead to door-to-door canvassing on behalf of fraudulent causes. In order to protect the public from such invasion of individual privacy, cities have passed laws restricting the right to solicit. In some cases, the Supreme Court has weighed the right to solicit members against the right to be left undisturbed.

Cantwell v. Connecticut, 60 S.Ct. 900 (1940), is such a case. Newton Cantwell was convicted for conducting door-to-door solicitation on behalf of Jehovah's Witnesses in a predominantly Catholic neighborhood in New Haven, Connecticut. Cantwell had ignored a statute that required any person soliciting for a religious cause to apply for a certificate of approval with the Welfare Secretary, who then decided whether the cause conformed to "reasonable standards of efficiency and integrity." The Supreme Court overturned the conviction, noting that the law was prohibitory, not regulatory. It allowed an official to ban religious solicitation entirely. The statute established a prior restraint on First Amendment freedoms. If a state wanted to protect its citizens against door-to-door solicitation, it could enact a regulation directed specifically at that problem. For example, a state could grant a householder the right to terminate the solicitation by demanding that the visitor leave the premises. In addition, a state could regulate the time and manner of solicitation. In Cantwell, the Court found fault with the broad sweep of the law.

Five years later, in Thomas v. Collins, 65 S.Ct. 315 (1945), the Court upheld the right to solicit members. A Texas statute prohibited labor-union organizers from soliciting members unless they first obtained an identification card from a state official. R. J. Thomas, an officer of the United Automobile Workers, traveled to Texas to deliver a union organizing speech. The Attorney General obtained a restraining order enjoining Thomas from soliciting any union memberships. When Thomas appeared as scheduled and solicited the audience, he was arrested and convicted of contempt of court. He appealed. The Supreme Court reversed the conviction on the ground that solicitation could not be separated from the First Amendment rights of speech and assembly.

> If one who solicits for the cause of labor may be required to register as a condition to the exercise of his right to make a public speech, so may he who seeks to rally support for any social, business, religious, or political cause. We think a requirement that one must register before he undertakes to make a public speech to enlist support for a lawful movement is quite incompatible with the requirements of the First Amendment.

The issue was raised once more in Staub v. Baxley, 78 S.Ct. 277 (1958). The International Ladies Garment Workers Union was trying to organize the employees of a manufacturing company located near Baxley, Georgia. A city ordinance mandated that a permit had to be obtained prior to soliciting members for any organization that required the payment of dues. Rose Staub, an employee of the union, without applying for a permit, attended a meeting where she detailed the benefits of joining the union. She urged the women to get other workers to join; blank membership cards were distributed for that purpose. Staub was charged with soliciting without a permit. She was convicted and sentenced to spend 30 days in prison or pay a fine of $300. She appealed. The Supreme Court reversed the decision. The ordinance made freedom of association contingent upon the discretion of the Mayor and the City Council; the statute provided no definitive standards governing the action of city officials regarding the granting or withholding of a permit. The officials were free to act as they wished. The ordinance was unconstitutional. In Staub, as in Cantwell and Thomas, the Supreme Court rejected ordinances designed to control solicitation of members because those statutes placed arbitrary authority with local officials. Solicitation may be regulated, but only by a constitutional ordinance.

RIGHT TO RESTRICT MEMBERSHIP

Numerous organizations have adopted policies which restrict membership to a specific category of individuals. For example, membership in United States Jaycees, a nonprofit association which promotes young men's civic organizations, was limited to men between the ages of 18 and 35. Two chapters in Minnesota admitted women, and, as a result, were reprimanded by the national office. Kathryn Roberts, one of the female members, filed discrimination charges, alleging that the exclusion of women violated her civil rights. The Jaycees argued that forcing an organization to accept women violated both the intimate and expressive associational rights of men. The Supreme Court, per Justice William Brennan, held that requiring an organization to accept women as members did not abridge either the male members' freedom of intimate or expressive association. First, regarding intimate association, Brennan noted several features of the Jaycee organization which placed it outside the category of highly personal relationships which are entitled to such protection. For example, local chapters are neither small nor selective, activities central to the organization involve the participation of strangers, and numerous nonmembers of both genders participate in the activities. Second, regarding expressive association, that right is not absolute; an infringement is justified if it serves a compelling state interest. According to Brennan, that interest was the prohibition of gender discrimination in places of public accommodation.

> ...discrimination based on archaic and overbroad assumptions about the relative needs and capacities of the sexes forces individuals to labor under stereotypical notions that often bear no relationship to their actual abilities. It thereby both deprives persons of their individual dignity and denies society the benefits of wide participation in political, economic, and cultural life.

In Roberts v. United States Jaycees, 104 S.Ct. 3244 (1984), the Court affirmed Minnesota's interest in eradicating discrimination against its female citizens. A few years later, in Board of Directors of Rotary International v. Rotary Club of Duarte, 107 S.Ct. 1940 (1987), and in New York State Club Association v. City of New York, 108 S. Ct. 2225 (1988), the Court reached similar decisions applicable to discrimination based on gender, race, or creed.

In Dallas v. Stanglin, 109 S.Ct. 1591 (1989), the Court supported the restriction of membership according to age. The case involved a Dallas ordinance which authorized the licensing of "Class E" dance halls, under the stipulation that admission be limited to persons between the ages of 14 and 18, and the hours of operation be restricted. The ordinance sought to provide a place where teenagers could socialize without being subjected to the detrimental influences of adults. Charles Stanglin operated the Twilight Skating Rink under a "Class E" license. He divided his establishment into two areas. On one side of a series of pylons, teens between ages 14 and 18 danced; on the other side, older individuals skated to the same music. By dividing the facility, Stanglin violated the ordinance. Stanglin challenged the ordinance in court, alleging that it violated the associational right of teens. The Supreme Court upheld the ordinance. The Court determined that recreational dancing "qualifies neither as a form of 'intimate association' nor as a form of 'expressive association' as those terms were described in Roberts." The teenagers who congregate in the dance hall are not members of any organization and most are strangers to one another. In addition, patrons do not adopt positions on public issues. The Court held that Dallas has a substantial interest in promoting the welfare of its teenagers. In this instance, restricting association on the basis of age furthered that interest.

In three cases, the Court decided that the First Amendment forbids government officials to discharge or threaten to discharge public employees solely because they refuse to support the political party in power. In Elrod v. Burns, 96 S.Ct. 2673 (1976), the Court decided that a sheriff could not engage in the patronage practice of replacing staff with members of his own party "when the existing employees lack or fail to obtain requisite support from, or fail to affiliate with, that party." The Court held that conditioning public employment on the willingness to support a political party "unquestionably inhibits protected belief and association." In Branti v. Finkel, 100 S.Ct. 1287 (1980), the Court prohibited a public defender from firing assistant public defenders because they did not have the support of a particular political party. In Rutan v. Republican Party of Illinois, 110 S.Ct. 2729 (1990), the Court held that promotions, transfers, and recalls based on political affiliation are impermissible infringements of the First Amendment. The case began when the Governor of Illinois issued an executive order proclaiming a hiring freeze for every state agency. Subsequently, the Governor's office operated a political patronage system which limited employment to members of the Republican Party. Writing for the majority in a 5-4 decision, Justice Brennan noted: "Under our sustained precedent, conditioning hiring decisions on political belief and association plainly constitutes an unconstitutional condition, unless the government has a vital interest in doing so.... We find no such government interest here."

In Hurley v. Irish-American Gay, Lesbian and Bisexual Groups of Boston, 115 S.Ct 2338 (1995), the Court considered a unique procedural issue. The case involved the Allied War Veterans Council, an association of individuals elected from various local veterans groups, which was authorized by the city of Boston to organize and conduct the St. Patrick's Day Parade. The Council refused a place in the 1993 parade to a group of openly gay, lesbian, and bisexual individuals of

Irish ethnicity. The group initiated court action alleging that the denial violated a state law which prohibited discrimination on account of sexual orientation in places of public accommodation. The Supreme Court, per Justice David Souter, held that application of the public accommodations law to require private citizens who organize a parade to include among the marchers a group conveying a message that the organizers did not wish to convey violated the First Amendment. The homosexual group's clear intention for marching in the parade was to celebrate their identity as gay, lesbian, and bisexual descendants of Irish immigrants, and to demonstrate that such individuals were in the community. The group sought to communicate its ideas as part of the existing parade, rather than staging one of its own. According to Souter, selection of parade participants was a form of protected expression because a parade included marchers who were making a collective point, not just to each other but to bystanders along the way. Requiring parade planners to alter their intended expressive content "violated the fundamental First Amendment rule that a speaker has the authority to choose the content of his own message and, conversely, to decide what not to say." In this case, the state law which prohibited discrimination could not be upheld without violating the First Amendment.

In the cases described in this section, the Supreme Court addressed a variety of attempts to restrict organizational membership. For the most part, the Court set aside such restrictions. The Court rejected efforts in Roberts, Rotary Club of Duarte, and New York State Club Association to restrict social membership on the basis of gender, race, or creed. It also turned back attempts in Elrod, Branti, and Rutan to regulate government employees on the basis of political affiliation. The Court, however, in Stanglin, upheld a local ordinance which restricted the associational rights of youths. And, in Hurley, the Court upheld a city's decision to deny participation in a parade to a specific group.

RIGHT TO ASSEMBLE

Most localities have ordinances that specify the conditions under which public assemblies may be held. Over the years, some of these laws have been upheld while others have been overturned. Several ordinances have been rejected because they permitted arbitrary or discriminatory procedures. Hague v. Committee For Industrial Organization, 59 S.Ct. 954 (1939) is such a case. A Jersey City, New Jersey ordinance authorized the Director of Public Safety to process applications for parades and public assemblies. A permit could be denied "for the purpose of preventing riots, disturbances or disorderly assemblage." The CIO, a labor union, was repeatedly refused permits on the ground that the individuals making the requests were Communists, a charge that CIO members denied. The union initiated court proceedings in order to challenge the ordinance. The Supreme Court noted that the right of assembly is not absolute; it may be regulated to protect general peace and order. Suppression of the right to assemble cannot, however, be substituted for the city's duty to maintain order. The New Jersey ordinance allowed city officials to arbitrarily consent to, or withhold, permission for public meetings. The ordinance was unconstitutional.

A decade later, the Court overturned a similar ordinance in Kunz v. New York, 71 S.Ct. 312 (1951). The ordinance made it illegal for an individual to hold a public worship meeting without obtaining a permit from the City Police Commissioner. In 1946, Carl Kunz, an ordained Baptist minister, obtained a permit to preach in New York City. Later that year, his permit was revoked because Kunz had ridiculed Catholics and Jews at his worship meetings. Kunz applied for a permit in 1947 and again in 1948, but both times his request was rejected. On September 11, 1948, Kunz was arrested for speaking without a permit. He was convicted and fined $10. Kunz appealed. The Supreme Court held the ordinance invalid — there was no mention of conditions under which a permit could be refused. The ordinance lacked standards to guide the action of the Commissioner — he had arbitrary power to control the right of persons to speak on religious matters.

In Niemotko v. Maryland, 71 S.Ct. 325 (1951), the Court rejected a discriminatory and arbitrary policy. Although no ordinance regulated the use of the park in Havre de Grace, Maryland, it had been customary for organizations to obtain a permit from the Park Commissioner. The Jehovah's Witnesses requested permission to use the park on four consecutive Sundays. Permission was refused even though no explanation was provided. The meeting was held anyway. Daniel Niemotko, who opened the meeting, was convicted on a disorderly conduct charge. He appealed. The Supreme Court noted that use of the park had been denied because the City Council disagreed with the opinions of the Jehovah's Witnesses. The city allowed other religious groups to use the park. To allow expression of religious beliefs by some and to deny the same privilege to others, merely because their views are unpopular, is a denial of equal protection of the law. The freedoms of speech and religion are entitled to firmer protection than that which depends upon the personal whims of local officials. According to Chief Justice Fred Vinson, "the lack of standards in the license issuing 'practice' renders that 'practice' a prior restraint." The conviction was overturned.

In <u>Cox v. New Hampshire</u>, 61 S.Ct. 762 (1941), the Court upheld a statute that properly regulated public assembly. On July 8, 1939, about 100 members of Jehovah's Witnesses participated in an informational march. The group marched, single file, along the sidewalks; marchers carried banners and handed out leaflets announcing a meeting to be held at a later time. Most were arrested and convicted for violating a New Hampshire statute prohibiting a "parade or procession" upon a public street without a permit. During the trial, the State pointed out that, every hour on a typical night, 26,000 people pass by the intersections where the defendants marched. The State claimed that the marchers had interfered with normal sidewalk travel. The Supreme Court upheld the statute:

> The authority of a municipality to impose regulations in order to assure the safety and convenience of the people in the use of public highways has never been regarded as inconsistent with civil liberties but rather as one of the means of safeguarding the good order upon which they ultimately depend.

The Court noted that the statute appropriately fixed time and place requirements. Equally important, the statute did not grant the permit board arbitrary "power"; discretion had to be exercised with uniform treatment. With respect to the meeting held by Jehovah's Witnesses, a change in time, place, and manner was necessary to avoid a public disturbance.

In three cases mentioned in this section — <u>Hague</u>, <u>Kunz</u>, and <u>Niemotko</u> — the Court overturned ordinances that allowed city officials to arbitrarily consent to, or withhold, permission for a public meeting. Specific guidelines are necessary to direct official action in determining whether permission will be granted or denied. In a fourth case, <u>Cox</u>, the Court acknowledged that a state may regulate public meetings on streets and in parks through a valid ordinance which specifies time, place, and manner of regulation.

RIGHT TO PICKET

The Supreme Court granted picketing First Amendment protection in 1940. The case originated when union organizer Byron Thornhill peacefully urged a group of strikebreakers not to cross a picket line. Thornhill was convicted of violating the Alabama antipicketing law. In <u>Thornhill v. Alabama</u>, 60 S.Ct. 736 (1940), the Supreme Court reversed the conviction and held that the right to picket enjoyed First Amendment protection. The Alabama antipicketing statute was deemed invalid because of two flaws — overbreadth and vagueness.

The statute was overbroad because it proscribed activities that were constitutionally protected, as well as activities that were not: "Whatever the means used to publicize the facts of a labor dispute, whether by printed sign, by pamphlet, by word of mouth or otherwise, all such activity without exception is within the inclusive prohibition of the statute." The Court also noted that "the dissemination of information concerning the facts of a labor dispute must be regarded as within that area of free discussion that is guaranteed by the Constitution." The statute was vague because the term "picket" was "nowhere delineated."

In Hughes v. Superior Court of California, 70 S.Ct. 718 (1950), the Court distinguished between picketing and speech, and in so doing placed limitations on the right to picket. The case began when a civil rights organization demanded that a grocery store hire blacks as soon as white clerks quit, until the proportion of black to white clerks approximated the proportion of black to white customers. When store officials refused this demand, picketers began to patrol in front of the store. The owner of the store obtained an injunction restraining the group from picketing. Upon appeal, the Supreme Court upheld the injunction, noting that the freedom to picket is less protected than freedom of speech.

> It has been amply recognized that picketing, not being the equivalent of speech as a matter of fact, is not its inevitable legal equivalent. Picketing is not beyond the control of a state if the manner in which the picketing is conducted or the purpose which it seeks to effectuate gives ground for its disallowance. A state is not required to tolerate in all places and circumstances, even peaceful picketing by an individual.

RIGHT TO DEMONSTRATE

In Edwards v. South Carolina, 83 S.Ct. 680 (1963), the Supreme Court recognized the right to demonstrate. On March 2, 1961, 187 black high school and college students walked to the South Carolina statehouse grounds where they protested discriminatory practices against blacks. A crowd of onlookers formed, and even though the crowd did not interfere with pedestrian or vehicular traffic, the police told the students to disperse within 15 minutes or they would be arrested. The students refused to disband. Instead, they sang patriotic and religious songs while stamping their feet and clapping their hands. After 15 minutes, they were arrested. The trial court convicted the students of disturbing the peace and imposed sentences ranging from a $10 fine or five days in jail to a $100 fine or 30 days in jail. They appealed. The Supreme Court, in reversing the convictions, ruled that

South Carolina infringed on the rights of the protestors. First, the students had a valid complaint in what they perceived to be the discriminatory laws. Second, the students assembled peaceably; at no time was there a threat of violence on the part of the students. Police protection was always ample. Third, the students had been arrested because "the opinions which they were peaceably expressing were sufficiently opposed to the views of the majority of the community to attract a crowd and necessitate police protection." The Court concluded that a state cannot ban the peaceful demonstration of unpopular views.

The right to demonstrate was reinforced in Gregory v. Chicago, 89 S.Ct. 946 (1969). Blacks in Chicago had become dissatisfied because the Superintendent of Schools was not moving speedily to desegregate public schools. A group of blacks began a march near the Chicago Loop and in an orderly fashion walked five miles to the neighborhood of Mayor Richard Daley's home. The blacks urged the Mayor to remove the Superintendent from his position. A crowd of about a thousand onlookers started shouting threats: "Goddamned nigger, get the hell out of here." Cars were stopped in the streets with their horns blowing. Ku Klux Klan signs were observable, and people started singing the Alabama trooper song. Afraid that the crowd was about to erupt, the police asked march leader Dick Gregory to leave the area. Gregory refused, and was eventually convicted of breaking the Chicago disorderly conduct law. The case reached the Supreme Court. Chief Justice Earl Warren noted that the demonstration had been orderly and that the conduct of the marchers was protected by the First Amendment. In their concurring opinion, Justices Hugo Black and William Douglas stressed that police may not stop a peaceful demonstration simply because a hostile crowd disagrees with the protestors. Police may stop a demonstration only if there is imminent threat of violence and the police have expended all reasonable efforts to protect the demonstrators. In Gregory, the police offered no protection for the demonstrators. In fact, the alleged "breach of the peace" occurred when the policeman in charge determined "that the hecklers...were dangerously close to rioting and that the demonstrators...were likely to be engulfed in that riot." So, he ordered Gregory to leave. Black and Douglas observed: "To let a policeman's command become equivalent to a criminal statute comes dangerously near making our government one of men rather than of laws." Such a possibility necessitated the reversal of Gregory's conviction.

RIGHT TO BOYCOTT

The Supreme Court acknowledged First Amendment protection for boycotting in NAACP v. Claiborne Hardware Company, 102 S.Ct. 3409 (1982). The case began when black citizens in Claiborne County, Mississippi presented white officials with a list of demands for racial equality. When the demands were ignored, several hundred NAACP members boycotted white merchants in the area. The merchants filed suit in court to recover losses caused by the boycott, and to forbid future boycott activity. The case reached the Supreme Court where the majority opinion of Justice John Stevens sided with the NAACP. Stevens stressed that "the boycott clearly involved constitutionally protected activity. The established elements of speech, assembly, association and petition, though not identical, are inseparable."

RIGHT TO LOITER

In 1992, Chicago enacted an anti-loitering law in an effort to clear the streets in gang-infested neighborhoods. The law made it a crime to "remain in any one place with no apparent purpose" while in the presence of a suspected gang member, when ordered by a police officer to move on. Violation of the ordinance was a misdemeanor carrying a fine of up to $500 or imprisonment of up to six months. Under the law, Chicago police arrested more than 42,000 people during the ensuing four years. Eventually, the law was challenged by the American Civil Liberties Union. The Supreme Court, in Chicago v. Morales, 119 S.Ct. 1849 (1999), acknowledged that the "freedom to loiter for innocent purposes" is constitutionally protected behavior. Furthermore, the Court declared the law unconstitutional because it gave the police too much discretion to single out innocent individuals. Stevens noted that a law which directly prohibited intimidating behavior of gang members would be constitutional but the Chicago ordinance "covers a significant amount of additional activity." Accordingly, the ordinance was "too vague." In a dissenting opinion, Justice Antonin Scalia criticized the plurality opinion because "it leaps far beyond any substantive due process atrocity we have ever committed by actually placing the burden of proof upon the defendant [Chicago] to establish that loitering is not a 'fundamental liberty'." In effect, the Morales decision protected the right to loiter.

REGULATING ASSOCIATION

State and local governments have attempted to regulate associations. Laws have been directed at groups whose goals and/or methods spark concern, as well as at the locations where groups gather. Of course, any statute is subject to constitutionality requirements. And, any individual or group that challenges a regulatory statute must follow certain procedures. These aspects are considered in the following section.

CONTROL OF ORGANIZATIONS

Over the past half-century, authorities have occasionally moved to control groups that pose real or imagined threats to national security. In 1944, the Supreme Court decided the constitutionality of an executive order that barred Japanese-American citizens from a specific geographical location. During recent decades, the Court considered the constitutionality of laws designed to control membership in the Communist Party, the organizational rights of prisoners, and the political contributions of corporations.

Japanese-Americans

On December 7, 1941, Japanese bombers attacked U.S. military bases at Pearl Harbor. President Franklin Delano Roosevelt declared war against Japan. At that time, about 112,000 persons of Japanese ancestry lived on the Pacific coast of the United States. The government declared that "the successful prosecution of the war requires every possible protection against...sabotage to national-defense material." Subsequently, President Franklin Delano Roosevelt issued an order which directed that all Japanese-Americans be excluded from the West Coast. Fred Korematsu was convicted for defying the order by remaining in California. Korematsu was placed on probation for five years. He appealed. The Supreme Court upheld the conviction. In the opinion of Justice Hugo Black, Korematsu was not excluded because of his race, rather, because military authorities feared an invasion on the West Coast. In Korematsu v. United States, 65 S.Ct. 193 (1944), the Court viewed the ban as encompassing military danger rather than social prejudice.

Communists

The Communist Party has been a target of government efforts to control "undesirable" groups. Through the years, the government has attempted to contain the growth of membership, identify persons affiliated with the organization, and control the activities of members. In 1950, at the start of the Korean War, Congress passed the McCarran Act over President Harry Truman's veto. Under the Act, Communist organizations were required to register with the Attorney General, giving names of the officers and members. When the Communist Party did not register, the Subversive Activities Control Board ordered it to do so. The Party appealed. In Communist Party v. Subversive Activities Control Board, 81 S.Ct. 1357 (1961), the Supreme Court upheld the order. In the opinion by Justice Felix Frankfurter, the Act was regulatory, not prohibitory, and the requirement to file the membership list was "demanded by rational interests high in the scale of National Concern." According to Frankfurter, this case differed from NAACP v. Alabama, 78 S.Ct. 1163 (1958), where such a requirement had been overturned. Requiring disclosure of membership lists is a reasonable regulation if the requirement is not aimed at prohibiting a particular group.

In another case heard that year, the Court emphasized that the right to organize is not absolute. Raphael Konigsberg refused, before the California State Committee of Bar Examiners, to answer questions relating to his membership in the Communist Party. Konigsberg was denied admission to the bar. He appealed. In Konigsberg v. State Bar of California, 81 S.CT. 997 (1961), the Supreme Court, using the balancing test, decided that California's interest in determining the fitness of applicants to the state bar outweighed free speech.

In 1971, the Court heard a case with similar facts, but provided a different result. When taking the Arizona bar examination, Sara Baird was asked whether she had ever been a member of the Communist Party or any organization "that advocates overthrow of the United States Government by force or violence." When she refused to answer this question, the bar committee recommended that she be denied admission. She appealed. In Baird v. State Bar of Arizona, 91 S.Ct. 702 (1971), the Supreme Court ruled that the First Amendment prohibits a state from excluding a person from a profession solely because that person is a member of a particular organization. In Baird, the Court, on balance, weighted the issue in favor of First Amendment freedoms.

United States v. Robel, 88 S.Ct. 419 (1967), involved the Subversive Activities Control Act of 1950, which prohibited members of communist groups from working in any defense facility. Eugene Robel, a member of the Communist Party who was employed as a machinist at the Todd Shipyards Corporation, was charged with violating the law. The case reached the Supreme Court. The Court ruled that the law was unconstitutional; it prevented employment because of guilt by mere association. According to Chief Justice Earl Warren, it was "precisely because that statute sweeps indiscriminately across all types of associations with communist-action groups, without regard to the quality and degree of membership, that it runs afoul of the First Amendment."

In <u>Communist Party of Indiana v. Whitcomb</u>, 94 S.Ct. 656 (1974), the Court again upheld the freedom to associate, while rejecting the practice of guilt by association. The Communist Party of Indiana applied for a place on the ballot during the 1972 general election. The application was rejected because the Party failed to submit an oath stating that it did not advocate the overthrow of the government by force or violence. The Party appealed. The Supreme Court held that the loyalty oath violated free-speech guarantees. The Court noted that "the right to associate with the political party of one's choice is an integral part" of protected First Amendment rights.

Government efforts to control communist groups have been interpreted rather consistently by the Supreme Court. In early cases — <u>Communist Party</u>, <u>Konigsberg</u> — the Court decided, on balance, that the nation's interests warranted the restrictions placed on associational rights. In more recent cases — <u>Baird</u>, <u>Robel</u>, <u>Whitcomb</u> — the Court stressed that guilt by mere association contradicts First Amendment guarantees. Over time, the Supreme Court acknowledged that the threat posed by the Communist Party has diminished.

Prisoners

The Supreme Court has determined that prisoners do not enjoy equal freedom of association as individuals who are not incarcerated. In <u>Jones v. North Carolina Prisoners' Labor Union</u>, 97 S.Ct. 2532 (1977), a union claimed that the First Amendment rights of prisoners were violated by regulations which prohibited prisoners from soliciting inmates to join the union, and which barred union meetings. The Supreme Court, per Justice William Rehnquist, noted that officials must be permitted to take "reasonable steps" to preserve order and authority in prisons. The regulations represented a constitutional method of maintaining a calm prison atmosphere.

> Perhaps the most obvious of the First Amendment rights that are necessarily curtailed by confinement are those associational rights that the First Amendment protects outside of prison walls. The concept of incarceration itself entails a restriction on the freedom of inmates to associate with those outside of the penal institution.

The Court concluded that the inmates' "status as a prisoner" and the "operational realities of a prison" justify restrictions on their associational rights.

Corporations

The Michigan Chamber of Commerce, a nonprofit corporation, funded its treasury through annual dues required of all members. The

Michigan Campaign Finance Act prohibited corporations from using treasury funds to support political candidates. Because the Chamber wished to use funds to advertise in support of a specific candidate, it initiated court action on the ground that the law violated the First Amendment. In <u>Austin v. Michigan Chamber of Commerce</u>, 110 S.Ct. 1391 (1990), the Supreme Court upheld the law as justified by a compelling state interest in preventing corruption. The law sought to reduce the potential for huge corporate treasuries to exert unfair influence on election outcomes. The Court determined that the law was not overbroad; it was narrowly tailored to achieve its goal. Although some corporations may not have accumulated significant amounts of wealth, the potential for distorting the political process justified general applicability to all corporations. Moreover,

> ...the Act does not impose an *absolute* ban on all forms of corporate political spending but permits corporations to make independent political expenditures through separate segregated funds. Because persons contributing to such funds understand that their money will be used solely for political purposes, the speech generated accurately reflects contributors' support for the corporation's political views.

LOCATIONAL CONSIDERATIONS

Does a group have the right to gather on private property? In several cases, the Supreme Court has answered that question in the negative. The freedom to associate which applies to public grounds does not pertain to private property.

Private buildings

The <u>Adderly v. Florida</u>, 87 S.Ct. 242 (1966), case involved about 200 students who protested against the prior arrest of fellow civil rights protestors. When the group blocked the entrance which was used to transport prisoners from the jail to the court nearby, the Sheriff notified the students that they should leave and that refusal would result in their arrest. Some students left, but the 32 who remained were arrested and convicted. They appealed. The Supreme Court upheld the convictions because the protest was lodged against a jail, traditionally closed to the public, and built for security purposes. Unlike the gathering in <u>Edwards</u>, where the protest was lodged on public grounds, the students in <u>Adderly</u> protested against private property, and for that reason were subject to prosecution.

Private residence

Individuals opposed to abortion picketed outside the Brookfield, Wisconsin residence of a doctor who performed abortions. In response to this activity, the Town Board passed an ordinance which prohibited "picketing before or about the residence or dwelling of any individual." The picketers initiated court action. In Frisby v. Schultz, 108 S.Ct. 2495 (1988), the Supreme Court upheld the ordinance. Justice Sandra O'Connor noted that the use of the singular form of the words "residence" and "dwelling" suggested that the ordinance was intended to prohibit picketing on a particular residence. General picketing through residential neighborhoods was not prohibited. As a result, the narrowly-drawn statute served a significant government interest.

> ...a special benefit of the privacy all citizens enjoy within their own walls, which the State may legislate to protect, is an ability to avoid intrusions. Thus, we have repeatedly held that individuals are not required to welcome unwanted speech into their own homes and that the government may protect this freedom.

Shopping-centers

In four cases decided between 1968 and 1980, the Supreme Court examined whether picketing is permissible in privately owned shopping areas. The first case involved Logan Valley Plaza, a shopping center located near Altoona, Pennsylvania. Signs were posted which prohibited trespassing or soliciting by anyone other than shopping-center employees. When members of a union began picketing the store, Logan Valley obtained a court order that required all picketing to be conducted along the roads outside the shopping-center. The Supreme Court overturned the order. Justice William Douglas noted that two types of activity were involved, one of which could be regulated: "Picketing is free speech, plus, the plus being physical activity that may implicate traffic and related matters. Hence, the latter aspects of picketing may be regulated." Douglas acknowledged that the provisions which prohibited picketers from interfering with employees, deliverymen, and customers were proper. Those provisions, however, that make "private property a sanctuary from which some members of the public may be excluded merely because of the ideas they espouse" were illegal. In Amalgamated Food Employees Union v. Logan Valley Plaza, 88 S.Ct. 1601 (1968), the Court concluded that trespass laws cannot be used to exclude members of the public from exercising their First Amendment picketing rights on premises that are freely accessible to the public.

In Lloyd v. Tanner, 92 S.Ct. 2219 (1972), the Court considered the issue again. Donald Tanner distributed handbills in the mall of Lloyd Center in Portland, Oregon. The handbills announced a meeting to protest the draft and the Vietnam War. Since the Lloyd Center had a strict no-handbilling regulation, security guards requested Tanner to stop. He complied, but brought the issue before the high court. The Supreme Court's opinion concluded that a privately owned shopping center had the right to prohibit the distribution of handbills on its property when the handbilling was unrelated to the shopping center's operation. The opinion cited some distinctions to free Lloyd from the precedent set by Logan Valley. In Logan Valley, the picketing was directed at a specific audience and concerned the use of shopping-center property. It had been upheld because of a lack of alternative opportunities for communicating the message to the intended audience. The handbilling in Lloyd Center, however, was unrelated to any activity within the center, and Tanner had alternative means of communication. Lloyd did not overrule Logan Valley; there were significant differences between the two cases.

In Hudgens v. National Labor Relations Board, 96 S.Ct. 1029 (1976), the Court overruled Logan Valley. When striking employees of the Butler Shoe Company peacefully picketed a store in a shopping plaza located outside Atlanta, Georgia, the manager told them that they could not picket within the mall or parking lot. The picketers left, but their union filed an unfair-labor practice complaint with the National Labor Relations Board. The Supreme Court decided that if the young man in Lloyd lacked First Amendment protection to enter the shopping center to distribute handbills concerning Vietnam, then the picketers in Hudgens "did not have a First Amendment right to enter this shopping center for the purpose of advertising their strike against the Butler Shoe Company."

In 1980, the Court heard a related case. It involved a group of high school students who conducted a petition in the privately owned PruneYard Shopping Center in Campbell, California. The students asked passersby to sign a petition opposing a United Nations resolution against Zionism. A security guard informed the students that shopping-center regulations prohibited any petitioning not directly pertinent to the center's commercial purposes. The students left the premises, but initiated court action. In PruneYard Shopping Center v. Robins, 100 S.Ct. 2035 (1980), the Supreme Court upheld a California statute that permitted citizens to exercise free speech and petition rights in a privately owned shopping center. The opinion noted a key difference between PruneYard and Lloyd: "In Lloyd...there was no state constitutional or statutory provision that had been construed to create rights to the use of private property by strangers, comparable to those found...here [in PruneYard]."

The four cases described above determined which regulations are applicable to picketing in privately owned shopping centers. In Lloyd and Hudgens, the Court set aside Logan Valley by denying the right of public picketing in privately-owned shopping areas. PruneYard, however, upheld the power of a state to protect picketing in such areas.

Inaccessibility exception

In Lechmere v. NLRB, 112 S.Ct. 841 (1992), the Court reiterated its stand regarding associational activity on private property. The specific behavior at issue involved union organizers placing handbills on employees' cars at a privately owned shopping plaza. Speaking through Justice Clarence Thomas, the Court held that an employer is not required to allow union organizers to distribute literature or solicit memberships. This form of trespass is protected only in rare cases where employees cannot be reached by other means. Thomas noted that the "inaccessibility exception" applies only "where the location of a plant and the living quarters of the employees place the employees beyond the reach of reasonable union efforts to communicate with them." In Lechmere, there were no "unique obstacles"; employees could be reached by numerous alternative methods such as mail, phone calls, home visits, newspaper advertising, or signs located at various points in the community.

STATUTORY REQUIREMENTS

Several cases already discussed in this chapter (Cantwell, Staub, Hague, Kunz, Niemotko, Thornhill, Robel, Whitcomb) involved statutes that were thrown out because they failed to meet constitutional requirements. Associational rights may not be regulated by an ordinance which is arbitrary, vague, overly broad, discriminatory, subject-matter oriented, or which judges guilt by association. Furthermore, a regulatory ordinance must specify time, place, and/or manner of restriction.

Arbitrary authority

During the spring of 1963, black citizens sought a permit authorizing the right to hold a parade to protest discrimination in Birmingham, Alabama. City Commissioner Eugene "Bull" Conner, citing a local ordinance, categorically denied the request. When the citizens held the parade without the permit, they were arrested, convicted, and sentenced to spend five days in jail and pay a $50 fine. In Shuttlesworth v. Birmingham, 89 S.Ct. 935 (1969), the Supreme Court overturned the ordinance because it subjected "the exercise of First Amendment freedoms to the prior restraint of a license, without narrow, objective, and definitive standards to guide the licensing authority." Decision making power rested with the arbitrary authority of a local official.

The Court cited the same reason in overturning an ordinance in Forsyth County, Georgia v. The Nationalist Movement, 112 S.Ct. 2395 (1992). The ordinance regulated the issuance of permits for private demonstrations and other uses of public property. The ordinance specified that, because the cost of protecting participants in such activities exceeds the cost of law enforcement, every permit applicant had to pay a fee. The county administrator was empowered to adjust the fee's amount to meet the expense in each case. After the county imposed a fee for a proposed demonstration in opposition to the Martin Luther King, Jr. federal holiday, the Nationalist Movement, an arm of the Ku Klux Klan, filed legal action. The Supreme Court found the ordinance to be unconstitutional.

> The decision how much to charge for police protection or administrative time — or even whether to charge at all — is left to the unbridled discretion of the administrator, who is not required to rely on objective standards or provide any explanation of his decision.

Vagueness, overbreadth, discriminatory

In Cameron v. Johnson, 88 S.Ct. 1335 (1960), the Court upheld a constitutional anti-picketing ordinance. The case began when a drive to increase voter registration of blacks was held at the courthouse in Hattiesburg, Mississippi. Black citizens maintained a picket line outside the courthouse throughout the campaign. Even though the Governor signed an anti-picketing law, the picketing continued. When some pickets were arrested, their colleagues sought to have the statute overturned. The Supreme Court held that the statute was constitutional. First, the law was not vague — it prohibited "only picketing in such a manner as to obstruct or unreasonably interfere with free ingress or egress to and from any county courthouses." The statute "clearly and precisely delineates its reach in words of common understanding." Second, the law was not overbroad — it banned "conduct subject to regulation so as to vindicate important interests in society." According to the Court, "the fact that free speech is intermingled with such conduct does not bring with it constitutional protection." Third, the law was not selectively enforced — it was not employed to harass any particular group. The law met statutory requirements.

In Schenck v. Pro-Choice Network of Western New York, 117 S.Ct. 855 (1997), the Court overturned a judicial order that imposed both "fixed" and "floating" regulatory zones. According to the Court, floating zones constituted an overly broad restriction. The case began when several upstate New York doctors, clinics, and organizations dedicated to maintaining access to abortion services filed a complaint seeking to prohibit protestors from engaging in blockades at the clinics. Various abortion clinics had been subjected to large scale blockades in which protestors marched in parking lot driveways and doorways, blocking cars from entering the lots, and preventing patients and employees from entering the clinics. The court issued a restraining order which banned any demonstrations within fifteen feet of entrances to clinic facilities (fixed buffer zones) or within fifteen feet of any person or vehicle seeking access to or leaving these facilities (floating buffer zones). In Schenck, the Supreme Court held that the fixed zones were constitutional but the floating zones were overly broad.

> We strike down the floating buffer zones around the people entering and leaving the clinics because they burden more speech than is necessary to serve the relevant government interests. The floating buffer zones prevent defendants...from communicating a message from a normal conversational distance or handing leaflets to people entering or leaving the clinics who are walking on the public sidewalks. This is a broad prohibition, both because of the type of speech that is restricted and the nature of location. Leafleting and commenting on matters of public concern are classic forms of speech that lie at the heart of the First Amendment, and speech in public areas is at its most protected on public sidewalks, a prototypical example of a traditional public forum.

Content-based

In 1972, in two cases, the Court held that an ordinance may regulate the time, place, and manner of public assembly, but not the subject matter. The first case, Police Department of Chicago v. Mosley, 92 S.Ct. 2286 (1972), involved a Chicago ordinance that banned picketing within 150 feet of any elementary or secondary school, except for peaceful picketing concerning a labor dispute. Earl Mosley initiated court action, arguing that the statute punished activity protected by the First Amendment. The Supreme Court held that the ordinance was unconstitutional because it made an impermissible distinction between labor picketing and other picketing. The ordinance did not limit picketing in terms of time, place, or manner, but rather in terms of subject matter.

> The central problem with Chicago's ordinance is that it describes permissible picketing in terms of its subject matter. Peaceful picketing on the subject of a school's labor-management dispute is permitted, but all other peaceful picketing is prohibited. The operative distinction is the message on the picket sign. But, above all else, the First Amendment means that government has no power to restrict expression because of its message, its ideas, its subject matter, or its content.

The second case, Grayned v. Rockford, 92 S.Ct. 2294 (1972), involved a demonstration in front of West Senior High School in Rockford, Illinois. Black students marched on the sidewalk around the school building; they carried signs that summarized their grievances. The picketers were arrested, tried, and convicted of violating an anti-picketing ordinance. The Supreme Court held that the ordinance, which banned all picketing of a school building except that related to a labor dispute, was unconstitutional for the same reasons given in Mosley. The convictions were reversed.

A similar case, Carey v. Brown, 100 S.Ct. 2286 (1980), concerned an Illinois statute that prohibited picketing of residences, but exempted picketing of a place of employment involved in a labor dispute. The Court found:

> On its face, the act accords preferential treatment to the expression of views on one particular subject; information about labor disputes may be freely disseminated, but discussion of all other issues is restricted. The permissibility of residential picketing under the Illinois statute is thus dependent solely on the nature of the message being conveyed. In these critical respects, then, the Illinois statute is identical to the ordinance in Mosley, and it suffers from the same constitutional infirmities.

Time, place, manner

In Clark v. Community for Creative Non-Violence, 104 S.Ct. 3065 (1984), the Court upheld a law which contained reasonable time, place, and manner restrictions. The case involved a National Park Service regulation which prohibited camping in certain parks. The case arose when the Community For Creative Non-Violence conducted a demonstration in Lafayette Park, in downtown Washington, D.C. The group, which gathered to demonstrate the plight of the homeless, had obtained a permit authorizing the erection of two symbolic tent cities as a means of expressing their point of view. The Park Service cited the anti-camping regulation in denying the group's request that demonstrators be permitted to sleep in the tents. Eventually, the

Supreme Court heard the case and upheld the ban.

> All those who would resort to the parks must abide by...valid rules for their use, just as they must observe the traffic laws, sanitation regulations, and laws to preserve the public peace. This is no more than a reaffirmation that reasonable time, place, and manner restrictions on expression are constitutionally acceptable.

The cases described in this section confirm that associational rights may be regulated by constitutionally drawn law. To pass such a test, the law must be clear, narrow, non-discriminatory, and content-neutral.

PROCEDURAL CONSIDERATIONS

The Supreme Court has decided several cases involving procedural questions. In <u>Poulos v. New Hampshire</u>, 73 S.Ct. 760 (1953), the Court stipulated the procedure a person must follow when challenging discriminatory enforcement of a valid statute. A Portsmouth, New Hampshire ordinance banned any parades or public meetings unless a license was obtained from the City Council. William Poulos, a Jehovah's Witness, was refused a permit for a religious meeting. No justification was provided for the refusal. Poulos, realizing that the ordinance had been applied in a discriminatory manner, held the meeting in a public park without a license. He was convicted and fined $20. On appeal, the Supreme Court affirmed that the ordinance was constitutional; it gave local authorities no arbitrary discretion in refusing permits. Rather, the ordinance instructed them to process all applications and to refuse licenses only when necessary to avert congestion in the public parks. Though Poulos would have been justified to disobey an unconstitutional ordinance, that issue was not relevant in this case. The Court noted that proof of a valid ordinance being applied in a discriminatory fashion does not justify disobedience. The only acceptable recourse in such instances is through the judicial system. Poulos' only legal remedy against discriminatory refusal by city officials to grant the permit would have been to obtain a judicial order to force issuance of the permit. Poulos had acted improperly when he ignored the denial of the license and held the gathering anyway. It is illegal to disobey a valid ordinance, even if it has been implemented in a discriminatory fashion.

In <u>Walker v. Birmingham</u>, 87 S.Ct. 1824 (1967), the Court faced another issue — are demonstrators required to obey a court injunction when the ordinance upon which it is based is unconstitutional? During the spring of 1963, sit-ins and marches were conducted by the black community to protest discrimination in Birmingham, Alabama. A court granted a temporary injunction enjoining the leaders of the demonstrations from conducting parades until they complied with a local ordinance and obtained a permit. The leaders applied for a permit, but the request was categorically refused without justification. Subsequently, demonstrations were held without any attempt to dissolve the injunction. Eight black ministers were arrested and held in contempt. They appealed, contending that the Birmingham law was unconstitutional; permission to demonstrate depended upon city administrators who had arbitrarily made it clear that no permission would be granted. The Supreme Court affirmed the convictions, noting that initial obedience is required of an unconstitutional court decree. The injunction must be overturned on appeal to a higher court. The opinion, prepared by Justice Potter Stewart, claimed:

> In the fair administration of justice no man can be judge in his own case, however exalted his station, however righteous his motives, and irrespective of his race, color, politics, or religion. This Court cannot hold that the petitioners were constitutionally free to ignore all the procedures of the law and carry their battle to the streets. One may sympathize with the petitioners' impatient commitment to their cause. But respect for judicial process is a small price to pay for the civilizing hand of law, which alone can give abiding meaning to constitutional freedom.

The Court concluded that a court order, even if almost certain to be reversed on appeal, must be obeyed until the order is set aside by a higher court.

In _Carroll v. President and Commissioners of Princess Anne County_, 89 S.Ct. 347 (1968), the Court considered whether a city has the authority to ban a demonstration, without granting a hearing to the demonstrators. On July 6, 1966, the National States Rights Party, a white supremacist organization, conducted a rally near the courthouse of Princess Anne, Maryland. Public speakers, amplified so that they could be heard for several blocks, insulted blacks and Jews. State policemen were brought in when the crowd became tense. The rally eventually broke up, but another gathering was scheduled for the following evening. The Princess Anne Commissioners then obtained a ten-day restraining order to prevent the rally. Joseph Carroll, on behalf of the Party, sought Supreme Court review of the order. The Court held the injunction to be unconstitutional. The proceedings that initially set up the injunction were _ex parte_; no notice was given to the States Rights Party to appear. The Carroll decision held that _ex parte_ orders restraining demonstrations are unconstitutional when it is possible to provide an opportunity for notice and a hearing to the demonstrating group, but no such opportunity is provided. In this case, officials were able, but not willing, to notify Carroll of the hearing on the injunction.

In <u>National Socialist Party v. Skokie</u>, 97 S.Ct. 2205 (1977), the Court weighed the issue of immediacy in granting appellate review. On April 29, 1977, the Circuit Court of Cook County, Illinois prohibited the National Socialist Party of America from performing any of the following actions within the predominantly Jewish village of Skokie: marching, walking, or parading in the uniform of the National Socialist Party of America; displaying the swastika on or off their persons; distributing pamphlets that incite or promote hatred against persons of any faith, ancestry, race, or religion. The Party sued, arguing that no timetable had been set for judicial appeal. The Supreme Court decided that the injunction deprived the marchers of First Amendment rights. When a state imposes a restraint of this kind, "it must provide strict procedural safeguards, including immediate appellate review." In <u>Skokie</u>, the court injunction, by failing to provide for such review, was unconstitutional. The <u>Skokie</u> case, like <u>Carroll</u>, established procedural safeguards for demonstrators. <u>Carroll</u> affirmed the right of demonstrators to a hearing. <u>Skokie</u> affirmed the right of immediate appellate review.

CONCLUSION

The following principles regulate communication law regarding ASSOCIATION:

1. The First Amendment protects the freedom to associate, the right to solicit members, and the right to assemble publicly.

2. The First Amendment protects the rights of petition, picketing, boycotting, loitering, and mass demonstration.

3. Associational rights may be restricted or denied when they lead to a breach of the peace — that is, the gathering interferes with public comfort, convenience, peace, or order.

4. The right to associate has been subject to greater control during time of war and national crisis than during peace time.

5. Associational rights may be regulated by a constitutionally drawn ordinance — that is, one which specifies time, place, and manner restrictions.

6. Associational rights may not be regulated by an ordinance which is arbitrary, vague, overbroad, discriminatory, subject-matter oriented,

or which judges guilt by association.

7. Any individual or group, seeking to overturn either a regulatory statute or a judicial decision, must abide by procedural rights and responsibilities.

KEY DECISIONS

1939 —   HAGUE — upheld the right of a group to assemble publicly, so long as the meeting is peaceful

1940 —   CANTWELL — supported the right of an organization to solicit members

1940 —   THORNHILL — determined that picketing enjoyed First Amendment protection

1958 —   NAACP— acknowledged that an organization has the right to protect membership lists

1963 —   EDWARDS — acknowledged the right of demonstration

1966 —   ADDERLEY — restricted demonstrations directed against private property

1972 —   MOSLEY — overturned an ordinance that restricted picketing in terms of subject matter, rather than in terms of time, place, or manner

1976 —   HUDGENS — denied public picketing in privately owned shopping centers

1977 —   SKOKIE — held that when a state restrains a gathering, strict procedural safeguards, including immediate appellate review, must be provided

1982 —   CLAIBORNE HARDWARE — acknowledged that boycotting enjoyed First Amendment protection

1984 —   ROBERTS — rejected practice by social organizations of restricting membership on basis of gender

1995 —   HURLEY — overturned a state law which, while prohibiting discrimination in public parades, also violated the First Amendment

1997 —   SCHENCK — held that "fixed" regulatory zones are constitutional but "floating" zones are overly broad

RECOMMENDED READING

Easterbrook, Frank H. "Implicit and Explicit Rights of Association," Harvard Journal of Law and Public Policy 10 (1987), 91-100.

Fellman, David, The Constitutional Right of Association. Chicago: University of Chicago Press, 1963.

Fellman, David, "Constitutional Rights of Association," Supreme Court Review (1961), 74-134.

Haiman, Franklyn S., "Nonverbal Communication and the First Amendment: The Rhetoric of the Streets Revisited," Quarterly Journal of Speech 68 (November, 1982), 371-83.

Haiman, Franklyn S., "The Rhetoric of the Streets: Some Legal and Ethical Considerations," Quarterly Journal of Speech 53 (April, 1967), 99-114.

Johnson, Robert, "Redefining Associational Rights," Bringham Young University Law Review (1988), 141-59.

Stone, Geoffrey R., "Content-Neutral Restrictions," University of Chicago Law Review 54 (1987), 46-118.

CHAPTER 4

ACADEMIC FREEDOM

Sidney Hook defined academic freedom as "the freedom of professionally qualified persons to inquire, discover, publish, and teach the truth as they see it in the field of their competence." This freedom "is subject to no control or authority except the control or authority of the rational methods by which truths or conclusions are sought and established in these disciplines."[1] Hook emphasized the rights of faculty members. Academic freedom, however, also concerns the interests of administrators, legislators, school boards, parents, and students. At times, these interests are in competition and resolution of the conflict is left to the courts.

ADMINISTRATION RIGHTS

Over the years, various groups have attempted to influence classroom curricula, methods, materials, and activities. Such endeavors have been evaluated by the Supreme Court, and as a result, a body of case law has emerged that establishes guidelines regarding the rights and responsibilities of school administrators.

CONTROL OF CURRICULUM

The curriculum includes all the subject matter offered by an educational institution. Some legislative attempts to control the curriculum have reached the Supreme Court; two such efforts involved the teaching of a foreign language and the use of a textbook that explained the theory of evolution.

Foreign language

Following World War I, Nebraska passed a law that banned the teaching of any subject in a language other than English. Robert Meyer, an instructor at a parochial school, was convicted for teaching his class in German. He appealed. In Meyer v. Nebraska, 43 S.Ct. 625 (1923), the Court determined that a state may not forbid the teaching of subjects or the use of teaching methods that are not injurious to the health or morals of children. The Court ruled that knowledge of the German language was not harmful, that perhaps it was even desirable. The United States contained a large foreign-born population, residing in localities that routinely used foreign languages. Students could be hindered in achieving their maximum usefulness as citizens in their communities if they were deprived of the use of a foreign language. The Court found the Nebraska law unconstitutional since it violated the teacher's right to instruct. Later that year, the Court declared similar ordinances unlawful in Bartels v. Iowa and Bohning v. Ohio, 43 S.Ct. 628 (1923).

Evolution

In 1925, Tennessee passed a law that forbade the teaching of Darwin's theory of evolution. The constitutionality of the act was upheld in Scopes v. State, 289 S.W. 363 (1927). In 1928, Arkansas adopted a similar law which specified that any teacher who promoted Darwinism faced dismissal. This law was challenged in Epperson v. Arkansas, 89 S.Ct. 266 (1968), a case that concerned selection of a biology textbook. The text that had been used for decades at Little Rock Central High School did not contain a section on the Darwinian theory. In 1965, acting upon the recommendation of the biology teachers, the administration adopted a text that included material about evolution. Susan Epperson, a tenth-grade biology teacher, faced a dilemma. She was instructed by school officials to use the new book, but to do so could subject her to dismissal. Epperson instituted court action to determine whether the Arkansas statute was illegal. The Supreme Court unanimously declared the statute to be unconstitutional. According to the Court, the First Amendment's command was to protect the fundamental rights of free speech and inquiry, which are nowhere more vital than in the educational system. The Arkansas law prevented teachers from discussing the theory of evolution. It thereby hindered the quest for knowledge and restrained the freedom to teach.

SCHOOL RITUALS

Two school rituals that were practiced frequently, in some instances daily, until the mid-twentieth century were the flag salute and prayer. During the 1940s, the Supreme Court first upheld, then overturned the flag-salute ritual. Two decades later, the Court declared that school-prayer exercises violated the Constitution.

Flag salute

Lillian and William Gobitis were expelled from the public school for refusing to pledge allegiance to the U.S. flag as part of a daily school ritual. These children, as Jehovah's Witnesses, had been raised to believe that saluting any flag was forbidden by the Bible. Their father initiated suit to stop the school from requiring participation in the flag salute. The Supreme Court weighed the freedom of conscience versus the power of school authorities. After deliberation, the Court upheld the authority of the administrators, who claimed that the flag salute was an effective means of promoting patriotism. In Minersville School District v. Gobitis, 60 S.Ct. 1010 (1940), the Court approved the flag salute as a required ritual.

Three years later, in West Virginia State Board of Education v. Barnette, 63 S.Ct. 1178 (1943), the Court reversed its position. When a group of Jehovah's Witnesses refused to salute the flag, they were expelled from school and their parents were prosecuted. Ultimately, the case reached the Supreme Court. The opinion, written by Justice Robert Jackson, stressed four differences between this case and Gobitis. First, in Gobitis, the Court supported the notion that a government must be stronger than the liberties of its people. In Barnette, the Court preferred individual freedom of mind over officially disciplined uniformity. Second, in Gobitis, the Court thought that to interfere with educational decisions would make the Supreme Court the school board for the nation. In Barnette, the Court acknowledged that while boards of education have vital functions, none may be performed in violation of the Constitution. Third, in Gobitis, the justices reasoned that the Court had no competence in the field of education and that the controlling influence should rest with legislatures and the public. In Barnette, the Court ruled that the rights of free speech and press are not subject to political debate or public votes. Fourth, Gobitis supported the view that "national unity is the basis of national security," and that school authorities have a right to decide how to attain that unity. In Barnette, the Court questioned whether a compulsory flag salute was an appropriate means of instilling national unity. According to the Court, "to believe that patriotism will not flourish if patriotic ceremonies are voluntary and spontaneous instead of a compulsory routine is to make an unflattering estimate of the appeal of our institutions to free minds." In Barnette, the Court set aside the mandatory flag-salute exercise.

Prayer

The school-prayer issue came before the Supreme Court in several cases. Engel v. Vitale, 82 S.Ct. 1261 (1962), involved parents who initiated court action when the Board of Education required a prayer composed by the New York Board of Regents to be said aloud at the beginning of every school day. A year later, in School District of Abington v. Schempp, 83 S.Ct. 1560 (1963), the Court considered a Pennsylvania law which required high school students to hold religious exercises at the start of each day. Participation in the exercises was voluntary; students could leave the room if they wanted, or they could remain in the room and not participate. The Edward Schempp family, members of the Unitarian Church, brought the issue before the courts, arguing that the exercise contradicted their religious beliefs. Schempp considered having his children excused from the exercises, but decided against it because he thought that the relationship between his children and their teachers would be adversely affected. A companion case, Murray v. Curlett, involved a Baltimore Board of School Commissioners' rule that religious services be held at the beginning of the school day. Madalyn Murray and her son, both atheists, argued that the exercise threatened their religious freedom "by placing a premium on belief as against nonbelief" and subjected their "freedom of conscience to the rule of the majority." In Engel, Schempp, and Murray, the Court ruled that both the Establishment and Free Exercise Clauses of the Constitution had been violated.

The Court reinforced this line of thinking in Stone v. Graham, 101 S.Ct. 192 (1981). The case involved a Kentucky statute that required the posting of a copy of the Ten Commandments on the wall of each public classroom in the state. The Superintendent of Public Instruction justified the posting on the ground that the purpose was secular. The Supreme Court disagreed.

> The pre-eminent purpose for posting the Ten Commandments on schoolroom walls is plainly religious in nature. The Ten Commandments are undeniably a sacred text in the Jewish and Christian faiths, and no legislative recitation of a supposed secular purpose can blind us to that fact. The Commandments do not confine themselves to arguably secular matters, such as honoring one's parents, killing or murder, adultery, stealing, false witness, and covetousness. Rather, the first part of the Commandments concerns

the religious duties of believers: worshipping the Lord God alone, avoiding idolatry, not using the Lord's name in vain, and observing the Sabbath Day.

Lee v. Weisman, 112 S.Ct. 2649 (1992), is a related case. It began when principals in the public school system invited members of the clergy to offer invocation and benediction prayers as part of graduation ceremonies. The father of one of the graduates initiated court action, arguing that the practice violated the Establishment Clause. He noted that the Constitution guarantees that government may not coerce students to participate in activities which "establish" a religious faith, or "tend to do so." Speaking for the Court, Justice Anthony Kennedy agreed:

> The undeniable fact is that the school district's supervision and control of a high school graduation ceremony places public pressure, as well as peer pressure, on attending students to stand as a group or, at least, maintain respectful silence during the Invocation and Benediction. This pressure, though subtle and indirect, can be as real as any overt compulsion.

According to Kennedy, the government may not exact religious conformity from a student as the price of attending his or her own graduation. In Lee, as in other cases cited in this section, the Court rejected the idea of compulsory religious rituals in public schools.

TEACHER FITNESS

In several states, committees have been formed to establish standards for judging teacher fitness. As a result, teachers have been required to testify before an investigative committee, banned from holding membership in certain organizations, and asked to take an oath of loyalty. In numerous cases, the Supreme Court has been called upon to evaluate punitive actions taken against teachers who have refused to comply with these standards.

Refusal to testify

Slochower v. Board of Higher Education, 76 S.Ct. 637 (1956), involved a New York City law which stipulated that a city employee could be fired for invoking the Fifth Amendment to avoid answering a question related to his or her employment behavior. Harry Slochower, an Associate Professor of German at Brooklyn College, was suspended when he refused to answer questions. He brought suit. The Supreme Court agreed with the purpose and intent of the law, but found fault with the procedure. Summary dismissal denied due process; the law was unconstitutional because it translated an employee's claim of Fifth

Amendment privilege "into a conclusive presumption of guilt."

A related case, Beilan v. Board of Public Education, 78 S.Ct. 1317 (1958), involved a teacher with 22 years of service. Herman Beilan was called to the Superintendent's office and asked whether he had been an officer in the Communist Party; the Superintendent stressed that he was investigating "a real question of the fitness of Beilan to be a teacher." When Beilan refused to answer, he was dismissed for "incompetency." He appealed. The Supreme Court determined that the questions asked by the Superintendent were relevant to the issue of teacher fitness. When Beilan accepted the teaching position, he had agreed to be cooperative in answering questions related to his fitness to teach. The Court concluded that Beilan was removed from his job, not for his Fifth Amendment claim or his membership in the Communist Party, but because his refusal to answer questions constituted evidence of unreliability and incompetency. In both Slochower and Beilan, the Court affirmed the power of authorities to inquire into a teacher's fitness, as long as the procedures conform to due process requirements.

Membership

Teacher fitness has also been evaluated in terms of membership in certain organizations. For instance, the New York Feinberg Law required that the Board of Regents prepare a list of all organizations that advocated overthrow of the government by force or violence. Membership in a listed organization constituted *prima facie* evidence for disqualification from holding a teaching position in New York schools. In Adler v. Board of Education, 72 S.Ct. 380 (1952), the Supreme Court considered the constitutionality of this statute. According to the Court, if teachers did not choose to work on the reasonable terms laid down by authorities, they were free to retain their associations, and go elsewhere. Justice Sherman Minton's opinion upheld the right of New York to oversee the associational habits of teachers.

> A teacher works in a sensitive area in a school room. There he shapes the attitude of young minds towards the society in which they live. In this, the state has a vital concern. It must preserve the integrity of the schools. That the school authorities have the right and the duty to screen the officials, teachers, and employees as to their fitness to maintain the integrity of the schools as a part of ordered society cannot be doubted.

A similar case, Wieman v. Updegraff, 73 S.Ct. 215 (1952), involved an Oklahoma law that required state employees to take an oath that they were not members of the Communist Party or of any organization that advocated the overthrow of the government. Under the statute, membership alone disqualified a teacher from employment. The Supreme Court found the law to be unconstitutional for two reasons. First, membership could be innocent — a person might join a forbidden organization unaware of its purposes. Second, a group might be innocent at the time it was formed and might later adopt illegitimate ends. Conversely, an organization that was formerly subversive might subsequently reject such influences. The Court found the oath denied due process because "the fact of association alone determines disloyalty and disqualification; it matters not whether association existed innocently or knowingly."

Shelton. v. Tucker, 81 S.Ct. 247 (1960), involved an Arkansas law that compelled teachers to file annually a list of organizations to which they belonged. B. T. Shelton, a teacher in the Little Rock school district for 25 years, declined to submit the list. His contract for the next school year was not renewed. Shelton initiated court action, which ultimately reached the high court. Citing Adler, the Court affirmed that "there can be no doubt of the right of a state to investigate the competence and fitness of those whom it hires to teach in its schools." The Court found, however, that the Arkansas law was very "unlimited and indiscriminate," in that it required a teacher to list "every conceivable kind of associational tie — social, professional, political, avocational, or religious," many of which might "have no possible bearing upon the teacher's occupational competence or fitness." In Shelton, the Court held the law unconstitutional because its "comprehensive interference with associational freedom" went beyond what could be justified in the exercise of a state's "inquiry into the fitness and competency of its teachers."

Loyalty oaths

During the 1960's, the Supreme Court struck down several statutes that established loyalty oaths as a measure of teacher fitness. The Florida statute required state employees to swear that they had never lent their "aid, support, advice, counsel or influence to the Communist Party." In Cramp v. Board of Public Instruction, 82 S.Ct. 275 (1961), the Court overturned the law because of the vagueness of its terms. A similar case is Baggett v. Bullitt, 84 S.Ct. 1316 (1964). All teachers at the University of Washington were required to swear allegiance to the laws of the United States and of the state of Washington. Teachers also had to disclaim membership in the Communist Party or any other subversive organization. In Baggett, the Court declared the loyalty oath unconstitutional because the language of the statute was unduly vague, uncertain, and broad. In <u>Keyishian v. Board of Regents</u>, 87 S.Ct. 675 (1967), the Court evaluated a New York law which required teachers to sign a certificate indicating that they were not Communists. The Court found the law to be overly broad since dismissal was based on mere membership without any showing of a teacher's intent to further the unlawful aims of the Communist Party. Clearly, New York's intent was to keep subversives out of the teaching ranks; but the loyalty-oath procedure stifled personal liberties and posed potential harm to academic freedom.

> The classroom is peculiarly the "marketplace of ideas." The Nation's future depends upon leaders trained through wide exposure to that robust exchange of ideas which discovers truth "out of a multitude of tongues [rather] than through any kind of authoritative selection."

<u>Whitehill v. Elkins</u>, 88 S.Ct. 184 (1967), involved a Maryland loyalty oath which required teachers to pledge that they were "not engaged in one way or another in the attempt to overthrow the Government." The Supreme Court noted the ambiguity of the act. The Court, in overturning the requirement, decided that "the continuing surveillance which this type of law places on teachers is hostile to academic freedom."

In cases cited in this section, the Court supported the right of a legislature to inquire into the fitness of public-school teachers, but it has been strict concerning the procedures such tests of fitness may follow. In <u>Slochower</u> and <u>Beilan</u>, the Court opposed penalizing a teacher for merely invoking the Fifth Amendment. In <u>Wieman</u>, a law was judged to violate due process because it did not recognize that association with a subversive organization might be innocent. In <u>Shelton</u>, a law was declared unconstitutional because it required a teacher to reveal associational ties that might have no bearing whatsoever upon a teacher's fitness. In <u>Cramp</u>, <u>Baggett</u>, <u>Keyishian</u>, and <u>Whitehill</u>, the Court overturned mandatory loyalty oaths because of obscurity in the wording of such oaths. It seems clear, however, that the Supreme Court would uphold inquiry into teacher fitness if conducted in a legal manner — that is, without ambiguity, discrimination, or overbreadth.

CAMPUS SPEAKERS

During the late 1960s and early 1970s, state courts heard numerous cases that involved campus bans on outside speakers. In several cases — <u>Dickson v. Sitterson</u>, 415 F.2d 228 (1969), <u>Stacy v. Williams</u>, 306 F.Supp 963 (1973), <u>Molpus v. Fortune</u>, 311 F. Supp 240 (1970),

Brooks v. Auburn University, 296 F.Supp 188 (1969), Duke v. Texas, 327 F.Supp 1218 (1971) — courts overturned regulations that were vague or overbroad. The courts rejected any system of prior restraint and any denial of speech that was not based on proof of danger to the orderly operation of the university.

Stacy provides a notable example because the court formulated six rules that a university administration should follow in regulating campus speakers: 1) any request had to be made by a student or faculty group; 2) no invitation could be sent without prior written permission from the head of the school; 3) any request had to include, in writing, the name of the sponsoring group, the proposed date, time, and location, the expected size of the audience, and the topic of the speech; 4) a request could be denied by the head of an institution only if the proposed speech would constitute a clear and present danger to orderly operation; 5) a campus review committee, composed of faculty and students, would hear the appeal of an aggrieved sponsoring group — further appeal could be sought through the courts; and 6) upon approval of the speaker, the sponsoring organization had to submit a written report indicating whether, and when, the invitation was accepted. In subsequent cases, the Stacy standards were cited as a model to test the acceptability of campus-speaker regulations.

BANNING BOOKS

In recent decades, groups have attempted to prohibit certain books from school classrooms and libraries. In the 1950s, super-patriotic groups compiled lists of "undesirable" books which were alleged to advocate communistic theories or contain subversive ideas. In the 1960s and 1970s, civil-rights groups tried to ban books that pictured minorities in an unfavorable light. In the 1980s and 1990s, parents and school boards sought to censor "pornographic" and "vulgar" books. Even though efforts to ban "offensive" books have been commonplace, only one case, Island Trees v. Pico, 102 S.Ct. 2799 (1982), was heard by the Supreme Court. The case began in September, 1975, when members of the Board of Education of Island Trees Union Free School District attended a conference sponsored by a politically conservative organization. At the conference, the Board members obtained a list of books described as "improper fare for school students." The Board members decided that nine of the books, housed in the high-school library, should be removed from the shelves. Several students initiated court action, claiming that the Board action denied First Amendment rights. The Island Trees opinion reflected the thinking of a deeply divided Supreme Court. The majority acknowledged that while local school boards have broad discretion in the management of school affairs, students do not relinquish their rights to free speech at the schoolhouse gate. According to Justice William Brennan, students enjoy "the right to receive information and ideas"; the school board must not violate the students' freedom "to inquire, to study and to evaluate, to gain new maturity and understanding. The school library is the principal locus of such freedom." Brennan continued:

> Petitioners [School Board] argue that they must be allowed unfettered discretion to "transmit community values" through the Island Trees schools.... We think that petitioners' reliance upon that duty is misplaced where, as here, they attempt to extend their claim of absolute discretion beyond the compulsory environment of the classroom, into the school library and the regime of voluntary inquiry that there holds sway.

Brennan admitted that school boards possess significant discretion to determine the content of school libraries; however, "that discretion may not be exercised in a narrowly partisan or political manner." In Island Trees, the school board's decision to remove books may have "rested decisively upon disagreement with constitutionally protected ideas in those books, or upon a desire...to impose upon the students...a political orthodoxy to which petitioners and their constituents adhered." According to Brennan,

> ....local school boards may not remove books from school library shelves simply because they dislike the ideas contained in those books and seek their removal to prescribe what shall be orthodox in politics, nationalism, religion, or other matters of opinion.

Brennan, however, noted that nothing in the Island Trees decision affects the authority of a school board to choose books to add to the school libraries; the decision affects only the authority to remove books. The dissenting opinion, written by Chief Justice Warren Burger, criticized the majority's reasoning.

> Today the plurality suggests that the Constitution distinguishes between school libraries and school classrooms, between removing unwanted books and acquiring books. Even more extreme, the plurality concludes that the Constitution requires school boards to justify to its teenage pupils the decision to remove a particular book from a school library. I categorically reject this notion that the Constitution dictates that judges, rather than parents, teachers, and local school boards, must determine how the standards of morality and vulgarity are to be treated in the classroom.

Nonetheless, the thrust of Island Trees is that while school boards have considerable authority to determine the content of school libraries, that authority may not be exercised in a partisan manner.

FACULTY RIGHTS

In 1915, a group of scholars founded the American Association of University Professors in order to further the interests of faculty members in higher education. In its "Statement of Principles on Academic Freedom and Tenure," the AAUP claimed that a teacher is entitled to 1) full freedom in research and in publication of the results, 2) freedom in the classroom in discussing his or her subject, and 3) freedom from institutional censorship or discipline when he or she communicates as a citizen.[2] While the AAUP lobbies in support of academic freedom, the organization lacks legislative clout or judicial authority. Accordingly, the courts ultimately have had to shape policies affecting faculty concerns. Some specific areas involved teaching methods, expression of views, and due process.

TEACHING METHODS

High-school English teacher Robert Keefe assigned an article that contained the word "mother-fucker" in its text. In class, Keefe discussed the article and the word's relevance to the article. Keefe stated that any student who found the assignment distasteful could have an alternative. Keefe was called before a school committee and asked to defend his use of the article. Following his explanation, the committee asked Keefe if he would agree not to use it again. He replied that he could not, in good conscience, comply with the request. Keefe was suspended, and he pursued court action. The court of appeals had to determine whether a teacher may, for educational reasons, use a "dirty" word. The judges agreed that no proper study of the article could avoid consideration of the word. The judges also noted that the word was known to many students and was used by young protesters throughout the country. In addition, the judges found that five books containing the word were housed in the school library. It was difficult "to think that any student could walk into the library and receive a book, but that his teacher could not subject the content to serious discussion in class." In light of such inconsistencies, the Keefe v. Geanakos, 418 F.2d 359 (1969), court supported Keefe's use of the article as a classroom assignment.

Marilyn Parducci assigned to her English classes Kurt Vonnegut's short story, "Welcome to the Monkey House." Subsequently, the School Board notified Parducci that she had been dismissed for assigning material that had a "disruptive" impact on the school. Parducci initiated suit, and the court considered two questions. First, was the assigned story inappropriate for high-school juniors? The court noted that it was not obscene under either the standards of <u>Roth v. United States</u>, 77 S.Ct. 1304 (1957), or the stricter standards for minors established in <u>Ginsberg v. New York</u>, 88 S.Ct. 1274 (1968). Second, did a substantial threat of disruption exist? The court noted that only three of the 90 students in the class objected to the assignment. There was no evidence that the assignment caused a significant disruption. In <u>Parducci v. Rutland</u>, 316 F.Supp. 352 (1970), the court ordered that Parducci be reinstated as a teacher.

In <u>Mailloux v. Kiley</u>, 448 F.2d 1242 (1971), another challenge to teaching method came before the courts. During one of his classes, English teacher Roger Mailloux briefly discussed taboo words, and cited the word "fuck" as an example. Mailloux never used the word orally; he wrote it on the blackboard. When a parent complained, the principal conducted an investigation and after a hearing, school officials dismissed Mailloux on the charge of "conduct unbecoming a teacher." Mailloux initiated court action. The district court noted that <u>Keefe</u> and <u>Parducci</u> had upheld two kinds of academic freedom for the teacher: the right to choose a teaching method that served an educational purpose, and the right not to be fired for using a teaching method that was not prohibited by a clearly articulated regulation. The court analyzed the particulars of <u>Mailloux</u> in the light of these criteria and made several observations: 1) the topic of taboo words is relevant to the teaching of high-school English; 2) the word "fuck" is relevant to a discussion of taboo words; 3) students in an eleventh-grade class should be able to treat the word from a serious educational viewpoint; 4) the class might be less disturbed by having the word written than if it had been spoken, since most students had seen the word even if they had not used it; 5) Mailloux's calling for a volunteer to define the word was a reasonable teaching technique that avoided involving anyone who did not wish to participate; and 6) the word "fuck" is in books in the school library. Then, the court acknowledged that experts disagreed about the appropriateness of the teaching method Mailloux employed. The court decided that, in such cases, authorities "may suspend or discharge a teacher for using the method," but only if the teacher "was put on notice either by a regulation or otherwise that he should not use the method." In <u>Mailloux</u>, there was no regulation warning the teacher not to use the method. The court concluded that Mailloux's discharge violated due process.

EXPRESSION OF VIEWS

The Supreme Court has evaluated unpopular statements of teachers in order to determine if restraints might be placed on such expression.

Though the Court has generally upheld academic freedom, the decisions have been inconsistent. The earliest case, <u>Sweezy v. New Hampshire</u>, 77 S.Ct. 1203 (1957), involved a New Hampshire law which declared "subversive persons" ineligible for employment by the state government. The law authorized the Attorney General to investigate alleged violations. Paul Sweezy, a visiting lecturer at the University of New Hampshire, was summoned to appear. Sweezy admitted to being a "classical Marxist" and a "Socialist," but he denied that he had ever been a member of the Communist Party or that he had ever been part of any effort to overthrow the government. Sweezy refused to answer several questions which he claimed were not pertinent to the inquiry and which he thought violated his First Amendment rights. Sweezy was judged in contempt and sentenced to the county jail until he cooperated. The Supreme Court overturned the verdict because the law had not authorized the specific questions asked of Sweezy. In addition, the Court took a solid stand in favor of academic freedom: "To impose any strait-jacket upon the intellectual leaders in our colleges and universities would imperil the future of our Nation." Chief Justice Earl Warren observed,

> Scholarship cannot flourish in an atmosphere of suspicion and distrust. Teachers and students must always remain free to inquire, to study, and to evaluate, and to gain new maturity and understanding otherwise our civilization will stagnate and die.

In <u>Pickering v. Board of Education</u>, 88 S.Ct. 1731 (1968), the Court strengthened the freedom of expression for teachers. Marvin Pickering, a high school teacher, sent a letter to the editor of a local newspaper, criticizing the manner in which the Board of Education and the Superintendent of Schools had handled proposals to raise educational funding. Pickering had neglected to comply with the requirement that material submitted to local newspapers should be checked with the Principal. The Board held a hearing, at which it was charged that Pickering's letter could foment controversy and dissension among teachers, administrators, and the residents of the district. The Board dismissed Pickering because his letter was detrimental to the efficient operation of the schools. On appeal, the Supreme Court ruled for Pickering. The justices agreed that Pickering's message was not shown "to have in any way either impeded the teacher's proper performance of his daily duties in the classroom or to have interfered with the regular operation of the schools." The opinion continued:

> In these circumstances we conclude that the interest of the school administration in limiting teachers' opportunities to contribute to public debate is not significantly greater than its interest in limiting a similar contribution by any member of the general public.

In <u>Pickering</u>, the Court established an important principle by emphasizing that "statements by public officials on matters of public concern must be accorded First Amendment protection." Pickering should be allowed "to speak freely on such questions [school funding] without fear of retaliatory dismissal."

The Lux v. Board of Regents of New Mexico Highlands University, 622 P.2d 266 (1980), case involved William Lux, a tenured Academic Dean at New Mexico Highlands University. When Lux delivered a speech to the Board of Regents, in which he engaged in "vituperation and personal vilification" against the school's administration, he was relieved of his duties as Academic Dean. The court of appeals cited the Pickering test as the basis for restricting Lux's free-speech rights. The court noted that a statement is protected only if it deals with matters "of legitimate public concern." Lux's "diatribe did not serve to foster rational discourse, exchange of ideas, and meaningful discussion about a matter of legitimate public interest." Accordingly, Lux's speech was not protected by the First Amendment. The Supreme Court denied certiorari.

Meinhold v. Clark County School District, 506 P.2d 420 (1973), is another case in which a court limited the right of faculty members to express their views. Alvin Meinhold, a public-school teacher, was dismissed for "unprofessional conduct," because he privately stated to his own children that he did not believe in compulsory school attendance. Meinhold did not state his views in the classroom, nor did he encourage his students to be truants. The Nevada Supreme Court ruled that "a teacher's right to teach cannot depend solely upon his conduct in the classroom," and upheld the firing. The Supreme Court refused to hear the case. In effect, the Meinhold decision punished a teacher for comments made in the privacy of his home.

City of Madison v. Wisconsin Employment Commission, 97 S.Ct. 421 (1976), involved the question of whether a teacher may speak in opposition to a union proposition at a public school board meeting. During 1971, the Madison Board of Education and a teachers union were negotiating a collective-bargaining agreement. The union submitted several proposals. At a school board meeting, a portion of the time was devoted to expression of public opinion regarding the proposals. A Madison teacher was among those who addressed the meeting. The union filed a complaint with the Wisconsin Employment Relations Commission, arguing that the Board had violated proper labor practices by allowing the teacher to speak at the meeting. The union claimed that by so doing the Board had engaged in negotiations with a member of the bargaining unit, other than the exclusive bargaining representative. The Supreme Court ruled that the circumstances did not present a danger to labor-management relations that would justify curtailing freedom of speech. The Union alone was authorized to negotiate with the Board of Education. The teacher's brief statement could not be considered as negotiation. The Board meeting at which the teacher spoke was open to the public; the teacher spoke not merely as one of the Board's employees but also as a concerned citizen, seeking to express his views on an important issue. The Court noted that in Pickering it had held that teachers may not be "compelled to relinquish the First Amendment rights they would otherwise enjoy as citizens to comment on matters of public interest in connection with the operation of the public school in which they work."

In Mt. Healthy City School District Board of Education v. Doyle, 97 S.Ct. 568 (1977), the Court heard another challenge to the right of a teacher to express his views. The case involved Fred Doyle, an untenured teacher, who became involved in several incidents — he argued with another teacher until the teacher slapped him, he disputed with employees of the school cafeteria over the amount of spaghetti he had received, he referred to students as "sons of bitches," and he made an obscene gesture to two girls who disobeyed him. Also, Doyle telephoned a Cincinnati radio station to report that his principal had established a dress and appearance code for teachers. The station reported the information as a news item. At the spring meeting of the Board of Education, Doyle's contract was not renewed because of "a notable lack of tact in handling professional matters." All of the above instances were cited. Doyle initiated court action, seeking reinstatement. The Supreme Court held that Doyle's telephone call to the radio station was protected by the First Amendment. Because it had played a "substantial part" in the decision not to rehire Doyle, he was entitled to reinstatement with back pay. The Court stressed that an important determination was whether the Board of Education would have reached the decision of non-renewal without consideration of the telephone call. With such a determination, the decision not to rehire Doyle would have been constitutional.

A related case, Givhan v. Western Line Consolidated School District, 99 S.Ct. 693 (1979), involved Bessie Givhan, who had been dismissed from her junior-high-school teaching job. Givhan sought reinstatement on the ground that nonrenewal of her contract violated her right of free speech. In order to justify its decision to dismiss Givhan, school officials offered evidence of a series of private encounters between Givhan and the school principal, in which Givhan allegedly made "petty and unreasonable demands" in a manner described by the principal as "insulting," "hostile," "loud," and "arrogant." The case reached the Supreme Court. The unanimous decision, per Justice

William Rehnquist, stressed two points. First, Rehnquist noted that a public employee, like Givhan, who arranges to communicate privately with her employer rather than spread her views before the public, does not forfeit her freedom of speech. In effect, the Court overturned the thrust of the Meinhold decision. Second, Rehnquist affirmed the Mt. Healthy standard. He noted that once an employee shows that his or her constitutionally protected conduct played a "substantial" role in the employer's decision to dismiss, the employer is required to show by a preponderance of evidence that the same decision would have been reached, even in the absence of protected conduct. Since, in Givhan, the lower court found that "criticism" was the "primary" reason for the failure to rehire, the Mt. Healthy standard required that the school district show that the decision to terminate Bessie Givhan would have been made, even if her encounters with the principal had never occurred. Without such a showing, Bessie Givhan would have to be reinstated.

Generally, the Supreme Court has defended the right of teachers to express their views. Early Court decisions, Sweezy and Pickering, supported the right of teachers to express their personal views outside of the classroom. The Pickering decision established an important standard regarding the speech of teachers — a statement about matters of legitimate public concern is entitled to First Amendment protection. In Lux, the Court restricted personal expression that failed to deal with matters of public concern. In Meinhold, an unusual decision, the Court refused to hear a case involving a teacher's dismissal for comments made in the privacy of his own home. More recently, in City of Madison, Mt. Healthy, and Givhan, the Court has protected the right of teachers to express their views in both private and public contexts.

DUE PROCESS

In 1972, the Supreme Court decided two cases that involved faculty claims of due-process violation. Both concerned nontenured members of a university faculty. The first case is Board of Regents v. Roth, 92 S.Ct. 2701 (1972). In 1968, David Roth accepted a position as Assistant Professor of Political Science at Wisconsin State University — Oshkosh. He was hired for a fixed term of one year. According to school policy, Roth was notified in writing that he would not be rehired for the next year. He was given no reason for the decision and no opportunity to challenge it at any type of hearing. Roth initiated court action on the ground that the decision infringed upon his rights. He claimed that the failure to provide him with reasons for non-retention and an opportunity for a hearing violated due process. According to Justice Potter Stewart, the terms of Roth's appointment secured absolutely no interest in re-employment for the next year.

> The respondent [Roth] surely had an abstract concern in being rehired, but he did not have a *property* interest sufficient to require the University authorities to give him a hearing when they declined to renew his contract of employment.

In Roth, the opinion concluded that, while it might be "appropriate or wise" to provide a statement of reasons for non-retention, Roth, a non-tenured professor, was not constitutionally entitled to such procedure.

A companion case involved Robert Sindermann, who between 1959 and 1969 taught in the state college system of Texas. After teaching for two years at the University of Texas and four years at San Antonio Junior College, he taught social science at Odessa Junior College for four years under one-year contracts. During the 1968-69 academic year, conflict developed between Sindermann and the college administration. In May, 1969, the Regents voted not to offer Sindermann a contract for the next academic year. The Regents issued a press release alleging insubordination, but they provided to Sindermann no official statement of the reasons for non-renewal, and they offered him no opportunity for a hearing. Sindermann initiated court action, alleging that the Regents decided not to rehire him because of his criticism of the administration, and this infringed his right to free speech. He also claimed that the failure to provide him an opportunity for a hearing violated procedural due process. The Supreme Court referred to its Roth ruling, which established that there is no right to a hearing before the non-renewal of a nontenured teacher's contract, unless it could be shown "that he had a 'property' interest in continued employment, despite the lack of tenure or a formal contract." Sindermann alleged that this interest, though not secured by a contractual tenure provision, was secured by an understanding fostered by the administration. Sindermann claimed that the college had a *de facto* tenure program, and that he had tenure under the program. He cited a provision in the college's official faculty guide.

> Teacher tenure: Odessa College has no tenure system. The administration of the college wishes the faculty member to feel that he has permanent tenure as long as his teaching services are satisfactory and as long as he displays a cooperative attitude toward his co-workers and his superiors, and as long as he is happy in his work.

Sindermann also referred to guidelines established by the Coordinating Board of the Texas College and University System, which provided that a teacher who had been employed in the state system for seven years or more has some form of job tenure. Sindermann claimed that a teacher, with his length of service, had no less a "property" interest in continued employment than a formally tenured teacher at other colleges.

The Court acknowledged Sindermann's claim as a "legitimate claim of entitlement to job tenure." In Perry v. Sindermann, 92 S.Ct. 2717 (1972), the Court concluded:

> Proof of such a property interest would not, of course, entitle him to reinstatement. But such proof would obligate college officials to grant a hearing at his request, where he could be informed of the grounds for nonretention and challenge their sufficiency.

In Sindermann, as in Roth, the Court reiterated that non-tenured faculty have considerably less right to procedural safeguards than tenured members of the faculty.

In University of Pennsylvania v. Equal Employment Opportunity Commission, 110 S.Ct. 577 (1990), the Court rendered a decision which at the same time both weakened and protected the tenure process. The case began in 1985 when the University denied tenure to an associate professor, who then filed a charge of discrimination with the EEOC. The professor argued that the decision violated Title VII of the Civil Rights Act, that her qualifications were equal to or better than those of five male faculty members who had received more favorable treatment. The Commission issued a subpoena seeking the professor's tenure-review file and the files of the five male members. The University objected, asserting a First Amendment right of academic freedom against wholesale disclosure of the documents. The University cited Sweezy v. New Hampshire, 77 S.Ct. 1203 (1957), in which the Court recognized that a university possesses a First Amendment right to "determine for itself on academic grounds who may teach." The University contended that it exercises this right through the process of awarding tenure. The University also maintained that

> ...the peer review process is the most important element in the effective operation of a tenure system. A properly functioning tenure system requires the faculty to obtain candid and detailed written evaluations of the candidates peers at the university and from scholars at other institutions. These evaluations...traditionally have been provided with express or implied assurances of confidentiality. It is confidentiality that ensures candor and enables an institution to make its tenure decisions on the basis of valid academic criteria.

The University also argued that requiring the disclosure of peer review evaluations will undermine the existing process of awarding tenure because a "chilling effect" on candid evaluations will result.

> And as the quality of peer review evaluations declines, tenure committees will no longer be able to rely on them. This will work to the detriment of universities, as less qualified persons achieve tenure causing the quality of instruction and scholarship to decline. Compelling disclosure of materials also would result in divisiveness and tension, placing strain on faculty relations and

impairing the free interchange of ideas that is a hallmark of academic
freedom.

The Court rejected the University's argument. According to Justice
Harry Blackmun, the Court could not create a new, expanded privilege
against the disclosure of peer review materials. Blackmun foresaw "a
wave of similar privilege claims by other employers who play
significant roles in furthering speech and learning in society...[such as]
writers, publishers, musicians, lawyers." The Court decided to hold
academic institutions to the same standard as is applicable to other
agencies and organizations. In the University of Pennsylvania case, the
Court accepted the EEOC claim that access to personnel documents
was necessary in order to determine whether or not discrimination had
taken place.

Court decisions described in this section establish specific due
process rights of faculty members. The Roth decision held that non-
tenured professors enjoy fewer rights than their tenured colleagues.
Sindermann acknowledged that some faculty members may be entitled
to due process under a "de facto" tenure policy. The University of
Pennsylvania decision held that personnel files must be made available
for public scrutiny in order to determine whether discrimination
occurred in the tenure process.

STUDENT RIGHTS

Between 1969 and 1975, the U.S. Supreme Court heard five
significant cases involving student rights. In Tinker, Papish, Healy,
Goss, and Wood, the Court upheld the academic freedoms of students.
In more recent cases, Hazelwood and Fraser, the Court denied student
complaints, and upheld administrative policies.

PROTEST

In Tinker v. Des Moines Independent Community School District,
89 S.Ct. 733 (1969), the Supreme Court established a standard — the
forecast rule — that had an impact on later court decisions concerning
the right of students to protest. Tinker involved the suspension of
school children who refused to remove black armbands they were
wearing to protest U.S. participation in the Vietnam War. The parents
sought an injunction that would restrain school officials from punishing
their children. The Supreme Court, per Justice Abe Fortas, established
guidelines to help school authorities determine when expression may
be restricted.

Schools exist to carry out educational benefits at several levels one
of which involves interpersonal communication among the students.

> Whenever a student is at school no matter what the hour or the activity that student is free to express his or her views as long as they do not materially and substantially interfere with the operation of the school.

In Tinker, the Court found no evidence "which might reasonably have led school authorities to forecast substantial disruption of or material interference with school activities." The students simply wore black armbands to protest Vietnam involvement and to influence others to adopt their views. The Court stressed that under the Constitution, students are "persons," and they cannot be treated as "closed-circuit recipients of only that which the State chooses to communicate."

In Guzick v. Drebus, 431 F.2d 594 (1970), a federal court applied the Tinker guidelines. Thomas Guzick, a student at Shaw High School, was instructed to remove an antiwar button he was wearing. Guzick refused to remove the button, and undertook court action. The court distinguished Guzick from Tinker. First of all, in Guzick, the principal applied a long-standing rule: the wearing of buttons, badges, scarves, or any other symbol whereby the wearers identified themselves as supporters of a particular cause, or which contained messages unrelated to education, was prohibited. The rule was established because buttons were potentially divisive in that they set a student apart from other students. In recent years, black and white students attempted to wear buttons expressing racially inflammatory messages. Because buttons contributed to the polarization of student groups, officials enforced the anti-button rule. In Tinker, school authorities did not prohibit the wearing of all political symbols, only the black armbands worn in opposition to the Vietnam War. Such a policy was discriminatory. Second, the cases differed in their settings. No potential racial conflict was evident in Tinker, whereas the changing racial composition of Shaw High School from all-white to 70 percent black made the no-symbol rule important for maintaining order. According to the court, enforcing the symbol ban helped to achieve meaningful integration of the public schools. In Guzick, the court concluded:

> We must be aware in these contentious times that America's classrooms and their environs will lose their usefulness as places in which to educate our young people if pupils come to school wearing the badges of their respective disagreements, and provoke confrontations with their fellows and their teachers. The buttons are claimed to be a form of speech. Unless they have some relevance to what is being considered or taught, a school classroom is no place for the untrammeled exercise of such rights.

The anti-button policy at Shaw High School was upheld. In 1971, the U.S. Supreme Court refused to hear the case.

During the years of protest against racial discrimination and U.S. involvement in the Vietnam War, students used leaflets, posters, pamphlets, and newspapers to proclaim their grievances. Most schools adopted regulations to cover the use of such printed matter. In two cases heard in the early 1970s, district courts analyzed specific regulations in the light of the Tinker guidelines. In Eisner v. Stamford Board of Education, 440 F.2d 803 (1971), high-school students challenged the policy of the Board of Education of Stamford, Connecticut which banned a person from distributing any printed material in any school building without prior approval by the administration. The district court cited Tinker in acknowledging that protected expression in public secondary schools may be banned "if school authorities reasonably forecast substantial disruption of or material interference with school activities." The Eisner court stressed that prior restraints requiring official approval before distribution of underground student newspapers were constitutional, but requirements for prior submission of publications must be accompanied by procedural safeguards. Based on that principle, the court declared the Stamford policy unconstitutional because of three procedural deficiencies. First, the policy failed to provide an expeditious review procedure. Second, the policy failed to specify to whom and how material could be submitted for approval. Third, the ban against "distributing" material without prior consent was unconstitutionally vague. The word "distributing" might mean nothing more than one student passing to a fellow student a copy of a magazine or textbook. If students were required to obtain prior approval before exchanging magazines among themselves, "the resultant burden on speech might very likely outweigh the very remote possibility that such activities would ever cause disruption."

In Fujishima v. Board of Education, 460 F.2d 1355 (1972), a court of appeals disagreed with the Eisner court's interpretation of Tinker. At stake was a Chicago Board of Education regulation which provided that "no person shall be permitted...to distribute on the school premises any books, tracts or other publications...unless the same shall have been approved by the General Superintendent of Schools." Because the rule required prior approval of publications, the Fujishima court declared the policy unconstitutional as a prior restraint. The judges believed that the Eisner court had erred "in interpreting Tinker to allow prior restraint on publication — long a constitutionally prohibited power — as a tool of school officials in 'forecasting' substantial disruption of school activities." According to the judges in Fujishima, the Tinker "forecast rule" was designed as a formula for determining when the requirements of school discipline justify punishment of students for exercise of their First Amendment rights. It was not a rationale "for establishing a system of censorship and licensing designed to prevent the exercise of First-Amendment rights."

In Tinker, the Court upheld the right of students to express their opinions, as long as they did not interfere with the operation of the school. Yet, because of the vagueness of the "forecast rule," state courts applied Tinker somewhat inconsistently in Guzick, Eisner, and Fujishima.

SCHOOL-RELATED SPEECH AND PRESS

Barbara Papish, a graduate student in journalism at the University of Missouri, was expelled for distributing a campus newspaper that contained "forms of indecent speech." The specific issue in question was objectionable in two ways. First, on the front cover the publishers had reproduced a political cartoon depicting a policeman raping the Statue of Liberty and the goddess of justice. The caption read, "With Liberty and Justice for All." Second, the issue contained an article entitled "Mother-Fucker Acquitted," which discussed the trial of a student-member of an organization known as "Up Against the Wall, Mother-Fucker." Papish claimed that her dismissal violated the First Amendment. According to the Supreme Court, the issue was whether the material was obscene. The school newspaper could not be censored simply because of "indecent speech." The Papish v. Board of Curators, 93 S.Ct. 1197 (1973), majority felt that neither the political cartoon nor the story could be labeled as constitutionally obscene. The University was ordered to reinstate Papish as a student.

In two cases concerning high school expression, the Supreme Court limited the academic freedom of students. In Bethel School District v. Fraser, 106 S.Ct. 3159 (1986), the Court restricted public speech which contained sexual references. Matthew Fraser, a high school student, delivered a speech nominating a fellow student for elective office. The speech contained an abundance of sexual innuendo. Approximately 600 students attended the assembly and heard the speech. During Fraser's delivery of the speech, some students hooted and yelled; others appeared to be bewildered and embarrassed. The next day, the assistant principal notified Fraser that he had violated a disciplinary rule which prohibited the use of obscene or profane language or gestures in the school. After a hearing, Fraser was suspended for three days and his name was removed from the list of candidates for speaker at commencement exercises. Fraser initiated court action. The Supreme Court opinion, prepared by Chief Justice Burger, observed a marked distinction between the political message represented by the armbands in <u>Tinker</u> and the sexual content in Fraser's speech. Burger upheld the action of the school administration.

> Under the First Amendment, the use of an offensive form of expression may not be prohibited to adults making what the speaker considers a political point, but it does not follow that the same latitude must be permitted to children in a public school. It is a highly appropriate function of public school education to prohibit the use of vulgar and offensive terms in public discourse. Nothing in the Constitution prohibits the states from insisting that certain modes of expression are inappropriate and subject to sanctions. The inculcation of these values is truly the work of the school, and the determination of what manner of speech is inappropriate properly rests with the school board.

In <u>Hazelwood School District v. Kuhlmeier</u>, 108 S.Ct. 562 (1988), the Court upheld restrictions placed on a high school press. The case involved a principal's order that stories regarding teen pregnancy and divorce be withheld from publication in the school newspaper. Students initiated court action upon the ground that the principal's action violated the First Amendment. The Supreme Court distinguished between two types of student speech — a student's personal expression that occurs on the school premises, and school-sponsored publications and expressions.

> Educators are entitled to exercise greater control over this second form of student expression to assure that participants learn whatever lessons the activity is designed to teach, that readers or listeners are not exposed to material that may be inappropriate for their level of maturity, and that the views of the individual speaker are not erroneously attributed to the school. Hence, a school may in its capacity as publisher of a school newspaper or producer of a school play "disassociate itself"...from speech that is, for example, ungrammatical, poorly written, inadequately researched, biased or prejudiced, vulgar or profane, or unsuitable for immature audiences.

The Court held that educators do not offend the First Amendment by exercising editorial control over the style and content of student speech in school-sponsored expressive activities so long as their actions "are reasonably related to legitimate pedagogical concerns." The Court concluded that the principal could reasonably have concluded that the students who had written and edited the withheld articles had not sufficiently mastered those aspects of the Journalism curriculum that pertained to the treatment of controversial issues, the need to protect the privacy of individuals, and the legal and ethical restrictions imposed upon journalists within a school setting that included adolescent readers. In <u>Hazelwood</u>, as in <u>Bethel</u>, the Court upheld restrictions on free expression within the high school setting.

ASSOCIATION

The ability of students to organize was essential for conducting protests during the 1960s and 1970s. In response, school administrators attempted to regulate both the membership and activities of campus organizations. The Supreme Court heard a challenge to such a policy in Healy v. James, 92 S.Ct. 2338 (1972). In 1969, students at Central Connecticut State College attempted to organize a local chapter of Students for a Democratic Society. The request for official recognition listed three purposes of the organization: 1) to provide "a forum of discussion and self-education for students developing an analysis of American society," 2) to serve as "an agency for integrating thought with action so as to bring about constructive changes," and 3) to provide a "coordinating body for relating the problems of leftist students" with other groups on campus and in the community. The Student Affairs Committee expressed concern that the group might become associated with the national SDS organization — an active force for student activism throughout the decade. The students stated that their group would remain completely independent of the national organization. The Committee recommended that the organization be awarded official recognition. The President of the college, however, denied recognition to SDS because, in his view, the organization's philosophy was opposed to Central Connecticut State's policies. The group's survival was difficult without official recognition. Members were not allowed to announce activities in the student newspaper. They could not post notices on campus bulletin boards. They were prohibited from meeting in campus buildings. The group started court action. The Supreme Court decided that First Amendment principles had been denied to the group, but since the judges could not decide whether the students were willing to abide by reasonable campus regulations, the case was remanded for reconsideration. The Court acknowledged that a college administration could require "that the group seeking official recognition affirm in advance its willingness to adhere to reasonable campus law." Participation in the internal life of an academic community may be refused to an organization that reserves the right to violate campus regulations.

In Widmar v. Vincent, 102 S.Ct. 269 (1981), the Court affirmed its belief that the rights of free speech and association extend to university campuses. The case involved the University of Missouri at Kansas City, which made its facilities available for the activities of student groups. When a student religious group was denied the use of campus buildings or grounds "for purposes of religious worship or religious teaching," the group alleged that the ban violated its First Amendment rights. The Supreme Court agreed:

> The basis for our decision is narrow. Having created a forum generally open to student groups, the University seeks to enforce a content-based exclusion of religious speech. Its exclusionary policy violates the fundamental principle that a state regulation of speech should be content-neutral.

In Widmar, the Court determined that UMKC had used a content-oriented policy to discriminate against a student group which sought to use a "generally open forum" to engage in speech and association behavior that is protected by the First Amendment. Such a policy is unconstitutional.

In Board of Education of the Westside Community Schools v. Mergens, 110 S.Ct. 2356 (1990), the Court upheld the associational rights of high school students. Policy at Westside High School in Omaha, Nebraska permits students to join clubs, all of which meet after school hours on school premises. Bridget Mergens requested permission to form a Christian club at the school. The club's purpose would have been to allow students to discuss the Bible, to enjoy fellowship, and to pray. Membership would have been voluntary and open to all students regardless of religious affiliation. The Principal denied the request. The case reached the Supreme Court. The Court found that the refusal violated the Federal Equal Access Act, which prohibits public secondary schools that maintain a "limited open forum" from denying "equal access" to students on the basis of the "religious, political, philosophical, or other content" of their speech. According to Justice Sandra O'Connor:

> Although the school apparently permits respondents to meet informally after school, they seek equal access in the form of official recognition, which allows clubs to be part of the student activities program and carries with it access to the school newspaper, bulletin boards, public address system, and annual Club Fair. Since denial of such recognition is based on the religious content of the meetings respondents wish to conduct within the school's limited open forum, it violates the Act.

DUE PROCESS

Two Supreme Court cases established student rights of due process in disciplinary actions. The first case was Goss v. Lopez, 95 S.Ct. 729 (1975). During a period of local unrest and disturbances, several high-school students were suspended from school for up to ten days without a hearing. The students argued that the statute permitting such suspensions was unconstitutional. The Supreme Court determined that the students were denied due process because they were "suspended without hearing prior to suspension or within a reasonable time thereafter." The Court made it clear that a student facing temporary suspension qualifies for protection of the due-process clause. The student must be given notice of the charges, and, if he or she denies the charges, the student must be provided with an explanation of the evidence the officials have, as well as with an opportunity to respond. In most cases, the disciplinarian could informally discuss the charges with the student, minutes after the offense occurred. In Goss, the Court concluded that the due-process clause "requires at least these rudimentary precautions against unfair or mistaken findings of misconduct and arbitrary exclusion from school."

In the second case, Wood v. Strickland, 95 S.Ct. 992 (1975), the due-process rights of students were extended by the Court. Two students were expelled for the use of intoxicating beverages at school activities. They were suspended from school for a two-week period; but after a meeting of the School Board the students were expelled for the remainder of the semester. The students brought suit, claiming that expulsion infringed upon their right to due process. Before the Supreme Court, the School Board argued that Board members enjoy an absolute immunity from liability. The Board maintained that its members could not be held accountable for decisions which violated student rights. The Court disagreed, holding that a Board member is not immune from liability for damages "if he knew or reasonably should have known that the action he took within his sphere of official responsibility would violate the constitutional rights" of the student, or "if he took the action with the malicious intention to cause a deprivation of constitutional rights or other injury to the student." The Wood decision held that a School Board member was indeed responsible for any improper behavior.

CONCLUSION

The following principles regulate communication law regarding ACADEMIC FREEDOM:

1. Administrators have certain rights and responsibilities:
   a. legislative efforts to control the curriculum have been overturned when such efforts hindered the quest for knowledge or the freedom to teach,
   b. school rituals, in the forms of required flag-salute and prayer, have been declared unconstitutional
   c. legislatures may inquire into teacher fitness, but only if such investigation is conducted in a legal manner — that is, without

ambiguity, discrimination, or overbreadth,
  d. administrators may regulate campus speakers, but only with
     statutes that are legally drawn — that is, without ambiguity,
     discrimination, or overbreadth,
  e. school boards have considerable authority to determine the
     content of school libraries, but that authority may not be
     exercised in a narrowly partisan or political manner.

2. Faculty have certain rights and responsibilities:
  a. authorities may suspend a teacher for using a controversial
     teaching method, but only if the teacher is notified that he or she
     should not use the method,
  b. teachers enjoy First Amendment protection to express their
     views in both private and public contexts,
  c. non-tenured faculty enjoy less right to procedural due process
     than tenured members of the faculty.

3. Students have certain rights and responsibilities:
  a. students enjoy the right to express their views as long as they do
     not interfere with the operation of the school,
  b. administrators may exercise greater control over school
     sponsored student expression than over personal student
     expression,
  c. students enjoy First Amendment associational rights as long as
     the organization adheres to valid campus regulations,
  d. students are entitled to due process — including notice of
     charges and a timely hearing.

NOTES

1. Hook, Sidney, <u>Academic Freedom and Academic Anarchy</u> New
   York: Cowles Book Company, 1970, p. 34.

2. Joughin Louis (ed.), <u>Academic Freedom and Tenure</u>: <u>A Handbook
   of the American Association of University Professors</u> Madison:
   University of Wisconsin Press, 1969, pp. 33-36.

KEY DECISIONS

1943 —   <u>BARNETTE</u> — overturned mandatory flag-salute statute

1968 —   <u>PICKERING</u> — upheld a teacher's right to speak on
          issues of public importance

1969 —   TINKER — affirmed the right of students to express their views, as long as they do not substantially disrupt school activities (forecast rule)

1972 —   ROTH — stressed that non-tenured faculty have fewer rights than tenured faculty members

1972 —   SINDERMANN — acknowledged the existence of an "informal" tenure system, which entitled faculty members, with considerable length of service, to procedural safeguards when facing non-renewal

1972 —   HEALY — acknowledged student rights of association

1973 —   PAPISH — upheld right of college students to operate uncensored school press

1975 —   GOSS — recognized students' right to due process

1975 —   WOOD — held that school administrators are responsible for any improper behavior; they are not entitled to good faith immunity

1979 —   GIVHAN — acknowledged right of teachers to express views in both private and public contexts

1982 —   ISLAND TREES — determined that while school boards have considerable authority to determine the content of school libraries, that authority may not be exercised in a partisan manner

1986 —   FRASER — restricted offensive expression by high school students

1987 —   KUHLMEIER — upheld right of principal to control school-sponsored publications and expressions

1990 —   UNIVERSITY OF PENNSYLVANIA — recognized that outside access to tenure files was necessary to determine instances of discrimination

RECOMMENDED READING

Daughtrey, Jr., William H., "The Legal Nature of Academic Freedom in United States Colleges and Universities," University of Richmond Law Review 25 (1991), 233-271.

Fischer, Louis, David Schimmel, and Cynthia Kelly, Teachers and the Law New York: Longman, 4th. Ed., 1995.

Hall, Daniel E., "The First Amendment Threat to Academic Tenure," University of Florida Journal of Law and Public Policy 10 (1998), 85-102.

Hickman, Michael J., "The Supreme Court and the Decline of Student's Constitutional Rights: A Selective Analysis," Nebraska Law Review 65 (Winter 1986), 161-187.

O'Shea, Kevin F., "First Amendment Cases in Higher Education," Journal of College and University Law 26 (1999), 193-219.

Rabban, David M., "A Functional Analysis of 'Individual' and 'Institutional' Academic Freedom Under the First Amendment," Law and Contemporary Problems 53 (1990), 227-301.

Reynolds, Janis L., "Free Speech Rights of Public School Teachers: A Proposed Balancing Test," Cleveland State Law Review 30 (Fall, 1981), 673-710.

Schulman, Carol Hernstadt, "Employment of Nontenured Faculty: Implications of Roth and Sindermann," Denver Law Journal 51 (1974), 215-33.

Smith, Norman B., "Constitutional Rights of Students, Their Families, and Teachers in the Public School," Campbell Law Review 10 (1988), 353-409.

Van Alstyne, William W., Freedom and Tenure in the Academy Durham: Duke University, 1993.

Van Alstyne, William W., "Academic Freedom and the First Amendment in the Supreme Court of the United States: An Unhurried Historical Review," Law and Contemporary Problems 53 (1990), 79-154.

CHAPTER 5

OBSCENITY

Even though numerous laws defined obscenity as a crime, prosecutions were rare prior to the post-Civil War period. In the 1870s, Anthony Comstock, an ardent crusader for decency, formed the New York Society for the Suppression of Vice. The organization sought an increase in obscenity convictions, and passage of stronger federal legislation. Comstock campaigned relentlessly, and largely through his efforts, new obscenity legislation was adopted which provided a maximum penalty of a $5,000 fine, or a five-year prison term, or both, for anyone who was caught sending obscene material through the mail. Comstock helped implement the new statute as a special agent of the Post Office Department. Until his death in 1915, Comstock and his colleagues seized tons of obscene materials, and prosecutions for obscenity law violations increased steadily.

TESTS OF OBSCENITY

Determining exactly what "obscenity" is has proven to be a difficult problem for the courts. Over the years, "obscenity" has been defined and regulated according to various criteria. The major standards have been the Hicklin, Roth, Redrup, and Miller tests.

HICKLIN TEST

An English court case, Regina v. Hicklin, L.R. 3Q.B. 360 (1868), had a significant effect on the regulation of obscenity in the United States. The case involved a court declaration that an anti-Catholic pamphlet was unconstitutional because it contained explicit descriptions of statements recited in the confessional. The case was appealed to the Queen's Bench which ruled the pamphlet to be obscene and offered the following test of obscenity:

> The test of obscenity is this, whether the tendency of the matter charged as obscenity is to deprave and corrupt those whose minds are open to such immoral influences and into whose hands a publication of this sort may fall.

The Hicklin test emphasized three ideas. First, printed material did not have to offend an "average person." If a work had a bad effect on "those whose minds are open to such immoral influences" — whether the individual was a child, an abnormal adult, or any member of the subclass of society — the work could be seized. Second, the material was not evaluated in terms of its impact as a whole; rather, if any portion of the work was found to be obscene, it was judged obscene in total. This aspect gave rise to the practice of judging a literary work by examining passages taken out of context. Third, obscenity was determined on the basis of a work's intent. Judges speculated about the thoughts induced by the material. They banned any work that produced "thoughts of a most impure and libidinous character" without any concern whether antisocial behavior would result from exposure to the material.

The Hicklin ruling was accepted by courts in the United States, and vigorously approved by Anthony Comstock. Throughout the next century, courts declared obscene such books as Casanova's Homecoming by Arthur Schnitzler (People v. Seltzer, 203 N.Y.S. 809 (1924), The Well of Loneliness by Radclyffe Hall (People v. Friede, 233 N.Y.S. 565 (1929), An American Tragedy by Theodore Dreiser (Commonwealth v. Friede, 171 N.E. 472 (1930), Lady Chatterly's Lover by D.H. Lawrence (People v. Dial Press, 182 Misc. 416 (1944), and both Tropic of Cancer and Tropic of Capricorn by Henry Miller (Besig v. United States, 208 F.2d 142 (1953). In these cases, the "selected passages" approach of the Hicklin test was used to determine obscenity; the determination was based on allegedly obscene sections of the work in which the language described an illicit sexual relationship.

Objections arose to the Hicklin test. In United States v. Kennerly, 209 F.119 (1913), Judge Learned Hand questioned whether "men will regard that as obscene which is honestly relevant to the adequate expression of innocent ideas," and he suspected that "shame will long prevent us from adequate portrayal of some of the most serious and beautiful sides of human nature." Judge Hand urged that obscenity be determined by considering the "present critical point in the compromise between candor and shame at which the community may have arrived." By acknowledging that societal tolerance of sexual matters varies over time, Judge Hand recognized the importance of "contemporary community standards" in a test of obscenity.

In <u>United States v. One Book Called "Ulysses,"</u> 72 F.2d 705 (1934), censors attempted to bar entry of James Joyce's <u>Ulysses</u> into the United States. Judge J. Woolsey noted that the work contained explicit descriptions of sexual acts, as well as coarse language which was commonly considered obscene. Yet, such literary techniques were necessary in order that Joyce accomplish his purpose. The words would be naturally used by the types of characters Joyce described. Woolsey concluded that in spite of its unusual frankness, <u>Ulysses</u> was not obscene and could enter the United States. Even though the book tended to excite "sexual impulses or lustful thoughts," its net effect was a powerful commentary on the inner lives of men and women. Woolsey departed from the practice of using excerpts to determine obscenity. He recognized the literary value of the entire work, apart from the existence of specific words or descriptions. In <u>Ulysses</u>, as in <u>Kennerly</u>, the groundwork was laid for a new test.

ROTH TEST

New York businessman Samuel Roth published and sold books, photographs, and magazines, some of which authorities considered to be obscene. When Roth advertised in an effort to solicit sales of these materials, he was arrested and convicted for violating the federal obscenity statute. In <u>Roth v. United States</u>, 77 S.Ct. 1304 (1957), the Court confronted the issue of whether obscenity is protected by the First Amendment. The majority opinion, written by William Brennan, concluded that obscenity was outside the protection intended for speech and press. Brennan examined the nature of obscenity and offered a definition — obscenity involves "whether to the average person applying contemporary community standards, the dominant theme of the material taken as a whole appeals to prurient interest." The <u>Roth</u> test stressed four elements. First, the Court noted differences between sex and obscenity. Obscene material must deal with sex, but must do so in a manner that appeals to prurient interest. The portrayal of sex, in and of itself, is insufficient reason to define obscenity. Second, the test applies to the average person. The material must be capable of affecting somebody other than a particularly susceptible individual. It must be applicable to "normal" persons. Third, the material must violate "contemporary community standards." Yet, the Court did not clarify what was meant by "community." Fourth, the material must be considered as a whole. It is not judged merely by the effect of an isolated passage. Concern must be with the dominant theme of the work. Brennan noted:

The Hicklin test, judging obscenity by the effect of isolated passages upon the most susceptible persons, might well encompass material legitimately with sex, and so it must be rejected as unconstitutionally restrictive of the freedoms of speech and press.

The Roth test set forth standards that safeguarded against the abuses associated with Hicklin.

During the following years the Supreme Court clarified the Roth test. In Manual Enterprises v. Day, 82 S.Ct. 1432 (1962), Justice John Harlan claimed that an obscenity-statute violation required proof of two elements — "patent offensiveness and prurient-interest appeal." In his view, both elements "must conjoin before challenged material can be found obscene." The Manual Enterprises case involved magazines that contained photographs of nude male models. It was read primarily by homosexuals. Justice Harlan noted:

> These magazines cannot be deemed so offensive on their face as to affront current community standards of decency — a quality that we shall hereafter refer to as "patent offensiveness...." Lacking that quality, the magazines cannot be deemed legally "obscene."

Even though the material was patently offensive to some, and it did have prurient appeal to a group of homosexuals, it was not patently offensive to a substantial portion of the community. Even though the pictures might be considered as unpleasant and uncouth, they were not obscene.

In Jacobellis v. Ohio, 84 S.Ct. 1676 (1964), the Court applied the Roth test in a case involving the obscenity conviction of a motion-picture-theatre manager who showed a film with an explicit love scene. Justice Brennan clarified two points of his Roth opinion. He indicated that an obscene work is "utterly without redeeming social importance"; the portrayal of sex in art, literature, and scientific works is not itself sufficient cause to deny constitutional protection. Brennan also noted that any suggestion that the "contemporary community standards" aspect of Roth involves a case-by-case determination of obscenity based on local standards "is an incorrect reading of Roth." The meaning of "community standards" referred to "national standards."

> We thus reaffirm the position taken in Roth to the effect that the constitutional status of an allegedly obscene work must be determined on the basis of a national standard. It is, after all, a national Constitution we are expounding.

The Roth test was further defined in Mishkin v. United States, 86 S.Ct. 958 (1966), when the Court heard an appeal from a bookstore operator whose publishing specialty dealt with sadism and masochism. Mishkin's defense was based on the idea that the books did not appeal to the prurient interest of an average person. Mishkin argued that instead of being stimulated, the average person would be disgusted and sickened by such works. The Court rejected this argument as an unrealistic interpretation of the "prurient-appeal requirement." When material is designed for and primarily disseminated to a clearly defined deviant sexual group, rather than the public at large, "the prurient-appeal requirement...is satisfied if the dominant theme of the material taken as a whole appeals to the prurient interest of the members of the group." In upholding Mishkin's conviction, the Court noted:

> No substantial claim is made that the books depicting sexually deviant practices are devoid of prurient appeal to sexually deviant groups. The evidence fully establishes that these books were specifically conceived and marketed for such groups. Mishkin instructed his authors and artists to prepare the books expressly to induce their purchase by persons who would probably be sexually stimulated by them.

In Memoirs v. Attorney General, 86 S.Ct. 975 (1966), Justice Brennan further clarified the Roth test. Three criteria must be established to determine obscenity: the dominant theme of the material taken as a whole must appeal to a prurient interest in sex; the material must be patently offensive because it affronts contemporary community standards; and the material must be utterly without redeeming social value. Each of the criteria must be applied independently; the social value of the book can neither be weighed against nor canceled by its prurient appeal or patent offensiveness. In Memoirs, using these three criteria, the Court decided that even though John Cleland's Fanny Hill possessed only a modicum of social value, it could not be judged obscene. The book was not obscene because it was not "unqualifiably worthless."

REDRUP REVERSALS

Despite numerous efforts to clarify Roth, the justices could not agree about the specifics of obscenity regulation. In 1967, in Redrup v. New York, 87 S.Ct. 1414 (1967), the Court wrote an opinion that summarized differences in the thinking of justices.

> Two members of the Court have consistently adhered to the view that a State is utterly without power to suppress, control or punish the distribution of any writings or pictures upon the ground of their "obscenity." A third has held to the opinion that a State's power in this area is narrowly limited to a distinct and clearly identifiable class of material. Others have subscribed to a not dissimilar standard, holding that a State may not constitutionally inhibit the distribution of literary material as obscene unless "a) the dominant theme of the material taken as a whole appeals to a prurient interest in sex; b) the material is patently offensive because it affronts contemporary community standards relating to the description or

representation of sexual matters; and c) the material is utterly without redeeming social value," emphasizing that the "three elements must coalesce," and that no such material can "be proscribed unless it is found to be utterly without redeeming social value."

In Redrup, the Court reversed obscenity convictions in three cases, noting that no matter which form of judicial thinking was applied, the convictions could not stand. Thus began a six-year policy of issuing summary reversals, without opinion, of any conviction that at least five justices, each applying his own standard, found to be under the protection of the First Amendment. From 1967 to 1973, the Court determined 31 cases in this manner. These cases became known as the "Redrup reversals" and marked a period of minimal regulation of obscenity.

MILLER TEST

The obscenity test established by the Earl Warren Court in Roth was overturned in 1973, when President Richard Nixon appointees Lewis Powell, Harry Blackmun, William Rehnquist, and Warren Burger were joined by Byron White to constitute a majority in Miller v. California, 93 S.Ct. 2607 (1973). Marvin Miller was convicted of distributing sexually explicit advertisements to unwilling recipients. The advertising brochures depicted men and women engaging in a variety of sexual activities, often with genitals prominently displayed. In Miller, the Supreme Court reexamined and revised its test of obscenity. The majority opinion, written by Chief Justice Burger, stressed three standards. First, the Court redefined the term "community." No longer were contemporary "community" standards to be considered as "national" in scope. It was not realistic to view the First Amendment as requiring that people of one state accept conduct found intolerable in another state. People in different states vary in their tastes and attitudes. According to the Court, this "diversity is not to be strangled by the absolutism of imposed uniformity." Appeal to "prurient interest" should be decided with reference to "contemporary community standards." Second, the Court retained the patent-offensiveness standard. Obscenity could be determined when "the work depicts or describes, in a patently offensive way, sexual conduct specifically defined by the applicable state law." The Court then identified specific examples of what might be regulated as "patently offensive": representations of normal or perverted, actual or simulated ultimate sexual acts, descriptions of masturbation and/or excretory functions, and lewd exhibition of the genitals. Third, the work "taken as a whole," must lack "serious literary, artistic, political, or scientific value." The Court thereby rejected the "utterly without redeeming social value" element of the Roth test and substituted the words "does not have serious literary, artistic, political or scientific value."

Ensuing Court decisions clarified the provisions of the Miller test. In three cases, the Court clarified the meaning of "contemporary community standards." In Smith v. United States, 97 S.Ct. 1756 (1977), the Supreme Court had to decide whether a jury is entitled to rely on its own knowledge of community standards, or whether a state legislature may declare what the community standards shall be, and when such a declaration has been made, whether it is binding in a federal prosecution. Justice Blackmun, writing for the majority, noted that it is impossible for a state legislature to define contemporary community standards, largely because of that body's isolation from a particular community. The Court admitted that there was room for state legislation regarding the obscenity issue, but "the question of the community standard to apply, when appeal to prurient interest and patent offensiveness are considered, is not one that can be defined legislatively." Blackmun concluded that "though state legislatures are not completely foreclosed from setting substantive limitations for obscenity cases, they cannot declare what community standards shall be."

In Pinkus v. United States, 98 S.Ct. 1808 (1978), the Court decided whether a trial court had erred by instructing the jury to include children and sensitive persons within the definition of "community," by whose standards obscenity was to be judged. Writing for the Court, Chief Justice Burger noted that "children" should not have been included: "A jury...might very well reach a much lower average when children are part of the equation than it would if it restricted its consideration to the effect of allegedly obscene materials on adults." Inclusion of "sensitive persons" was appropriate, however. The "community" includes all adults who compose it, and a jury should consider all adults in determining community standards. Yet, the Court noted that it would be incorrect for a jury to focus "upon the most susceptible or sensitive members rather than...merely including them...along with all others in the community." In Pinkus, the Court held that "children" are not to be included as part of the "community," but "sensitive persons" are.

In Pope v. Illinois, 107 S.Ct. 1918 (1987), the Court decided that a jury should not be instructed to apply "community standards" in deciding the question of the material's value.

> Only the first and second prongs of the Miller test — appeal to prurient interest and patent offensiveness — should be decided with

reference to "contemporary community standards." The ideas that a work represents need not obtain majority approval to merit protection, and the value of that work does not vary from community to community based on the degree of local acceptance it has won.

According to the Court, the proper inquiry is not whether an "ordinary member" of the community would find value in the material, but whether a "reasonable person" would find such merit.

Two cases clarified the meaning of the term "patently offensive." In Jenkins v. Georgia, 94 S.Ct. 2750 (1974), the Court evaluated the movie "Carnal Knowledge." In the unanimous opinion, Justice Rehnquist noted that the main theme of the movie is sex. There are scenes in which sexual acts are "understood" to be occurring. Yet, the camera does not focus on actors at sexually critical moments, and "ultimate sexual behavior" is only intimated. The Court emphasized that even though the film shows occasional nudity, "nudity alone does not render material obscene under Miller's standards." The Court found nothing in the movie to fall within the patently-offensive standards established in Miller.

The Court further expounded upon the "patently offensive" provision in Ward v. Illinois, 97 S.Ct. 2085 (1977). The defendant, Wesley Ward, asserted that sadomasochistic materials may not be constitutionally proscribed because they were not expressly included in the examples of sexually explicit materials that the Court had cited in Miller. Justice White noted that those specifics were offered merely as "examples" and "were not intended to be exhaustive"; they "were not intended to extend constitutional protection to the kind of flagellatory materials that were among those held obscene in Mishkin." Ward's conviction was affirmed.

The history of obscenity prosecutions has been shaped around three distinctly different tests. Hicklin stipulated that any printed material that was thought to have a corruptive influence on minors or sexually deviant adults was prohibited. According to Roth, a work was considered obscene if an average person, applying national standards, would find the dominant theme of the complete material appealing to prurient interest. According to Miller, localities were responsible for determining the prurient appeal of a work, obscene material must be "patently offensive," and the work must lack serious literary, artistic, political, or scientific value. While the Supreme Court has clarified the prurient appeal and patently offensive prongs of Miller, it has not elaborated about the social value prong. Miller is the current test of obscenity.

GUIDELINES FOR REGULATION

Several Supreme Court decisions have established guidelines for obscenity regulation. These decisions have considered a variety of issues.

NATURE OF FILM

In Mutual Film Corporation v. Industrial Commission of Ohio 35 S.Ct. 387 (1915), the Supreme Court held that film is a unique medium that does not warrant First Amendment protection. The justices offered two reasons. First, motion pictures are "capable of evil, having power for it...because of their attractiveness and manner of exhibition." Second, film has a commercial nature. According to the Court, "the exhibition of moving pictures is a business, pure and simple, originated and conducted for profit, like other spectacles, not to be regarded, nor intended to be regarded...as part of the press of the country, or as organs of public opinion." In Mutual Film Corporation, the Court refused to grant protection to the film medium.

In Burstyn v. Wilson, 72 S.Ct. 777 (1952), the Court changed its position. This case centered around Roberto Rossellini's "The Miracle." The film received mixed reviews. It was attacked as "a sacrilegious and blasphemous mockery of christian religious truth" by the National Legion of Decency. The National Board of Review recommended the film as "especially worth seeing." New York critics selected it as the best foreign film of 1950. After viewing the film, a committee censored it under a New York statute that permitted banning motion pictures that were "sacrilegious." When the case reached the Supreme Court, the justices considered the arguments offered in the Mutual Film Corporation case. First, with regard to the claim that motion pictures "posses a greater capacity for evil" than other modes of expression, the Court held that if this is true, the capacity for evil may be relevant in determining the scope of control, but it does not authorize "unbridled censorship." Second, it had been argued that film production, distribution, and exhibition was a large-scale business conducted for profit. The Court noted:

> That books, newspapers, and magazines are published and sold for profit does not prevent them from being a form of expression whose liberty is safeguarded by the First Amendment. We fail to see why operation for profit should have any different effect in the case of motion pictures.

In Burstyn, the Court recognized film as a significant medium for the communication of ideas. And, the importance of film as a vehicle of public opinion is not diminished when film is intended to entertain, as well as to inform. Regarding the specifics of "The Miracle," the Court concluded that a State may not bar a movie on the basis that it is "sacrilegious." The principal significance of Burstyn is that the justices recognized film as a medium warranting First Amendment protection.

PRIOR RESTRAINT

Prior restraint involves censorship of obscene material before its appearance in print or exhibition at a theatre. This form of censorship is effective because it prevents the obscenity from ever reaching the audience. In Freedman v. Maryland, 85 S.Ct 734 (1965), the Court established specific standards for regulating prior restraint. The case began when Ronald Freedman challenged the constitutionality of a Maryland statute by showing a film without first submitting the film to the Board of Censors. When the case reached the Supreme Court, the justices established three standards that authorities must meet when censoring a film. First, the burden of proving obscenity rests on the censoring agency; the censor has the burden of initiating judicial proceedings. Second, any restraint prior to judicial review can be for only a brief period to preserve the status quo. Third, there must be assurance of a prompt judicial review. In Freedman, the Court overturned the Maryland law because it failed to provide adequate safeguards. It constituted an invalid prior restraint.

The Court reinforced the Freedman safeguards in Southeastern Promotions v. Conrad, 95 S.Ct. 1239 (1975). In Chattanooga, Tennessee, promoters sought to present "Hair," a rock musical that had played for three years on Broadway and had been performed in nearly 150 cities in the United States. Even though city officials had not seen the play or read the script, they rejected the request on the ground that allowing the performance would not be "in the best interest of the community." The Supreme Court rejected this action. The justices noted that refusing the use of facilities had been decided by personal judgment about the play's content, and this constituted prior restraint. Furthermore, the restraint was final; it was not merely a temporary ban while judicial proceedings took place. According to Freedman, prior restraint can be acceptable only when "it takes place under procedural safeguards designed to obviate the dangers of a censorship system." In Southeastern Promotions, the safeguards were lacking. First, the promoter, rather than the censor, bore the burden both for obtaining judicial review and for disproving obscenity. Second, the restraint altered the status quo because review of the request did not occur until more than five months later. The promoter was forced to schedule the performance at a later date. Third, the system failed to provide a procedure for judicial determination. In Southeastern Promotions, the Court reinforced the notion that prior restraint can be employed only when the Freedman criteria are met.

In Vance v. Universal Amusement, 100 S.Ct. 1156 (1980), the Court again reinforced its thinking on prior restraint. A county attorney attempted to close Carol Vance's indoor, adult motion-picture theatre in order to prevent the showing of obscene films. The action was taken under "public nuisance" statutes which approved the closing of premises on which forbidden "habitual uses" occurred. In this case, since obscene films had been shown in the past, authorities sought to close Vance's theatre in order to prevent the future exhibition of films that had not yet been determined to be obscene. Vance appealed. The Supreme Court declared the laws unconstitutional; "they authorized prior restraints that are more onerous than is permissible under Freedman and Southeastern."

In FW/PBS v. City of Dallas, 110 S.Ct. 596 (1990), the Court again applied the Freedman safeguards. Under dispute was an ordinance which regulated sexually oriented businesses through licensing. An adult bookstore operator challenged the ordinance for failing to set a time limit within which the licensing authority must act. The Court applied the first two Freedman safeguards in noting that the ordinance was unconstitutional because it failed to provide an effective time limitation on the licensing decision, and because it neglected to provide for prompt judicial review. The Court noted, however, that the third safeguard was not vital in FW/PBS.

> Unlike the Freedman censor, Dallas does not engage in presumptively invalid direct censorship of particular expressive material, but simply performs the ministerial action of reviewing the general qualifications of each license applicant. It therefore need not be required to carry the burden of going to court or of there justifying a decision to suppress speech. Moreover, unlike the motion picture distributors considered in Freedman — who were likely to be deterred from challenging the decision to suppress a particular movie if the burdens of going to court and of proof were not placed on the censor — the license applicants under the Dallas scheme have every incentive to pursue a license denial through court, since the license is the key to their obtaining and maintaining a business.

Based on Southeastern, Vance, and FW/PBS, it seems clear that the Court will tolerate prior restraint of obscene materials only when authorities comply with the Freedman safeguards.

Alexander v. United States, 113 S.Ct. 2766 (1993), is a somewhat related case that involved a claim of prior restraint. After a criminal trial, Ferris Alexander, the owner of several businesses dealing in sexually explicit materials, was convicted of violating obscenity laws and the Racketeer Influenced and Corrupt Organizations Act (RICO). In addition to receiving a prison term and fine, Alexander was also required to forfeit his businesses and $9 million acquired through racketeering activity. Alexander appealed, arguing that the sentence constituted a prior restraint. The Supreme Court disagreed. Chief Justice Rehnquist noted that "prior restraint" describes orders forbidding communications that are issued before the communications occur. In this case, Alexander was not forbidden to engage in any expressive activities in the future, nor was he required to obtain prior approval.

> Unlike the injunctions in Near, Keefe, and Vance, the forfeiture order in this case imposes no legal impediment to — no prior restraint on — petitioner's ability to engage in any expressive activity he chooses. He is perfectly free to open an adult bookstore or otherwise engage in the production and distribution of erotic materials; he just cannot finance these enterprises with assets derived from his prior racketeering offenses.

SEARCH AND SEIZURE WARRANTS

Saul Heller managed a movie theatre in the Greenwich Village area of New York City. The theatre showed a film depicting a nude couple engaged in sexual acts. Three police officers saw part of the film, and requested a judge to see the performance. At the end of the showing, the judge signed a search warrant for the seizure of the film and the arrest of the theatre manager. When Heller was found guilty of displaying obscenity, he claimed that his rights had been violated. In Heller v. New York, 93 S.Ct. 2789 (1973), the Supreme Court identified the acceptable procedure for obtaining a search warrant and for providing a hearing for cases involving motion pictures. According to the opinion prepared by Chief Justice Warren Burger, there was no necessity of holding an adversary hearing prior to the seizure of one copy of a film for use as evidence. Burger noted, however, that a film cannot be seized by police until a warrant is issued by a judge who has viewed the film and judged it to be obscene. Following seizure, a prompt adversary hearing must be held to determine if the movie is obscene. The theatre owner must be given the opportunity to be represented at the hearing. The theatre owner could continue to show the film if he has a second copy, and, if there were no other copies available, the owner might make a copy so that it could be shown pending the adversary proceeding. Thus, the Court approved the procedure followed in the Heller case.

...the film was not subjected to any form of "final restraint," in the sense of being enjoined from exhibition or threatened with destruction. A copy of the film was temporarily detained in order to preserve it as evidence. There has been no showing that the seizure of a copy of the film precluded its continued exhibition. Nor, in this case, did temporary restraint in itself "become a form of censorship."

In Roaden v. Kentucky, 93 S.Ct. 2796 (1973), a case decided on the same day as Heller, the Court reaffirmed the notion that seizure of a film cannot occur without the issuance of a warrant following judicial determination of obscenity. The case involved a sheriff who, after viewing a movie, determined that it was obscene, went to the projection room, seized the film, and arrested the theatre manager. There was no warrant and no prior determination of obscenity. When the theatre manager was convicted, he appealed. The Supreme Court decided that the seizure was illegal.

The importance of correct procedure was stressed again in Fort Wayne Books v. Indiana, 109 S.Ct. 916 (1989). The pretrial seizure of an entire bookstore and its contents was deemed improper. According to the Court, while a single copy of a book or film may be seized and retained for evidentiary purposes based on a finding of probable cause, "books or films may not be taken out of circulation completely until there has been a determination of obscenity after an adversary hearing." The risk of prior restraint renders such seizure invalid. Justice White maintained: "Probable cause to believe that there are valid grounds for seizure is insufficient to interrupt the sale of presumptively protected books and films." The presumption that expressive materials are protected by the First Amendment is not rebutted until justification for seizure of such materials is properly established in an adversary proceeding. Based on Heller, Roaden, and Fort Wayne Books, it is clear that in the event of seizing a film or book, judicial activity must occur prerequisite to police action. And, an adversary hearing on the issue of obscenity must be held promptly after seizure.

SCIENTER

Scienter refers to the amount of knowledge that an individual must have in order to be held legally responsible for the consequences of his or her action. In Smith v. California, 80 S.Ct. 215 (1959), the Court applied the concept of *scienter* to obscenity. Eleazar Smith was convicted for possessing obscene material in his Los Angeles bookstore. No element of *scienter*, that is, knowledge by Smith of the obscene nature of the book, was considered. Smith appealed. Writing for the Court, Justice Brennan pointed out that elimination of the *scienter* requirement may place a substantial restriction on freedom of speech and press. A bookseller who is held liable, while unaware of any obscene content, will probably restrict the volume of books to those that have been personally inspected. Distribution of books that are both obscene and not obscene would be impeded. Thus, a law that ignores *scienter* "tends to impose a severe limitation on the public's access to constitutionally protected matter." In Smith, the Court decided that an obscenity conviction can be obtained only when the accused is aware of the obscenity.

The question of *scienter* was also addressed in United States v. X-Citement Video Inc., 115 S.Ct. 464 (1994). The owner of a video store was convicted of violating the Protection of Children Against Sexual Exploitation Act, which punished any person who "knowingly" transported or shipped "any visual depiction, if...the producing of such visual depiction involves the use of a minor engaging in sexually explicit conduct." The owner argued that the grammatical reading of the Act suggested that the term "knowingly" modified only the verbs "transports" and "ships." The word did not modify the element of minor age of the performer. The elements were set forth in independent clauses separated by interruptive punctuation. The Supreme Court, per Chief Justice Rehnquist, held that the term applied to both the verbs and the minority element.

> If the term "knowingly" applies only to the relevant verbs...transporting, shipping, receiving, distributing and reproducing — we would have to conclude that Congress wished to distinguish between someone who knowingly transported a particular package of film whose contents were unknown to him, and someone who unknowingly transported that package. It would seem odd, to say the least, that Congress distinguished between someone who inadvertently dropped an item into the mail without realizing it, and someone who consciously placed the same item in the mail, but was nonetheless unconcerned about whether the person had any knowledge of the prohibited contents of the package.

Rehnquist also observed that the Court's reluctance to follow the most grammatical reading of the statute was heightened by precedent cases which interpreted criminal codes to broadly include *scienter* requirements, even when the code did not specifically contain such language.

DISTRIBUTION BY MAIL

The second-class mail privilege provides a competitive advantage for a magazine publisher. With it, the publisher pays substantially lower postal rates. Legislation entitles periodical publications to the second-class provision if they are "published for the dissemination of information of a public character, or devoted to literature, the sciences, arts, or some special industry." Obscene material does not qualify for the second-class privilege. Over the years, Court cases have involved efforts at controlling "alleged" obscenity by restricting the use of the mails.

In Hannegan v. Esquire, 66 S.Ct. 456 (1946), the Postmaster General revoked the second-class permit for Esquire magazine. The issues under challenge contained recurrent offensive features: jokes, cartoons, pictures, articles, and poems that emphasized sex. He claimed that some "writings and pictures may be indecent, vulgar, and risque and still not be obscene in a technical sense"; but in order to enjoy unique mail privileges, a publisher was bound to do more than refrain from disseminating obscene material. The publisher was obliged to contribute to the public welfare. It was on these grounds that the Postmaster General revoked the second class privilege. The Supreme Court rescinded the order because Congress had not given the Postmaster General such power of censorship.

> From the multitude of competing offerings the public will pick and choose. What seems to one to be trash may have for others fleeting or even enduring values. But to withdraw the second-class rate from this publication today because its contents seemed to one official not good for the public would sanction withdrawal of the second-class rate tomorrow from another periodical whose social or economic views seemed harmful to another official.

In Rowan v. U.S. Post Office Department, 90 S.Ct. 1484 (1970), the Court approved the right of an individual to censor his or her own mail, with the help of the post office. During the 1960s, public concern was aroused over the use of mail facilities to distribute unsolicited pornographic advertisements. Complaints to the Postmaster General about such activity had reached almost 250,000 annually, when Congress passed the Postal Revenue and Federal Salary Act of 1967. According to the Act, when an individual notifies the postmaster that erotically arousing or sexually provocative advertisements have been received, the postmaster orders the sender to stop any future mailings of such materials to the individual. Daniel Rowan initiated court action after receiving several notices from the postmaster. He claimed the law violated his right of free speech. Chief Justice Burger, writing for the Court, recognized that people are inescapably captive audiences for many purposes, but a person must be free to exercise control over unwanted mail. The right of every person "to be let alone" must be measured against the right of others to communicate. In Rowan, the Court decided that the right to communicate stops at the mailbox of an unreceptive individual. The Court rejected the notion that a vendor has a right to send unwanted material into the home of another.

PANDERING

In <u>Ginzburg v. United States</u>, 86 S.Ct. 942 (1966), the Court upheld an obscenity conviction based on pandering. Bookdealer Ralph Ginzburg sold sex-oriented publications through the mail. In order to advertise these materials, Ginzburg sought mailing privileges from the postmasters of Intercourse and Blue Ball, Pennsylvania. These towns were selected because of the value their names had for selling the publications. The postal facilities in these localities were inadequate to handle the anticipated volume of mail, so the requests were denied. Mailing privileges were then obtained from Middlesex, New Jersey. Shortly thereafter, several million circulars soliciting subscriptions for the publications were mailed from the Middlesex Post Office. The advertising boasted about the sexual candor of the publications. Ginzburg was convicted for violating the federal obscenity statute. The prosecution admitted that the materials in and of themselves might not be obscene, but in the context of the advertising campaign commercial exploitation had made them obscene. The Supreme Court agreed. Justice Brennan held that the question of obscenity may include consideration of the setting in which the materials are advertised. In <u>Ginzburg</u>, the materials were sold as part of the sordid business of pandering, that is, "the business of purveying textual or graphic matter openly advertised to appeal to the erotic interest of their customers." Brennan noted that "where the purveyor's sole emphasis is on the sexually-provocative aspects of his publications, that fact may be decisive in the determination of obscenity." Deliberate representation of the publications as erotically arousing "stimulated the reader to accept them as prurient." On the basis of pandering, the Court upheld Ginzburg's conviction.

A decade later, in <u>Splawn v. California</u>, 97 S.Ct. 1989 (1977), the Court affirmed that "there is no doubt that...evidence of pandering to prurient interests in the creation, promotion, or dissemination of material is relevant in determining whether the material is obscene."

YOUTH

Supreme Court opinions have considered regulations that apply to youth. In <u>Butler v. Michigan</u>, 77 S.Ct. 524 (1957), the Court declared unconstitutional a law that reduced adults to the level of youth. At issue was a Michigan statute that made it a crime to offer to the general public a book that could incite youth to violent, depraved, or immoral acts. Alfred Butler was convicted of selling such a book to a policeman. He appealed. The Supreme Court noted that the law prevented distribution of books to the general public because of the undesirable influence they might have upon youth. The adult population was reduced to reading only what was fit for children. According to the Court, the overly broad law was "not reasonably restricted to the evil with which it is said to deal." The Court reversed Butler's conviction. The Butler decision is significant because it freed adult literature from obscenity tests that might be appropriate for children's literature.

In Ginsberg v. New York, 88 S.Ct. 1274 (1968), the Court upheld a statute that outlawed the sale to minors of material defined as specifically obscene for them. The case began when Sam Ginsberg was arrested for selling magazines which contained pictures of female nudity to a 16-year-old boy, without attempting to ascertain the youth's age. A judge held that the pictures represented nudity in a manner that predominantly appeals to the prurient interest of minors, and is utterly without redeeming social importance to minors. Ginsberg was tried and found guilty. The Supreme Court recognized the constitutionality of the statute that regulated the sale of pornography to children through special standards, broader than those designed for adults. The State has an interest in protecting the "welfare of children," and seeing that they are "safeguarded from abuses."

In New York v. Ferber, 102 S.Ct. 3348 (1982), the Court examined the "sexploitation" of youth in America. Throughout the 1970s, the exploitive use of children in the production of pornography became a serious national problem. To combat this situation, New York passed a law that "prohibits persons from knowingly promoting a sexual performance by a child under the age of 16 by distributing material which depicts such a performance." The law defined "sexual performance" to include such conduct as actual or simulated sexual intercourse, deviate sexual intercourse, sexual bestiality, masturbation, sado-masochistic abuse, or lewd exhibition of the genitals. When bookstore proprietor Paul Ferber was convicted for selling films depicting young boys masturbating, he appealed on the basis that the law infringed upon First Amendment rights. The Supreme Court disagreed. The opinion, per Justice White, acknowledged that "the use of children as subjects of pornographic materials is harmful to the physiological, emotional, and mental health of the child." Therefore, New York was entitled to considerable leeway in regulating pornographic depiction of children. The Court noted that the Miller test was not a satisfactory solution to the child pornography problem.

The Miller standard, like all general definitions of what may be banned as obscene, does not reflect the State's particular and more compelling interest in prosecuting those who promote the sexual exploitation of children. Thus, the question under the Miller test of whether a work, taken as a whole, appeals to the prurient interest of the average person bears no connection to the issue of whether a child has been physically or psychologically harmed in the production of the work. Similarly, a sexually explicit depiction need not be "patently offensive" in order to have required the sexual exploitation of a child for its production. In addition, a work which, taken on the whole, contains serious literary, artistic, political, or scientific value may nevertheless embody the hardest core of child pornography.... We therefore cannot conclude that the Miller standard is a satisfactory solution to the child pornography problem.

In Ferber, the Court upheld the New York law which excluded child pornography from First Amendment protection.

In Osborne v. Ohio, 110 S.Ct. 1691 (1990), the Court upheld the constitutionality of another child pornography law. The statute prohibits possession of material which depicts a nude minor, unless the material is presented for a *bona fide* purpose, or if the minor's parents consent in writing to such depiction. The defendant argued that the Stanley principle was applicable; the First Amendment protected the private possession of child pornography. The Supreme Court rejected that argument on the ground that the material in Osborne affects more than the mind of the viewer; it affects the physical and psychological well being of the minor. The Court noted the importance of the statute:

Given the importance of the State's interest in protecting the victims of child pornography, we cannot fault Ohio for attempting to stamp out this vice at all levels in the distribution chain.... Since the time of our decision in Ferber, much of the child pornography market has been driven underground; as a result, it is now difficult, if not impossible, to solve the child pornography problem by only attacking production and distribution. Indeed, 19 States have found it necessary to proscribe the possession of this material.

The decisions in this section confirm that the Supreme Court has consistently applied a different standard to youths than to adults. In Butler, the Court refused to judge adult literature by the same standard that is applied to reading material fit for children. Ginsberg punished the sale of material that was legally non-obscene for adults, but offensive to children. Ferber and Osborne found the Miller test inadequate in dealing with youths — child pornography is outside the protection of the First Amendment.

VENDING MACHINES

The court system continued to apply different standards for youth and adults in Crawford v. Lungren, 96 F.3d 380 (1996), a case which tested the constitutionality of a California law which banned the sale of "harmful matter" in public sidewalk vending machines. The statute defined harmful matter as that which violated the three prongs of the Miller test, as they apply to minors. The constitutionality of the statute was challenged by publishers, distributors, and users of the vending service on the ground that the statute makes it "commercially infeasible" to operate the vending business. The court of appeals noted that the purpose of the law was to shield minors from the influence of adult-oriented literature by limiting their access. The court recognized "a compelling interest in protecting the physical and psychological well-being of children" and that "this interest extends to shielding minors from the influence of literature that is not obscene by adult standards." In upholding the law, the court noted that adults could easily obtain the material elsewhere. The Supreme Court denied certiorari.

WOMEN

In an effort to protect women from the impact of pornographic materials, the Indianapolis City Council passed an ordinance which punished "the graphic sexually explicit subordination of women, whether in pictures or words" when such depictions viewed women as any of the following: sexual objects who enjoy pain or humiliation, sexual objects who experience sexual pleasure in being raped, or women as being penetrated or mutilated. A national organization of booksellers initiated judicial action. The district court noted that the ordinance did not apply to "categories of speech, such as obscenity and child pornography which have been excepted from First Amendment protections" but went on to attempt to establish a new category. Indianapolis argued that this ordinance should not be judged by the Miller test, but rather by other established guidelines found in New York v. Ferber, 102 S.Ct. 3348 (1982), Federal Communications Commission v. Pacifica Foundation, 98 S.Ct. 3026 (1978), and Young v. American Mini Theatres, 96 S.Ct. 2440 (1976). The court distinguished the current case from these precedents. Ferber was not compelling because "adult women as a group do not...stand in need of the same type of protection which has long been afforded children." In contrast to Pacifica, "if an individual is offended...the logical thing to do is avoid it [pornography], an option frequently not available to the public with material disseminated through broadcasting." Young was inapplicable because the Indianapolis ordinance did not attempt "to restrict the time, place, and manner in which 'pornography' may be distributed." Turning to the ordinance, the court noted several flaws. It was vague in its use of particular phrases as well as its generalized prohibitions. According to the court, "persons subjected to this ordinance cannot reasonably steer between lawful and unlawful conduct, with confidence that they know what its terms prohibit." The ordinance was overbroad; it "goes beyond legally obscene material in imposing its control." In addition, it constituted a prior restraint, failing to meet the first prong of Freedman; the law "does not preserve the status quo nor allow for prompt judicial review." For all of these reasons, the court in American Booksellers Association v. Hudnut, 598 F. Supp. 1316 (1984), found the ordinance to be unconstitutional. The court concluded that although a city has an interest in "prohibiting sex discrimination, that interest does not outweigh the constitutionally protected interest of free speech." The Supreme Court, without comment, upheld the decision by a six to three vote in Hudnut v. American Booksellers Association, 106 S.Ct. 1172 (1986).

PRIVACY

The Supreme Court has explored the relationship between obscenity and privacy. The Stanley v. Georgia, 89 S.Ct. 1243 (1969), decision is relevant to this issue. Government agents, armed with a search warrant, entered Robert Stanley's home and found three films that showed "successive orgies by nude men and women engaging in repeated acts of seduction, sodomy, and intercourse." Stanley was convicted of possessing obscene material. Before the Supreme Court, Stanley claimed the right to privacy in his own home. He demanded freedom from inquiry into the contents of his private library. The Court unanimously supported Stanley, ruling "that a State has no business telling a man, sitting alone in his own home, what books he may read or what films he may watch." According to Justice Thurgood Marshall,

> Georgia asserts the right to protect the individual's mind from the effects of obscenity. We are not certain that this argument amounts to anything more than the assertion that the State has the right to control the moral content of a person's thoughts. To some, this may be a noble purpose, but it is wholly inconsistent with the philosophy of the First Amendment.

The Court held that the First Amendment "prohibits making mere private possession of obscene material a crime."

In the following years, in United States v. Thirty Seven

Photographs, 91 S.Ct. 1400 (1971), United States v. Reidel, 91 S.Ct. 1410 (1971), United States v. Orito, 93 S.Ct. 2674 (1973), and United States v. 12 200-ft Reels, 93 S.Ct. 2665 (1973), the Court limited the scope of the Stanley principle. In Thirty Seven Photographs, the Court heard the case of Milton Luros, who, upon returning to the United States from Europe, had in his luggage photographs that customs agents seized as obscene. In terms of Stanley, the Supreme Court ruled that Luros' situation did not involve the privacy of his home. At the same time, the Court heard the Reidel case. Norman Reidel had been convicted for mailing a copy of an illustrated booklet. The Court ruled that the Stanley principle was not relevant; it did not sanction the use of the channels of commerce to disseminate obscene matter, nor did it sanction the postal service to be a party to such activity. In Orito, the Court further restricted the scope of Stanley. George Orito was convicted for knowingly transporting on the airlines films which authorities called "lewd, lascivious, and filthy materials." In court, Orito argued that the Stanley case had established the right to possess obscene material in the privacy of the home and that there existed a correlative right to receive, transport, and distribute such material. The Supreme Court rejected "the idea that some zone of constitutionally-protected privacy follows such material when it is moved outside the home area protected by Stanley."

> It is sufficient to reiterate the well-settled principle that Congress may impose relevant conditions and requirements on those who use the channels of interstate commerce in order that those channels will not become the means of promoting or spreading evil, whether of a physical, moral or economic nature.

In the 12 200-ft Reels case, movies, photographs, color slides, and other printed and graphic materials were seized by customs officers at the Los Angeles Airport. The importer was convicted. He appealed. The Supreme Court held that the focus in Stanley was on freedom of thought and mind in the privacy of the home, and a port of entry is not a traveler's home. In 12 200-ft Reels, as in Orito, Reidel, and Thirty Seven Photographs, the Court restricted the "privacy" ruling in Stanley. The Court upheld governmental power to regulate interstate transportation, delivery through the mails, or the importation from abroad of obscene materials for personal use. The Stanley principle applies only to the home.

PASSERBY VISIBILITY

During the 1970s, the Court, on at least two occasions, examined the question of passerby visibility. Specifically, the Court was presented situations in which passersby were exposed to offensive, if not obscene, films at an outdoor theatre. The first case, Rabe v. Washington, 92 S.Ct. 993 (1972), involved a drive-in theatre operator who was convicted for exhibiting an X-rated picture on a screen visible to passersby and nearby residents. The Supreme Court reversed the conviction on the ground of vagueness. The law did not mention that the "context" of the exhibition of a film was an "element of the offense somehow modifying the word obscene." The Court held that the showing at a drive-in theatre of a motion picture cannot be criminally punished unless the law gives a fair notice that the location of the showing is a vital element.

The issue arose again in Erznoznik v. Jacksonville, 95 S.Ct. 2268 (1975). The case involved a code which prohibited displaying nudity in a film shown by a drive-in theatre with a screen visible from a public street. The Court determined that the code was overbroad because it discriminated among movies solely on the bases of content. The ordinance deterred drive-in theatres from showing films containing any nudity, even if the film was innocent or educational. The ordinance was not directed specifically against legally-obscene or sexually-explicit nudity. The Court concluded "that the limited privacy interest of persons on the public streets cannot justify this censorship of otherwise protected speech on the bases of its content."

ZONING

In many larger cities throughout the United States pornographic activity is located in a specific section of town. In Young v. American Mini Theatres, 96 S.Ct. 2440 (1976), the Supreme Court considered whether a city could legally restrict pornography to a particular "zone." The Young Court upheld a Detroit ordinance that regulated the geographic location of motion-picture theatres that exhibit non-obscene but sexually-oriented films. According to the opinion written by Justice John Stevens, a "municipality may control the location of theatres as well as the location of other commercial establishments, either by confining them to certain specified commercial zones or by requiring that they be dispersed throughout the city." In Young, the Court actually upheld the regulation of protected expression that is sexually-oriented, but not obscene. The Court also affirmed the right of a city to determine locational requirements for adult theatres. It is the city's business to decide whether to "require adult theaters to be separated rather than concentrated in the same areas."

Schad v. Borough of Mount Ephraim, 101 S.Ct. 2176 (1981), is a related case. James Schad operated an adult bookstore in the commercial zone of Mount Ephraim, New Jersey. The store included a coin-operated machine that allowed customers to view a live, nude dancer, performing behind a glass panel. Schad was convicted of violating a zoning ordinance that banned live entertainment within the commercial zone. Upon appeal, the Supreme Court declared the statute overbroad. By excluding live entertainment, the ordinance had prohibited a type of expression that was entitled to First Amendment protection. Justice White emphasized that the Young decision was not controlling in Schad. In Young,

> ...the restriction did not affect the number of adult movie theaters that could operate in the city; it merely dispersed them. The Court did not imply that a municipality could ban all adult theatres — much less all live entertainment or all nude dancing — from its commercial districts citywide.

In Schad, the Court acknowledged that the power of local governments to control land use is essential to achieving satisfactory quality of life in the community. Nonetheless, "the zoning power is not infinite and unchallengeable; it must be exercised within constitutional limits." The ban in Schad had exceeded those limits.

A few years later, the Court heard City of Renton v. Playtime Theatres, 106 S.Ct. 925 (1986). The case involved a challenge to the zoning ordinance enacted by Renton, Washington. It prohibited adult motion-picture theatres from locating within 1,000 feet of any residential zone. The Court compared this case with related cases. The Renton ordinance, like the one in Young, did not ban adult theatres altogether, but merely regulated their location: "We...find no constitutional defect in the method chosen by Renton to further its substantial interests. Cities may regulate adult theatre by dispersing them, as in Detroit, or by effectively concentrating them, as in Renton." The decision also compared the Renton ordinance with the one in Schad, noting that the Renton statute was "narrowly tailored" to affect only that "category of theatres shown to produce the unwanted secondary effects." In this way, the ordinance avoided "the flaw that proved fatal to the regulations in Schad." The Renton ordinance was a valid form of time, place, and manner regulation. Furthermore, the ordinance was a valid governmental response to the serious problems created by adult theatres.

In Arcara v. Cloud Books, 106 S.Ct. 3172 (1986), the Supreme Court determined the constitutionality of a statute which regulated sexually-oriented business activities. The Court affirmed that a city has considerable power to control obscene and other illegal activities. Cloud Books Company operated an adult bookstore that sold sexually-explicit printed materials. In addition, booths were available for viewing sexually-explicit films. Police investigated reports of illicit sexual activities occurring at the bookstore. A deputy sheriff observed instances of prostitution, masturbation, fondling, and fellatio by patrons of the store. All of the activities took place within the observation of the store's proprietor. Subsequently, an action was initiated under the New York Public Health Law to close the store for one year on the ground that it was a public nuisance, that is, a "place used for the purpose of lewdness, assignation, or prostitution." Cloud Books asserted that the closure of the store interfered with their First Amendment right to sell books. The closure order was much broader than necessary to restrict illicit commercial sexual activities. The Supreme Court disagreed for two reasons. First, the bookstore proprietor was free to sell books at another location. Second, the closure order was directed at unlawful conduct having nothing to do with protected expressive activity. According to the Court,

> Bookselling in an establishment used for prostitution does not confer First Amendment coverage to defeat a valid statute aimed at penalizing and terminating illegal uses of premises. The legislature properly sought to protect the environment of the community by directing the sanction at premises knowingly used for lawless activities.

In Barnes v. Glen Theatre, Inc., 111 S.Ct. 2456 (1991), the Court upheld a public indecency law which required dancers in adult entertainment establishments to wear pasties and G-strings. Applying the four-part O'Brien test, the Court found, first, that the law was within the government's constitutional power. Second, it furthered a substantial governmental interest in protecting societal order and morality. Third, that interest was unrelated to the suppression of expression. The evil being addressed was not erotic messages, but public nudity. In fact, an erotic performance could be presented without any interference, so long as the performers wore a scant amount of clothing. Fourth, the incidental restriction on freedom of expression was no greater than is essential to further the governmental interest of banning public nudity.

The lesson of Arcara and Barnes is that a city has wide latitude in regulating obscene and illegal business activities. The lesson of Young, Schad, and Renton is that a city may regulate non-obscene, pornographic businesses by either concentrating or dispersing them, but only if the regulations provide constitutional safeguards.

INTERNET

The United States v. Hibbler, 159 F.3d 233 (1998), decision affirmed the conviction of an individual who used the internet to possess and distribute child pornography. James Hibbler, a middle school principal, had purchased a home computer and opened an account with America Online. Using the screen name SHIGUY, he created a false profile and began to trade in visual images depicting child pornography. He was arrested when an FBI investigation uncovered these illegal practices. At trial, Hibbler claimed that he was "investigating" the accessibility of pornography in cyberspace because his school was in the process of going on-line. Further investigation revealed that Hibbler was not a member of, or a consultant to, the committee responsible for upgrading computer services. The court rejected Hibbler's contention that his conduct was protected by the First Amendment because he was simply investigating the evils of the internet in order to protect his students. The. U.S. Supreme Court denied certiorari.

FEDERALLY-FUNDED INDECENCY

For years, the National Endowment for the Arts enjoyed substantial discretion in awarding financial grants to support the arts. The NEA selected broad funding priorities, based on such criteria as "artistic significance," "cultural diversity," "professional excellence," and "public education." When controversial photographs appeared in two NEA-funded exhibits, a public outcry led Congress to pass legislation which directed that "artistic excellence and artistic merit are the criteria by which [NEA] applications are judged, taking into consideration general standards of decency and respect for the diverse beliefs and values of the American public." Various performance artists initiated legal action, challenging the provisions as vague and viewpoint biased. The artists argued that the provisions constituted viewpoint discrimination because it rejected artistic speech that failed to respect mainstream values or which offended standards of decency. In National Endowment for the Arts v. Finley, 118 S.Ct. 2168 (1998), the Supreme Court disagreed with the artists. The majority opinion, prepared by Justice Sandra O'Connor, noted that the provision was merely hortatory, falling well short of an absolute restriction. It did not preclude awards to projects that might be deemed "indecent" or "disrespectful," nor did it "specify that those factors must be given any particular weight in reviewing an application." O'Connor also rejected the vagueness argument, stressing that the provision "merely adds some imprecise considerations to an already subjective selection process." According to the Court, the provisions did not infringe on First Amendment rights.

CONCLUSION

The following principles regulate communication law regarding OBSCENITY:

1. The three-part <u>Miller</u> test of obscenity requires that the material:
   a. appeals to the prurient interest in sex as determined by contemporary community standards,
   b. depicts sexual conduct in a patently offensive way,
   c. lacks serious literary, artistic, political, or scientific value.

2. The <u>Freedman</u> procedure for censoring obscenity requires:
   a. burden of proof rests with the censor,
   b. restraint prior to judicial review can be for only a brief period,
   c. prompt judicial review.

3. The distributors and users of obscenity are entitled to rights:
   a. seizure of material requires a properly obtained warrant,
   b. conviction must consider scienter,
   c. obscenity is protected in the privacy of the home.

4. The regulators and opponents of obscenity are entitled to rights:
   a. child pornography is outside the protection of the First Amendment,
   b. individuals can order the post office to stop distribution of materials that appear to be obscene,
   c. pandering may be decisive in determining obscenity,
   d. citizens may restrict non-obscene, pornographic business activities by either concentration or dispersion,
   e. federal financing of artistic excellence should consider standards of decency.

KEY DECISIONS

1957 —   <u>ROTH</u> — concluded that obscenity is outside the protection of the First Amendment

1965 —   <u>FREEDMAN</u> — established standards regulating prior restraint

1966 —   <u>GINZBURG</u> — upheld obscenity conviction based on pandering

1967 — REDRUP — summarized differences in the thinking of Supreme Court justices regarding standards for obscenity regulation

1969 — STANLEY — allowed obscenity in the privacy of the home

1970 — ROWAN — held that vendor has no constitutional right to send unwanted material through the mail

1973 — MILLER — redefined obscenity; introduced a period of intensified regulation

1976 — YOUNG — upheld right of city to determine locational requirements for "adult" theatres

1977 — SMITH — indicated that the jury, rather than the state legislature, has responsibility for determining what is obscene

1978 — PINKUS — held that "children" are to be excluded and "sensitive persons" should be included as part of "community standards" for determining obscenity

1982 — FERBER — upheld a state law that excluded child pornography from First Amendment protection

1986 — HUDNUT — overturned an ordinance designed to punish the graphic sexually explicit subordination of women

1998 — NATIONAL ENDOWMENT FOR THE ARTS — held that funding priorities should be based on such criteria as artistic excellence and general standards of decency

RECOMMENDED READING

Benston, George, "Government Constraints on Political, Artistic, and Commercial Speech," Connecticut Law Review 20 (1988), 303-24.

Dauber, Eric L., "Child Pornography: A New Exception to the First Amendment," Florida State University Law Review 10 (Winter, 1983), 684-701.

Gard, Stephen W., "Obscenity and the Right to be Let Alone: The Balancing of Constitutional Rights," Indiana Law Review 6 (1973), 490-508.

Grunes, Rodney A., "Justice Brennan and the Problem of Obscenity," Seton Hall Law Review 22 (1992), 789-813.

Main, Edward J., "The Neglected Prong of the Miller Test for Obscenity: Serious Literary, Artistic, Political, or Scientific Value," Southern Illinois University Law Journal 11 (Summer 1987), 1159-1177.

Makau, Josina M., and J. P. Williams, "Perspectives on Pornography and Free Speech," Free Speech Yearbook (1984),109-22.

Nahmod, S. H., "Artistic Expression and Aesthetic Theory: The Beautiful, The Sublime and the First Amendment," Wisconsin Law Review (1987), 221-63.

Rubin, Susan A., and Laurence B. Alexander, "Regulating Pornography: The Feminist Influence," Communications and the Law 18 (1996), 73-94.

Schauer, Frederick, The Law of Obscenity. Washington D.C.: Bureau of National Affairs, 1976.

Schauer, Frederick, "The Return of Variable Obscenity?" Hastings Law Journal 28 (July, 1977), 1275-91.

Stern, Ronald M., "Sex, Lies, and Prior Restraints: 'Sexually Oriented Business' — The New Obscenity," University of Detroit Law Review 68 (1991), 253-285.

Van Dyke, Michael S., "Regulation of Pornography: Is Erotica Self-Expression Deserving of Protection?" Loyola Law Review 33 (1987), 445-468.

CHAPTER 6

SILENCE

The First Amendment clearly guarantees the freedom to communicate. Does it also guarantee the freedom not to communicate? Does it guarantee the freedom not to be communicated with, or the freedom to be let alone? The Supreme Court has, in several cases, answered these questions in the affirmative. Yet, while the right to silence is constitutionally protected, it is not absolute. Under certain conditions, an individual may be required to communicate, or to be communicated with, contrary to his or her will. In other situations, the individual enjoys a constitutional right to silence.

FREEDOM NOT TO COMMUNICATE

U.S. citizens, in a variety of situations, have claimed a right to refuse to communicate. Some have refused to sign loyalty oaths. Others have declined to answer questions before investigative committees. Writers have sought to remain anonymous. Some individuals have objected to systems of government surveillance. The Supreme Court has been the final arbiter in many of these instances.

LOYALTY OATHS

Chapter 4 contained explication of several cases in which loyalty oaths, required as an indication of a teacher's fitness to work in the public-school system, were struck down on the grounds of ambiguity and overbreadth. Loyalty oaths have been required of state employees other than teachers. These oaths have been tested in the courts. In Elfbrandt v. Russell, 86 S.Ct. 1238 (1966), the Court considered the constitutionality of an Arizona act which subjected any employee who took the oath, and "knowingly" belonged to an organization that sought to overthrow the government, to dismissal from his or her position. The Court found fault with the law. Justice William Douglas noted that a member who does not participate in an organization's unlawful activities poses no threat. Laws that are not restricted to members who join with the "intent" to further illegal action presume that all members share the unlawful goals of the organization. Such laws are based on "guilt by association." The law was unconstitutional. Five years later, in Connell v. Higginbotham, 91 S.Ct. 1772 (1971), the Court declared unconstitutional another oath that rested on the assumption of "guilt by association."

In Cole v. Richardson, 92 S.Ct 1332 (1972), the Court approved a Massachusetts oath that did not contain these flaws. The oath in question required an individual to "uphold and defend" the constitutions of the United States and of Massachusetts, and "to oppose the overthrow" of the government. The Court determined that this oath merely sought a commitment from employees not to use illegal action to change the constitutional system. The Supreme Court upheld the oath because it was constitutionally valid.

INVESTIGATIVE COMMITTEES

The Watkins, Barenblatt, and Uphaus cases involved an individuals's right to refuse to answer questions before a governmental investigating committee. In 1954, John Watkins was subpoenaed as a witness before the House Committee on UnAmerican Activities. In recent years, HUAC had intensified its efforts to curb Communist Party activities. Before the committee, Watkins claimed that he was not then nor had he ever been a card-carrying member of the Communist Party. Watkins was then confronted with the names of several people who were suspected of having been members of the Party. Watkins said he would answer questions about himself and about persons whom he believed to still be members of the Communist Party. He would not, however, answer questions about persons who may have belonged to the Party in the past, but who had since terminated their membership. He did not believe that HUAC had any right to publicly expose persons because of their past activities. Watkins was found guilty of contempt, and fined $100. The Supreme Court, per Chief Justice Earl Warren, expressed concern about compelling an unwilling witness to testify about past beliefs and associations that are "judged by current standards rather than those contemporary with the matters exposed." HUAC had "no congressional power to expose for the sake of exposure." Warren emphasized that when First Amendment rights are involved, "the delegation of power to the committee must be clearly revealed in its charter." In <u>Watkins v. United States</u>, 77 S.Ct. 1173 (1957), the investigative committee did not state the subject under inquiry and did not show the pertinence of the questions to the investigation. Watkins' conviction violated due process.

In <u>Barenblatt v. United States</u>, 79 S.Ct. 1081 (1959), the Court upheld the conviction of Lloyd Barenblatt, who had objected to HUAC's inquiry into his possible membership in and association with the Communist Party. He was convicted of contempt, sentenced to six months' imprisonment, and fined $250. The Court upheld the conviction on three grounds. First, it was within HUAC's authority to compel testimony. Second, unlike <u>Watkins,</u> the questions asked by the committee were pertinent to HUAC's investigation. Third, the action of the committee did not violate the First Amendment. The Court compared the protections of the First and Fifth Amendments, noting that "the protections of the First Amendment, unlike a proper claim of the privilege against self-incrimination under the Fifth Amendment, do not afford a witness the right to resist inquiry in all circumstances."

A related case, <u>Uphaus v. Wyman</u>, 79 S.Ct. 1040 (1959), involved an effort to investigate subversive activities within New Hampshire. Willard Uphaus, Executive Director of a summer camp, was asked by the Attorney General to produce a list of the names of all the camp's employees and the names of all persons who attended the camp. When Uphaus refused to comply, he was judged to be in contempt and was sent to jail until he provided the names. The case reached the Supreme Court. The justices acknowledged that the Attorney General was commissioned to determine if there were any subversive people in New Hampshire. The obvious starting point for such an inquiry was to learn what persons were in the state. Any requests for lists of persons related directly to the purpose of the probe, and thus the inquiries were "pertinent." The committee's demand for the lists was legitimate and the contempt citation for refusing to produce the lists was valid. The conviction was upheld. In <u>Watkins</u>, <u>Barenblatt</u>, and <u>Uphaus</u>, the Court noted that a witness before a federal commission may be required to testify about personal matters and associational activities when the questions have "obvious pertinence" to the investigation.

ANONYMOUS PUBLICATION

In two decisions, the Supreme Court defended the right of anonymous publication. The first case involved a Los Angeles ordinance which provided that no person could distribute any leaflet that did not have printed on its face the names and addresses of the persons who had written and distributed it. When Michael Talley distributed leaflets void of the required information, he was arrested, convicted, and fined $10. He appealed. The Supreme Court, in the opinion of Justice Hugo Black, decided that the law violated Talley's right to free speech and press.

> There can be no doubt that such an identification requirement would tend to restrict freedom to distribute information and thereby freedom of expression. Liberty of circulating is as essential to that freedom as liberty of publishing; indeed, without the circulation, the publication would be of little value.

Justice Black noted that, throughout history, persecuted groups have been able to criticize their oppressors either by anonymous means, or not at all. According to Black, anonymity must be protected, because it had "sometimes been assumed for the most constructive of purposes." In Talley v. California, 80 S.Ct. 536 (1960), the Court supported Talley's freedom to refuse to communicate the required information.

In McIntyre v. Ohio Elections Commission, 115 S.Ct. 1511 (1995), a pamphleteer who distributed anonymous leaflets criticizing a proposed school tax was fired by the Ohio Elections Commission for violating a statute which prohibited the distribution of campaign literature that did not contain the name and address of the person or campaign official issuing the literature. The Supreme Court acknowledged that the limitation under review was narrow when compared with the restriction in Talley; it applied only to unsigned documents designed to influence voting in an election. Nonetheless, the Court rejected both interests Ohio raised in support of the statute. First, Ohio's interest in preventing fraudulent or libelous anonymous messages could be dealt with more directly; a broad prohibition was not warranted. Second, the state's interest in providing the electorate with relevant information does not justify requiring a writer to make disclosure he or she would otherwise omit. Writing for the majority, Justice John Stevens reviewed the rationale for protecting anonymous publications.

> Under our Constitution, anonymous pamphleteering is not a pernicious, fraudulent practice, but an honorable tradition of advocacy and of dissent. Anonymity is a shield from the tyranny of the majority.... It thus exemplifies the purpose behind the Bill of Rights, and of the First Amendment in particular: to protect unpopular individuals from retaliation — and their ideas from suppression — at the hand of an intolerant society. The right to remain anonymous may be abused when it shields fraudulent conduct. But political speech by its nature will sometimes have

unpalatable consequences, and, in general, our society accords greater weight to the value of free speech than to the dangers of its misuse.

SURVEILLANCE

In 1967, the U.S. Army was asked to assist local authorities in quelling civil disorders. To enhance its effort, the army developed a data-gathering system which included the collection of information about public activities that were thought to have potential for civil disorder. The information was then stored in a data bank at army intelligence headquarters. Arlo Tatum, a conscientious objector, argued that the army was conducting illegal surveillance of civilian political activity. He also claimed that the activity had a "chilling" effect which resulted from the potential abuse of military power and the potential later misuse of gathered data. The Court, per Chief Justice Warren Burger, held that "allegations of a subjective 'chill' are not an adequate substitute for a claim of specific present objective harm or a threat of specific future harm." Army surveillance could be challenged in court, but only if individuals could demonstrate "actual or threatened injury." Tatum had failed to demonstrate any actual injury. In effect, the Laird v. Tatum, 92 S.Ct. 2318 (1972), ruling approved of the government's right to gather information that an individual did not wish to communicate.

REQUIRED SUBSIDATION

Lehnert v. Ferris Faculty Association, 111 S. Ct. 1950 (1991), involved a challenge to Michigan's Public Employment Relations Act which provided that a union shall serve as the exclusive collective-bargaining representative of public employees. The Act permitted a union and a government employer to enter into an arrangement under which employees who declined to become members of the union were compelled to pay a "service fee" to the union. Employees at Ferris State College objected to the use of their fees for purposes other than negotiating and administering a collective-bargaining agreement. They argued that such practices violated the First Amendment. The Court, per Justice Harry Blackmun, held that a local bargaining representative may charge objecting employees for their share of the costs associated with activities of its state and national affiliates, even if those activities were not performed for the direct benefit of the objecting employees' bargaining unit. Blackmun added the following qualifications:

This conclusion, however, does not serve to grant a local union *carte blanche* to expend dissenters' dollars for bargaining activities wholly unrelated to the employees in their unit.... There must be some indication that the payment is for services that may ultimately inure to the benefit of the members of the local union by virtue of their membership in the parent organization.

In University of Wisconsin v. Southworth, No. 98-1189 (2000), the Supreme Court decided that as long as a public academic institution remains "viewpoint neutral" it can use student activity fees to fund organizations whose views are offensive to some students. The suit was brought by a conservative student who objected to supporting gay, socialist, and feminist organizations. Justice Anthony Kennedy noted that the purpose of the fees was to facilitate open exchange of ideas.

FREEDOM NOT TO BE COMMUNICATED WITH

The Supreme Court has considered whether an individual enjoys a freedom to prevent incoming communication. In Saia, Kovacs, and Rock Against Racism, the Court considered whether restrictions could be placed on the public use of sound amplification equipment. In Pollak, the Court decided whether a public transportation company could broadcast a radio program over loudspeakers on its vehicles.

SOUND AMPLIFICATION

A local ordinance prohibited the use of sound-amplification devices, except with the permission of the Chief of Police. Complying with this law, Samuel Saia, a minister of the Jehovah's Witnesses, obtained permission to use sound equipment, mounted atop his car, to amplify speeches on religious topics. When his permit expired, Saia applied for another, but his request was refused because several complaints had been received concerning the "noise." Saia then used his equipment without permission, and was arrested. The case reached the Supreme Court. According to Justice Douglas, the ordinance contained several flaws. It provided no standards to guide the police chief in granting permission. It did not regulate the hours of use of loudspeakers, nor did it specify the volume of sound allowed. Douglas's opinion noted that "any abuses which loudspeakers create can be controlled by narrowly drawn statutes." The ordinance, however, failed to satisfy this requirement. Douglas also feared the power of censorship inherent in the ordinance. Douglas noted that, in Saia's case, a permit was denied because some persons found the sound annoying. In future cases, a permit might be denied because some people found the ideas annoying. According to Douglas, "annoyance at ideas can be cloaked in annoyance at sound." In Saia v. New York, 68 S.Ct. 1148 (1948), the Court declared the ordinance to be unconstitutional.

A year later, in <u>Kovacs v. Cooper</u>, 69 S.Ct 448 (1949), the Court supported a Trenton, New Jersey ordinance that forbade the use, on city streets, of mobile sound devices that send out loud and raucous noises. Charles Kovacs was convicted for violating this ordinance by speaking into an amplifier in order to comment upon a labor dispute. Kovacs appealed. The Supreme Court noted that sound amplification in public places was subject to reasonable regulation. The majority opinion, per Justice Stanley Reed, acknowledged that "city streets are recognized as a normal place for the exchange of ideas by speech or paper. But this does not mean the freedom is beyond all control." Reed expressed concern that "such distractions would be dangerous to traffic" and that "in the residential thoroughfares the quiet and tranquility so desirable for city dwellers would likewise be at the mercy of advocates of particular religious, social or political persuaders." The minority opinion, written by Justice Black, argued that an ordinance could be written that protected a community from unreasonable use of amplifying systems without absolutely denying the use of this avenue of communication. An ordinance could restrict the volume of sound or the hours during which amplification was permitted — without infringing upon free speech. The majority, however, ruled that the Trenton statute was a constitutionally-valid method of protecting the right not to be communicated with.

In <u>Ward v. Rock Against Racism</u>, 109 S.Ct. 2746 (1989), the Court upheld a New York City noise regulation policy. The case began when the group Rock Against Racism furnished its own sound equipment and technicians while sponsoring programs of rock music at the bandshell in Central Park. Area residents voiced numerous complaints about excessive noise. At other bandshell events, audiences became disappointed and unruly when musical groups were unable to provide sufficient amplification levels. In an effort to correct the problem, New York adopted guidelines which specified that the city would furnish high quality sound equipment and retain an experienced sound technician for all performances in the bandshell. Rock Against Racism initiated court action which sought to strike down the guidelines. The Supreme Court approved the guidelines as a reasonable content neutral regulation of the time, place, and manner of protected speech. The Court found that the guidelines served two significant governmental interests:

> That the city has a substantial interest in protecting citizens from unwelcome and excessive noise, even in a traditional public forum such as a park, cannot be doubted. Moreover, it has a substantial interest in ensuring the sufficiency of sound amplification at Bandshell events in order to allow citizens to enjoy the benefits of the park, in light of the evidence that inadequate amplification had

resulted in the inability of some audiences to hear performances.

FORCED LISTENING

In March, 1948, Capital Transit Company, a privately owned transportation system that operated in the District of Columbia, initiated "music-as-you-ride" radio programs which were played through loudspeakers in streetcars and buses. The programs consisted of about ten percent commercial announcements on behalf of Capital Transit and 90 percent musical selections. Franklin Pollak and Guy Martin initiated court action on the grounds that the radio programs interfered with their freedom of conversation by making it necessary for them to compete against the programs in order to be heard, and that the First Amendment guarantees a right to listen only to those points of view an individual wishes to hear. When the case reached the Supreme Court, the justices decided that the radio programs violated neither the right to free speech nor the right to privacy. The Court found no evidence of a free speech violation because the programs had not "been used for objectionable propaganda." The Court also found that the programs did not violate an individual's right to privacy because a passenger on a public vehicle is not entitled to privacy equal to that which is available at home. No matter how complete the right to privacy is at home, it is limited by the rights of others when a person travels on public transit. Under the conditions present in Public Utilities Commission v. Pollak, 72 S.Ct. 813 (1952), an individual did not enjoy the right to prevent incoming communication.

FREEDOM TO BE LET ALONE

The Supreme Court has heard claims based on the right to be let alone. Some of these cases involved ordinances that were designed to regulate door-to-door and community-wide solicitation and distribution. Some involved access to public and nonpublic forums. Others concerned laws that control an individual's freedom to travel.

SOLICITATION AND DISTRIBUTION

During the past several decades, the Supreme Court has been asked to balance the freedoms of solicitors and distributors against the right of citizens to be free from uninvited intrusions at the front doors of their homes, on the streets of their cities, or at various places throughout their communities.

Door-to-door

The Court has evaluated the constitutionality of numerous local ordinances which regulated door-to-door solicitation and distribution. In Lovell v. Griffin, 58 S.Ct. 666 (1938), the Court considered an ordinance that prohibited the distribution of any kind of literature in Griffin, Georgia, without the permission of the City Manager. The Supreme Court declared that the ordinance was unconstitutional. It was not restricted to "literature" that was obscene or offensive to public morals, or that advocated unlawful conduct. Instead, the ordinance prevented the distribution of literature of any kind, at any place, and in any manner, without a permit. The ordinance was too broad in its restrictions.

In Martin v. Struthers, 63 S.Ct. 862 (1943), the Court examined an ordinance that banned the distribution of literature to residences in Struthers, Ohio. According to the Court, a city does not have the power to prevent a person from going from residence to residence in order to distribute information. Even though such distribution causes inconvenience, this is a small price to pay for the protection of free expression. An occupant could, however, post a notice on the door indicating his or her desire not to be disturbed by uninvited solicitors or distributors. The Struthers ordinance was overturned because it "in effect, makes a person a criminal trespasser if he enters the property of another for an innocent purpose without an explicit command from the owners to stay away." In Martin, the Court determined that a notice to stay away is necessary to stop intrusions by "harmless" distributors.

At stake in Murdock v. Pennsylvania, 63 S.Ct. 870 (1943), was an ordinance prohibiting persons from soliciting in Jeanette, Pennsylvania, without first obtaining a license and paying a tax. The justices found fault with the ordinance because it required religious colporteurs to pay a tax as a condition for the pursuit of their activities. The ordinance was unconstitutional because it restrained in advance the freedoms "of press and religion and inevitably tends to suppress their exercise." The tax did not acquire validity simply because it was "non-discriminatory."

In Breard v. Alexandria, 71 S.Ct. 920 (1951), the Court approved an ordinance that placed limitations on door-to-door solicitation. Jack Breard supervised a crew of solicitors who went door-to-door seeking subscriptions for several nationally known magazines. While soliciting in Alexandria, Louisiana, Breard was arrested and convicted for violating an ordinance that required solicitors to obtain prior consent from the owners of the residences solicited. He appealed. The Supreme Court, per Justice Reed, compared the facts in Breard with those in Martin and concluded that door-to-door solicitation for commercial purposes could be prohibited by local ordinance. The Court decided that "subscriptions may be made by anyone interested in receiving the magazines without the annoyance of house-to-house canvassing." According to Reed, "communities that have found these methods of sale obnoxious may control them by ordinance."

In Hynes v. Borough of Oradell, 96 S.Ct. 1755 (1976), the Court considered an Oradell, New Jersey ordinance that required any individual wishing to solicit door-to-door for a charitable or political cause to register with the police department for identification purposes. When State Assemblyman Edward Hynes wished to campaign for reelection by canvassing door-to-door and speaking with voters, he initiated suit. Hynes claimed that the ordinance restricted First Amendment freedoms. The Supreme Court rejected the ordinance because it lacked specific standards to be used by authorities who would apply the ordinance. There was also no clue as to what qualified as a "recognized charity" or a "political cause." The ordinance was unconstitutional because of vagueness.

In Schaumburg v. Citizens For A Better Environment, 100 S.Ct. 826 (1980), the Court evaluated the constitutionality of an ordinance prohibiting door-to-door or on-street solicitation of contributions by charitable organizations not using at least 75 percent of their receipts for "charitable purposes." When a nonprofit, environmental-protection group was denied a permit because it could not meet the "75 percent requirement," the group sought relief in the courts. The Supreme Court, per Justice Byron White, decided that the requirement was illegal. Although the 75 percent requirement might be enforceable against "traditional" charities, it was not applicable to organizations whose main purpose is not to provide money or services for the poor, but to gather and disseminate information about matters of public concern. Such organizations characteristically use paid employees.

The Court rejected a similar law in Secretary of State of Maryland v. Joseph H. Munson Company, 104 S.Ct. 2839 (1984). Justice Blackmun noted that the statute operated on a mistaken premise that high solicitation costs are an accurate measure of fraud.

> ...there is no necessary connection between fraud and high solicitation and administrative costs. A number of other factors may result in high costs; the most important of these is that charities often are combining solicitation with dissemination of information, discussion, and advocacy of public issues, an activity clearly protected by the First Amendment.

In Riley v. National Federation of the Blind of North Carolina, 108 S.Ct. 2667 (1988), the Court rejected the "reasonable fee" provision of the North Carolina Charitable Solicitation Act. Citing the rulings of

Schaumburg and Munson, the Court reaffirmed that "using percentages to decide the legality of the fundraiser's fee is not narrowly tailored to the States' interest in preventing fraud." The Act was impermissibly insensitive to the realities faced by small or unpopular charities which must often pay high percentages of the receipts due to the difficulty of attracting donors. In addition, the threat that fund-raisers will face potential litigation over the "reasonableness" of the fee "must necessarily chill speech in direct contravention of the First Amendment's dictates."

The cases considered in this section indicate that the personal inconvenience that results from unsolicited distribution of literature is generally outweighed by the public interest in maintaining a free flow of information. The cases also indicate that an ordinance which limits door-to-door solicitation must be constitutionally valid; that is, it must *not* grant arbitrary power, be vague or overbroad, or provide prior restraint. The Court decided, however, in Martin, that an individual may restrict uninvited solicitors by posting a notice to stay away. And, in Breard, the Court held that door-to-door solicitation for commercial purposes may be restricted. In these cases, the Supreme Court recognized an individual's right to be let alone.

Community-wide

In Marsh v. Alabama, 66 S.Ct. 276 (1946), the Supreme Court deliberated whether Alabama could forbid an individual from distributing literature on the premises of a company-owned town. Chickasaw, a suburb of Mobile, was owned by the Gulf Shipbuilding Corporation. There was nothing to differentiate Chickasaw from any other town, except that the title to the property belonged to a private corporation. In Chickasaw, stores were posted with a notice that declared the area "private property," and prohibited any distribution or solicitation without written permission. A Jehovah's Witness was told by town officials that she could not distribute religious literature without a permit, and that no permit would be issued. The case reached the Supreme Court. The opinion, per Justice Black, noted that people who live in company-owned towns must make decisions that affect the welfare of their community and nation. They must have access to information and the distribution of literature is vital to such access. In Marsh, Justice Black concluded that when the rights of property owners are balanced against First Amendment freedoms, "the latter occupy a preferred position."

In Organization For A Better Austin v. Keefe, 91 S.Ct. 1575 (1971), the Court again evaluated a community-wide ban on distribution. Organization For A Better Austin (OBA), a racially integrated organization in the Austin neighborhood of Chicago, was formed in order to "stabilize" the racial ratio in the area. For several years, the boundary of the black segregated area of Chicago had moved progressively west toward Austin. OBA, in its efforts to "stabilize" the area, opposed such real-estate tactics as "blockbusting" and "panic peddling." OBA contended that Jerome Keefe, a real-estate broker, had engaged in such activities and thereby aroused fear in white residents that blacks were moving into the area. Then by exploiting the reactions of whites, Keefe was able to secure listings and sell homes to blacks. OBA members met with Keefe to attempt to convince him to alter his practices, but he argued that he was entitled to solicit real-estate business as he wished. Subsequently, OBA members distributed throughout Westchester, the city in which Keefe resided, leaflets that criticized Keefe's real-estate activities. Keefe obtained an injunction that prohibited OBA from distributing leaflets in Westchester. The case reached the Supreme Court. In the opinion of Chief Justice Burger, the injunction constituted an impermissible restraint on First Amendment freedoms. The injunction operated "not to redress alleged private wrongs, but to suppress, on the basis of previous publications, distribution of literature 'of any kind'." In Organization For A Better Austin, as in Marsh, the Court overturned community-wide bans that violated the free speech of solicitors and distributors.

PUBLIC FORUMS

In recent years, the Supreme Court has determined the conditions under which certain properties may serve as public forums. In these cases, the Court examined free-speech rights and responsibilities of such institutions as military bases, prisons, airports, the postal service, corporations, the work place, school facilities, public lands, and public broadcasting stations. In these cases, the Court determined whether properties could be classified as any of three types of public forums: 1) a public place that has been established by tradition as open for public assembly and discussion at all times and for all purposes, 2) a public land that has been opened by legislative enactment for the purpose of expressive activity, or 3) a public property that has not been designated as open to public communication. Out of these Court decisions emerged a body of communication law applicable to the public forum.

Military bases

In four cases, the Supreme Court examined whether the First Amendment rights of petition and distribution may be regulated more extensively at military installations than at other facilities. One such case was Flower v. United States, 92 S.Ct. 1842 (1972). John Flower, a member of the American Friends Service Committee, was arrested by military police while quietly distributing leaflets on New Braunfels Avenue within the limits of Fort Sam Houston. He had previously been barred from the base when he attempted to distribute "unauthorized" materials. Flower was convicted under a federal law for reentering a military base in violation of an order not to do so. Upon appeal, the Supreme Court noted that the base commander had not barred vehicular or pedestrian traffic from the street where Flower was arrested. Therefore, New Braunfels Avenue was a public thoroughfare.

> Under such circumstances the military has abandoned any claim that it has special interests in who walks, talks, or distributes leaflets on the avenue. The base commandant can no more order petitioner [Flower] off this public street because he was distributing leaflets than could the city police order any leafleteer off any public street.

The Greer v. Spock, 96 S.Ct. 1211 (1976), case arose when the base commander at Fort Dix denied Dr. Benjamin Spock — a candidate of the People's Party for the office of President — permission to visit the post in order to distribute campaign literature and discuss election issues with the servicemen and their families. Base regulations banned "demonstrations, picketing, sit-ins, protest marches, political speeches, and similar activities" and allowed the posting of handbills and the distribution of leaflets only with the written approval of the base commander. Spock initiated court action, contending a violation of First Amendment rights. The Supreme Court supported the Fort Dix policy "of keeping official military activities there wholly free of entanglement with partisan political campaigns of any kind." According to the Court, per Justice Potter Stewart, the policy of banning speeches was "consistent with the American Constitutional tradition of a politically neutral military establishment under civilian control." Stewart emphasized that "the notion that federal reservations, like municipal streets and parks, have traditionally served as a place for free public assembly and communication of thoughts by private citizens is...historically and constitutionally false." In Spock, the Court emphasized that a military base is not a public forum and that Fort Dix did not abandon the right to regulate distribution of leaflets, as did the base in Flower. In Flower, the street in question was a public thoroughfare and the military had abandoned any right to ban civilian traffic. In Spock, the base was not a public forum and civilian access could be restricted.

In 1980, the Supreme Court reiterated its position in two cases — Glines and Huff. The Brown v. Glines, 100 S.Ct. 594 (1980), case involved air-force regulations that require military personnel to obtain authorization from their commanders prior to circulating petitions on bases. When Captain Albert Glines distributed petitions to members of Congress and to the Secretary of Defense, in which he complained about grooming standards, he was removed from active duty. Glines brought suit. The Supreme Court upheld the regulations. According to Justice Lewis Powell, "a base commander may prevent the circulation of material that he determines to be a clear threat to the readiness of his troops." In a similar case, Secretary of the Navy v. Huff, 100 S.Ct. 606 (1980), the Court upheld navy and marine-corps regulations that required military personnel on overseas bases to obtain approval before circulating petitions addressed to members of Congress. Both Glines and Huff affirmed the position established in Spock — military regulations may require members of the armed forces to secure approval before circulating petitions or distributing leaflets within a military base.

Prisons

The Supreme Court affirmed that prisoners' First Amendment rights may be restricted in Thornburgh v. Abbott, 109 S.Ct. 1874 (1989). Even though the Court acknowledged that prisoners may generally receive publications from the outside, it approved a regulation which allowed wardens to reject incoming publications that are judged "to be detrimental to the security, good order, or discipline of the institution or if it might facilitate criminal activity." The Court stressed that prison officials may not reject a publication because its content is political, unpopular, or repugnant, or establish a list of banned publications, but must "review each issue of a subscription separately." Otherwise, the practice would constitute prior restraint.

Airports

Board of Airport Commissioners of Los Angeles v. Jews For Jesus, 107 S.Ct. 2568 (1987), involved the question of access to airport grounds. The Board of Airport Commissioners adopted a resolution banning all "First Amendment activities" within the Los Angeles International Airport. Jews for Jesus, a nonprofit religious corporation, challenged the resolution's constitutionality. The Airport Commissioners justified the resolution on the grounds that the Airport was a nonpublic forum, and that the policy was intended to reach only expressive activity unrelated to airport purposes. The Court found the resolution to be overly broad since it prohibited all expression and did not merely regulate expressive activity that might create problems such as congestion or disruption. Under such a sweeping ban, virtually every individual who entered the airport could be found to violate the resolution by engaging in some "First Amendment activity." The ban would be unconstitutional even if the airport were a non-public forum because no conceivable governmental interest would justify such an absolute prohibition of speech.

International Society For Krishna Consciousness v. Lee, 112 S.Ct 2701 (1992), raised a similar issue. It involved a regulation by the Port Authority of New York and New Jersey, which owns and operates three major airports in the New York City area. The regulation banned solicitation of money within airport terminals. Solicitation was permitted on the sidewalks outside the airport buildings. The Society for Krishna Consciousness brought suit, arguing that the terminals were public forums and that any regulation had to support a compelling governmental interest. The Supreme Court determined that an airport terminal is a nonpublic forum, and "a ban on solicitation need only satisfy a reasonableness standard." It need not be the "most" reasonable or the "only" reasonable limitation. Furthermore, the ban does not have to serve a compelling interest. According to the Court, the ban was reasonable. Solicitors might have a disruptive effect "by slowing the path of both those who must decide whether to contribute and those who must alter their paths to avoid the solicitation." Furthermore, solicitors had access to the general public via the sidewalk outside the terminals — an area frequented by an overwhelming percentage of airport users.

Postal service

Four cases involved efforts to control the distribution of information through the postal service. Each case took place within a different context. In Rowan v. U.S. Post Office Department, 90 S.Ct. 1484 (1970), a case considered in Chapter 5, the Court approved a system of post-office-assisted self-censorship. According to the statute, when an individual notifies the postmaster that pornographic advertisements have been received, the postmaster orders the sender to stop any future mailings of such materials to the individual. The Act was challenged in Court, where the justices held that a person must be free to exercise control over unwanted mail. The right of every person "to be let alone" must be measured against the right of others to communicate. In Rowan, the Court decided that the right to communicate stops at the mailbox of an unreceptive individual.

In Procunier v. Martinez, 94 S.Ct. 1800 (1974), the Court evaluated regulations that allowed authorities to censor the mail of prison inmates.   As Director of the California Department of Corrections, Raymond Procunier established rules that directed inmates not to write letters in which they "unduly complain" or "magnify grievances," express "inflammatory...views or beliefs," describe "criminal activity," are "obscene or defamatory," include "foreign matter," or contain material that is "otherwise inappropriate." Prison employees screened both incoming and outgoing mail to determine violations. The inmates challenged the regulations. The Supreme Court decided that censorship of prisoner mail is justified when two criteria are met.

> First,...they must show that a regulation authorizing mail censorship furthers one or more of the substantial governmental interests of security, order, and rehabilitation. Second, the limitation of First Amendment freedoms must be no greater than is necessary or essential to the protection of the particular governmental interest involved.

On the basis of these criteria, the Court found that Procunier's regulations "invited prison officials and employees to apply their own personal prejudices and opinions as standards for prisoner mail censorship." The regulations allowed censorship that was "far broader than any legitimate interest in penal administration demands." In Procunier, the Court acknowledged that censorship of prisoner mail is justifiable, but only under specific guidelines.

In United Postal Service v. Council of Greenburgh Civil Associations, 101 S.Ct. 2676 (1981), the Court considered the question of letter-box use. Council of Greenburgh Civic Associations, an umbrella organization for several civic groups, was notified that the practice of delivering messages to local residents by placing unstamped notices in the letter boxes of private homes violated a federal ordinance. Council members filed suit, contending that enforcement of the ordinance would deny free-speech and free-press rights. The case reached the Supreme Court. Justice William Rehnquist noted that the Court was not confronted with a regulation that prohibits individuals from going door-to-door, or that prohibits individuals to use the mails to distribute their messages. The issue was solely the constitutionality of an ordinance that makes it unlawful for a person to use, without paying a fee, a letter box that has been designated as an "authorized depository" of mail by the postal service. Rehnquist noted that once a letter box becomes an "authorized depository," it does not undergo transformation into a "public forum" with First Amendment guarantees of access to all. In Greenburgh, the Court concluded that the ordinance did not abridge First Amendment rights because the ordinance was not aimed at the content of the messages; rather, it was aimed at the place of deposit.

Perry Education Association v. Perry Local Educator's Association, 103 S.Ct. 948 (1983), involved the issue of privileged access to mailboxes. Perry Educational Association was the exclusive bargaining representative for the teachers in the local school district. A collective bargaining agreement provided the association with access to the interschool mail system and to teacher mailboxes. No other union was granted access. A rival union initiated court action. The issue was whether the First Amendment was violated when a union that had been elected by teachers as their exclusive bargaining representative was granted access to certain means of communication while access was denied to a rival union. The Supreme Court noted that an "interschool mail system is not a traditional public forum." Consequently, there is no constitutional obligation to let every organization use the mailboxes.

> Implicit in the concept of the nonpublic forum is the right to make distinctions in access on the basis of subject matter and speaker identity. These distinctions may be impermissible in a public forum but are inherent and inescapable in the process of limiting a nonpublic forum to activities compatible with the intended purpose of the property.

The differential access provided to the union was reasonable because it enabled the association to perform its obligations as the representative of local teachers.

In the cases cited in this section, the Supreme Court determined that, under specific conditions, individuals have differential access to the postal system as a means of distributing information. In Procunier, the Court acknowledged that prisoner mail may be censored if specific guidelines are met. In Greenburgh, the Court determined that the letter box was not a public forum and that it could be restricted to those who were willing to pay a fee. In Perry Education Association, the Court approved differential access; a labor union that was the exclusive bargaining representative for teachers enjoyed privileged access to those teachers' mailboxes.

Corporations

In three cases, the Supreme Court considered the First Amendment rights of corporations. In these cases, the Court examined conditions under which corporations could distribute information. First National Bank of Boston v. Bellotti, 98 S.Ct. 1407 (1978), involved a Massachusetts law that prohibited corporations from making contributions for the purpose of influencing political issues other than those "materially affecting any of the property, business or assets of the corporation." A corporation that violated the law could receive a fine of $50,000. When two national banking associations and three business corporations wanted to publicize their views on a proposed constitutional amendment, they started court action to have the law declared unconstitutional. The Supreme Court acknowledged that a corporation enjoys First Amendment rights of free expression.

> If the speakers here were not corporations, no one would suggest that the State could silence their proposed speech. It is the type of speech indispensable to decision-making in a democracy, and this is no less true because the speech comes from a corporation rather than an individual. The inherent worth of the speech in terms of its capacity for informing the public does not depend upon the identity of its source, whether corporation, association, union, or individual.

In Consolidated Edison Company of New York v. Public Service Commission of New York, 100 S.Ct. 2326 (1980), the Court again examined corporate free-speech rights. Consolidated Edison placed a pamphlet in its billing envelopes. The pamphlet stated the company's views on "the benefits of nuclear power," saying that they "far outweigh any potential risk" and that nuclear power plants are safe, economical, and clean. Shortly thereafter, an anti-nuclear-power group requested Consolidated Edison to enclose a rebuttal, prepared by the group, in its next billing envelope. When the request was refused, the Public Service Commission was asked to intervene. After deliberation, the Commission prohibited "utilities from using bill inserts to discuss political matters." The Supreme Court overturned the ban for three reasons. First, the restriction could not be upheld on the ground that the company was not entitled to freedom of speech. In First National Bank of Boston, the Court had "rejected the contention that a State may confine corporate speech to a specified issue." Second, the ban was not a valid time, place, or manner restriction; it was related to subject matter.

> The First Amendment's hostility to content-based regulation extends not only to restrictions on particular viewpoints, but also to prohibition of public discussion of an entire topic. As a general matter, the First Amendment means that government has no power to restrict expression because of its message, its ideas, its subject matter, or its content.

Third, the ban was not justified by a compelling state interest. The ban was not necessary to avoid forcing Consolidated Edison's views on a captive audience; customers could escape exposure simply by throwing the insert into a wastebasket.

Pacific Gas and Electric Company v. Public Utilities Commission, 106 S.Ct. 903 (1986), is a similar case. For six decades, the Pacific Gas and Electric Company had distributed a newsletter in its monthly billing envelopes. The newsletter contained political editorials, feature stories on matters of public interest, tips on energy conservation, and information about utility services and bills. At the insistence of a group of ratepayers, the Public Utilities Commission decided that the company should not use billing envelopes to distribute political editorials because the customers should not bear the expense of the company's political speech. In an effort to work out a compromise, the Commission permitted the ratepayers to include a counter-message in the envelopes. Pacific Gas and Electric Company appealed. The Supreme Court held that the billing envelopes were the property of the company, which should not be forced to use its own property to disseminate views with which it disagreed. A corporation, just like an individual, has the choice of what not to say as well as the choice of what to say. The Court anticipated that, under the compromise, there might be a chilling effect on communication altogether — the company might conclude that the safe course would avoid any controversy, thus reducing the free flow of all information. In Pacific Gas and Electric Company, as in First National Bank of Boston and Consolidated Edison of New York, the Court upheld the First Amendment right of corporations to distribute information, while denying access to the messages of special interest groups.

Work place

Sheila Myers, an Assistant District Attorney in New Orleans, objected to her supervisors when informed that she would be transferred. Myers then distributed a questionnaire soliciting the views of fellow staff members concerning office transfer policy and office morale. Upon learning of this behavior, District Attorney Harry Connick told Myers that she was being terminated. She was told that her distribution of the questionnaire was considered an act of insubordination. Myers initiated legal action, contending that her employment was terminated because she had exercised her right of free speech. In Connick v. Myers, 103 S.Ct. 1684 (1983), the majority opinion, written by Justice White, sided with Connick. White noted that when an employee personally confronts an immediate superior, institutional efficiency may be threatened not only by content but by the manner, time, and place in which it is delivered. In this case, Myers' questionnaire was prepared and distributed at the office; the manner of distribution required employees to set aside their work in order to complete the forms. According to White, the fact that Myers "exercised her rights of speech at the office supports Connick's fears that the functioning of his office was endangered." White concluded:

The limited First Amendment interest involved here does not require that Connick tolerate action which he reasonably believed would disrupt the office, undermine his authority, and destroy close working relationships. Myers' discharge therefore did not offend the First Amendment.

The Connick principle was applied in Rankin v. McPherson, 107 S.Ct. 2891 (1987). In McPherson, a data-entry employee in a county constable's office was fired for remarking to a co-worker after hearing about an attempt on President Ronald Reagan's life: "If they go for him again, I hope they get him." Her statement was made during a private conversation in a room not easily accessible to the public. She brought suit, alleging that her discharge violated the First Amendment. The Supreme Court, in a five to four decision, held that the statement dealt with a matter of "public concern." A statement threatening to kill a president would not be protected, but the remark at issue in this case could not be criminalized. Although the statement was made in the work place, there was no proof that it disrupted the efficient functioning of the office. Nor was there any danger that the employee had discredited the office by making the statement in public. The Court concluded that the constable's interest in discharging the employee did not outweigh the employee's right to free speech.

In a related case, Waters v. Churchill, 114 S.Ct. 1878 (1994), Cheryl Churchill, a registered nurse, was fired from her position at a public hospital because of statements she made to a co-worker during a work break. Hospital administrators maintained that Churchill made disruptive statements, critical of her department and of administrators. According to Churchill, her speech was nondisruptive, though critical of hospital policies which she believed threatened patient care. Churchill sued, claiming that her speech was protected under the Connick test which protected a government employee's speech if it covered a matter of public concern and if the speech did not impair the efficiency of the public services performed by the institution's employees. The plurality opinion, written by Justice Sandra Day O'Connor, held that a government employer can discharge an employee for unprotected speech only after it conducts a reasonable investigation. In this case, the hospital had undertaken an adequate investigation to determine that Churchill's speech was not protected. In a concurring opinion, Justice Antonin Scalia claimed that disciplining of an employee violated the First Amendment only if it was in retaliation for an employee's protected speech on a matter of public concern. Scalia would not require that an employer conduct an investigation prior to taking action. Justice Stevens offered a dissenting opinion. He viewed the plurality's rule as inviting discipline rather than discussion, thus contradicting an essential function of the First Amendment. Clearly, the <u>Churchill</u> opinion represented considerable disagreement among the justices but the plurality's interpretation of the <u>Connick</u> test remains applicable to the work place.

The <u>United States v. National Treasury Employees Union</u>, 115 S.Ct. 1003 (1995), decision also had an impact on communication law regarding the work place. In 1989, Congress enacted a law that prohibited federal employees from accepting compensation for making speeches or writing articles. The ban applied even when neither the topic of the speech or article nor the group paying for it had any connection with the employees' official duties. Two unions challenged the law as an abridgement of free speech. Justice Stevens delivered the opinion of the Court. He noted that several famous authors — Nathanial Hawthorne, Herman Melville, Bret Harte, Walt Whitman — as federal employees, wrote for publication in their spare time. Stevens distinguished the speech under question in this case with that found punishable in <u>Connick</u>.

> ...expressive activities in this case fall within the protected category of citizen comment on matters of public concern rather than employee comment on matters related to personal status in the work place. The speeches and articles for which they received compensation in the past were addressed to a public audience, were made outside the work place, and involved content largely unrelated to their government employment.

Stevens concluded that the law violated the First Amendment. The prohibition on compensation imposed a significant burden on employees' expressive activity by inducing them to curtail their expression if they wished to remain employed. The prohibition also imposed a significant burden on the public's right to read and hear what the employees might otherwise have written and said. Stevens acknowledged that Congress could assume that payments on honoria to high-ranking officials in the Executive Branch might generate the appearance of improper influence. Congress could not, however, extend that assumption to low-level federal employees with negligible power to confer favors on anyone who might pay to hear them speak or to read their articles. Stevens noted that any law would have to distinguish among various degrees of influence posed by respective levels of government employment.

School facilities

New York law authorized local school boards to allow the after-hours use of school property for groups that held meetings and entertainments as long as they did not advance religious purposes.

When the pastor of an evangelical church sought to use school facilities to show a religious-oriented film series on family values and child-rearing, his application was denied. He sued. In Lamb's Chapel v. Center Moriches Union Free School District, 113 S.Ct. 2141 (1993), the Supreme Court held that denying the church group access to school premises violated the First Amendment. Allowing the film to be shown would not constitute an establishment of religion since the film would not be shown during school hours, nor would it be school sponsored, and it would be open to the public. There was no danger of citizens thinking that the community was endorsing religion or any particular creed. According to the Court, the New York statute was viewpoint based.

> That Rule 7 [New York statute] treats all religions and religious purposes alike does not make its application in this case viewpoint neutral, however, for it discriminates on the basis of viewpoint by permitting school property to be used for the presentation of all views about family issues and child rearing except those dealing with the subject from a religious standpoint. Denial on this basis is plainly invalid.

In Lamb's Chapel, the Court reaffirmed the principle that the First Amendment forbids the government to regulate expression in ways that favor some viewpoints at the expense of others.

A related case is Rosenberger v. Rector and Visitors of the University of Virginia, 115 S.Ct. 2510 (1995). At issue was a university policy of authorizing payment from the student activities fund to cover printing costs for a variety of publications. A student organization which published a newspaper with a christian editorial viewpoint initiated court action when the university withheld authorization for payment solely because the organization engaged in "religious activity" that "primarily promoted or manifests a particular belief in or about a deity or an ultimate reality." Justice Arthur Kennedy noted that once it had opened a limited forum, the university could exclude speech only when the exclusion was "reasonable in light of the purpose served by the forum." Kennedy cited the possible basis for exclusion: viewpoint discrimination was permissible if it preserved the purposes of the forum, but impermissible when directed against otherwise protected expression. Kennedy concluded that in Rosenberger, as in Lamb's Chapel, the exclusion constituted viewpoint discrimination. The university did not exclude religion as a subject matter but selected for disfavored treatment those student journalistic efforts with religious editorial viewpoints. In Rosenberger, "the prohibited perspective, not the general subject matter, resulted in the refusal to make...payments, for the subjects discussed were otherwise within the approved category of publications."

Public lands

In several cases, the Supreme Court considered the extent to which expression can be limited on public lands. One of these cases was Heffron v. International Society For Krishna Consciousness, 101 S.Ct. 2559 (1981). Each year, the Minnesota Agricultural Society operates a state fair on a 125-acre, state-owned tract located in St. Paul. The fair is a major public event and attracts people from all over Minnesota, as well as from other parts of the country. A regulation of the fair specified that any non-profit, charitable, or commercial organization could conduct its sales, distribution, or solicitation only in a rented booth, from a fixed location on the fair grounds. Representatives could walk about the grounds and promote their organization's views in face-to-face discussions but all distribution and solicitation were to be done from the fixed locations. One day prior to the opening of the 1977 Minnesota State Fair, International Society For Krishna Consciousness filed suit in court, seeking a declaration that the regulation violated the First Amendment. Specifically, the society asserted that the regulation suppressed the practice of Sankirtan, a religious ritual that enjoins members to go into public places to distribute or sell religious literature and to solicit donations for the support of the Krishna religion. The Supreme Court, in the opinion written by Justice White, acknowledged that oral and written dissemination of the Krishna views is protected by the First Amendment. The First Amendment does not, however, guarantee the right to communicate those views at all times and places or in any manner that may be desired. According to Justice White, the Minnesota rule was a permissible restriction on the place and manner of communication.

> The Rule applies even-handedly to all who wish to distribute and sell written materials or to solicit funds. No person or organization, whether commercial or charitable, is permitted to engage in such activities except from a booth rented for those purposes.

Justice White recognized that because the fair attracted large crowds, "the State's interest in the orderly movement and control of such an assembly of persons is a substantial consideration." Since the flow of the crowd and demands for safety were vital, Minnesota was justified in regulating distribution and solicitation rights on the state fair grounds.

A related case involved a state-owned plaza surrounding the statehouse in Columbus, Ohio. For more than a century, the plaza had been available for public speeches, gatherings, and festivals advocating and celebrating a variety of causes. A local board was responsible for regulating public access. The Capital Square Review and Advisory Board v. Pinette, 115 S.Ct. 2440 (1995), case began when the board denied a request by the Ku Klux Klan to display a cross in the plaza during the Christmas season. The board claimed that permitting the cross would violate the Establishment Clause of the First Amendment. The Supreme Court disagreed. Justice Scalia, in a plurality opinion, noted that precedent cases — Lamb's Chapel, Mergens, Widmar, Heffron — established that private religious speech was fully protected by the Free Speech Clause. Furthermore, the right to use government property depended on whether the property had by law or tradition been given the status of a public forum. Scalia applied these criteria to the Klan's request.

> Religious expression cannot violate the Establishment Clause where it 1) is purely private and 2) occurs in a traditional or designated public forum, publicly announced and open to all on equal terms. Those conditions are satisfied here, and therefore the State may not bar respondents' cross from Capital Square.

In United States v. Grace, 103 S.Ct. 1702 (1983), the Court examined a statute that prohibited the distribution of leaflets and the display of banners on the Supreme Court grounds. The statute identified the surrounding streets and sidewalks as part of the grounds. Court action was initiated by two citizens. Thaddeus Zywicki filed a suit when he was prohibited from distributing leaflets concerning such topics as the removal of unfit judges and oppression in Central America. Mary Grace sought relief when she was not allowed to display a sign on which was inscribed the text of the First Amendment. The Supreme Court decided that the section of the statute "which totally bans the specified communicative activity on the public sidewalks around the Court grounds cannot be justified as a reasonable place restriction." According to Justice White:

> Traditional public forum property occupies a special position in terms of First Amendment protection and will not lose its historically recognized character for the reason that it abuts governmental property that has been dedicated to a use other than as a forum for public expression.... The public sidewalks forming the perimeter of the Supreme Court grounds, in our view, are public forums and should be treated as such for First Amendment purposes.

In United States v. Kokinda, 110 S.Ct. 3115 (1990), the Supreme Court determined that the premises of the Postal Service are not a public forum. The case began when members of a political advocacy group set up a table on the sidewalk near the entrance to a post office building. The group solicited contributions, sold subscriptions to a newspaper, and distributed literature on a variety of issues. When the group refused to leave, members were arrested and convicted for violating a regulation which prohibits solicitation on postal property. The case reached the Supreme Court. According to Justice O'Connor, the sidewalk in this case differed from the one in Grace; it was not a traditional public forum.

> The postal sidewalk at issue does not have the characteristics of public sidewalks traditionally open to expressive activity. The municipal sidewalk that runs parallel to the road in this case is a public passage-way. The Postal Service's sidewalk is not such a thoroughfare. Rather, it leads only from the parking area to the front door of the post office.

The sidewalk was constructed solely to provide for the passage of persons engaged in postal business. The sidewalk was private property, subject to regulation. It was not designed for First Amendment activity.

Burson v. Freeman, 112 S.Ct. 1846 (1992), concerned public streets surrounding a polling place. Mary Freeman, the treasurer for a political campaign, brought legal challenge against a Tennessee code which prohibited the solicitation of votes and the display or distribution of campaign materials within 100 feet of the entrance to a polling place. Freeman argued that the statute limited her ability to communicate with voters and thereby violated the First Amendment. Justice Blackmun noted that this case presented a particularly difficult conflict between the right to engage in political discourse and the fundamental right to vote. Blackmun noted that the statute was content-based; whether individuals could exercise their free-speech rights near polling places depended entirely on whether that speech was related to political campaigning. The statute did not ban other categories of expression. Blackmun stated that for a content-based regulation to receive the Court's approval, the state must show that the regulation served a compelling interest and was narrowly drawn to achieve that end. The Court accepted Tennessee's rationale that the regulation protected the citizens' right to vote freely for the candidates of their choice in an election conducted with integrity and reliability. This was an especially compelling interest in a country with a persistent history of voter intimidation and election fraud. The only remaining question was how large a restricted zone was permissible. The Court concluded that Tennessee's 100-foot boundary was narrowly-drawn and therefore constitutional.

The Madsen v. Women's Health Center, 114 S.Ct. 2516 (1994), case involved public streets surrounding a health clinic. After anti-abortion protestors threatened to picket and demonstrate around an abortion clinic, a Florida court prohibited any blockage or interference with public access to the clinic. Upon learning that access was still being impeded, the court issued an injunction which specified conditions that applied to the protestors. In assessing the constitutionality of the injunction, the Supreme Court, per Chief

Justice Rehnquist, differentiated between an ordinance (legislative promotion of societal interests) and an injunction (remedy imposed for violation of legislative or judicial decree). Then, Rehnquist considered two issues. First, the prohibition under question was not content- or viewpoint-based simply because it restricted only the expression of antiabortion protestors.

> An injunction, by its very nature, does not address the general public, but applies only to particular parties, regulating their activities, and perhaps their speech, because of their past actions in the context of a specific dispute. The fact that this injunction did not prohibit activities by persons demonstrating in favor of abortion is justly attributable to the lack of such demonstrations and of any consequent request for relief. Moreover, none of the restrictions at issue were directed at the content of petitioners' antiabortion message.

Second, Rehnquist noted that in evaluating a content-neutral injunction, the standard was whether its "provisions burden no more speech than necessary to serve a significant government interest." The Court found that some provisions were acceptable — buffer around the clinic as well as the limited noise restrictions. Other provisions — buffer zone applied to private property near the clinic and around staff residences — went beyond the controls needed to protect the tranquility and privacy of the clinic. The Court affirmed and reversed portions of the injunction.

Boos v. Barry, 108 S.Ct. 1157 (1988), involved a District of Columbia law which regulated First Amendment activity directed against a foreign embassy. The law contained two clauses. The display clause prohibited the display of any sign within 500 feet of an embassy if the sign brought that government into "public disrepute." The congregation clause prohibited any gathering of three or more persons within 500 feet of an embassy. The law was challenged in court. The Supreme Court found the display clause in violation of the First Amendment because it was a content-based restriction on political speech in a public forum. The law prohibited an entire category of speech — signs critical of foreign governments. Furthermore, the law was not narrowly tailored to serve a compelling state interest. Even if the protection of the dignity of foreign diplomats is a "compelling" interest, there are less restrictive alternatives. For example, a law could prohibit harassment or obstruction of foreign officials in the performance of their duties. The Court held that the congregation clause was acceptable; it permitted dispersal of congregations only when the police believed that the embassy's "security or peace" were threatened. The clause regulated the place and manner of demonstrations, was site-specific to areas within 500 feet of embassies, and did not prohibit peaceful gatherings.

At issue in the Members of the City Council of the City of Los Angeles v. Taxpayers For Vincent, 104 S.Ct. 2118 (1984), case was a Los Angeles law that prohibited the posting of signs on public property. Roland Vincent, a candidate for election to the Los Angeles City Council, posted signs with his name on them on utility poles at various locations. When city employees routinely removed the posters, Vincent's supporters sought an injunction against enforcement of the law. The case reached the Supreme Court. The decision, per Justice Stevens, upheld the law for three reasons. First, there was no hint of bias; the law did not seek to suppress certain ideas while favoring others. Second, Los Angeles's interest in avoiding visual clutter justified the prohibition of public postings. Third, other effective means of communication were available to Vincent's supporters.

> The Los Angeles ordinance does not affect any individual's freedom to exercise the right to speak and to distribute literature in the same place where the posting of signs on public property is prohibited. To the extent that the posting of signs on public property has advantages over these forms of expression, there is no reason to believe that these same advantages cannot be obtained through other means. To the contrary, there are ample alternative modes of communication in Los Angeles.

Lakewood v. Plain Dealer Publishing Company, 108 S.Ct. 2138 (1988), also involved access to public property. On the strength of a local ordinance, Lakewood, Ohio denied the Plain Dealer Publishing Company permission to place its coin-operated newspaper dispensing machines on city sidewalks. The Company brought legal action and Lakewood was ordered to amend its law. The revised ordinance, however, fared no better than the original because it gave the Mayor unbounded authority to grant or deny applications for newsrack permits. The provision allowed prior restraint.

In this section, cases have been cited in which individuals, groups, corporations, and governments have sought communication access to various public and nonpublic forums. The cases suggest that a non-public forum is subject to greater regulation than a public forum. Any regulation, however, must protect a substantial governmental interest through a non-discriminatory, content-neutral, time-place-manner-specific ordinance.

Public broadcasting

The Arkansas Educational Television Commission, a pubic broadcasting agency, sponsored a debate between the major party

candidates for a congressional seat in the 1992 election. When Paul
Forbes, an independent candidate with little popular support was
denied permission to participate in the debate, he initiated court action
and claimed that the First Amendment entitled his participation. In
Arkansas Educational Television Commission v. Forbes, 118 S.Ct.
1633 (1998), the Supreme Court sided with the broadcaster. In
reaching its decision, the Court had to determine the type of forum
involved in this political debate. The justices held that the event could
not be classified as either a "traditional" or "designated" public forum;
rather, it was a "nonpublic" forum. According to Justice Arthur
Kennedy: "Access to a nonpublic forum can be restricted if the
restrictions are reasonable and are not an effort to suppress expression
merely because public officials oppose the speaker's views." Kennedy
noted that the broadcaster's decision to exclude Forbes was a
"reasonable viewpoint-neutral exercise of journalistic discretion
consistent with the First Amendment." Forbes was denied a role, not
for his viewpoint, but because he had not generated appreciable public
interest.

PERSONAL RESIDENCE

In December, 1990, Margaret Gilleo placed on her front lawn a 24-
by 36-inch sign printed with the words "Say No to War in the Persian
Gulf, Call Congress Now." She initiated court action upon learning
that the sign was illegal. At issue was a city ordinance which
prohibited all signs except residential identification signs, for sale
signs, church and school postings, and some on-site advertisements.
The policy was justified on the grounds that the prohibited signs
created ugliness and clutter, impaired property values, impinged upon
privacy, and caused traffic safety hazards. The Supreme Court identified
reasons why the local policy violated an individual's right of free
speech. Although the city had a valid interest in achieving its stated
goals, the policy almost completely foreclosed "an important and
distinct medium of expression to political, religious, or personal
messages." According to the Court, other media were inadequate
substitutes.

> Displaying a sign from ones' own residence carries a message quite
> distinct from placing the same sign someplace else, or conveying the
> same text or picture by other means, for it provides information about
> the speaker's identity, an important component of many attempts to
> persuade. Residential signs are also an unusually cheap and
> convenient form of communication. Furthermore, the audience
> intended to be reached by a residential sign — neighbors — could
> not be reached nearly as well by other means.

In <u>City of Ladue v. Gilleo</u>, 114 S.Ct. 2038 (1994), the Supreme Court recognized that even though the local law under question was free of content or viewpoint discrimination, it offended the First Amendment by eliminating a common means of expression.

TRAVEL

Is there a First Amendment freedom of movement? In several cases, the Supreme Court has examined the travel rights of U.S. citizens. In <u>Kent</u>, <u>Aptheker</u>, <u>Zemel</u>, <u>Agee</u>, and <u>Wald</u>, the issue involved the right of U.S. citizens to travel abroad. In <u>Mandel</u>, the Court considered the right of a foreigner to enter the United States.

When Rockwell Kent wanted to attend a meeting in Helsinki, Finland, his application for a passport was denied by the Secretary of State on the ground that Kent was a Communist. Kent initiated court action. The Supreme Court decided that freedom of movement was a part of the U.S. heritage.

> Freedom of movement across frontiers in either direction, and inside the country, may be as close to the heart of an individual as the choice of what he eats, or hears, or reads. Freedom of movement is basic in our scheme of values.

According to the Court, the Secretary of State was not entrusted with the power to grant or withhold the right to travel. In <u>Kent v. Dulles</u>, 78 S.Ct. 1113 (1958), the ban on travel was reversed.

In <u>Aptheker v. Secretary of State</u>, 84 S.Ct. 1659 (1964), the Court established a link between the right to travel and First Amendment freedoms. The case involved Section Six of the Subversive Activities Control Act of 1950. The Act provided that a member of a Communist organization could not apply for or use a passport. Herbert Aptheker challenged the Act, arguing that Section Six deprived him of his constitutional right to travel. The Supreme Court, per Justice Arthur Goldberg, declared Section Six unconstitutional because its sweep was too broad and too indiscriminate. The Act neglected such relevant considerations as the individual's "knowledge, activity, commitment, and purposes in and places for travel." Justice Goldberg also noted that "freedom of travel is a constitutional liberty closely related to rights of free speech and association." In a concurring opinion, Justice Black claimed that Section Six denied Aptheker "the freedom of speech, press, and association which the First Amendment guarantees."

In <u>Zemel v. Rusk</u>, 85 S.Ct. 1271 (1965), the Court upheld a restriction on travel. Until 1961, no passport was required to travel anywhere in the Western Hemisphere. In that year, the State Department eliminated Cuba from the list of places for which passports were not required and declared all passports invalid for travel to Cuba unless approved by the Secretary of State. In 1964, Louis Zemel requested permission to travel to Cuba in order to satisfy his "curiosity about the state of affairs in Cuba" and make him "a better informed citizen." When his request was denied, he appealed. Chief Justice Earl Warren, writing for the Court, upheld the restriction on travel. Warren contrasted the facts in Zemel with those in earlier decisions. The issue in Kent and Aptheker had been whether a person could be refused a passport because of political beliefs or associations. In Zemel, the issue was whether a passport could be denied to an individual "because of foreign policy considerations affecting all citizens." In Warren's opinion, the ban on travel was justified. Warren admitted that the denial of travel to Cuba "renders less than wholly free the flow of information concerning that country," but pointed out that "the right to speak and publish does not carry with it the unrestrained right to gather information."

In Haig v. Agee, 101 S.Ct. 2766 (1981), the Court again upheld a ban on travel. Court action was initiated by Philip Agee, whose passport was revoked when, though employed by the Central Intelligence Agency, he announced his intention to oppose the goals and expose the agents of the CIA. The Supreme Court, per Chief Justice Burger, acknowledged that the Secretary of State may revoke a passport on the ground that the passport holder's activities in foreign countries were likely to cause serious damage to the national security or foreign policy of the United States.

> The mere fact that Agee is also engaged in criticism of the Government does not render his conduct beyond the reach of the law. To the extent the revocation of his passport operates to inhibit Agee, "it is an inhibition of *action*," rather than of speech. Agee is as free to criticize the United States Government as he was when he held a passport.

The Regan v. Wald, 104 S.Ct. 3026 (1984), decision also upheld a regulation that curtailed general tourist and business travel to Cuba. The Court noted that Cuba, with the political, economic, and military backing of the Soviet Union, had provided widespread support for armed violence and terrorism in the Western Hemisphere. There was an adequate basis "to sustain the President's decision to curtail the flow of hard currency to Cuba — currency that could then be used in support of Cuban adventurism — by restricting travel." The lesson that emerges from the Wald, as well as the Kent, Aptheker, Zemel, and Agee decisions is that while travel is a fundamental right, restrictions may be imposed in the interest of national security.

Unlike the five previous cases, which involved the right of a U.S.

citizen to travel abroad, <u>Kleindienst v. Mandel</u>, 92 S.Ct. 2576 (1972), examined the right of a foreign journalist to enter the United States. Ernest Mandel, a Belgian journalist and Marxist theorist, was invited to attend academic meetings in the United States. He was refused permission to enter the country under a provision of the Immigration and Nationality Act of 1952, which refuses entry to anyone who advocates "the economic, international and governmental doctrines of world communism." The Attorney General could have waived ineligibility, but declined to do so because, on a 1968 trip to the United States, Mandel had spoken at more universities than his visa application indicated. In <u>Mandel</u>, the Supreme Court acknowledged that Congress has absolute power to grant or deny entry to aliens. The lesson of <u>Mandel</u> is that the freedom U.S. citizens enjoy to travel abroad does not apply similarly to foreigners wishing to enter the United States. The First Amendment interest of citizens seeking communication with an alien is secondary to the Executive's authority to regulate entry.

CONCLUSION

The following principles regulate communication law regarding SILENCE:

1. Individuals enjoy the right to silence — the freedom not to communicate, the freedom not to be communicated with, and the freedom to be let alone.

2. The right to silence can be regulated by a validly constructed ordinance designed to protect a substantial governmental interest.

3. The following principles apply to the right to silence:
   a. a witness may be required to testify before a governmental investigative committee when the questions have obvious pertinence to the investigation,
   b. an individual may restrict uninvited solicitors by posting a notice to stay away,
   c. a nonpublic forum is subject to greater regulation than a public forum,
   d. the right to travel may be restricted in the interest of national security,
   e. the freedom of U.S. citizens to travel abroad does not apply similarly to foreigners wishing to enter the United States.

KEY DECISIONS

1943 — <u>MARTIN</u> — determined that a notice to stay away is necessary to stop intrusions by "harmless" distributors and solicitors

1946 — <u>MARSH</u> — rejected a community-wide ban on solicitation and distribution

1949 — <u>KOVACS</u> — ruled that sound amplification in public places was subject to reasonable restraint

1951 — <u>BREARD</u> — concluded that door-to-door solicitation for commercial purposes may be prohibited by local ordinance

1960 — <u>TALLEY</u> — upheld the right of anonymous publication

1964 — <u>APTHEKER</u> — established a link between the right to travel and First Amendment freedoms

1976 — <u>SPOCK</u> — upheld a military installation's ban on petition and distribution of materials without prior written approval from the base commander

1978 — <u>FIRST NATIONAL BANK OF BOSTON</u> — acknowledged that a corporation enjoys First Amendment rights of free expression

1981 — <u>INTERNATIONAL SOCIETY FOR KRISHNA CONSCIOUSNESS</u> — upheld statute regulating distribution and solicitation on state fair grounds

1983 — <u>CONNICK</u> — protected government employees' speech if it covered a matter of public concern and did not impair the efficiency of the work place

1990 — <u>KOKINDA</u> — clarified the nature of a public forum

1994 — <u>GILLEO</u> — upheld the right to display a sign from one's own residence

2000 — <u>SOUTHWORTH</u> — decided that public academic

institutions may use student fees to fund campus groups as long as the institution remains "viewpoint neural"

RECOMMENDED READING

Fiss, Owen M., "Silence on the Street Corner," Albany Law Review 55 (1992), 713-23.

Freedman, Warren, Freedom of Speech on Private Property New York: Quorum, 1988.

Haiman, Franklyn S.,"Speech v. Privacy: Is There a Right not to be Spoken to?" Northwestern University Law Review 67 (May-June, 1972), 153-99.

Halbert, Terry Ann, "The First Amendment in the Work place: An Analysis and Call for Reform," Seton Hall Law Review 17 (1987), 42-72.

Hershkoff, Helen, and Adam S. Cohen, "Begging to Differ: The First Amendment and the Right to Beg," Harvard Law Review 104 (1991), 896-916.

Kanzer, Adam M., "Misfit Power, the First Amendment and the Public Forum: Is There Room in America for the Grateful Dead?" Columbia Journal of Law and Social Problems 25 (1992), 521-65.

Rice, George P. Jr., "The Right to be Silent," The Quarterly Journal of Speech 47 (December, 1961), 349-54.

Sanders, Wayne, "The First Amendment and the Government Work Place: Has the Constitution Fallen Down," Western Journal of Speech Communication 47 (Summer, 1983), 253-276.

CHAPTER 7

DEFAMATION

Supreme Court justices have identified defamation as a form of expression that is outside the scope of First Amendment protection. Justice Frank Murphy, in Chaplinsky v. New Hampshire, 62 S.Ct. 766 (1942), referred to libel and defamation as a class of expression that is subject to "prevention and punishment." Justice William Brennan, in Roth v. United States, 77 S.Ct. 1304 (1957), affirmed that libel falls "outside the protection intended for speech and press." Adjudication of this form of unprotected expression is subject to specific procedures and doctrines.

PROCEDURES

Defamatory statements may have a crippling effect on an individual's ability to relate to his or her associates in personal, social, or professional ways. Appropriate legal relief is available to anyone so harmed. This section focuses on the procedural aspects of a defamation court action.

FORMS OF DEFAMATION

Defamation may be classified in two ways. First, it may be classified according to the medium of expression. Libel consists of defamatory words that are either written or broadcast. Slander is a defamatory statement that is spoken. Slander tends to be less harmful than libel, since it is not permanently recorded and cannot be effectively transmitted to a larger audience after its utterance. Second, defamation may be classified according to impact. Two types have been recognized by the courts — defamation *per se* and defamation *per quod*.

Defamation *per se*

Defamation *per se* involves a statement that is injurious on its face. The harm resulting from the statement is immediately apparent. Words that have been held defamatory *per se* include "hog" (Solverson v. Peterson, 25 N.W. 14 (1885), "hypocrite" (Overstreet v. New Nonpareil Company, 167 N.W. 669 (1918), "liar" (Smith v. Lyons, 77 So. 896 (1918), "drunkard" (Smith v. Fielden, 326 S.W.2d 476 (1959), "communist" (Toomey v. Farley, 138 N.E.2d 221 (1956), "fascist" (Buckley v. Littel, 394 F.Supp. 918 (1975), and "criminal" (Hornby v. Hunter, 385 S.W.2d 473 (1964). The Hornby case provides an example. The suit alleged that a newspaper article, claiming that a car had been stolen and that a warrant had been issued in connection with the theft, implied "criminality." The court decided that the article was not true, and was defamatory. The article did "impute to [plaintiff] the commission of a crime for which punishment by imprisonment in jail or the penitentiary may be imposed and is, therefore, libelous *per se*."

Defamation *per quod*

Defamation *per quod* is not immediately apparent. The words themselves are not defamatory, but become so when facts are associated with them. Defamation *per quod* is indirect, and dependent on the context in which the words are expressed. The Karrigan v. Valentine, 184 Kansas 783 (1957), case illustrates this type of defamation. The case involved a news item, printed in a morning newspaper, announcing the birth of a baby girl to Mr. and Mrs. "Phillip" Karrigan. In response to this news item, a certain "Philip" Karrigan sued, claiming the announcement, innocent on its face, was defamatory because he was a bachelor, the only person in the vicinity with this name, and because the article made readers think that he "was married to a woman of ill repute." The Court ruled in favor of Karrigan.

BURDENS — all 4

A successful defamation action must satisfy four requirements: publication, identification, injury, and fault. Without sufficient evidence proving each of these burdens, the plaintiff cannot recover damages.

Publication

Of the four, publication is easiest to prove. The plaintiff need only demonstrate that a third person heard, read, or viewed the statement, and interpreted it in a defamatory sense. In the age of mass media and information technology, a statement printed in a newspaper, broadcast over radio or television, or posted in cyberspace constitutes publication. In instances involving limited audiences, the question of what comprises publication is less clear, and it is up to the courts to decide the matter. For example, in Davis v. Schuchat, 510 F.2d 731 (1975), the court held that publication occurred when statements were made to a friend of the plaintiff during a private conversation. Likewise, in Arvey Corporation v. Peterson, 178 F.Supp. 132 (1959), the judges decided that a letter sent by an individual to a lawyer had been published in two ways — the dictation of the letter to a stenographer and the receipt of the letter by the attorney. In both ways, the defamation had been received by a third party. In Davis and Arvey Corporation, the court acknowledged that publication can occur when a message is communicated to a limited audience.

Identification

In regard to identification, the plaintiff must prove that the defamatory reference is to the plaintiff — whether by name, nickname, pseudonym, caricature, or unique circumstance. Sometimes, a typographical error, wrong initials, an incorrect address, or identical names may connect an innocent person to an undesirable event. In such cases, the courts must decide whether identification occurred. Hope v. Hearst Consolidated Publications, 294 F.2d 681 (1961), provides an example. The case involved a Palm Beach attorney who demonstrated identification in the statement: "...one of the resort's richest men caught his blonde wife in a compromising spot the other day with a former FBI agent." To prove identification, the man argued that he was known primarily as an ex-agent, and that he was the only former FBI man who traveled in high-society circles. In addition to his own statements, he offered the testimonies of other citizens of Palm Beach. According to the court, this evidence supported the claim that identification had occurred.

The E.W. Scripps Company v. Cholmondelay, 569 S.W.2d 700 (1978), case centered around a newspaper article which erroneously stated that an "older boy" pounded the decedent's head against the pavement until he was "beaten into insensibility." In actuality, the older boy hit the decedent on the head a single blow after which he fell into a coma and died a year later. The court found the article to be libelous *per se* even though the article did not name the older boy. According to the court, the older boy's friends and acquaintances who were familiar with the incident were certain to recognize him as the perpetrator of the offense. Identification had been established.

Liquori v. Republican Company, 396 N.E.2d 726 (1979), provides another example. A news reporter wrote a story about Anthony Liquori, an admitted criminal. The reporter used an incorrect address by relying on a local telephone book, rather than conducting a more extensive investigation. The criminal Anthony Liquori had moved to a different city; the Anthony Liquori listed in the phone book successfully sued for libel. The Liquori case demonstrates the importance of both thorough research and complete identification. A reporter who includes as identifiers the full name, address, occupation, and age of an individual is likely to avoid defamation suits stemming from inadequate identification.

Injury

To demonstrate injury, the plaintiff must show that the words in question belong to one of four classes that the courts have recognized as actionable. The first category involves words that lower one's public esteem. Of the various ways in which words may damage a person's esteem, none has brought more libel suits than a false charge of criminality. Roth v. Greensboro News Company, 6 S.E.2d 882 (1940), involved this type of claim — a newspaper published a story that incorrectly reported a person as having been charged with a crime.

A second category of libelous words includes those that expose a person to public ridicule, scorn, or derision. Zybszko v. New York American, 228 App.Div. 277 (1930), provides an example. The case involved an illustrated newspaper article which compared a specific professional wrestler with a gorilla. The plaintiff asserted that, as a wrestler and businessman, he was brought into public ridicule and disgrace, and that he was shunned by a respectable segment of the community. The court held the publication libelous.

A third category includes words that cause a person to be avoided by a respectable segment of the community. Most notable in this category are words that falsely attribute venereal disease, mental illness, alcoholism, and other diseases. Such unfair attribution of physical or mental illness has been held defamatory in such cases as Sally v. Brown, 295 S.W. 890 (1927), and Cowper v. Vannier, 156 N.E.2d 761 (1959).

The fourth category of injurious words includes those that may cause damage in one's occupation or profession. Mistakenly attributing a "single instance" of error to a professional person is not sufficient to cause damage. There must be a claim of general incompetency. Such was the finding in Blende v. Hearst Publications, 93 P.2d 733 (1939). The "single instance" rule, however, does not protect words that impute to an individual questionable ethics in business practices. In Nichols v. Bristow Publishing Company, 330 P.2d 1044 (1957), the court decided that a sole article accusing an individual of "shady ethics" and of operating on a "sneak basis" caused sufficient injury to a professional reputation to justify a finding of libel.

Fault

Fault, the fourth burden in a defamation action, applies differently to "public" and "private" persons. A "public" person must demonstrate that the material was published with "actual malice." According to New York Times Company v. Sullivan, 84 S.Ct. 710 (1964), actual malice is knowledge of falsity or reckless disregard for the truth. The specific cases that established and clarified this doctrine are discussed later in this chapter.

A "private" person, on the other hand, must show that the material was printed through "negligence." While the Supreme Court has not defined "negligence," it has provided some examples. In St. Amant v. Thompson, 88 S.Ct. 1323 (1968), the Court noted that "failure to investigate" constituted negligent reportorial behavior. In Time v. Pape, 91 S.Ct. 633 (1971), the Court identified the failure to use the word "alleged" as a "nonmalicious error in judgment." In Milkovich v. Lorain Journal Company, 110 S.Ct. 2695 (1990), the Court determined that a reporter could not avoid a finding of negligence by claiming a constitutional privilege for his "opinion." Lower courts have provided broad definitions of "negligence." In Gobin v. Globe Publishing Company, 531 P.2d 76 (1975), the court noted that "the norm usually is the conduct of the reasonably careful person under the circumstances"; in Martin v. Griffin Television, 549 P.2d 85 (1976), the court required "ordinary care" which was defined as "that degree of care which ordinary prudent persons engaged in the same kind of business usually exercise under similar circumstances"; in Taskett v. King Broadcasting Company, 546 P.2d 81 (1976), the court held that a news anchor should exercise "reasonable care"; in Karp v. Miami Herald Publishing Company, 359 So.2d 580 (1978), the court required that a reporter make "reasonable efforts" to verify a story; in Memphis Publishing Company v. Nichols, 569 S.W.2d 412 (1978), the test was whether a "reasonably prudent person" would do likewise under the same circumstances; and in Jones v. Sun Publishing Company, 292 S.E.2d 23 (1982), the justices held a reporter legally at fault for departing from "acceptable standards." These cases suggest that reporters are well advised to check all sources thoroughly, and to clearly indicate which statements are allegations, impressions, and/or opinions.

DAMAGES

If the four burdens — publication, identification, injury, and fault — are adequately proven, the court may assess monetary damages against the offender. Depending on the nature of the case, four types of damages may be awarded: compensatory, actual, punitive, and nominal.

Compensatory

Compensatory damages are intended as reimbursement for injury to one's reputation. Such damages were awarded in Dalton v. Meister, 52 Wis.2d 173 (1971), a case in which libelous statements caused an individual to suffer transfer from his position, disfavor with his superior, loss of reputation as a criminal investigator, abuse of his character as a lawyer, and public contempt, ridicule, disgrace, and humiliation. The jury awarded compensatory damages.

Actual

Actual damages represent the real monetary loss suffered by the plaintiff as a result of a defamatory statement. The MacLeod v. Tribune Publishing Company, 343 P.2d 36 (1959), case involved actual damages. When a publication imputed that a dentist was a "communist sympathizer," he argued that he had suffered monetary loss in his profession because a large percentage of established patients canceled appointments and there had been a sharp decline in the number of new patients. The court awarded actual damages.

Punitive

Punitive damages are designed to punish past defamatory behavior and to discourage similar conduct in the future. A high degree of fault is necessary to sustain an award for punitive damages. In United Press International v. Mohs, 381 S.W.2d 104 (1964), a news item was judged to be malicious because even though the reporter was cognizant of possible inaccuracies in the story, he never attempted to verify the story. Even though the need for more investigation was suggested, the reporter "was so pleased with a funny story holding [the plaintiff] up to ridicule that he forthwith sent it out for all to read and be amused." The court concluded that "fabrication of this libelous story was a willful and wanton act sufficient to support a finding of malice." The court awarded punitive damages.

Nominal

Nominal damages are token damages awarded when there has been a defamation, but no serious harm to the plaintiff's reputation or financial position. Nominal damages were awarded in <u>Goldwater v. Ginzburg</u>, 90 S.Ct. 1085 (1970). When writer Ralph Ginzburg could not document claims that Senator Barry Goldwater suffered from "repressed homosexuality," experienced "infantile fantasies of revenge and dreams of total annihilation of his adversaries," and displayed "paralyzing, deepseated irrational fear," the court punished Ginzburg by awarding punitive damages. In addition, since Goldwater had neither pleaded nor proved any actual damages, the jury granted one dollar in nominal compensation.

DEFENSES

A publisher of an alleged defamation is not helpless in the face of a lawsuit. There are four complete and six partial defenses. In most states, the following are complete defenses: truth, absolute privilege, qualified privilege, and fair comment. Partial defenses include use of reliable source, retraction and apology, right of reply, settlement out of court, bad reputation of plaintiff, and provocation.

Truth

Demonstrating the truth of a defamatory statement is a complete defense in most states. In some states, truth is a defense only if the statement is published with good motives; intent to cause harm destroys the defense. In establishing this defense, even though it is unnecessary to show that every detail is accurate, substantial proof is required in order to exonerate the defendant. <u>Empire Printing Company v. Roden</u>, 247 F.2d 8 (1957), suggests the extent to which the defense must prove the truth of its expression. The case concerned an issue of the <u>Daily Alaska Empire</u> which detailed how the Territorial Board of Road Commissioners purchased and operated parts of the state road system. The story consisted of "sensationalized" written copy, headlines, and a photograph, all of which implied dishonesty on the part of the commissioners. The defense cited truth as justification for the story. The court noted that the establishment of truth must be as broad as the defamation. In this case, even though the defense demonstrated the truth of the words in the article, the truth of what the reader understood was not established. The court determined that the manner in which the front page was set up could be regarded as a deliberate defamation by insinuation and association. Readers of the newspaper could easily infer that the members of the board had been guilty of embezzlement. According to the court, "whatever a newspaper article actually says or carries to its readers must be judged by the publication as a whole. The headlines alone may be enough to make libelous *per se* an otherwise innocuous article." In addition, "an article may become libelous by juxtaposition with other articles or photographs." In Empire Printing Company, the defense was unable to demonstrate that the board members were guilty of any dishonesty or that they made any profit for their own use. In light of the failure to establish truth as a defense, the court awarded the verdict to the plaintiffs.

Absolute privilege

The courts have recognized three types of communications that are absolutely immune from defamation action: privileged communications, communications involving prior consent, and political broadcasts. Privileged communications apply to all transactions between husband and wife, attorney and client, doctor and patient, and priest and parishioner. Judges, jurors, witnesses, attorneys, and the parties in both civil and criminal cases are absolutely privileged. In addition, executive and legislative officials are immune from defamation that is communicated in the course of their official duties. For example, in Barr v. Matteo, 79 S.Ct. 1335 (1959), the Supreme Court granted immunity to an executive press release. The decision held that it was important that officials

> ...should be free to exercise their duties unembarrassed by the fear of damage suits...which would consume time and energies which would otherwise be devoted to governmental service and the threat of which might appreciably inhibit the fearless, vigorous, and effective administration of policies of government.

Consent constitutes a second type of absolute privilege. A person who consents to an expression that subsequently defames him or her cannot collect for the suffering. Consent can be granted directly through a written release indicating prior consent, or consent can be implied. In Langford v. Vanderbilt University, 318 S.W.2d 568 (1958), an individual in quest of publicity permitted journalists an extensive interview and photographing session. When a news story appeared, the individual sued for libel. The court held that when consent is implied through words or actions, the plaintiff is unable to collect for libel.

The judge stressed that the plaintiff had wanted and sought publicity. The publication was absolutely privileged.

A third type of communication that affords the defense of absolute privilege is political broadcast. Prior to 1959, broadcast stations that granted equal time to political candidates under section 315 of the Federal Communications Act were liable for any defamation in those broadcasts. Stations subsequently argued that if they were unable to edit libelous speeches, they should not be held responsible for damages. In Farmers Educational and Cooperative Union of America v. WDAY, 79 S.Ct. 1302 (1959), the Supreme Court agreed: "We cannot believe that it was the intent of Congress to compel a station to broadcast libelous statements and at the same time subject it to the task of defending actions for damages." The justices held that Section 315 grants a licensee an immunity from liability for libelous material it broadcasts. Since stations cannot control what candidates say over the air, they should not be held responsible for the statements. The candidates, however, can be sued.

Qualified privilege

The courts have also recognized the defense of qualified privilege. A news medium may publish an impartial report of judicial, legislative, executive, or other public proceedings. In Stice v. Beacon Newspaper Corporation, 340 P.2d 396 (1959), the court upheld the right of the press to publish articles regarding the investigation of crime. The Court noted that the news stories were based upon interviews with police officers and reports of the police department concerning the operation of a burglary ring. Excerpts from the articles were attributed to law-enforcement agents and agencies; for example, qualifiers such as "police investigation had revealed," "detectives disclosed," "investigations are continuing," and "according to the police evidence," accompanied the articles. Noting the accuracy of the reports and the absence of malice, the court decided in favor of the newspaper. In Dorsey v. National Enquirer, 952 F.2d 250 (1991), a celebrity entertainer initiated defamation action after a newspaper reported that the mother of the entertainer's child claimed that the entertainer had AIDS. The court found the article was a "fair and true report" of the judicial proceeding. In Stice and Dorsey, the articles enjoyed a qualified privilege.

Fair comment

Another complete defense is fair comment. Reporters may comment on people or institutions that offer their work for public approval or public interest. This principle was applied in Oswalt v. State-Record Company, 158 S.E.2d 204 (1967). A newspaper had criticized a police officer for pursuing a car at high speed. The fleeing driver crashed broadside into another car, killing two young occupants. The editorial claimed that there was no "sense or justification" for police to race with offenders on public highways to the danger of citizens' lives. The editorial concluded by calling for officials to hire qualified persons to be law-enforcement officers. The officer brought suit. According to the court, a citizen or newspaper may criticize acts and qualifications of a public official without being liable for damages, so long as the criticism is fair and honest, and made without malice.

Use of reliable source

In addition to the complete defenses available to defendants in a libel action, there are also partial defenses. For example, a defendant can claim reliance on a trustworthy source. When a publisher can show that he or she accurately reprinted a story from a major news source, the court may be influenced to reduce damages. In Wood v. Constitution Publishing Company, 194 S.E. 760 (1937), the court did not excuse "an untruthful and libelous statement...that was communicated to the person making the statement by an authority [Associated Press] having a reputation for truth and accuracy." The court decided, however, that evidence regarding the AP being a reliable organization tended to show lack of malice. The evidence constituted a partial defense.

Retraction and apology

A full and prompt retraction and apology will usually mitigate the amount of damages. Such a good-faith effort indicates that publication was not made with malice. Yet, retraction is not a complete defense. Some people who saw the original story may not see the retraction. There is no guarantee that the retraction will offset the harm already suffered. Nonetheless, retraction and apology usually saves money for a publisher guilty of libel. Brush-Moore Newspapers v. Pollit, 151 A.2d 530 (1959), provides an example. The judge acknowledged that defamation had occurred, but noted that the newspaper's attempt to retrieve copies containing the error, as well as publication of a correction, tended to mitigate damages.

Right of reply

The right of reply extends to legitimate spokespersons for someone who has been defamed. This could be the defamed individual, a public relations person, an attorney, the secretary of an organization, or a family member. A victim of defamation may respond with a defamatory reply, provided that the reply is in direct response to a defamatory attack and the reply does not exceed the scope of the original defamation. In addition, a newspaper may transmit libelous remarks when it supports a person replying to an attack, or when it is in a role of news gatherer. The Dickins v. International Brotherhood of Teamsters, 171 F.2d 21 (1948), case involved a series of accusations between a military officer and members of a union. The court held:

> The appellant testified that, before the publication of which he here complains, he himself released to the press his own charges that members of the union assaulted him and his companion. His act in so doing cast upon the union the moral duty and consequently conferred upon it the legal right to publish a reply which, even if it were false, was privileged unless the plaintiff proved the defendant knew it to be false or otherwise proved actual malice in the publication.

Settlement out of court

A defendant may reduce the amount of damages by settling out of court. There are advantages to out-of-court settlement. Court costs are eliminated. Moreover, harmful publicity is avoided and the matter is resolved quickly and comparatively painlessly. The amount of monetary damages sought by the plaintiff can be reduced through negotiation. Furthermore, the defendant usually agrees to publish an apology or allows the plaintiff an opportunity to reply. A case that was settled out of court, Dempsey v. Time, 43 Misc.2d 754 (1964), involved a cover story in Sports Illustrated. The article, based on a source of questionable veracity, accused Jack Dempsey of using "loaded" gloves in his title fight with Jess Willard. Dempsey initiated court action, but settled out of court for an undisclosed sum.

Bad reputation of plaintiff

Another partial defense is proof of bad reputation of the plaintiff. Demonstration that the plaintiff's reputation is so bad that a new libel cannot harm it will mitigate damages. Nichols v. Philadelphia Tribune Company, 22 F.R.D. 89 (1958), involved such a claim. The judges stressed that the connection between the bad reputation and the defamation must be close. The defendant cannot establish the bad reputation by showing misconduct at a time and place far removed from the setting of the defamation. Though the defense of bad reputation may mitigate damages, it cannot fully exonerate the defendant.

Provocation

Statements uttered in the heat of the moment or provoked by the plaintiff may constitute a partial defense. Farrell v. Kramer, 193 A.2d 560 (1963), provides an illustration. This case concerned a dispute between a registered nurse and a surgeon. The nurse criticized postoperative treatment given to a patient who was under the care of the physician. The nurse also lodged a series of complaints with hospital officials. The complaints touched off a personal feud which continued for more than a year. Eventually, the nurse was dismissed from employment at the hospital, but was later rehired. The doctor then telephoned a hospital administrator and asked why he "would stoop so low as to hire that creep, that malignant son of a bitch, back to work." The nurse sued. In court, the judge noted that the nurse had begun the feud. A nurse should know that criticism of this type will almost certainly induce anger on the part of a doctor. As a result, the doctor was forced to defend himself before a grievance committee of the medical association. The court concluded: "Although the slander is not thereby excused, such provocation will substantially diminish both the public interest in the punishment of the defendant and the plaintiff's right to have severe punishment inflicted."

DOCTRINES

During the past few decades the Supreme Court has formulated several doctrines that relate to defamation. While most of these doctrines deal with the effect of slander and libel on individuals, the Court has recognized that groups and corporations can also be damaged by defamatory statements.

ACTUAL MALICE

The doctrine of "actual malice" was enunciated for the first time in New York Times v. Sullivan, 84 S.Ct. 710 (1964). On March 29, 1960, the Times published an advertisement entitled "Heed Their Rising Voices." The ad charged that black students "are being met by an unprecedented wave of terror by those who would deny and negate that document [constitution] which the whole world looks upon as setting the pattern for modern freedom." The ad illustrated the "wave of terror" by describing specific events, such as lockouts and expulsion from school, use of armed police and tear gas, and bombings of homes.

The ad concluded with an appeal for funds to aid the student movement, the struggle for the right to vote, and the legal defense of Dr. Martin Luther King, Jr., who at the time was under arrest in Montgomery, Alabama. The ad was signed by more than 100 people, many widely known for their work in public affairs and the performing arts. L. B. Sullivan, the Supervisor of Montgomery's Police Department, requested that the Times print a retraction. When the Times failed to do so, Sullivan initiated a libel suit. He argued that the ad contained inaccuracies. In fact, several statements were not accurate. For example, black students who protested on the state capitol steps sang the national anthem and not "My country, Tis of Thee." Nine students were expelled, not for conducting a protest, but for demanding service at the courthouse lunch counter. Not the entire student body, but most of it, protested the expulsion. The campus dining room had not been padlocked, and the only students barred from eating there were those who had not obtained a meal ticket. Even though police were deployed near the campus in large numbers, they never did "ring" the campus. Dr. King had been arrested only four times, not seven. Although Dr. King's home had been bombed twice, the police were acquitted of the bombings. Based on the inaccuracies, the jury awarded Sullivan damages of $500,000. The U.S. Supreme Court, per Justice William Brennan, unanimously overturned the decision and established the doctrine of "actual malice."

> The constitutional guarantees require, we think, a federal rule that prohibits a public official from recovering damages for a defamatory falsehood relating to his official conduct unless he proves that the statement was made with "actual malice" — that is, with knowledge that it was false or with reckless disregard of whether it was false or not.

In the New York Times case, the Court did not find "actual malice." First, there was no evidence that the individuals who had authorized the use of their names were aware of any erroneous statements or were "reckless" in that regard. Second, whether the statements were "substantially correct" was not relevant in deciding whether the Times had acted in good faith. Third, in response to Sullivan's request for a retraction, the Times letter to Sullivan reflected reasonable doubt that the advertisement referred to Sullivan at all. It was not a final refusal, since it asked for an explanation from Sullivan, a request that Sullivan ignored. Fourth, negligence in failing to discover misstatements is insufficient ground to demonstrate the recklessness that is required for a finding of "actual malice."

Later that year, the Supreme Court further developed its "actual malice" doctrine in Garrison v. Louisiana, 85 S.Ct. 209 (1964). This libel action centered around a dispute between James Garrison, the District Attorney of Orleans Parish, and eight justices of the Criminal District Court. The disagreement was over disbursements of a fund which was used to defray expenses of the District Attorney's office. When the judges denied Garrison use of the fund for conducting investigations of commercial vice, Garrison held a press conference at which he harshly criticized the conduct of the judges. Specifically, Garrison attributed the large backlog of criminal cases to the inefficiency, laziness, and excessive vacations of the judges. He also claimed that, by refusing to cover the expenses of investigations, the judges had hampered his efforts to enforce the vice laws. In addition, Garrison implied that racketeer influences shaped the judges' behavior. The judges brought suit. Garrison was tried and convicted under the Louisiana defamation statute. He appealed. The Supreme Court unanimously reversed, noting that the "reasonable belief" standard set forth in the law did not measure up to the "actual malice" requirement.

> A reasonable belief is one which an ordinary prudent man might be able to assign a just and fair reason for; the suggestion is that under this test the immunity from criminal responsibility in the absence of ill-will disappears on proof that the exercise of ordinary care would have revealed that the statement was false.

The Court stressed that the test it set down in New York Times was "not keyed to ordinary care; defeasance of the privilege is conditioned, not on mere negligence, but on reckless disregard for the truth." In Garrison, the Court rejected the concept of "reasonable belief" and insisted that public officials show "actual malice" in order to win libel suits.

In Beckley Newspapers Corporation v. Hanks, 88 S.Ct. 197 (1967), the Court again emphasized the "actual malice" requirement. The case arose when the Clerk of Courts in Raleigh County, West Virginia, initiated a libel action over three newspaper editorials that criticized his official conduct. At trial, the jury was instructed that a newspaper could be found guilty if the editorials had been published "with bad or corrupt motive" or "from personal spite, ill will or a desire to injure plaintiff." The jury returned a verdict for the plaintiff and awarded $5,000 damages. The Supreme Court reversed the decision because the judge's instructions were inadequate; nothing in the court record revealed "the high degree of awareness of probable falsity" demanded by the New York Times decision.

Harte-Hanks Communications v. Connaughton, 109 S.Ct. 2678 (1989), affirmed the relevance of the New York Times standard for determining actual malice. When a defendant newspaper lost a libel case, the newspaper's publisher appealed on the ground that the judge had applied an incorrect test of actual malice. According to the publisher, the court had not applied the New York Times standard, but instead had used a less severe professional standard rule that merely required a showing of "highly unreasonable conduct constituting an extreme departure from the standards of investigation and reporting ordinarily adhered to by responsible publishers." The Supreme Court, per Justice John Stevens, stressed that "there is no question that public figure libel cases are controlled by the New York Times standard and not by the professional standards rule." Stevens acknowledged that the less severe standard had been used, but after applying the New York Times standard, he found that the paper had been guilty of actual malice. In Harte-Hanks Communication, as in Garrison and Beckley Newspapers, the Court stressed that the New York Times standard must be used to determine actual malice in defamation cases involving public figures.

Knowledge of falsity

According to the New York Times guidelines, a public figure may demonstrate actual malice in either of two ways: knowledge of falsity, or reckless disregard for truth. The first of these standards has never been applied by the Supreme Court in a clear and direct manner. It has been used indirectly by the Court in Masson v. New Yorker Magazine, 111 S.Ct. 2419 (1991). The case involved an article which depicted world-famous psychoanalyst Jeffery Masson in an unflattering light. The article was based on several taped interviews the author conducted with Masson. In court, Masson claimed that the author of the piece, with full knowledge of the inaccuracies, used quotation marks to attribute to Masson statements he had not made. The lower court sided with the author on the ground that the quotations were "rational interpretations" of actual statements. The Supreme Court, per Justice Arthur Kennedy, found fault with the author's literary technique.

> In general, quotation marks indicate a verbatim reproduction, and quotations add authority to a statement and credibility to an author's work. A fabricated quotation may injure reputation by attributing an untrue factual assertion to the speaker, or by indicating a negative personal trait or an attitude the speaker does not hold.

Justice Kennedy noted that in this instance the author gave the reader "no clue" that the quotations were anything but the reproduction of actual conversations, and the work was published in a magazine that "enjoyed a reputation for scrupulous factual inquiry." These factors "could lead a reader to take the quotations at face value." According to Kennedy, the "rational interpretation" analysis was not applicable because "the quotation marks indicate that the author is not interpreting the speaker's ambiguous statement, but is attempting to convey what the speaker said."

Reckless disregard

While the "knowledge of falsity" standard has had limited application as the basis of Supreme Court decisions, the "reckless disregard" standard has received considerable attention. In the Curtis Publishing Company v. Butts and Associated Press v. Walker, 87 S.Ct. 1975 (1967), companion cases, the Court offered an interpretation of "reckless disregard," and also discussed the concept of "hot news." The Butts case involved an article in the Saturday Evening Post, which reported a telephone conversation between Wally Butts, athletic director of the University of Georgia, and Paul "Bear" Bryant, head football coach at the University of Alabama, in which the two men allegedly conspired to "fix" a football game between the two schools. The source of the story was George Burnett, who, because of an electronic error, had overheard the conversation when he picked up a telephone. The Post story compared this "fix" to the Chicago "Black Sox" scandal of 1919, and went on to describe the presentation of Burnett's notes to University of Georgia officials, and Butt's subsequent resignation. The article concluded:

> The chances are that Wally Butts will never help any football team again.... The investigation by university and Southeastern Conference officials is continuing; motion pictures of other games are being scrutinized; where it will end no one so far can say. But careers will be ruined, that is sure.

Butts sued. In court, the Post argued truth as its defense, but the evidence contradicted its version of the event. Butts argued that his conversation with Bryant had been general football talk. Expert witnesses supported Butt's position after analyzing films of the game. The jury awarded Butts $60,000 in compensatory damages and $3 million in punitive damages. On appeal, the Supreme Court, per Justice John Harlan, noted: "the Butts story was in no sense 'hot' news and the editors of the magazine recognized the need for a thorough investigation of the serious charges." Necessary precautions were ignored, however. The Post knew that Burnett was on probation in connection with bad-check charges but published his story without verification. Burnett's notes were not even analyzed by any of the magazine's personnel. An individual who was with Burnett when the phone call was overheard was not interviewed. No attempt was made to view the game film to see if Burnett's information was accurate.

The evidence supported a finding of "highly unreasonable conduct constituting an extreme departure from the standards of investigation and reporting ordinarily adhered to by responsible publishers." The Court found "reckless disregard," and affirmed the trial court's decision.

The Walker case further developed the concept of "hot news." The case involved a news release about General Edwin Walker's involvement in the events surrounding the entry of James Meredith into the University of Mississippi. The Associated Press report stated that Walker had taken command of the violent crowd and had led a charge against federal marshals. Walker initiated court action, seeking to collect damages from newspapers and broadcasting stations that carried the AP reports. A trial court awarded Walker $500,000 in compensatory damages. The case was appealed to the Supreme Court. The Court determined that Walker was a public figure because he had thrust his personality into an important public controversy. Moreover, in contrast to the Butts article, the Walker dispatch contained news that required immediate dissemination. AP received the information from a reporter who was present at the scene and who gave every indication of being trustworthy and competent. The story seemed reasonable to anyone familiar with Walker's previous publicized statements on the controversy. The court determined that "considering the necessity for rapid dissemination, nothing in this series of events gives the slightest hint of a severe departure from accepted publishing standards." The Court did not find "reckless disregard," and concluded that Walker was not entitled to damages.

In St. Amant v. Thompson, 88 S.Ct. 1323 (1968), the Court distinguished between "negligence" and "reckless disregard." The St. Amant case involved a televised political broadcast in which Phil St. Amant, a candidate for public office, delivered a speech that contained numerous quotations of a second person's opinions of St. Amant's political opponents. One of the opponents initiated suit for defamation, claiming that the broadcast had "inferred conduct of the most nefarious nature." The Louisiana Supreme Court ruled that St. Amant had "recklessly" broadcast false information, though not knowingly. St. Amant had failed to verify the facts because he mistakenly believed that he had no responsibility for the broadcast since he was merely quoting another person's words. The Supreme Court, in the opinion of Justice Byron White, reversed the decision. Justice White wrote:

> Reckless conduct is not measured by whether a reasonably prudent man would have published, or would have investigated before publishing. There must be sufficient evidence to permit the conclusion that the defendant in fact entertained serious doubts as

to the truth of his publication. Publishing with such doubts shows reckless disregard for truth or falsity and demonstrates actual malice. The Supreme Court found no evidence that St. Amant was aware of the probable falsity of the statement about his opponent. St. Amant had verified some of the statements. There was no reason to doubt the veracity of the source. The Court concluded that there was no reason to find "reckless disregard" for the accuracy of the statements. Failure to investigate does not, in itself, establish bad faith. Negligence, even though undesirable, does not constitute "reckless disregard."

In Time v. Pape, 91 S.Ct. 633 (1971), the issue was whether the failure to use the word "alleged" constituted "reckless disregard." In 1961, Time's report of the findings of the U.S. Commission on Civil Rights claimed that 13 Chicago police officers, led by Detective Frank Pape, broke through the doors of a family's apartment, woke the parents with flashlights, and forced them at gunpoint to stand naked in the center of the living room. The report claimed that Pape struck the father with a flashlight and called him "nigger" and "blackboy" while his six children watched. After police ransacked the apartment, the report continued, the father was taken to the police station, where he was neither advised of his rights nor permitted to call an attorney. He was subsequently released without criminal charges being filed against him. The allegations in the Commission's report had not been proven, and the Time article failed to make clear it was reporting mere allegations. Pape sued. The case reached the Supreme Court. The opinion of Justice Potter Stewart held that the article, at worst, reflected an error in judgment. According to Stewart, media that maintain professional standards should not be subject to financial liability for nonmalicious errors in judgment. The Court felt that if the freedoms of expression were to have "the breathing space that they need to survive, misstatements of this kind must have the protection of the First and Fourteenth Amendments." In Pape, the Court refused to punish a harmful, yet nonmalicious, statement.

The Butts, Walker, St. Amant, and Pape decisions indicate that individuals have generally free reign to publish statements about public officials, figures, or issues, as long as such publication is not made with "reckless disregard" for the truth. To prove "reckless disregard," public officials must establish more than mere negligence — they must demonstrate an uncaring and malicious disregard on the part of the writer and/or publisher.

Public official

The New York Times Company v. Sullivan, 84 S.Ct. 710 (1964), case stipulated that "public officials must show actual malice in order to win a defamation case. Ensuing Supreme Court cases clarified the nature of "public officials," and then distinguished them from "private persons." Rosenblatt v. Baer, 86 S.Ct. 669 (1966), provided an initial definition. The case involved Frank Baer, Supervisor of the Belkamp [Minnesota] Recreation Area. Baer won a libel suit against a news reporter who had charged him with mismanagement of operations. Upon appeal, the Supreme Court overturned the decision and clarified the concept of "public official." Justice Brennan noted that in the New York Times case, the Court did not determine how far down into the lower ranks of government employees the "public official" designation would extend. In Rosenblatt, the Court decided:

> Criticism of government is at the very center of the constitutionally protected area of free discussion. Criticism of those responsible for government operations must be free, lest criticism of government itself be penalized. It is clear, therefore, that the "public official" designation applies at the very least to those among the hierarchy of government employees who have, or appear to the public to have, substantial responsibility for or control over the conduct of government affairs.

The Court provided further clarification in Monitor Patriot Company v. Roy, 91 S.Ct. 621 (1971). The case involved Alphonse Roy, a candidate for the U.S. Senate who objected to a column which described him as a "former small-time bootlegger." Roy felt the column was a contributing factor when he lost his bid for election in the primary. Roy argued that since the alleged criminal conduct had occurred in the 1920s and had involved his private life rather than his performance as a public servant, the newspaper was guilty of libel. A jury agreed and awarded damages of $10,000. The Supreme Court reversed. According to Justice Stewart, the principal task of a candidate consisted of putting before the electorate every aspect of his or her public and private life that might lead the voters to form a favorable impression. A candidate who vaunts a spotless record before the electorate cannot cry "Foul!" when an industrious reporter attempts to demonstrate the contrary. Subsequently, the Court ruled that a charge of criminal conduct, no matter how remote in time or place, is relevant to a candidate's fitness for office. Accordingly, the remarks applied to Roy as a "public official," and a showing of "actual malice" was essential for Roy to win the suit.

Ocala Star-Banner Company v. Damron, 91 S.Ct. 628 (1971), is a related case. A newspaper reported that the Mayor of Crystal River, Leonard Damron, who was then a candidate for County Tax Assessor, had been charged with perjury in a civil-rights case. It was, however, Damron's brother who had been accused of perjury. An editor had changed the first name in the story to the Mayor's. Damron lost the election, which was held two weeks after the story appeared. At trial, the judge instructed the jury that the "actual malice" rule did not apply because the error did not involve Damron's official conduct. The jury found the newspaper guilty of negligence, and awarded Damron $22,000 in compensatory damages. The Supreme Court unanimously reversed the decision, viewing Leonard Damron as a "public official" in two ways — as the Mayor and as a candidate for the office of County Tax Assessor. The Court stressed that under the New York Times rule a "public official" cannot recover damages for a defamatory falsehood without proof of "actual malice." The Court was unimpressed with Damron's claim that the New York Times rule should apply only to "official conduct." Citing the Monitor decision, the Court reiterated that a charge of criminal conduct against an official or candidate, no matter how remote in time or place, was always "relevant to his fitness for office," for purposes of applying the Times rule.

Private person

In a series of cases throughout the 1970s, the court distinguished between the terms "public official" and "private person." Rosenbloom v. Metromedia, 91 S.Ct. 1811 (1971), was such a case. In Rosenbloom, two separate allegations of defamation came before the Supreme Court. The events of this case began when George Rosenbloom was arrested for distributing nudist magazines. The event was broadcast over a local radio station; the reporter stated that vice-squad officers had confiscated 1,000 "allegedly obscene" books at Rosenbloom's house and another 3,000 "obscene" books at a barn near his home. Rosenbloom brought suit against the news media on the ground that the magazines were not obscene. A trial court eventually acquitted Rosenbloom of this charge. A second instance of allegedly defamatory radio broadcasts related to news reports of the lawsuit itself. None mentioned Rosenbloom by name. The broadcasts did mention that "the girlie-book peddlers say the police crackdown and continued reference to their borderline literature as smut or filth is hurting their business." Rosenbloom argued that the characterization of him and his associates as "smut distributors" and "girlie-book peddlers" was defamatory. The court awarded $25,000 in compensatory damages and $250,000 in punitive damages. The court of appeals reversed the decision on the grounds that the broadcasts concerned matters of public interest and that they involved "hot news" prepared under deadline pressure. Rosenbloom took the case to the Supreme Court. The issue Rosenbloom raised was whether, since he was not a public official or a public figure, he had to establish "actual malice" on the part of the radio station. The Court noted:

> If a matter is a subject of public or general interest, it cannot suddenly become less so merely because a private individual is involved. The public's primary interest is in the event; the public focus is on the conduct of the participant and the content, effect, and significance of the conduct, not the participant's prior anonymity or notoriety. In that circumstance we think the time has come forthright to announce that the determinant whether the First Amendment applies to state libel actions is whether the utterance involved concerns an issue of public or general concern.... Drawing a distinction between "public" and "private" figures makes no sense in terms of the First Amendment guarantees.

In effect, Rosenbloom held that no person — public or private — who becomes involved in an event of "public interest" could collect libel damages without proof of "actual malice."

Three years later the Court overturned the Rosenbloom rule. In Gertz v. Welch, 94 S.Ct. 2997 (1974), the Court ruled that private citizens have greater protection against libelous statements than do public officials. This case began when a Chicago policeman shot and killed a young man. Authorities prosecuted the policeman and ultimately obtained a conviction for second-degree murder. The victim's family then retained Elmer Gertz, an attorney, to represent them in civil litigation. Shortly thereafter, American Opinion, a monthly vehicle for the opinions of the conservative John Birch Society, printed a story which alleged that the policeman had been framed. The article contained several falsehoods. For example, the article charged that Gertz had a criminal record, that he had taken part in planning the 1968 demonstrations in Chicago, and that he was a "Leninist" and a "Communist-fronter." The editor of American Opinion made no effort to verify the charges. He included a photograph of Gertz and wrote a caption under it which linked Gertz to the communist philosophy. Gertz brought suit, claiming that the falsehoods injured his reputation. The jury awarded him $50,000. The court of appeals, referring to Rosenbloom, ruled that the New York Times standard was applicable in this case and that Gertz failed to demonstrate that the editor had acted with "actual malice." Gertz appealed to the Supreme Court. The primary issue was whether a different degree of constitutional privilege applied to defamatory falsehoods about a private citizen than to those about a public official. According to Justice Lewis Powell,

> ...we conclude that the state interest in compensating injury to the reputation of private individuals requires that a different rule should obtain with respect to them.... The first remedy of any victim of

defamation is self help — using available opportunities to contradict the lie or correct the error and thereby minimize its adverse impact on reputation. Public officials and public figures usually enjoy significantly greater access to the channels of effective communication and hence have a more realistic opportunity to counteract false statements than private individuals normally enjoy. Private individuals are therefore more vulnerable to injury, and the state interest in protecting them is correspondingly greater.

In Gertz, the Court decided that a libel action by a private person required a showing of "negligence" as contrasted with a showing of "actual malice." A secondary issue was whether Gertz was a private person or a public figure. The Court noted that Gertz was not a public figure; even though he was "well-known in some circles, he had achieved no general fame or notoriety in the community." The Court acknowledged that the public-figure question should be considered by looking to the extent of a person's participation in the issue giving rise to the defamation. In this light, Gertz was not a public figure. His involvement with the issue related only to his representation of a client. He took no part in the criminal prosecution. He never discussed the litigation with the press. He did not thrust himself into the center of this issue, nor did he engage the public's attention in an effort to influence its outcome. The Court concluded that the "actual malice" standard was inapplicable to Gertz, who was a private citizen.

The Court reaffirmed this view in Time v. Firestone, 96 S.Ct. 958 (1976). After the Mary Alice and Russell Firestone divorce proceedings, Time magazine printed a note in the "Milestones" section which stated that the separation was granted "on grounds of extreme cruelty and adultery," and that the "trial produced enough testimony of extramarital adventures on both sides...to make Freud's hair curl." Mary Alice Firestone brought suit against Time, claiming that the descriptions were "false, malicious, and defamatory." The trial court granted, and the Supreme Court of Florida affirmed, a $100,000 award of damages. Time appealed, alleging that since Mrs. Firestone was a "public figure," the article deserved the protection of the New York Times standard. The U.S. Supreme Court, in the opinion of Justice William Rehnquist, held that the "actual malice" standard was inapplicable in this case. Mrs. Firestone was not a public figure. In applying the Gertz decision, Rehnquist noted that Mrs. Firestone had not assumed a role of "especial prominence in the affairs of society" and had not been "thrust to the forefront of particular public controversies in order to influence the resolution of the issues involved." The Court emphasized that a private person, like Firestone, should not forfeit protection against defamation simply by being drawn into court.

> Imposing upon the law of private defamation the rather drastic
> limitations worked by New York Times cannot be justified by
> generalized references to the public interest in reports of judicial
> proceedings. The details of many, if not most, courtroom battles
> would add almost nothing toward advancing the uninhibited debate
> on public issues.

Rehnquist noted that "Gertz provides an adequate safeguard for the
constitutionally protected interests of the press and affords it a tolerable
margin for error in requiring some type of fault." Rehnquist concluded
that since the divorce court had not found Mrs. Firestone guilty of
adultery, as reported by Time, the lower court had properly found the
reporting to be inaccurate. The magazine was guilty of negligence in
its treatment of a "private person."

The Court further delineated its concept of "public figure" in
Hutchinson v. Proxmire, 99 S.Ct. 2675 (1979), a case that involved an
alleged defamation by a government official. William Proxmire, U.S.
Senator from Wisconsin, initiated the "Golden Fleece of the Month
Award" to publicize examples of wasteful government spending. One
of these awards criticized several government agencies for spending half
a million dollars to fund Professor Ronald Hutchinson's research of
animals that had been exposed to aggravating, stressful stimuli. The
federal agencies were interested in this project for resolving problems
associated with confining humans in close quarters in space and
undersea exploration. In presenting the award, Proxmire delivered a
speech in which he declared:

> Dr. Hutchinson's studies should make the taxpayers as well as his
> monkeys grind their teeth. In fact, the good doctor has made a
> fortune from his monkeys and in the process made a monkey out of
> the American taxpayer.... It is time for the Federal Government to get
> out of this "monkey business." In view of the transparent
> worthlessness of Hutchinson's study of jaw-grinding and biting by
> angry or hard-driving monkeys, it is time we put a stop to the bite
> Hutchinson and the bureaucrats who fund him have been taking of
> the taxpayer.

Hutchinson filed suit, alleging that he suffered a loss of respect in his
profession, extreme mental anguish, and a loss of ability to earn
income. The case reached the Supreme Court. The opinion, written
by Chief Justice Warren Burger, noted that Hutchinson would not have
become a public figure without Proxmire's action. In fact,
Hutchinson's pubic profile was much like that "of countless members
of his profession." His publications reached "a relatively small
category of professionals concerned with research in human behavior."
Hutchinson did not enjoy the access to the media that "is one of the
accouterments of having become a public figure." Burger's opinion

stressed that Hutchinson became a limited public figure only as a consequence of the Golden Fleece Award. Burger then argued: "Clearly, those charged with defamation cannot, by their own conduct, create their own defense by making the claimant a public figure." The Court concluded that Hutchinson was not a "public figure" and therefore a demonstration of "actual malice" was not necessary in this case.

The Court provided definitive explanation of the terms "public figure" and "private individual" in Wolston v. Reader's Digest Association, 99 S.Ct. 2701 (1979). The case concerned a Reader's Digest publication which listed Ilya Wolston as a Soviet agent and claimed that he had been indicted for espionage. Wolston brought suit, claiming that the charges were false and defamatory. The lower courts decided that Wolston was a "public figure" and that the "First Amendment precluded recovery unless Wolston proved that the book was written with actual malice." When the case reached the Supreme Court, Justice Rehnquist summarized the Court's decisions of the previous decade.

> We identified two ways in which a person may become a public figure for purposes of the First Amendment: For the most part those who attain this status have assumed roles of especial prominence in the affairs of society. Some occupy positions of such persuasive power and influence that they are deemed public figures for all purposes. More commonly, those classed as public figures have thrust themselves to the forefront of particular public controversies in order to influence the resolution of the issues involved.

Rehnquist then argued that Wolston did not qualify as a "public figure" in either sense of the term. First, Wolston was not "one of that small group of individuals who are public figures for all purposes." Second, even though Wolston was investigated in regard to Soviet espionage in the United States, he had not "voluntarily thrust" or "injected" himself into the forefront of the public controversy. Instead, Rehnquist felt it would be more accurate to say that Wolston "was dragged unwillingly into the controversy." In Wolston, the Court concluded:

> A private individual is not automatically transformed into a public figure just by becoming involved in or associated with a matter that attracts public attention. To accept such reasoning would in effect re-establish the doctrine advanced by the plurality opinion in Rosenbloom...which concluded that the New York Times standard should extend to defamatory falsehoods relating to private persons if the statements involved matters of public or general concern. We repudiated this proposition in Gertz and in Firestone, however, and we reject it again today. A libel defendant must show more than

mere newsworthiness to justify application of the demanding burden of New York Times.

Rehnquist's opinion was unequivocally clear — the interpretation of the First Amendment that was set forth in Rosenbloom had been overturned by subsequent decisions. A "private person" did not have to demonstrate "actual malice" in order to win a libel suit.

EVIDENTIARY CONSIDERATIONS

The courts have examined various evidentiary questions related to the defamation trial. The issues of neutral reportage, scope of discovery, and burden of proof raise potential questions for a defamation suit.

Neutral reportage

In 1977, a district court considered the question of whether a reporter, supplied with information from a usually reliable source that appears unreliable in this instance, can publish an account of the information without fear of punishment for "actual malice." In rendering its opinion in Edwards v. National Audubon Society, 556 F.2d 113 (1977), the court established the doctrine of "neutral reportage." The case involved a story, written by John Devlin, which appeared in the New York Times. Devlin's interest in the story was first aroused when an official publication of the National Audubon Society claimed that any scientists who supported the use of DDT were "paid liars." Devlin researched the story; he requested verification from the Audubon Society, and he sought response from the scientists. Even though he did not receive complete data from either side in the controversy, he published a story entitled "Pesticide Spokesman Accused of 'Lying' on Higher Bird Count." The story accurately reported the information he had obtained from his sources. Dr. J. Gordon Edwards and other scientists filed a libel suit. The trial judge instructed the jury that the Times could be found guilty of "actual malice" if Devlin had serious doubts about the truth of the "paid liars" claim, even if he had no doubts that he was reporting his source's allegations faithfully. Accordingly, the jury returned a verdict against the Times and awarded Edwards $21,000. The district court overturned the award. Judge Irving Kaufman wrote:

> At stake in this case is a fundamental principle. Succinctly stated, when a responsible, prominent organization like the National Audubon Society makes serious charges against a public figure, the First Amendment protects the accurate and disinterested reporting of those charges, regardless of the reporter's private views regarding

their validity. What is newsworthy about such accusations is that they were made. We do not believe that the press may be required under the First Amendment to suppress newsworthy statements merely because it has serious doubts regarding their truth.

In Edwards, Kaufman formulated the doctrine of "neutral reportage." The Supreme Court denied certiorari in the Edwards case.

In ensuing decisions, the lower courts applied the doctrine inconsistently. In Dickey v. CBS, 583 F.2d 1221 (1978), a court of appeals opposed the "neutral reportage" doctrine. In this case, a person, during a televised debate, was accused by a congressman of having accepted a bribe. The accused initiated a libel suit against the television station that presented the debate. The Dickey court decided that the "neutral reportage" concept violates the St. Amant v. Thompson, 88 S.Ct. 1323 (1968), decision. In St. Amant, the Supreme Court ruled that an individual who publishes information while entertaining serious doubts as to the truth of the publication "shows reckless disregard for truth or falsity and demonstrates actual malice." Influenced by this opinion, the Dickey court concluded: "A constitutional privilege of neutral reportage is not created...merely because an individual newspaper or television or radio station decides that a particular statement is newsworthy."

Another case which rejected the doctrine of neutral reportage is McCall v. Courier-Journal and Louisville Times, 623 S.W.2d 882 (1981). The case involved a published allegation that an attorney was guilty of intent to bribe a judge. A third party had made the allegation, which was corroborated by another individual. Even though reporters doubted the allegation, they printed it as stated. In McCall, the judge rejected neutral reportage arguments because "this doctrine has not been approved by the Supreme Court of the United States and has not received approval in other jurisdictions." Using a negligence test, the court found the reporters guilty because, in the exercise of "reasonable care," they should have known that the statement was false or would create a false impression. They were guilty for failing to do "what a reasonably prudent person would...have done under the same or similar circumstances.

In Re United Press International, 16 Med. L. Rptr. 2401 (1989), the court applied the neutral reportage doctrine. The case involved a wire service report stating that a Valley Isle, Hawaii newspaper had published an article in which the brother of a missing environmentalist activist had said that the activist had named a particular individual as the "godfather" of local organized crime. The named individual initiated a defamation action. In supporting the neutral reportage doctrine, the court noted:

The undisputed facts indicate that [reporter] did make adequate efforts to verify the *Valley Isle* story. His stories did no more than repeat *only* that which he had verified; as noted above, he reported only that individuals (who he named) had made statements to the *Valley Isle*, and that the *Valley Isle* had published those statements. In light of the constitutional concerns underlying the neutral reportage doctrine, the Court finds these efforts legally sufficient.

The cases discussed in this section illustrate that, since Edwards, courts have inconsistently applied the neutral reportage doctrine. In any event, a determination of the constitutionality of "neutral reportage" must await a hearing by the U.S. Supreme Court.

Scope of discovery

In Herbert v. Lando, 99 S.Ct. 1635 (1979), the Supreme Court determined that a plaintiff in a libel action may probe a journalist's mind during the discovery procedure. The libel action in this case was brought by Colonel Anthony Herbert, who had received widespread media attention as a result of his bringing Vietnam war crimes to public attention. In an episode of the television program "60 Minutes," various contradictions in Herbert's story were highlighted. Shortly thereafter, Barry Lando, the producer of "60 Minutes," made the same claims in an article for Atlantic Monthly. Herbert's libel suit alleged that the program and article "falsely and maliciously portrayed him as a liar." Since Herbert was a "public figure," he had to show "actual malice" in order to recover damages. In order to prove his case, Herbert questioned Lando at length. Lando answered numerous questions, but refused to respond in some instances on the ground that "the First Amendment protected against inquiry into the state of mind of those who edit, produce, or publish, and into the editorial process." The district court decided that Lando's state of mind was of "central importance" to the issue of "actual malice." The court ruled that the questioning procedure was "entirely appropriate to Herbert's efforts to discover whether Lando had any reason to doubt the truth of any of his sources." When the court of appeals reversed this decision, Herbert took the case to the Supreme Court. Justice White, writing for the Court, observed that recent Supreme Court decisions made it essential for recovering damages "that the plaintiff focus on the conduct and state of mind of the defendant." According to White, "the thoughts and editorial processes of the alleged defamer" are vital to the discovery process. White concluded: "According an absolute privilege to the editorial process of a media defendant in a libel case is not required, authorized, or presaged by our prior cases, and would substantially enhance the burden of proving actual malice." In Herbert, the Supreme

Court determined that the First Amendment does not bar a plaintiff from inquiring into the state of mind of those responsible for publication.

Burden of proof

In Philadelphia Newspapers v. Hepps, 106 S.Ct. 1558 (1986), the Court considered whether the plaintiff or defendant should demonstrate a burden of proof. The case involved a series of articles which linked Maurice Hepps to organized crime, and suggested that he used those links to influence governmental processes. Hepps initiated suit for defamation, and the case eventually reached the Supreme Court. The majority opinion, written by Justice Sandra O'Connor, noted the difficult task associated with assigning the burden of proof. O'Connor acknowledged that if the plaintiff bears the burden of showing falsity, there will be some cases in which plaintiffs cannot meet their burden, even though the speech is in fact false. Conversely, under an alternative rule placing the burden of showing truth on defendants, there would be some cases in which the defendants could not meet the burden, despite the fact that the speech is in fact true. After weighing the problem, Justice O'Connor noted:

> In a case presenting a configuration of speech and plaintiff like the one we face here, and where the scales are in such an uncertain balance, we believe that the Constitution requires us to tip them in favor of protecting true speech. To ensure that true speech on matters of public concern is not deterred, we hold that the common-law presumption that defamatory speech is false cannot stand when a plaintiff seeks damages against a media defendant for speech of public concern.

Even though the Court recognized "that requiring the plaintiff to show falsity will insulate from liability some speech that is false, but unprovably so," it was necessary to "protect some falsehood in order to protect speech that matters." The plaintiff is obligated to meet the burden of proof.

TOLERABLE DEFAMATION

The Supreme Court has decided whether certain forms of expression are so important in a free society that some level of defamation should be tolerated. Forms of speech and press which warrant special protection include robust debate, parody, and on-line republication. Communications about private concerns and libelous petition do not enjoy special protection.

Robust debate

In Greenbelt Publishing Association v. Bresler, 90 S.Ct. 1537 (1970), the Supreme Court enunciated the doctrine of "robust debate." The case involved negotiations between Charles Bresler, a prominent local real-estate developer, and the Greenbelt City Council. These negotiations produced substantial controversy and several stormy city-council meetings. The meetings were reported at length in the Greenbelt News Review. The articles claimed that some citizens had described Bresler's negotiating position as "blackmail." Bresler brought suit. The jury awarded Bresler $5,000 in compensatory damages and $12,500 in punitive damages. Upon appeal, the Supreme Court reversed the decision on the ground that the news stories were accurate accounts of the public debates.

> It is simply impossible to believe that a reader who reached the word "black-mail" in either article would have not understood exactly what was meant: It was Bresler's public and wholly legal negotiating proposals that were being criticized. No reader could have thought that either the speakers at the meetings or the newspaper articles reporting their words were charging Bresler with the commission of a criminal offense. On the contrary, even the most careless reader must have perceived that the word was no more than rhetorical hyperbole, a vigorous epithet used by those who considered Bresler's negotiating position extremely unreasonable. Indeed, the record is completely devoid of evidence that anyone in the city of Greenbelt or anywhere else thought Bresler had been charged with a crime.

In Greenbelt, the Court emphasized that the societal interests in providing for "robust debate" of subjects of substantial concern took precedence over a person's interest in maintaining his or her good name.

The doctrine of "robust debate" was reaffirmed in Bose Corporation v. Consumer Union of United States, 104 S.Ct. 1949 (1984). The case involved an article in Consumer Reports that evaluated the quality of numerous brands of loudspeakers, including the Bose 901. The article presented a critical assessment of the model and claimed that "individual instruments heard through the Bose system seemed to grow to gigantic proportions and tended to wander about the room." The article urged consumers not to buy the model unless they "were sure the system would please [them] after the novelty value had worn off." The Bose corporation initiated court action on the ground that the article constituted libelous product disparagement. The district court found "actual malice" because the claim that instruments tended to wander "about the room" was false. Actually, listeners perceived "movement back and forth along the wall in front of them and between the two speakers." They did not perceive movement "about the room." The Supreme Court, per Justice Stevens, overturned the decision. Stevens noted that the statement under question "represents the sort of inaccuracy that is commonplace in the forum of robust debate."

> ...adoption of the language chosen was "one of a number of possible rational interpretations" of an event "that bristled with ambiguities" and descriptive challenges for the writer. The choice of such language, though reflecting a misconception, does not place the speech beyond the outer limits of the First Amendment's broad perceptive umbrella.

The Bose Corporation decision acknowledged that erroneous statements are inevitable in the system of free and "robust debate."

Parody

Jerry Falwell, a nationally known minister and commentator on politics and public affairs, sued Hustler magazine to recover damages for two separate charges — libel and intentional infliction of emotional distress. The court action arose from the publication of a parody of an advertisement which was entitled "Jerry Falwell talks about his first time." The parody was modeled after Campari Liqueur ads that included interviews with various celebrities about their "first times." Although it was apparent by the end of each interview that this meant the first time they sampled Campari, the ads clearly played on the sexual double entendre of the notion of "first time." The Hustler "first time" parody portrayed Falwell as having engaged in a drunken incestuous rendezvous with his mother in an outhouse. In small print at the bottom of the page, the ad contained the disclaimer, "ad parody — not to be taken seriously." The jury found in favor of Hustler on the libel charge, specifically finding that the ad parody could not "reasonably be understood as describing actual facts...or actual events." The jury ruled for Falwell on the intentional infliction of emotional distress claim, and awarded $100,000 in compensatory damages and $50,000 in punitive damages. The case reached the Supreme Court where Falwell argued that the parody was so "outrageous" as to distinguish it from similar characterizations. The Court sided with "Hustler," rejecting outrageousness as a valid criterion for determination of libel.

> "Outrageousness" in the area of political and social discourse has an inherent subjectiveness about it which would allow a jury to impose liability on the basis of the juror's tastes or views, or perhaps on the basis of their dislike of a particular expression. An

"outrageousness" standard thus runs afoul of our longstanding refusal to allow damages to be awarded because the speech in question may have an adverse emotional impact on the audience.
In Hustler Magazine v. Falwell, 108 S.Ct. 876 (1988), the Court also decided that public figures may not recover damages for intentional infliction of emotional distress without a showing of "actual malice." Since the jury had ruled against Falwell in that the parody could not "reasonably be understood as describing actual facts...or actual events" in which Falwell participated, the Court reversed the jury damages award.

On-line republication

In Zeran v. America On-line, 129 F.3d 327 (1997), the court determined that an on-line computer service cannot be held liable for third-party defamatory statements that are published through that service. Kenneth Zeran sued the service when his name and phone number were included in a series of bulletin board notices that advertised T-shirts and other items glorifying the 1995 bombing of the federal building in Oklahoma City. The information was posted as part of an anonymously perpetrated prank. Zeran subsequently received a high volume of calls, comprised primarily of angry, derogatory, and threatening messages. The court of appeals ultimately cited the Communications Decency Act of 1996 in holding that computer service providers are immune "for liability for information that originates with third parties."

The opinion was reaffirmed in Blumenthal v. Drudge and America On-line, 992 F. Supp 44 (1998). Sidney Blumenthal, an Assistant to President Bill Clinton, initiated legal action when the electronic publication called the Drudge Report accused Blumenthal of "spousal abuse" and "wife-beating." The court concluded:

> It is undisputed that the Blumenthal story was written by Drudge without any substantive or editorial involvement by AOL. AOL was nothing more than a provider of an interactive computer service on which the Drudge Report was carried, and Congress has said quite clearly that such a provider shall not be treated as a "publisher or speaker" and therefore may not be held liable.

So, while Drudge could be held accountable, the computer service provider was immune from fault.

Private concerns

On July 26, 1976, Dun and Bradstreet sent a credit report to five subscribers, indicating that Greenmoss Builders had filed a voluntary petition for bankruptcy. This report was false and grossly misrepresented Greenmoss Builder's assets and liabilities. When Dun and Bradstreet realized that its report was false, it issued a corrective notice to the subscribers who had received the report. Greenmoss, nonetheless, initiated a defamation action, alleging that the false report had injured its reputation. After trial, the jury awarded $50,000 in compensatory and $300,000 in punitive damages. Dun and Bradstreet appealed on the ground that the court had erred in not requiring a finding of actual malice. In Dun and Bradstreet v. Greenmoss Builders, 105 S.Ct. 2939 (1985), the Supreme Court stressed that not all speech is of equal First Amendment importance; matters of public concern are at the heart of constitutional protection, while matters of private concern are of less importance. In this case, the credit report concerned no public issue but was speech solely in the individual interest of the communicator and the business audience. According to the Court, "this particular interest warranted no special protection when it was wholly false and damaging to the victim's business reputation." In light of the reduced constitutional protection for expression of purely private concern, the state interest in compensating individuals for injury to their reputation may be satisfied by awarding damages without a showing of actual malice.

Libelous petition

In McDonald v. Smith, 105 S.Ct. 2787 (1985), the Court examined the meaning of the Petition Clause of the First Amendment. Robert McDonald filed a libel action against David Smith on the ground that while McDonald was being considered for the position of U.S. Attorney, Smith maliciously wrote letters to President Ronald Reagan and other officials that contained "false slanderous, libelous, inflammatory and derogatory statements" concerning his qualifications for public office. McDonald claimed that the letters had their intended effect; he was not appointed and his reputation and career were injured. Smith argued that the Petition Clause of the First Amendment, which provides the right to petition the government for a redress of grievances, guarantees "absolute immunity from liability." The Supreme Court, in an opinion written by Chief Justice Warren Burger, disagreed.

> Although the values in the right of petition as an important aspect of self government are beyond question, it does not follow that the Framers of the First Amendment believed that the Petition Clause provided absolute immunity from damages for libel.

Burger ruled that the Petition Clause "was inspired by the same ideas of liberty and democracy that gave us the freedoms to speak, publish, and assemble." Burger maintained that there was no sound basis to grant greater First Amendment protection to petition than to other forms of expression.

GROUP LIBEL

The concept of group libel has been recognized by state courts since early in the twentieth century. In <u>Crane v. State</u>, 166 P. 1110 (1917), an Oklahoma appeals court noted: "The law of libel forbids the writing, publication, or circulation of libelous matter against a class as much so as against individuals." The doctrine of group libel was further clarified by the Supreme Court of Illinois in <u>People v. Spielman</u>, 149 N.E. 466 (1925). The court noted that

> ...a libel upon a class or group has as great a tendency to provoke a breach of the peace or to disturb society as has a libel on an individual, and such a libel is punishable, even though its application to individual members of the class or group cannot be proved.

The notion of group libel was applied by the U.S. Supreme Court in <u>Beauharnais v. Illinois</u>, 72 S.Ct. 725 (1952). The libelous material was prepared by Joseph Beauharnais, the President of the White Circle League, a racist "neighborhood improvement group." Beauharnais and his volunteers distributed, in downtown Chicago, leaflets that called on the Mayor "to halt the further encroachment, harassment and invasion of white people, their property, neighborhoods and persons, by the Negro." The leaflets warned: "If persuasion and the need to prevent the white race from becoming mongrelized by the negro will not unite us, then the aggression...rapes, robberies, knives, guns and marijuana of the Negro surely will." When Beauharnais was convicted of violating an Illinois law by distributing publications that subjected black citizens to contempt and derision, he appealed. The Supreme Court, in the opinion written by Justice Felix Frankfurter, supported the Illinois law. The Court noted that Illinois had a history of tension between races, which had often flared into violence and destruction. It seemed clear that the Illinois legislature acted within reason in attempting "to curb false or malicious defamation of racial and religious groups, made in public places and by means calculated to have a powerful emotional impact on those to whom it was presented." Justices Hugo Black and William Douglas opposed the law as a form of censorship. They argued that "this act sets up a system of state censorship which is at war with the kind of free government envisioned by those who forced adoption of our Bill of Rights." The majority of the Court, however, upheld Beauharnais's conviction for group libel. Though the doctrine has not been frequently invoked, the concept of "group libel" stands as a reminder to publishers that groups may seek retribution for libelous statements.

CORPORATE LIBEL

Each company has a reputation to protect. The doctrine of "corporate libel" recognizes that companies enjoy the same rights to plead for damages as do individuals. In Neiman-Marcus Company v. Lait, 107 F.Supp. 96 (1952), the company brought suit against the publishers of a book on the ground that statements made about company-employed models and sales personnel were libelous. The publication referred to employees as "call girls — the top babes in town" and as "expensive imported faggots." The corporation sought $2 million in compensatory and punitive damages. The district court determined that while a corporation has no reputation in a personal sense, its prestige and position are capable of being damaged by aspersive language. A corporation could be defamed by statements directed at its employees, if they discredit the method in which business is conducted. The court concluded that a corporation could be "damaged in a business way by a publication that it employs seriously undesirable personnel."

A decade later, the doctrine was affirmed in Cosgrove Studio and Camera Shop v. Pane, 182 A.2d 751 (1962). Cosgrove Studio and Camera Shop advertised that it would offer a free roll of film for every roll brought to it for developing. The next day, its business competitor placed an advertisement which urged consumers to "use common sense — you get nothing for nothing." The ad went on to state that "we will not inflate the price of your developing to give you a new roll free." Cosgrove initiated a suit for libel, alleging that the competitor's advertisement suggested dishonest business practices. The court found that any language that "unequivocally, maliciously, and falsely imputes to an individual or corporation want of integrity in the conduct of his or its business is actionable." In arriving at this decision, the court acknowledged that identification of the defamed corporation need not be by name; a company may be identified by description or circumstances. In Cosgrove Studios, as in Neiman-Marcus Company, the court found "corporate libel."

CONCLUSION

The following principles regulate communication law regarding DEFAMATION:

1. Defamation law seeks to compensate an individual, group, or corporation whose reputation has been wrongfully damaged.

2. In order to win a case, the plaintiff must prove all of the burdens.
   a. publication,
   b. identification,
   c. injury,
   d. fault — actual malice for public persons, negligence for private persons.

3. If a plaintiff proves the burdens, four types of damages may be awarded:
   a. compensatory — award for injury to reputation,
   b. actual — reimbursement of real monetary loss,
   c. punitive — punishment of past behavior and discouragement of future defamation,
   d. nominal — token damages in case of no serious harm.

4. A defendant may successfully contest a defamation charge by employing:
   a. complete defenses — truth, absolute privilege, qualified privilege, fair comment,
   b. partial defenses — reliable source, retraction and apology, right of reply, settlement out of court, bad reputation of plaintiff, provocation.

KEY DECISIONS

1952 — BEAUHARNAIS — recognized the concept of group libel

1959 — FARMERS EDUCATIONAL AND COOPERATIVE UNION OF AMERICA — determined that broadcast stations are not liable for defamatory statements made over their facilities by political candidates

1964 — NEW YORK TIMES COMPANY — established "actual malice" doctrine

1967 — BUTTS — noted that when a story does not involve "hot news," the reporter has adequate time for thorough investigation of the charges

1968 — ST. AMANT — distinguished between "negligence" and "reckless disregard"

1970 — GREENBELT — stressed the value of "robust debate" about subjects of substantial concern

1974 — GERTZ — ruled that private citizens have greater protection against libelous statements than do public figures

1979 — WOLSTON — clarified the Court's meaning of the term "public figure"

1979 — HERBERT — determined that a plaintiff in a defamation action may inquire into the state of mind of those responsible for publication

1984 — BOSE CORPORATION — acknowledged that erroneous statements are inevitable in a system of free and robust debate

1988 — FALWELL — held that potentially-defamatory parody could not be understood as describing actual events

1997 — ZERAN — computer service cannot be held liable for third-party defamatory statements

RECOMMENDED READING

Batterman, Jamie D., "The First Amendment Protection of the Freedoms of Speech and the Press and its Effect on the Law of Defamation as Seen Through the Eyes of Justice Brennan: His Impact and its Future," Whittier Law Review 13 (1992), 233-84.

Bezanson, Randall P., "The Libel Tort Today," Washington and Lee Law Review 45 (1988), 535-556.

Carlson, Marian L., "A Logical Product of the New York Times Revolution," Denver University Law Review 61 (Winter, 1987), 65-80.

Cohen, J. and A. C. Gunther, "Libel as Communication Phenomena," Communications and the Law 9 (1987), 9-30.

Lawhorne, Clifton O., The Supreme Court and Libel. Carbondale: Southern Illinois University Press, 1981.

Matheson, Scott M., "Procedure in Public Person Defamation Cases: The Impact of the First Amendment," Texas Law Review 66 (1987), 215-302.

Minnick, Wayne C., "The United States Supreme Court on Libel," Quarterly Journal of Speech 68 (November, 1982), 384-96.

Sanford, Bruce W., et. al., Libel and Privacy Englewood Cliffs, N.J.: Prentice Hall, 2nd Ed., 1991.

Tiersma, Peter Meijes, "The Language of Defamation," Texas Law Review 66 (1987), 303-50.

CHAPTER 8

PRIVACY

The framers of the Constitution did not provide for a "right to privacy." After all, in the 1700's, most citizens lived in their own homes, in relatively small communities, and did not feel a pressing need for securing their privacy. The legal basis for a right to privacy in the United States was initially outlined in the late nineteenth century by two law partners, Samuel Warren and Louis Brandeis.[1] Since that time, the right to privacy has been recognized by legislatures and courts in several states. One of the most important legislative enactments, the Privacy Act of 1974 (P.L. 93-579), was designed to regulate the collection and dissemination of personal information by federal agencies. There is no equivalent legislation which applies to privacy and the media or privacy and the general citizenry. Resolution of disputes in those areas is often left to the courts. The privacy torts include: 1) intrusion of physical solitude, 2) public disclosure of private facts, 3) placing an individual in a false light in the public eye, and 4) appropriation of some element of an individual's personality for commercial use.[2] Each of the torts will be discussed in this chapter.

INTRUSION

Intrusion is the act of thrusting oneself upon the peace and into the private life of another. It can occur through numerous techniques, which include photography, hidden electronic devices, physical entry, and statutory restriction.

PHOTOGRAPHY

Galella v. Onassis, 487 F.2d 986 (1973), involved intrusion which stems from an individual's being unwillingly photographed. The case involved freelance photographer Ronald Galella, who made a living photographing celebrities. His favorite subject was Jacqueline Onassis, whom he photographed continuously. Mrs. Onassis filed a claim, seeking injunctive relief against Galella's interference with the former first lady and her children. According to Onassis, Galella continually stalked her, popped up everywhere, and emitted "grunting" sounds that terrified her. Galella argued that he had a right to photograph Onassis, a "camera shy" and "uncooperative" public person. The court held that Galella's snooping violated Mrs. Onassis's right of privacy.

> Of course legitimate countervailing social needs may warrant some intrusion despite an individual's reasonable expectation of privacy and freedom from harassment. However, the interference allowed may be no greater than that necessary to protect the overriding public interest. Mrs. Onassis was properly found to be a public figure and thus subject to news coverage. Nonetheless, Galella's action went far beyond the reasonable bounds of news gathering.

The court enjoined Galella from approaching within 300 feet of the Onassis and Kennedy homes, as well as the school attended by the children. He was required to remain 30 feet from the children and 25 feet from Mrs. Onassis at all other places. In addition, Galella was instructed not to put the family under surveillance or to attempt to communicate with them. In Galella, the court upheld the freedom from harassment associated with being unwillingly photographed.

HIDDEN ELECTRONIC DEVICES

Dietemann v. Time, 449 F.2d 245 (1971), involved invasion of privacy through the use of a hidden camera and electronic recording equipment. A. A. Dietemann, a minimally educated, disabled veteran, illegally practiced medical healing through the use of clay, minerals, and herbs. Life magazine employees Jackie Metcalf and William Ray, in collaboration with the District Attorney's office, visited Dietemann in order to obtain facts and pictures concerning his activities. Dietemann, while examining Metcalf, was photographed with a hidden camera. One picture showed Dietemann with his hand on Metcalf's breast while he was holding a wand in his hand. Metcalf had told Dietemann that she had a lump in her breast. Dietemann concluded that she had eaten some rancid butter 11 years previously. The conversation was carried by a radio transmitter hidden in Metcalf's purse to a tape recorder in an automobile occupied by a member of the District Attorney's office. Dietemann was arrested on a charge of practicing medicine without a license; he pled no contest. Shortly thereafter, Life carried a story claiming that Dietemann was a quack.

Pictures and information obtained by Metcalf and Ray were used to prepare the article. Dietemann initiated an invasion-of-privacy suit. He claimed that he conducted his practice in his home, which is not open to the public. Life's employees had gained entrance by a subterfuge. The court concluded that Metcalf and Ray had invaded Dietemann's privacy; the judge awarded $1,000 in compensatory damages for injury to Dietemann's feelings and peace of mind. Before the court of appeals, Life claimed that the First Amendment immunized it from liability for invading Dietemann's home with hidden devices because its employees were gathering news. Life argued that such equipment constituted indispensable tools of investigative reporting. The court disagreed — the First Amendment was not a license to trespass by electronic means into another's home or office even if the person was suspected of committing a crime.

A few years later, the courts heard a related case — Cassidy v. American Broadcasting Companies, 377 N.E.2d 126 (1978). During 1975, Arlyn Cassidy and other Chicago police officers acted as undercover agents in the investigation of a massage parlor, for alleged solicitation and obscenities. As part of the investigation, Cassidy paid a $30 admission fee to see "deluxe" lingerie modeling. He was taken to a small room by a model who changed her lingerie several times. Cassidy arrested the model for solicitation after she established "sufficient" physical contact with him. At that point, the door to an adjacent room opened, revealing that a camera crew had filmed the entire scene. A newsman for a local television station claimed that the news crew had reported to the massage parlor in response to a call from the manager, who had complained that his establishment was the subject of police harassment. The film crew installed a two-way mirror which provided visual access to the activities involving Cassidy and the model. Cassidy initiated court action, alleging an invasion of privacy. The court noted that Cassidy was not a private citizen engaged in conduct that pertained only to himself. He was a public official performing a public duty concerning a newsworthy event. The court held that "under these circumstances no right of privacy against intrusion can be said to exist with reference to the gathering and dissemination of news concerning discharge of public duties." In Cassidy, the Dietemann principle was not applicable because Dietemann was a private individual, while Cassidy was a public official.

PHYSICAL ENTRY

The Pearson v. Dodd, 410 F.2d 701 (1969), case involved

accusations that two newspaper reporters received stolen property which was eventually used in a published article. On several occasions, employees of Senator Thomas Dodd entered his office without permission and took documents from his files, made duplicates, replaced the originals, and turned the copies over to newspapermen Drew Pearson and Jack Anderson. The reporters knew how the copies had been obtained. Pearson and Anderson used this information in publishing articles about Dodd's alleged relationship with lobbyists for foreign interests. Dodd sued, claiming invasion of privacy. The court ruled that a news medium that published information received through physical intrusion cannot be held responsible for the behavior of the intruders. The court stressed that injuries from intrusion and injuries from publication should be considered separately. Pearson and Anderson had not committed an act of physical intrusion. Furthermore, they had published information that was of general public interest. Their activity was not subject to suit for invasion of privacy.

In People v. Kunkin, 107 Cal.Rptr. 184 (1973), Arthur Kunkin, editor of the Los Angeles Free Press, was indicted for receiving a copy of a document that had been stolen by a clerk in the office of the Attorney General. The document was the personnel roster of the Bureau of Narcotic Enforcement. It listed the names, addresses, and telephone numbers of undercover narcotics agents throughout the state. It was not marked "secret" or "confidential." The Free Press published the roster verbatim under the headline "Know your local Narc." When Kunkin was convicted of receiving stolen property, he appealed. The California Supreme Court noted that the conviction could not stand unless substantial evidence demonstrated that 1) the property was received by the accused, 2) the property had been obtained by theft or extortion, and 3) the accused knew that the property had been stolen. The court decided that the first two requirements were satisfied, then considered whether there was substantial evidence from which the jury could reasonably draw an inference that Kunkin knew the roster was stolen. The court considered five circumstances which, the Attorney General argued, established Kunkin's knowledge that the roster was stolen. In each circumstance, the court concluded that the evidence was insufficient to sustain a conviction. First, the sensitive nature of the information, although cause for outrage at Kunkin's gross irresponsibility in publishing it, gave no basis for presuming that he knew the roster was stolen. Second, the list of inferences that might reasonably be drawn about a person who hands over a roster of names of undercover narcotics agents and wishes to remain anonymous does not include the inference of theft. Third, recognition that publication might cause trouble does not warrant an inference of theft. Fourth, Kunkin's willingness to pay for the information was without significance because he was willing to pay similar amounts for other information. Fifth, knowledge of the theft could not be discerned by Kunkin's refusal to surrender the roster after its publication. The court concluded that there was no substantial evidence to indicate that Kunkin knew the roster was stolen. The conviction was reversed. The courts sided with the press in Kunkin, as in Pearson. In so doing, the courts made it difficult to obtain the conviction of a reporter who publishes information obtained through physical intrusion.

In Wilson v. Layne, 119 S.Ct. 1692 (1999), the Supreme Court ruled that police officers violate individual privacy by bringing news reporters or other third parties into a private home to observe and record the execution of a warrant. The case began when a circuit court issued an arrest warrant for a person suspected of probation violations. The police invited members of the media to join them when they approached the location thought to be the home of the suspect. In reality, it was the residence of the suspect's parents, who were confronted and accosted by police officers. The parents sued for monetary damagers. The Court, per Chief Justice William Rehnquist, held that a media "ride along" violates the Fourth Amendment.

> Surely the possibility of good public relations for the police is simply not enough, standing alone, to justify the ride-along intrusion into a private home. And even the need for accurate reporting on police issues in general bears no direct relation to the constitutional justification for the police intrusion into a home.

STATUTORY RESTRICTION

Courts have evaluated statutes which intrude into aspects of personal life, including sexual mores, the abortion question, personal appearance, and drug use.

Sexual mores

An example is Griswold v. Connecticut, 85 S.Ct. 1678 (1965). Estelle Griswold, Executive Director of the Planned Parenthood League of Connecticut, gave advice and supplies to married couples regarding methods of birth control. Griswold was arrested for violating a law that prohibited any person from counseling others concerning the use of contraceptives. When she was found guilty and fined $100, Griswold appealed. The Supreme Court noted that "the First Amendment has a penumbra where privacy is protected from governmental intrusion." The law, by restricting the use of contraceptives, intruded upon an individual's privacy surrounding the marriage relationship. The Court stressed that the First Amendment protects not only the right to speak and print, but also the right to distribute, to receive, to read, to teach, and to associate, as well as the freedom of thought and inquiry. In Griswold, the Court determined that married persons were entitled to access to contraceptives.

Seven years later, in Eisenstadt v. Baird, 92 S.Ct. 1029 (1972), the Court approved of access to contraceptives for unmarried persons. The case involved William Baird, who was convicted for displaying contraceptive materials during a lecture to students at Boston University, as well as for giving a package of vaginal foam to a young woman at the end of his presentation. When the case reached the Supreme Court, the justices cited Griswold and noted that "whatever the rights of the individual to access to contraceptives may be, the rights must be the same to the unmarried and married alike." The Court stressed that a married couple is not an independent entity with one mind and heart, but an association of two persons, each with an individual intellectual and emotional makeup. Accordingly, "if the right of privacy means anything, it is the right of the individual, married or single, to be free from unwarranted governmental intrusion into matters so fundamentally affecting a person as the decision whether to bear or beget a child."

Abortion

Throughout the 1970s, a heated debate took place between religious groups dedicated to protecting human life and environmental organizations determined to control population growth. In several cases, the Supreme Court considered the constitutionality of state abortion statutes. Roe v. Wade, 93 S.Ct. 705 (1973), was the classic case. In Roe, an unmarried, pregnant woman challenged a Texas law that prohibited anyone from destroying a fetus except on "medical advice for the purpose of saving the life of the mother." The woman claimed that the law intruded upon her privacy by denying her the right to choose to terminate her pregnancy. Texas countered with the claim that the power to protect prenatal life constituted a compelling state interest. When the case reached the Court, the justices concluded that "the right of personal privacy includes the abortion decision, but that this right is not unqualified and must be considered against important state interests in regulation." The Court acknowledged that, at some point, "the woman's privacy is no longer sole and any right of privacy she possesses must be measured accordingly." The "compelling" point was at the end of the first trimester. From this point, a state could regulate abortion. In Roe, the Court declared the Texas law to be too broad because it failed to distinguish between abortions performed early and those performed later in pregnancy, and because the law banned abortion in all cases except those involving risk to the mother's life.

In Doe v. Bolton, 93 S.Ct. 739 (1973), an indigent, pregnant woman challenged the validity of Georgia's abortion statute. The law allowed abortion only in cases of danger to the woman's life, likelihood of a serious birth defect, or pregnancy that resulted from rape. Justice Harry Blackmun, writing for the Court, reaffirmed the position taken in Roe, noting that a pregnant woman did not possess an absolute constitutional right to an abortion on demand. The Court overturned the Georgia law, however, because of several faulty provisions — those requiring that abortions be conducted in hospitals, that abortions be approved by a hospital committee, that two other physicians confirm the finding of the pregnant women's doctor, and that abortions be available only to Georgia residents.

In Planned Parenthood of Central Missouri v. Danforth, 96 S.Ct. 2831 (1976), the Court analyzed and upheld several provisions of the Missouri abortion law. For example, the Court upheld the requirement that a woman must provide written consent prior to an abortion during the first trimester. In addition, records must be kept by physicians and health facilities that perform abortions. On the other hand, the Court declared some provisions unconstitutional. A state cannot require written consent of the spouse of a woman seeking an abortion, nor can it require consent of the parent of an unmarried woman under 18. In these situations, the abortion decision must be left to the medical judgement of the attending physician. In Planned Parenthood, the Court reinforced its Roe decision by holding that the abortion right "must be considered against important state interests."

Toward the end of the 1980s, pro-life groups crusaded ardently on behalf of the unborn child. They were optimistic when the Court heard a challenge to a Missouri anti-abortion statute. In Webster v. Reproductive Health Services, 109 S.Ct. 3040 (1989), the Court approved statutory restrictions on the use of public employees and facilities to perform non-therapeutic abortions. The Court, however, explicitly noted that Webster did not overrule Roe.

> Both appellants and the United States...have urged that we overrule our decision in Roe v. Wade. The facts of the present case, however, differ from those at issue in Roe. Here, Missouri has determined that viability is the point at which its interest in potential human life must be safeguarded. In Roe, on the other hand, the Texas statute criminalized the performance of *all* abortions, except when the mother's life was at stake. This case therefore affords us no occasion to revisit the holding in Roe.

Rust v. Sullivan, 111 S.Ct. 1759 (1991), afforded the Court another opportunity to restrict abortion, without overturning Roe. In 1988, the Secretary of Health and Human Services issued regulations that prohibited government-funded projects from suggesting abortion as a method of family planning. Fund recipients as well as doctors who supervised such projects filed suit, challenging the validity of the policy on the ground that it violates the First Amendment by imposing "viewpoint-discriminatory conditions on government subsidies." The Court, per Justice William Rehnquist, disagreed.

> Here the Government is exercising the authority it possesses...to subsidize family planning services which will lead to conception and childbirth, and declining to "promote or encourage abortion." The Government can, without violating the Constitution, selectively fund a program to encourage certain activities it believes to be in the public interest without at the same time funding an alternate program which seeks to deal with the problem in another way. In so doing, the Government has not discriminated on the basis of viewpoint; it has merely chosen to fund one activity to the exclusion of the other.

Pro-life supporters again had reason for optimism when the Court heard Planned Parenthood of Southeastern Pennsylvania v. Casey, 112 S.Ct. 2791 (1992), an examination of the Pennsylvania Abortion Control Act. The Court upheld three limitations on abortion — a woman must be provided with certain information at least 24 hours before the abortion is performed, a minor must obtain the informed consent of one parent, a married woman must notify her husband. Nonetheless, the Court affirmed the basic thrust of Roe.

> It must be stated at the outset and with clarity that Roe's essential holding, the holding we affirm, has three parts. First is a recognition of the right of the woman to choose to have an abortion before viability and to obtain it without undue interference from the State.... Second is a confirmation of the State's power to restrict abortions after fetal viability, if the law contains exceptions for pregnancies which endanger a woman's life or health. And third is the principle that the State has legitimate interests from the outset of the pregnancy in protecting the health of the woman and the life of the fetus that may become a child. These principles do not contradict one another; and we adhere to each.

In cases described in this section, the Supreme Court acknowledged that the government may play a role in regulating abortion. Accordingly, the Court upheld several statutory restrictions related to the abortion issue.

Appearance

Cases have dealt with personal aspects other than sexual mores. The <u>Kelley v. Johnson</u>, 96 S.Ct. 1440 (1976), case involved alleged intrusion concerning an individual's personal appearance. Police officers in Suffolk County, New York, were obligated to comply with grooming regulations which limited the length and appearance of hair, length and shape of sideburns, size and configuration of mustaches, and which prohibited beards, wigs, and hairpieces. A police officer initiated suit against the Commissioner of the Police Department. The suit argued that the grooming standards violated freedom of expression. The Supreme Court opinion, written by Justice Rehnquist, concluded that hair-grooming regulations did not deprive police officers of their constitutional rights. <u>Johnson</u>, as well as other cases cited in this section, indicates that freedom from intrusion is not absolute. Under certain conditions, the government can intrude into an individual's personal life-style.

Drug use

In <u>Chandler v. Miller</u>, 117 S.Ct. 1295 (1997), the Supreme Court protected personal freedom in overturning a policy designed to detect drug abuse. The Libertarian Party initiated court action, challenging a Georgia statute which required candidates for political office to certify that they had taken a urinalysis drug test within 30 days prior to qualifying for nomination and that the test result was negative. Writing for the majority, Justice Ruth Bader Ginsburg acknowledged that the law was motivated by Georgia's commitment to the struggle against drug abuse. The state, however, demonstrated no evidence of a drug problem among elected officials. Ginsburg decided that the law was "symbolic." She concluded that the constitution "shields society from state action that diminishes personal liberty for a symbol's sake."

PUBLIC DISCLOSURE

Invasion of privacy can involve the publication of truthful, private information about a person. Such information may concern tragedy, embarrassment, and intimacy. The most successful defense in such cases is a showing that the information is newsworthy, and of legitimate public interest.

TRAGEDY

In several cases, the courts rejected invasion-of-privacy suits that involved publication of photographs of victims who died as a result of accidents and injuries. The courts accepted the newspeople's defense because the photographs illustrated accurate news stories about events of legitimate public interest.

The Kelley v. Post Publishing Company, 98 N.E.2d 286 (1951), case began the day after the 15-year-old daughter of Mr. and Mrs. James Kelley was killed in an automobile accident, when a wide-circulation Boston newspaper printed an article about the accident. The story included a picture of the disfigured, dead body of the girl, referring to her as the daughter of the Kelleys. The parents sued, claiming an invasion of privacy that caused them to suffer bodily pain and mental anguish. The court recognized that the parents were obviously distressed and preferred to be spared the anguish of sensational publicity. The court also realized that if the Kelleys' claim was sustained, it would be difficult to fix the boundaries for news coverage.

> A newspaper account or a radio broadcast setting forth in detail the harrowing circumstances of the accident might well be as distressing to the members of the victim's family as a photograph of the sort described in the declaration. A newspaper could not safely publish the picture of a train wreck or of an airplane crash if any of the bodies of the victims were recognizable.

In this instance, the only reference to the Kelleys was that the girl whose body appeared in the photograph was their daughter. The court concluded that the publication of the photograph, while probably indelicate or lacking in good taste, did not constitute an actionable invasion of the Kelleys' privacy.

Costlow v. Cusimano, 311 N.Y.S.2d 92 (1970), is a similar case. Three-year-old Robert Costlow and his two-year-old sister Marion died by suffocation when they trapped themselves inside a refrigerator. Photographer Frederick Cusimano took pictures of the dead children and later published an article which he illustrated with the photographs. Mr. and Mrs. Robert Costlow initiated action, alleging an invasion of privacy. They claimed that Cusimano acted maliciously, with knowledge of the grief of the parents. The Costlows argued that they suffered severe mental anguish and emotional disturbance due to the publication of the photos. The court denied the invasion-of-privacy claim because the article, while unpleasant to the parents, was a matter of legitimate public interest. Furthermore, the cause of these deaths was brought to the attention of the public so that similar deaths might be prevented. The court found no actual malice; there was no evidence that the story falsely represented the actual occurrence. The court acknowledged that Cusimano probably exhibited his article with disregard for the emotional distress caused by the pictures but his main purpose was to make a profit and to enhance his professional reputation.

The complaint was dismissed.

In Jenkins v. Dell Publishing Company, 251 F.2d 447 (1958), the widow and children of David Jenkins, who had been kicked to death by the leader of a gang of teenagers, argued that an article and photograph about the incident, which appeared in Front Page Detective, invaded their privacy. The magazine publisher argued that the event was newsworthy. The court agreed. News consisted of "relatively current events such as in common experience are likely to be of public interest." The court noted:

> A large part of the matter which appears in newspapers and news magazines today is not published or read for the value or importance of the information it conveys. Some readers are attracted by shocking news. Others are titillated by sex in the news. Still others are entertained by news which has an incongruous or ironic aspect. Much news is in various ways amusing and for that reason of special interest to many people.

The court concluded that it was "neither feasible nor desirable" for a judicial body to "make a distinction between news for information and news for entertainment." The court sided with the publishing company.

A related case involved publication by a newspaper of the picture of a mass murder victim. Members of the victim's family initiated court action, claiming an invasion of privacy. The court noted that "although the caption accompanying the photograph...omits the name of the victim, few in our society would argue that publication and distribution of the photograph was not in poor taste, insensitive, and indelicate." However, the victim whose picture was published involuntarily became a legitimate subject of a newsworthy event and therefore the paper "clearly was authorized to publish the offending photograph on the ground that it involved a matter of legitimate public concern." The victim's family also argued that the "newsworthiness" defense was not available because the photograph resulted from a "blatant trespass." The court, however, noted that "the crime took place on public business premises, and news media personnel are customarily permitted access to such scenes whenever they involve events of great public concern." In Badger v. Courier Journal and Louisville Times Company, 20 Med. L. Rptr. 1189 (1991), the court sided with the press. In this case, as in Kelley, Costlow, and Jenkins, the court concluded that the tragic event was newsworthy.

EMBARRASSMENT

On several occasions, the courts have heard cases in which it was alleged that the publication of private information caused embarrassment. Daily Times Democrat v. Graham, 162 So.2d 474 (1964), is an example. Flora Graham, a middle-aged housewife, took her two sons to the county fair. Mrs. Graham accompanied the boys through the fun house, where her dress was blown up by ground-level air jets and her body was exposed from the waist down, with the exception of that portion covered by her underwear. At that moment, the photographer for the Daily Times Democrat snapped a picture of the situation. Four days later, the picture was published on the front page of the newspaper. Mrs. Graham sued, contending that this invasion of privacy was embarrassing. The Supreme Court of Alabama noted that an actionable invasion of one's privacy occurred upon "the wrongful intrusion into one's private activities, in such manner as to outrage or cause mental suffering, shame or humiliation to a person of ordinary sensibilities." An exception occurred in cases that involved the interest of the public to be informed. In Graham, the court stressed that "not only was this photograph embarrassing to one of normal sensibilities" but it also was "offensive to modesty or decency" and expressed "something which delicacy, purity, or decency forbid to be expressed." The court also argued:

> One who is a part of a public scene may be lawfully photographed as an accidental part of that scene in his ordinary status. Where the status he expects to occupy is changed without his volition to a status embarrassing to an ordinary person of reasonable sensitivity, then he should not be deemed to have forfeited his right to be protected from an indecent and vulgar intrusion of his right of privacy merely because misfortune overtakes him in a public place.

Jacova v. Southern Radio and Television Company, 83 S.2d 34 (1955), involved another alleged embarrassing invasion of privacy. In a newscast, a television station showed police raids on a hotel. Subsequently, John Jacova initiated a suit, claiming that his picture had been shown during the news film. Jacova said he was an innocent bystander. He was in the hotel during the time of the raid because he had stopped for a newspaper. The film showed Jacova standing against the wall with two men, presumably police officers, talking to him. While Jacova's picture was being shown an announcer said: "Carmen was arrested at his apartment by other officers. Then raiders visited the cigar shop of the Casablanca Hotel looking for a man reputedly accepting bets there." Jacova claimed that his right to privacy had been invaded. The station argued that since the telecast did not falsely depict Jacova as "being arrested as a gambler," it was privileged to publish his photograph because he became involved in a newsworthy event. The court agreed — a communication medium has a qualified privilege to use in its telecast the name or photograph of a person who had become an "actor" in a newsworthy event.

...certainly those of his friends and acquaintances who saw his picture on the screen would know that there was nothing sinister about his presence there. Further, the background of his picture clearly showed him to be at a newsstand and not at some residential apartment, and that he occupied the role that, in fact, was his. If not, a simple explanation by him would make this clear. We see nothing humiliating or embarrassing in such a role — shopping at a newsstand — nor anything that would offend a person of "ordinary sensibilities."

Williams v. KCMO Broadcasting Division, 472 S.W.2d 1 (1971), is a similar case. A Kansas City high-school student, Charles Williams, and five other youths were detained by police officers and searched with their hands against a police vehicle. News personnel for a local television station filmed the events. Williams was then booked at the police station and placed in a "line-up." He was released several hours later when police realized that he had not committed any crime. The film was shown on the evening newscast along with the following commentary:

> Kansas City police surrounded the Jackson County Court House today, and took six young men into custody following a search of the building. Three of them have since been released, but two adults and one juvenile remain in custody, and will be charged tomorrow in connection with last week's holdup of a finance company office.

Williams sued, charging that the film showed him in a humiliating position and that even though the event was a matter of legitimate public interest, his right of privacy had been invaded. The court noted that the newsperson's right to publicize matters of public interest applied "even though the individual publicized may have been drawn out of his seclusion and become involved in a noteworthy event involuntarily and against his will and over his protest." Matters concerning crime, police action, and apprehension of suspected criminals constitute proper public concern.

The court reached a similar decision in McNamara v. Freedom Newspapers, Inc., 802 S.W. 2d 901 (1991). The case involved Larry McNamara, a student whose genitalia could be seen in a photograph of two students running after a soccer ball during a high school game. He brought suit against the newspaper which published the photograph in conjunction with an article reporting on the game. McNamara argued that the newspaper violated the bounds of public decency and should have used one of its other numerous photographs in its article. The court sided with the press: "We hold that because the published photograph accurately depicts a public, newsworthy event, the First Amendment provides the Newspaper with immunity from its publication of McNamara's photograph." The court emphasized that a publication "does not lose its protected character simply because it may embarrass the persons to whom the publication refers." Unlike Graham, where there was no publication of a matter of legitimate public interest, McNamara was involved in a newsworthy event about which the public had a right to be informed. The court concluded that McNamara, for reasons like those stated in Jacova and Williams, had no cause for action against the newspaper.

INTIMACY

In Cox Broadcasting Corporation v. Cohn, 95 S.Ct. 1029 (1975), the Supreme Court heard arguments concerning the publication of private information which was of an intimate nature, but was already on the public record. The case involved the rape and murder of Martin Cohn's 17-year-old daughter. While covering the criminal proceedings against six youths who were indicted for the crime, a news reporter learned the victim's name by examining the indictments — public records available for inspection. He broadcast her name as part of a news report. In alleging that his privacy had been invaded, Cohn cited a Georgia law that makes it a misdemeanor to publicize the name of a rape victim. The Supreme Court decided that a state could not impose sanctions on the publication of the name of a rape victim obtained from records that were open to public inspection. The news media had great responsibility to report fully and accurately the proceedings of government. Concerning judicial matters in particular, "the function of the press serves to guarantee the fairness of trials and to bring to bear the beneficial effects of public scrutiny upon the administration of justice." The Court refused to uphold a system which made public records available to the media, but at the same time forbade their publication when offensive to the sensibilities of reasonable persons. Such a policy made it very difficult for the press to inform their readers about public events. According to the Court, "the prevailing law of invasion of privacy generally recognizes that the interests in privacy fade when the information involved already appears on the public record."

The Cox Broadcasting decision was applied in Howard v. Des Moines Register and Tribune Company, 283 N.W.2d 289 (1979). The case involved Robbin Howard who, while a minor confined in the Jasper County Home, was sterilized against her wishes. After her release from the home, she led a quiet life and made friends who were not aware of her surgery. Sometime later, the home's psychiatrist told a news reporter about the sterilization. She published this information in an article about the Jasper County Home. Howard initiated court action, charging that this article subjected her to public contempt, ridicule, humiliation, mental pain, and anguish. The court decided in favor of the newspaper on two grounds. First, the documents in question were public; the information they contained was in the public domain. As determined in Cox Broadcasting, there is no liability when a newspaper merely gives further publicity to information that is already public. Second, the information was newsworthy. It was vital to a thorough evaluation of the administration at Jasper Home.

> In the sense of serving an appropriate news function, the disclosure contributed constructively to the impact of the article. It offered a personalized frame of reference to which the reader could relate, fostering perception and understanding. Moreover, it lent specificity and credibility to the report.

Florida Star v. B. J. F., 109 S.Ct. 2603 (1989), is a related case. The Florida Star publishes a "Police Reports" section containing brief descriptions of local criminal incidents. A reporter went to the Police Department press room and copied the report of a robbery and sexual assault which identified the victim [B.J.F.] by her full name. Consequently, the name was included in the paper. B. J. F. filed suit, alleging that the newspaper had negligently violated a Florida statute which made it unlawful to publish the name of the victim of a sexual offense. The jury awarded B. J. F. compensatory and punitive damages. The verdict was appealed. The Supreme Court noted that "if a newspaper lawfully obtains truthful information about a matter of public significance then state officials may not constitutionally punish publication of that information absent a need to further a state interest of the highest order." In this case, the Star lawfully obtained the information; B. J. F.'s identity would never have come to light were it not for the inadvertent inclusion of her name in a report made available in a press room open to the public. Also, imposing liability on the Star would not serve a state interest of the highest order. Justice Thurgood Marshall claimed:

> Where, as here, the government has failed to police itself in disseminating information, it is clear under Cox Broadcasting...that the imposition of damages against the press for its subsequent publication can hardly be said to be a narrowly tailored means of safeguarding anonymity.

The Florida Star decision was cited in Macon Telegraph Publishing Company v. Tatum, 436 S.E.2d 655 (1993). The court action was filed by Nancy Tatum, who killed a man with a shotgun after he broke into her home. After investigating the incident, the police concluded that the killing was in self-defense. The investigating officers gave Tatum's name to two news reporters but admonished them not to publish it. Disregarding that advice, the reporter identified Tatum and the street where she lived in an article reporting the break-in and shooting. Tatum sued the newspaper for invasion of privacy. A jury awarded her $30,000 in compensatory damages and $70,000 in punitive damages. That decision was reversed. The court held:

> Under the facts of this case, we hold that Tatum, who committed a homicide, however justified, lost her right to keep her name private. When she shot Hill [the deceased], Tatum became the object of a legitimate public interest and the newspaper had the right under the Federal and State Constitutions to accurately report the facts regarding the incident, including her name.

FALSE LIGHT

Publication of false information about a person, whether the material is defamatory or not, can constitute an invasion of privacy. There are two components to false-light cases — fictionalization and actual malice.

FICTIONALIZATION

Fictionalization usually involves a writer who exaggerates while dramatizing a true happening. Strickler V. National Broadcasting Company, 167 F.Supp. 68 (1958), illustrates this form of invasion of privacy. Kenneth Strickler, a Commander on active duty with the U.S. Navy, was a passenger on a commercial airliner that developed engine trouble and was forced to make an emergency landing. Strickler and other passengers were rescued by a Coast Guard cutter. NBC telecast a show depicting in dramatized form Strickler's experiences. He claimed that the telecast, made without his consent, contained inaccuracies. He alleged that the program portrayed him in the highly personal act of praying during the emergency landing, that it showed him out of uniform and wearing a Hawaiian shirt, that it depicted him as smoking cigarettes, and that the program did not reflect the valuable assistance he provided in the evacuation of the plane. Strickler claimed that he was placed in a false light by the telecast and that as a result he experienced humiliation, embarrassment, and great mental pain and suffering. In Strickler, the court ruled that the network had embellished the incident in such a way as to constitute sufficient fictionalization to warrant an invasion of privacy.

Aquino v. Bulletin Company, 190 Pa. Super 528 (1959), is another case involving fictionalization. The case began when the daughter of Michael and Nancy Aquino secretly married a young man before a justice of the peace. The man promised the daughter that at a later date he would provide a home for her and marry her in a church. Later, the man said that he did not intend to keep his promises and that he had married the daughter only to spite her parents, who had opposed their courtship. The news media published several stories regarding both the marriage and subsequent divorce. The Aquinos initiated an invasion-of-privacy suit. The judge noted that the marriage and the divorce were newsworthy events; newspapers had a right to publish such information. The article in question, however, was in the form of a story, not a news article. It was in a Sunday supplement and not in the news section. It was bedecked with an "illustrated" drawing covering half of the page. The illustrated figures bore no resemblance to the daughter and the young man. According to the court, the author had allowed his imagination to roam through the facts so that "newsworthy events were presented in a style used almost exclusively by writers of fiction." Although the basic facts of the story were true, the author had fictionalized them.

The Carlisle v. Fawcett Publications, 20 Cal. Rptr. 405 (1962), case acknowledged that minor fictionalization does not constitute an invasion of privacy. An article in Motion Picture magazine described actress Janet Leigh's hasty marriage and eventual annulment. John Carlisle, the male party to the marriage, initiated action for invasion of privacy. The court noted that public figures, including actresses, have to some extent lost their right of privacy. Furthermore, people closely associated with such public figures "also to some extent lose their right to privacy that one unconnected with the famous or notorious would have." Carlisle claimed that the article contained errors, the two principal ones being that the date of the marriage was put back approximately a year to the attack at Pearl Harbor, and the age of the actress at the time of the marriage was reduced a year. These elements were altered, apparently for dramatic effect. According to the court, the mere fact that there were errors in the account did not constitute an invasion of privacy. Carlisle also contended that the article was fictionalized; it was not restricted to a "cold recital of the skeletal fact of the marriage and the annulment, but fills in the gaps with the supposed conversations and thoughts of the participants." The court disagreed: The article contained no "so-called revelations of any intimate details that would tend to outrage public [decency]." The circumstances in Carlisle differed considerably from those in Strickler and Aquino. In Carlisle, the fictionalization was minor and did not constitute an invasion of privacy.

The court reached a similar conclusion in Rinsley v. Brandt, 700 F.2d 1304 (1983), a case initiated by a man who claimed that certain statements in a book placed him in a false light. The court held that "the difference between the meaning conveyed and the actual truth is simply too slight to be actionable. To the author, and to many lay people, no doubt, the technical difference between 'instituting' a suit and going to see a lawyer about filing a suit is insignificant." The statement involved nothing more than minor fictionalization.

ACTUAL MALICE

In Time v. Hill, 87 S.Ct. 534 (1967), the Supreme Court ruled that the First Amendment does not shield the press from invasion-of-privacy suits involving matters of public interest when there is proof of "actual malice." The James Hill family became a front-page news story after being held hostage by three escaped convicts in their suburban home in Whitemarch, Pennsylvania, during September, 1952. The family was eventually released unharmed. In an interview with newsmen, Hill indicated that the convicts had treated the family courteously. Hill sought to keep his family out of the public eye by declining interviews with magazine writers and appearances on television. In an attempt to preserve their privacy, the family moved to Connecticut. In 1953, Joseph Hayes published The Desperate Hours, a novel depicting the experience of a family of four, held hostage by three escaped convicts in the family's suburban home. Contrary to Hill's experience, in Hayes' story the father and son are beaten and the daughter is subjected to verbal sexual assault. The book was made into a play, which was also entitled The Desperate Hours. In February, 1955, an article appeared in Life magazine which claimed that the Hill family had experienced a "desperate ordeal" by being held prisoners by three escaped convicts. The article noted that people throughout the country

> ...read about it in Joseph Hayes' novel, The Desperate Hours, inspired by the family's experience. Now they can see the story re-enacted in Hayes' Broadway play, based on the book, and the next year will see it in his movie, which has been filmed but is being held up until the play has had a chance to pay off.

The article described the play as "a heart-stopping account of how a family rose to heroism in a crisis." Life claimed to transport "some of the actors to the actual house where the Hills were besieged." Pictures on the following two pages included an enactment of the son being "roughed up" by one of the convicts, a picture of the "daring daughter" biting the hand of a convict to make him drop a gun, and a picture of the father throwing his gun through the door after a "brave try" to save his family is foiled. Hill sued on the ground that the article knowingly and falsely gave the impression that the play portrayed the Hill family experience. Attorneys for Life argued that the article concerned a topic of legitimate news interest and that it was "published in good faith without any malice whatsoever." The justices sided with the press.

The subject of the article — the opening of the new play — was a matter of public interest. The Court felt that sanctions against either innocent or negligent misstatements would instill in the press a fear of large verdicts in damage suits, which would inevitably cause publishers to "steer wider of the unlawful zone" and thus "create the danger that the legitimate utterance will be penalized." The Court concluded that the First Amendment shields the press from invasion-of-privacy suits involving matters of public interest unless there is proof of actual malice, that is, proof that the material was published with deliberate falsehood or reckless disregard of the truth. In Hill, such proof was absent. In subsequent cases, such proof was evident.

Varnish v. Best Medium Publishing Company, 405 F.2d. 608 (1968), provides an example. In 1963, Melvin Varnish's wife killed their three young children, and committed suicide. A few months later, an article entitled "'Happiest Mother' Kills Her Three Children and Herself" appeared in The National Enquirer. Varnish initiated an invasion-of-privacy suit, claiming that the portrayal of his wife and his relationship with her was fictionalized and placed him in a false and unfavorable light. He claimed that the "happy wife and mother" theme used throughout the article was fictitious and was intended, through the use or irony, to indicate Varnish's insensitivity and lack of caring for his wife. Varnish also claimed that, as a result of the article, he attempted suicide, required psychiatric attention, was unemployed, was shunned in his community, and became the victim of severe mental suffering. The case was tried before a jury, which awarded $5,000 compensatory and $15,000 punitive damages. The case was appealed. The judges found actual malice. The record showed that Mrs. Varnish was a despondent, depressed, and extremely unhappy woman. A suicide note addressed to her mother expressed her extreme unhappiness. The court noted that the article "presented a substantially false and distorted picture." It found sufficient evidence of recklessness because of the author's testimony that he had no basis except his own "presumption" for labeling Mrs. Varnish a happy wife and mother. Both the suicide note and the police reports, which the author had in his possession, indicated that the Varnishes did not have a happy home life. The article "was published with knowledge that it was false, or in reckless disregard for the truth." In Varnish, the Supreme Court denied certiorari.

In Cantrell v. Forest City Publishing Company, 95 S.Ct. 465 (1974), the Court determined that a reporter, through actual malice, had placed a family in a false light. In 1967, Margaret Cantrell's husband Melvin was killed, along with 43 other people, when a bridge collapsed. Joseph Eszterhas, a reporter for the Cleveland Plain Dealer, wrote a "news feature" that focused on the funeral of Melvin Cantrell and the impact his death had on the Cantrell family. Five months later, Eszterhas and a photographer returned to write a follow-up feature. Mrs. Cantrell was not at home, so the men talked with the Cantrell children and took 50 pictures. An article appeared in the Sunday magazine section of the newspaper. Mrs. Cantrell brought action for invasion of privacy; she claimed that the article placed the family in a false light through its many inaccuracies. For example, although Mrs. Cantrell was not present during the reporter's visit, Eszterhas wrote:

> Margaret Cantrell will talk neither about what happened nor about how they are doing. She wears the same mask of non-expression she wore at the funeral. She is a proud woman. She says that after it happened, the people in town offered to help them out with money but they refused to take it.

Other misrepresentations involved descriptions of the alleged poverty in which the Cantrells were living and the dirty and dilapidated condition of the Cantrell home. Mrs. Cantrell claimed the story made the family objects of pity and ridicule and caused them to suffer outrage, mental distress, shame, and humiliation. The jury returned a verdict against the paper, the reporter, and the photographer for compensatory damages. The Supreme Court, per Justice Potter Stewart, found actual malice in the actions of the reporter; Eszterhas must have known that a number of the statements in the story were untrue. His article implied that Mrs. Cantrell had been present during his visit to her home and that Eszterhas had observed her wearing "the same mask of non-expression" she wore at her husband's funeral. These were "calculated falsehoods." The jury was correct in finding that Eszterhas had portrayed the Cantrells in a false light through knowing or reckless untruth. In Cantrell, as in Varnish, the Court was willing to punish a publication that placed an individual in a false light through actual malice.

APPROPRIATION

Appropriation involves taking an individual's name, picture, photograph, or likeness without that person's permission and using it for commercial gain. It may take the form of advertising or publicity.

ADVERTISING

In most states, laws forbid using the name or picture of any living person for advertising purposes without obtaining consent from that person. Over the years, the courts have heard several cases involving alleged violations of such laws. In Sarat Lahiri v. Daily Mirror, 295 N.Y.S. 382 (1937), a court set forth guidelines concerning the use of photographs in newspaper advertising. The case involved a feature article about rope tricks performed by Hindu mystics. The article claimed that mystics, through hypnotic powers and the creation of an illusion, convinced viewers that the rope was rising into the air, when, in fact, it remained coiled upon the ground. The article was illustrated by several color photographs. One pictured Sarat Lahiri, a well-known Hindu musician, playing a musical instrument as accompaniment for a female Indian dancer. Lahiri initiated court action, claiming invasion of privacy. In Sarat Lahiri, the court set forth specific rules applicable to unauthorized publication of photographs in a single issue of a newspaper. The court determined that it was illegal to publish, without permission, a photograph as part of an advertisement, or to use such a photograph with a fictional article. It was, however, legal to publish a photograph in connection with an article of current news or public interest. Regarding Lahiri's claim, the court noted that the article concerned a legitimate news interest. A British society had offered a substantial prize to any person who was able to perform the famous rope trick. The author explained how the trick was allegedly performed in India and discussed the possibility that the society would have to pay the prize. The only issue was whether the picture had too tenuous a connection with the article. The court decided that the photograph illustrated one of the points made by the author — the mystical quality of the East. In the court's opinion, "it would be far-fetched to hold in this case that the picture was not used in an illustrative sense, but merely to promote the sale of the paper."

Another case involved actress Shirley Booth. While Miss Booth was vacationing at a prominent resort in Jamaica, a photographer for Holiday magazine took photographs to use with an article concerning the resort and its guests. Booth was photographed, to her knowledge, and without her objection. Booth, however, never gave written consent for publication. When the article appeared, a photograph showing Booth in the water up to her neck, wearing a brimmed, high-crowned street hat of straw, was given a prominent place in the story. This publication did not violate Booth's right of privacy because this was reproduction for news purposes. A few months later, Curtis Publishing Company reproduced the same photograph in a full-page advertisement. The ad presented Booth's photograph as a sample of the content of Holiday. Booth initiated court action, claiming that the procedure violated the privacy statute. The issue facing the court was whether a person's photograph, originally published in one issue of a periodical as a newsworthy subject, may be republished later as an advertisement for the periodical itself. The court noted that "contemporaneous or proximate advertising of the news medium, by way of extract, cover, dust jacket, or poster, using relevant but otherwise personal matter, does not violate the statute." In Booth v. Curtis Publishing Company, 15 A.D.2d 343 (1962), the court found "that so long as the reproduction was used to illustrate the quality and content of the periodical in which it originally appeared, the statute was not violated."

The Booth decision was applied in Namath v. Sports Illustrated, 363 N.Y.S.2d 276 (1975). In January, 1969, Sports Illustrated published newsworthy photographs of Joe Namath, star quarterback of the New York Jets. Three years later, Namath initiated an invasion-of-privacy suit, charging that the magazine had used these photographs in an advertising campaign designed to promote subscriptions. Namath argued that the magazine should not be permitted to use his name or photograph without consent and without remuneration. The court cited Booth, noting that as far as advertising is concerned, the "incidental use of a name or likeness" is not actionable.

> It is understandable that plaintiff [Namath] desires payment for the use of his name and likeness in advertisements for the sale of publications in which he has appeared as newsworthy just as he is paid for collateral endorsement of commercial products. This he cannot accomplish under the existing law of our State and Nation.

In Palmer v. Schonhorn Enterprises, 232 A.2d 458 (1967), the court granted relief to plaintiffs whose names and accomplishments had been used for financial gain. The case involved action by professional golfers who objected to the use of their names for marketing the Pro-Am Golf Game. The contents of the game included 23 sheets of paper, each of which contained the name of a well-known professional golfer, accompanied by a short biography. Each of the sheets contained accurate facts concerning the golfer's professional career. Arnold Palmer, Gary Player, Doug Sanders, and Jack Nicklaus, all of whom had never given permission for the use of their profiles by the company, sought an injunction. The golfers claimed that such use constituted an invasion of their privacy. The judges noted that the use of the names and biographies enhanced the marketability of the game. The company argued that the golfers "waived their rights of privacy because of their being well-known athletes who have deliberately invited publicity in furtherance of their careers." Since the data contained in the profiles were readily obtained public information, the company should be allowed to reproduce it. The court disagreed:

> Although the publication of biographical data of a well-known figure does not *per se* constitute an invasion of privacy, the use of that same data for the purpose of a commercial project other than the dissemination of news or articles or biographies does.

According to the court, it was unfair for a company to commercialize, exploit, or capitalize upon a person's name, reputation, or accomplishments merely because the accomplishments had been highly publicized.

A similar case involved action by professional baseball players who objected to the use of their names in the marketing of games. The games used statistical information, such as batting, fielding, earned run, and other averages of some 500 to 700 major-league players, identified by team, uniform number, and playing position. The players had not given permission for the use of their names or statistics. The Association of Major League Baseball Players sought an injunction, claiming that the company was guilty of "misappropriation and use for commercial profit of the names of professional major league baseball players without the payment of royalties." The court supported the legitimate interest a celebrity has in his public personality.

> A celebrity must be considered to have invested his years of practice and competition in a public personality which eventually may reach marketable status. That identity, embodied in his name, likeness, statistics and other personal characteristics, is the fruit of his labors and is a type of property.

In Uhlaender v. Henricksen, 316 F.Supp. 1277 (1970), the court determined that the defendants violated the athletes' "rights by the unauthorized appropriation of their names and statistics for commercial use."

A judgement for the plaintiff was also granted in Onassis v. Christian Dior-New York, Inc., 472 N.Y.S. 254 (1984). Well-known personality Jacqueline Onassis was granted an injunction to prohibit the use and distribution of a magazine advertisement containing a picture of a "look-alike" model. The court held that the ad was an appropriation without consent of Onassis' "portrait or picture" even though the picture was not of Onassis herself.

A similar case, Midler v. Ford Motor Company, 849 F.2d 460 (1988), involved an advertisement performed by a "sound alike" singer. When nationally known actress and singer Bette Midler turned down an offer to sing an edited version of one of her popular songs in an automobile commercial, the Ford Company turned to a singer who was told to "sound as much as possible like the Bette Midler record." After the commercial was aired, containing no use of Midler's name or picture, the entertainer initiated court action. In upholding Midler's claim of appropriation for commercial gain, the court stated:

> A voice is as distinctive and personal as a face. The human voice is one of the most palpable ways identity is manifested. We are all aware that a friend is at once known by a few words on the phone....
> A fortiori, these observations hold true of singing, especially singing by a singer of renown. The singer manifests herself in the song. To impersonate her voice is to pirate her identity.

In <u>Midler</u>, as in <u>Palmer</u>, <u>Uhlaender</u> and <u>Onassis</u>, the court protected a celebrity whose name, accomplishments, and/or likeness was used for commercial gain.

PUBLICITY

In several cases, the courts have considered whether a celebrity has the right to control his or her own publicity. <u>Paulsen v. Personality Posters</u>, 299 N.Y.S.2d 501 (1968), provides an example. Pat Paulsen, a well-known television comedian, conducted a mock campaign prior to the 1968 presidential election. Claiming to be the "Put-On Presidential Candidate of 1968," Paulsen ran under the banner of the Stag Party. Paulsen's satirical comments on various issues were aired with regularity on the nationally televised "Smothers Brothers" program. Paulsen received several votes in primary elections, and he participated in activities traditionally associated with political campaigning. In conjunction with this comedy routine, Paulsen granted an exclusive license to a company in connection with all campaign buttons, stickers, and posters relating to the "Pat Paulsen for President" campaign. Without obtaining Paulsen's permission, another company prepared for sale an enlargement of a photograph of Paulsen. Paulsen initiated action, claiming that distribution of the posters invaded his right of privacy. In <u>Paulsen</u>, the court noted that the privacy statute was not intended to limit the dissemination of news of public interest. Even though Paulsen was "only kidding," and his presidential activities were really only a "publicity stunt," they fell within the scope of constitutionally-protected matters of public interest. According to the court, "when a well-known entertainer enters the presidential ring, tongue in cheek or otherwise, it is clearly newsworthy and of public interest." The poster, which reflected the spirit in which Paulsen approached the role, was a form of public-interest presentation entitled to constitutional protection. The court noted that Paulsen was less concerned with the "right of privacy" than with the "right of publicity" — that is, the ability to control the financial benefits that attach to a person's name and picture. The court ruled that the right of publicity had no application in this case, which involved a matter of public interest. The use of the poster was constitutionally protected and superseded any privacy or publicity claims.

In 1970, the courts heard a similar case involving the right of publicity. Frank Man, a professional musician, mounted the stage at the Woodstock Festival in August, 1969, and played "Mess Call" on his flugelhorn before 400,000 people. The festival was of wide public interest and was extensively reported in news media. Over 120 hours of sound track and motion pictures of the event were recorded and later reduced to a length suitable for exhibition as a motion picture in theatres under the title "Woodstock." Man brought action, claiming that the producers of the film included his performance in the film without his consent, thereby violating his right to privacy. According to the court in Man v. Warner Brothers, 317 F.Supp. 50 (1970), "there can be no question that the Woodstock Festival was and is a matter of valid public interest." Furthermore, the New York privacy statute was never intended to apply to professional entertainers who are shown giving a performance before a public audience. Man placed himself in the spotlight of a sensational event that exposed him to publicity. That fact alone made him newsworthy and deprived him of any right to complain of a violation of his privacy.

Carson v. Here's Johnny Portable Toilets, Inc., 698 F.2d 831 (1983), also involved the publicity issue, but this time the court favored the plaintiff. The case dealt with the question of whether a celebrity's name or picture had to be used in an actionable invasion of privacy. Entertainer Johnny Carson, who used the phrase "Here's Johnny" as a method of introduction on "The Tonight Show," brought suit against a corporation engaged in renting and selling "Here's Johnny" portable toilets. The court sided with Carson: "If a celebrity's identity is commercially exploited, there has been an invasion of his right whether or not his 'name or likeness' is used. Carson's identity may be exploited even if his name...or his picture is not used."

In two cases, Lugosi v. Universal Pictures Company, 172 U.S.P.Q. 541 (1972), and Price v. Hal Roach Studios, 400 F.Supp. 836 (1975), the courts considered whether the right to control publicity terminates at death. The cases involved lawsuits claiming wrongful appropriation of the names, likenesses, and characterizations of film stars Bella Lugosi, Oliver Hardy, and Stanley Laurel. The suits were initiated by the beneficiaries of the wills of the deceased actors. The courts differentiated between two concepts — the right of privacy, which terminates upon death, and the right of publicity, which does not terminate upon death. Both courts decided in favor of the beneficiaries of the wills. The Lugosi opinion noted: "Bella Lugosi's interest or right in his likeness and appearance as Count Dracula was a property right of such character and substance that it did not terminate with his death but descended to his heirs." The Price decision claimed: "The present case [involving Laurel and Hardy] is easier to decide than Lugosi since we deal here with actors portraying themselves and developing their own characters rather than fictional characters which have been given a particular interpretation by an actor." These have been given a particular interpretation by an actor." These opinions recognize a distinction between termination of a right to privacy at death and survival of a right of publicity.

In Zacchini v. Scripps-Howard Broadcasting Company, 97 S.Ct. 2849 (1977), the Supreme Court upheld the right of a celebrity to control his own publicity. Hugo Zacchini performed a "human cannonball" act in which he was shot from a cannon into a net some 200 feet away. Zacchini performed his act on a regular basis at a county fair. The public was not charged a separate fee to observe his act. A television reporter videotaped the entire act even though Zacchini had asked him not to do so. This film clip, approximately 15 seconds in length, was shown on the news program that evening, along with favorable commentary. Zacchini brought action, alleging that the station "showed and commercialized the film of his act without his consent" and that such conduct constituted an "unlawful appropriation of plaintiff's professional property." Before the Supreme Court, Zacchini acknowledged that his appearance at the fair and his performance could be reported by the press as newsworthy items. He complained, however, that the reporter filmed and showed his entire act. This was an appropriation of his professional property. The Court noted that the broadcast of a film of Zacchini's entire performance posed a substantial threat to the economic value of that performance. Much of its economic value stemmed from the "right of exclusive control over the publicity given to his performance"; if the public could see the act free on television, they would be less willing to pay to see it performed elsewhere.

> There is no doubt that entertainment, as well as news, enjoys First Amendment protection. It is also true that entertainment itself can be important news.... But it is important to note that neither the public nor respondent will be deprived of the benefit of petitioner's performance as long as his commercial stake in his act is appropriately recognized. Petitioner does not seek to enjoin the broadcast of his performance; he simply wants to be paid for it.

In Zacchini, the Court recognized the right of celebrities to control their own publicity. Yet, as was demonstrated in Paulsen and Man, when a celebrity engages in an activity of legitimate public interest, that celebrity surrenders the right to control his or her own publicity regarding that activity.

CONCLUSION

The following principles regulate communication law regarding PRIVACY:

1. The courts have recognized the following types of invasion of privacy:
   a. intrusion of physical solitude,
   b. public disclosure of private facts,
   c. placing an individual in a false light in the public eye,
   d. appropriation of some element of an individual's personality for commercial use.

2. The courts have recognized the following defenses:
   a. newsworthiness or public interest,
   b. consent,
   c. information already on the public record,
   d. lack of actual malice (applicable in false light cases).

NOTES

1. Warren, Samuel D., and Louis D. Brandeis, "The Right to Privacy," Harvard Law Review 4 (December 15, 1890), 193-200.

2. Prosser, William L., "Privacy," California Law Review 48 (August, 1960), 383-423.

KEY DECISIONS

1965 — GRISWOLD — overturned a law that prohibited the advising of persons concerning the use of contraceptives; such a law intruded upon the privacy of the marriage relationship

1967 — HILL — ruled that the First Amendment shields the press from invasion of privacy suits involving matters of public interest, unless there is proof of "actual malice"

1972 — EISENSTADT — extended the Griswold rule to unmarried persons

1973 — ROE — acknowledged that even though the right of personal privacy includes the abortion decision, the government may play a role in regulating the abortion issue

1974 — CANTRELL — punished a reporter who, through actual malice, placed an individual in a false light

1975 — <u>COHN</u> — acknowledged that the interests in preserving privacy fade when the information involved already appears on the public record

1977 — <u>ZACCHINI</u> — upheld the right of a celebrity to control his or her own publicity

1989 — <u>FLORIDA STAR</u> — recognized press' immunity from punishment for truthful publication of lawfully-obtained newsworthy information

1999 — <u>WILSON</u> — determined that media personnel may not "ride along" with police officers to observe and report the execution of an arrest warrant at a private home

RECOMMENDED READING

Barinholtz, Aloe, "False Light Invasion of Privacy: False Tort?" <u>Southwestern University Law Review</u> 17 (1987): 135-85.

Emerson, Thomas I., "The Right of Privacy and Freedom of the Press," <u>Harvard Civil Rights —Civil Liberties Law Review</u> 14 (1979), 329-360.

Franklin, Kenneth, "Invasion of Privacy: False Light Offers False Hope," <u>Loyola Entertainment Law Journal</u> 8 (1988), 411-27.

Gormley, Ken, "One Hundred Years of Privacy," <u>Wisconsin Law Review</u> (1992), 1335-1441.

Haines, James Barr, "Developments in the Right of Publicity," <u>Annual Survey of American Law</u> (1989), 211-243.

Halpern, Sheldon W., and Robert A. Booth, <u>The Law of Defamation, Privacy, Publicity and 'Moral Rights': Case & Materials on Protection of Personality Interests</u>. New York: Amnesty International Publications, 1988.

Lasswell, Byran R., "In Defense of False Light: Why False Light Must Remain A Viable Cause of Action," <u>South Texas Law Review</u> 34 (1993), 149-179.

McKeever, Joyce, "Right to Privacy: Publication of True Information on the Public Record," <u>Duquesne Law Review</u> 14 (Spring, 1976), 507-20.

Pember, Don R., <u>Privacy and the Press: The Law, the Mass Media, and the First Amendment</u>. Seattle: University of Washington Press, 1972.

Sanford, Bruce W., *et. al.*, <u>Libel and Privacy</u> Englewood Cliffs, N.J.: Prentice Hall, 2nd Ed., 1991.

Zuckman, Harvey L., "Invasion of Privacy — Some Communicative Torts Whose Time Has Gone," <u>Washington and Lee Law Review</u> 47 (1990), 253-265.

CHAPTER 9

COPYRIGHT

Copyright law enables an author, artist, or composer to protect his or her work against plagiarism. This legal guarantee is subject to conflicting interpretation, which has sometimes been resolved in the courts. In this chapter, the history of copyright law, tests of infringement, and guidelines for "fair use" will be considered in light of judicial interpretation.

HISTORY OF COPYRIGHT LAW

In 1710, the English Parliament passed the Statute of Eight Anne, a law that granted authors exclusive right to their works, and restricted unauthorized reproduction and distribution of those works. Under this system authors were encouraged to write, safe in the knowledge that their creative efforts would be protected. The first copyright law adopted in the United States closely resembled the British statute. U.S. copyright law has had two historical sources — statutory and common law.

STATUTORY COPYRIGHT

Article 1, Section 8, of the Constitution provides the fundamental authority for copyright law. It gives Congress power "to promote the Progress of Science and useful Arts, by securing for limited Times to Authors and Inventors the exclusive Right to their respective Writings and Discoveries." Accordingly, Congress has enacted three copyright statutes — in 1790, 1909, and 1976.

The 1790 Copyright Act provided that any author of a map, chart, or book could control the right to publish and sell the work. The term of the copyright was 14 years, plus possible renewal for another 14-year term. In order to copyright a work, the title had to be deposited in the clerk's office of the district court where the author lived, for a fee of 60 cents. The author had to publish a copy of the record in a newspaper, and deposit a copy of the record with the Secretary of State. Any violation was subject to penalties which included forfeiture of all copies, and a fine of 50 cents per page. Half of the fine was given to the copyright owner and the other half was retained by the government. Court action had to begin within one year of the violation. Over the next century, the law was amended to provide protection to prints, musical compositions, photographs, and works of fine art. The term of protection was lengthened to 28 years, plus a renewal period of an additional 14 years.

In 1909, Congress revised the law. Copyrightable material included original books, periodicals, lectures, dramas, musical compositions, maps, works of art, reproductions, scientific drawings, photographs, prints, and motion pictures. Application for copyright had to be made to the Registrar of Copyrights in Washington, D.C. Two copies "of the best edition" of the work had to be "promptly deposited in the copyright office." The application fee for registration was six dollars. A published work had to contain a notice of copyright in the form of the symbol ©, the word "copyright," or the abbreviation "copr." It also included the name of the copyright owner and the date of publication. The original copyright period remained 28 years, but the renewal period was increased to an additional 28 years. Punitive damages for infringement were fixed; the minimum amount was $250 and the maximum was $5,000. In addition, the Act allowed a person to use copyrighted works without obtaining permission, so long as the use constituted a "fair use." Between 1909 and 1976, technological advancements produced minor amendments to the law — radio, film, tape recorders, television, computers, photocopying, cable television, and satellite communication systems came within the scope of copyright law.

The 1976 law provided some significant revisions. The 1909 Act provided that unpublished works were protected by common law; the 1976 Act discontinued that form of protection, but provides federal statutory protection from the time the work is fixed in a "tangible form." A work is "fixed in a tangible medium when it is sufficiently permanent or stable to permit it to be perceived, reproduced or otherwise communicated for a period of more than transitory duration." Under this law, unpublished works are entitled to statutory copyright. Unlike earlier statutes, the 1976 law protects the copyright even if publication occurs without notice. The 1976 law also established a

single term of copyright, the author's lifetime plus 50 years. The fee for registration of most works was established at ten dollars. The copyright owner has up to five years to register. The law clarified the doctrine of fair use, indicating that reproduction "for purposes such as criticism, comment, news reporting, teaching [including multiple copies for classroom use], scholarship, or research, is not an infringement of copyright." The act set forth the following criteria to help the courts determine whether a use is a "fair use":
1. the purpose and character of the use,
2. the nature of the copyrighted work,
3. the amount used,
4. the effect upon the value of the copyrighted work.
The 1976 law also set damages for infringement at not less than $250 and not more than $10,000. If, however, infringement was committed "willfully," the amount could be increased to as much as $50,000. If the infringer demonstrated that he or she was unaware that the act was an infringement, the fine could be as low as $100. In addition, the law specifies that the award may include recovery of actual damages, infringed profits, and attorney's fees. The courts have wide discretion on these matters.

In October, 1998, President Bill Clinton signed the Sonny Bono Copyright Extension Act which extended the length of copyright to the life of the author plus 70 years — 20 years beyond the time provided by the Act of 1976. The Bono Act also extended to 95 years the copyright on works created before the 1976 Copyright Act became effective.

COMMON-LAW COPYRIGHT

The 1976 Copyright Act provides for the termination of common-law copyright, which prior to that time had played a vital role in protecting an author's work. Under common-law copyright, automatic protection existed as soon as an author created a work, and it lasted as long as the work remained unpublished. It was especially useful for authors who chose not to publish their work. Common-law copyright was recognized by the courts in Chamberlain v. Feldman, 300 N.Y. 135 (1949). The focus of the alleged infringement was a story which was written by Samuel Clemens under the pen name Mark Twain. When Clemens died in 1910, the manuscript of the unpublished story was not found among his effects. In 1945, Lew Feldman bought the original manuscript at an auction. Feldman contacted Thomas Chamberlain, the owner of all Clemens' property, seeking permission to publish the story. When Chamberlain refused, Feldman started court action. The judge noted that, in Clemens' lifetime, the manuscript had been rejected for publication by the Atlantic Monthly and it could be inferred that Clemens decided that the manuscript was unsuitable for publication. Thus, Clemens never granted anyone the literary property.

> The common-law copyright, or right of first publication, is a right different from that of ownership of the physical paper; the first of those rights does not necessarily pass with the second; and the separate common law copyright or control of the right to reproduce belongs to the artist or author until disposed of by him.

The court decided that Clemens had never parted with the publication rights to the story. No matter how the manuscript left Clemens' possession, he apparently never intended that it be published. Therefore, Feldman had not purchased the publication rights when he bought the original manuscript.

In Estate of Hemingway v. Random House, 23 N.Y.2d 341 (1968), the courts again examined the nature of common-law copyright. During the 13 years prior to his death, Ernest Hemingway formed a close friendship with a young writer, A.E. Hotchner. In conversations with Hotchner, Hemingway revealed personal reminiscences which the young man carefully recorded on tape and on notecards. With Hemingway's approval, Hotchner wrote several articles in which he quoted material from the conversations. After Hemingway died, Hotchner authored Papa Hemingway, a biography which relied heavily on the conversations. The Hemingway family sued, alleging that Papa Hemingway consisted mainly of literary matter composed by Hemingway, in which he retained common-law copyright. A key issue in the Estate of Hemingway case was whether the common-law copyright extended to conversational speech. It had become a continuing practice in Hemingway's later years for Hotchner to write stories about Hemingway, approved by Hemingway, which were based largely on conversations between the two men. Under such circumstances, authority to publish was implied, thus negating any common-law copyright. The judge noted that it was possible for a speaker to reserve the common-law copyright — it could be stated in prefatory words or inferred from the circumstances in which the dialogue took place. In this case, Hemingway's words and behavior, "far from making any such reservation, left no doubt of his willingness to permit Hotchner to draw freely on their conversation in writing about him and to publish such material." In Estate of Hemingway and Chamberlain, the court acknowledged that works of authors, written and spoken, were entitled to common-law copyright. Such protection, however, is no longer available under the 1976 copyright statute.

TESTS OF INFRINGEMENT

The 1976 Copyright Act states that "anyone who violates any of the exclusive rights of the copyright owner...is an infringer of the copyright." The Act does not specify forms of infringement; that determination has been left to the courts. Some appropriate tests are originality, copying, substantiality, and access.

ORIGINALITY

Originality is the fundamental requirement of copyrightable material. In a copyright-infringement trial, the plaintiff seeks to show that the work in question is copied, while the defendant hopes to demonstrate originality. The meaning of the term "originality" was discussed by Judge Joseph Story in Emersen v. Davies, 8 Fed. Cas. 615 (1845).

> In truth, in literature, in science and in art, there are and can be, few, if any, things, which, in an abstract sense, are strictly new and original throughout. Every book in literature, science, and art, borrows, and must necessarily borrow, and use much which was well known and used before. No man creates a new language for himself, at least if he be a wise man, in writing a book. He contents himself with the use of language already known and used and understood by others. No man writes exclusively from his own thoughts, unaided and uninstructed by the thoughts of others. The thoughts of every man are, more or less, a combination of what other men have thought and expressed, although they may be modified, exalted, or improved by his own genius or reflection. If no book could be the subject of copyright which was not new and original in the elements of which it is composed, there could be no ground for any copyright in modern times, and we should be obliged to ascend very high, even in antiquity, to find a work entitled to such eminence.

In Story's opinion, an author necessarily incorporates parts of the ideas and style of another's work into his or her own work. Such effort constitutes sufficiently unique treatment to warrant copyright protection.

In numerous court cases, the question of infringement has centered around the issue of originality. Bleistein v. Donaldson Lithographing Company, 23 S.Ct. 298 (1903), involved the copying of three posters that advertised a circus. The defendant claimed that posters were not subject to copyright protection. The Supreme Court noted that the material could be copyrighted because it met the requirement of originality. According to Justice Oliver Wendell Holmes, "these prints in their ensemble and in all their details, in their design and particular combinations of figures, lines, and colors, are the original work" of the designer. The Court concluded that printing and engraving were original work, entitled to protection of copyright law.

The Amsterdam v. Triangle Publications, 189 F.2d 104 (1951), case concerned a map that appeared in a historical article in the Philadelphia Inquirer. Lewis Amsterdam, a publisher of maps, alleged that it was copied from his copyrighted map. The newspaper conceded the copying, but argued that the map was not entitled to copyright. The court stressed that "to be copyrightable a map must be the result of some original work." The court considered the manner in which Amsterdam had prepared the map. Amsterdam made no actual surveys of any roads, county lines, township lines, creeks, rivers, or railroad tracks; all such information had been obtained from other maps. The work of surveying, calculating, and investigating that was done by Amsterdam "was so negligible that it may be discounted entirely." The court concluded that, because Amsterdam's map lacked originality, it was not copyrightable.

In Donald v. Zack Meyer's T.V. Sales and Service, 426 F.2d 1027 (1970), the court considered the originality of a business form. O. W. Donald had registered with the copyright office a standard invoice form, which Donald printed and sold to television dealers and repairmen. When a competitor used the same language on his forms, Donald sued. The court noted that a copyright applicant did not have to demonstrate that a work was unique or novel, only that it was original. The material could be copyrighted even when it was based on a previously copyrighted work if the author added "some substantial, not merely trivial, originality." The court did not find the required originality in Donald's form. The word arrangement was a paraphrase of various portions of earlier forms and in copyright law paraphrasing is equivalent to outright copying. The court concluded: "The Copyright Act was not designed to protect such negligible efforts. We reward creativity and originality with a copyright but we do not accord copyright protection to a mere copycat."

Lipman v. Massachusetts, 475 F.2d 565 (1973), concerned the copyrightability of a court transcript. During the inquest into the drowning death of Mary Jo Kopechne, court stenographer Sidney Lipman was hired to record the testimony. Realizing the marketable value of the transcript, Lipman prepared several copies at his own expense. Senator Edward Kennedy, who had been driving the car in which Kopechne died, instituted proceedings in an attempt to prevent Lipman from selling the copies. The court noted that "since transcription is by definition a verbatim recording of another persons' statements, there can be no originality in the reporter's product." The report was not copyrightable. The court rejected Lipman's scheme to make a profit from the sale of the transcript.

Feist Publications v. Rural Telephone Service Company, 111 S.Ct. 1282 (1991), is another case determined on the ground of originality. Rural Telephone Service Company, a public utility providing telephone service to several communities in Kansas, distributes a typical telephone directory, consisting of white and yellow pages. The company obtains data for the directory from subscribers, who must provide their names and addresses to receive service. Feist Publications, a company that specializes in telephone directories covering large geographic areas, sought permission from the Rural Company to use its white page listings. Permission would have saved Feist Publications extensive independent investigation. When Rural refused to grant permission, Feist extracted the listings it needed for its directory. When the case reached the Supreme Court, the justices noted that the 1976 Copyright act leaves no doubt that originality, not "sweat of the brow," is the touchstone of copyright protection in directories and other fact-based compilations. In other words, the compiler must "display some minimal level of creativity." That was lacking in this case. The names, towns, and telephone numbers of subscribers were uncopyrightable facts, and "these bits of information were not selected, coordinated, or arranged in an original way." The Court concluded that Rural's compilation lacked "originality,...a constitutionally mandated prerequisite for copyright protection."

COPYING

The concepts of copying and originality are closely related. They represent different ways of asking the same question. In an infringement trial, a court might ask — Did the defendant create the work? Was it original? A court might also inquire — Did the defendant copy the plaintiff's work? The courts have determined which parts of a work may not be copied. They have held that while the facts cannot be copyrighted, the style and manner in which the facts are presented can be protected. This principle has been upheld in cases dealing with news stories, fiction, and works of art.

News stories

In International News Service v. Associated Press, 39 S.Ct. 68 (1918), the Court applied this principle to news stories. Associated Press and International News Service were competitors in the gathering and distribution of news. For a fee, newspaper companies throughout the United States obtained news of current events from these services.

In 1918, INS began to pirate information from AP. Subsequently, AP initiated court action. The Supreme Court examined the question of property in news. In the Court's opinion, per Justice Mahlon Pitney, the literary style of the news story was subject to protection, but the news element itself was not.

> The news element — the information respecting current events contained in the literary production — is not the creation of the writer, but it is a report of matters that ordinarily are *publici juris*, it is the history of the day. It is not to be supposed that the framers of the Constitution...intended to confer upon one who might happen to be the first to report a historic event the exclusive right for any period to spread the knowledge of it.

The Court concluded that, though the news element was not protected, the "pirating" by INS of the style of the news story was an infringement.

A few years later, in Chicago Record-Herald v. Tribune Association, 275 F. 797 (1921), the courts decided a similar case. The New York Tribune copyrighted and printed a news story about Germany's reliance upon submarines during World War I. The Tribune Company offered the story for simultaneous publication in the Chicago Herald, which declined, and the Chicago Daily News, which purchased. Although realizing that the story was copyrighted, the Herald printed a condensed version. The Tribune Association initiated court action. The court affirmed that news events were not subject to copyright protection, but insofar as the story involves "literary quality and style, apart from the bare recital of the facts or statement of news, it is protected by the copyright law." The exact or substantial copying or paraphrasing of a copyrighted news story constituted an infringement. The Herald had presented the facts of the Tribune article "in the very garb wherein the author clothed them, together with some of his deductions and comments thereon in his precise words."

In Wainwright Securities v. Wall Street Transcript Corporation, 558 F.2d 91 (1977), the court found a similar copyright violation. Wainwright Securities Company prepared in-depth analytical reports on industrial, financial, utility, and railroad corporations. The Wall Street Transcript Corporation published a weekly newspaper, concerned with economic news. One of the paper's features was the "Wall Street Roundup," a column containing abstracts of institutional research reports. A copyright infringement action was initiated when the paper published abstracts of Wainwright's research reports. The court noted that, while the "news event" may not be copyrighted, the style or manner of a news story is entitled to protection.

> What is protected is the manner of expression, the author's analysis or interpretation of events, the way he structures his material and

marshals facts, his choice of words and the emphasis he gives to particular developments. Thus, the essence of infringement lies not in taking a general theme or in coverage of the reports as events, but in appropriating the particular expression through similarities of treatment, details, scenes, events, and characterization.

In Wainwright, the court found infringement because the Wall Street Transcript Corporation copied "almost verbatim the most creative and original aspects of the reports." The paper's action "was not legitimate coverage of a news event; instead it was...chiseling for personal profit."

Fiction

In four cases decided in the late 1970s, courts considered the legality of copying the main idea of a story. In these cases, the judges affirmed that copyright protection extends only to the style and manner of expressing an idea, never to the idea itself. Author Rebecca Reyher sued the producers of "Sesame Street," claiming that a televised skit copied the story line for her children's book. In Reyher v. Children's Television Workshop, 533 F.2d 87 (1976), the court decided that even though both writings present the same idea, there was no copyright infringement because "the two stories are not similar in mood, details or characterization." In the second case, David Musto alleged that a substantial portion of The Seven Percent Solution was copied from an article Musto wrote for a medical journal. The Musto v. Meyer, 434 F.Supp 32 (1977), court concluded that "the copying involved only an 'idea' and not an 'expression of an idea' and therefore is not actionable under the copyright laws." In the third case, Margaret Alexander complained about similarities between her novel Jubilee and the book Roots written by Alex Haley. Each book purports to be based on the lives of the author's ancestors. The court rejected Alexander's suit because the similarities dealt with noncopyrightable elements — matters of historical fact, items of folk custom, characters and settings, and cliched language. Concerning language, the Alexander v. Haley, 460 F.Supp 40 (1978), court observed: "Words and metaphors are not subject to copyright protection; nor are phrases and expressions conveying an idea that can only be, or is typically, expressed in a limited number of stereotyped fashions." In the fourth case, Hoehling v. Universal City Studios, 618 F.2d 972 (1980), an author brought action against Universal Studios because of alleged similarities between his book Who Destroyed the Hindenburg? and the screenplay for a motion picture. The court noted that the idea at stake in this instance was an interpretation of an historical event, and "such interpretations are not copyrightable as a matter of law." The decision stated: "To avoid a chilling effect on authors who contemplate tackling an historical issue or event, broad latitude must be granted to subsequent authors who make use of historical subject matter, including theories or plots." In all four cases — Reyher, Musto, Alexander, Hoehling — the courts upheld the principle that facts are not copyrightable.

Works of art

In Franklin Mint v. National Wildlife Art Exchange, 575 F.2d 62 (1978), the court applied the principle to a work of art. The Franklin Mint Corporation was accused of infringing on the copyright of National Wildlife Art Exchange's painting, "Cardinals on Apple Blossom." The alleged copy was entitled "The Cardinal." Both paintings were done by artist Albert Gilbert. The court noted: "Since copyrights do not protect thematic concepts, the fact that the same subject matter may be present in two paintings does not prove copying or infringement." The judges accepted Franklin Mint Corporation's claim that the paintings were "variations on a theme."

> We do not find the phrase objectionable...because a "variation" probably is not a copy and if a "theme" is equated with an "idea," it may not be monopolized. We conceive of "variation on a theme," therefore, as another way of saying that an "idea" may not be copyrighted and only its "expression" may be protected.

SUBSTANTIALITY

Few infringement suits involve total and exact copying of the copyrighted work. Consequently, the test becomes whether there is substantial similarity between two works. The Henry Holt v. Liggett and Meyers Tobacco Company, 23 F.Supp. 302 (1938), case provides an example. In 1931, Henry Holt and Company published Dr. Leon Felderman's book, The Human Voice, Its Care and Development. Shortly thereafter, Liggett & Meyer Tobacco Company published a pamphlet entitled, "Some Facts about Cigarettes," in which the following statements were copied, though not exactly, from Felderman's book.

> Statistics have it that 80 per cent of physicians are smokers.... It appears unanimous that smoking is not nearly so injurious as over-eating.... From my experience with ear, nose and throat cases, I firmly believe that tobacco, when properly used, has no ill effect upon the auditory passages.

Henry Holt and Company sought an injunction, claiming that the use of Felderman's statements reflected negatively upon his professional ethics and hampered the sale of the book. The court emphasized that the whole, or even a large portion of a book, need not be copied to constitute an infringement. It was sufficient if a "material" and "substantial" part had been copied, even though it was but a small part of the whole. In Holt, only three sentences had been taken from Felderman's book; however, the material made up about one-twentieth of the pamphlet. Under these circumstances, the copied matter seemed substantial. The fact that the pamphlet acknowledged the source of the information did not excuse the infringement.

Independent research

In Toksvig v. Bruce Publishing, 181 F.2d 664 (1950), the court considered the importance of independent research in determining the question of substantiality. The case involved two books. The first, The Life of Hans Christian Anderson by Signe Toksvig, was written after three years of research done exclusively from Danish sources, which included the letters of Hans Christian Anderson. The second, Flight of the Swan, a novel by Margaret Hubbard, was based on a year's research which was confined to English sources including Toksvig's book. Toksvig sued for copyright violation. The court found substantial similarity — Hubbard had copied certain concepts about Anderson, his life, and his friends that were set down for the first time in Toksvig's work. In addition, Hubbard had copied 24 specific passages of the work — the copied materials were original translations made by Toksvig from Danish sources. Hubbard argued that she could have obtained the information from works originally researched by Toksvig. The court noted:

> The question is not whether Hubbard could have obtained the same information by going to the same sources, but rather did she go to the same sources and do her own independent research? In other words, the test is whether the one charged with the infringement has made an independent production, or made a substantial and unfair use of the complainant's work.

Since Hubbard could not read Danish, the use of Toksvig's book facilitated completion of her book in considerably less time than would have been possible with independent research. The book was a substantial infringement.

In Eisenschiml v. Fawcett Publications, 246 F.2d 598 (1957), the court found that substantial similarity in writings which contain historical facts and ideas did not constitute infringement. After extensive research, Otto Eisenschiml published two scholarly books about the death of Abraham Lincoln. In an issue of True magazine, Joseph Millard published an article about Lincoln's assassination entitled, "America's Greatest Unsolved Murder." The article contained no footnotes or bibliography. Eisenschiml initiated court action, claiming that the article copied substantial portions of his books. The judge concluded that Millard's article did not constitute copyright infringement. In historical writings, such as the events surrounding Lincoln's assassination, both writers described the same persons during a limited period of time. Some similarity of treatment would unavoidably result. The Eisenschiml decision, when compared with Toksvig, places less value on the practice of independent research.

Parody

In a series of cases which reached contradictory conclusions, the courts considered the substantiality requirement as it relates to parody. One such case is Columbia Pictures Corporation v. National Broadcasting Company, 137 F.Supp. 348 (1955). NBC broadcast over its national television network a 20-minute burlesque of Columbia Picture's movie, "From Here to Eternity." There were several similarities between the film and the skit — locale, characters, and some details. Columbia Pictures initiated court action. The court concluded that the use of the original work was permissible and did not constitute the taking of a substantial portion. According to the court, since a burlesque had to use the original to conjure up the subject matter being burlesqued, the law allowed more extensive utilization of the "predictable portion of a copyrighted work in the creation of a burlesque of that work than in the creation of other fictional or dramatic works not intended as a burlesque of the original."

A similar case, Columbia Broadcasting System v. Loew's, 78 S.Ct. 770 (1958), involved Jack Benny's use of Metro-Goldwyn-Mayer's film, "Gas Light." In 1945, after obtaining consent, Benny presented a 15 minute parody of "Gas Light" over a national radio network. Six years later, CBS produced a television show burlesquing "Gas Light," with Jack Benny in the leading role. Neither Benny nor CBS had obtained permission for the telecast. The court found that a substantial part of the film had been copied; that

> ...a "parodized or burlesque" taking is to be treated no differently from any other appropriation; that is, as in all other cases of alleged taking, the issue becomes first one of fact, i.e., what was taken and how substantial was the taking; and if it is determined that there was a substantial taking, infringement exists.

In CBS, the decision granted to burlesque less protection than that allowed in Columbia Pictures.

In Berlin v. E. C. Publications, 329 F.2d 541 (1964), the court held that musical lyrics, in the form of parody, did not constitute copyright infringement. When Mad Magazine published satiric parody lyrics for popular songs, the copyright holders initiated court procedures. The court noted that the theme and content of the parodies differed markedly from those of the originals. For example, "The Last Time I Saw Paris," originally written as a nostalgic ballad became "The First Time I saw Maris," a commentary upon a baseball hero. The court opinion read:

> We believe in any event that the parody lyrics involved in this appeal would be permissible under the most rigorous application of the "substantiality" requirement. The disparities in theme, content and style between the original lyrics and the alleged infringements could hardly be greater.

In Berlin, as in Columbia Pictures, the Court allowed substantial use of an original work in order to generate a "parody." This opinion differed from the CBS decision which had granted less protection to that form of expression.

The United States Supreme Court addressed the parody issue in Campbell v. Acuff-Rose Music, Inc., 114 S. Ct. 1164 (1994). The music company filed suit against the members of the rap group 2 Live Crew, claiming that their song "Pretty Woman" infringed upon Acuff-Rose's copyright in Roy Orbison's rock ballad "Oh Pretty Woman." 2 Live Crew argued that its song was a parody that made fair use of the original song. The Court applied the four criteria for determining fair use. Under the first, the purpose and character of the use, a parody may have "transformative" value, altering the original with new expression and meaning. In this case, 2 Live Crew's song contained parody, commenting on and criticizing the original work. The second criterion, the nature of the copyrighted work, was not much help in resolving a parody case because parodies almost invariably copy publicly known works. Under the third factor, the amount and substantiality of the use, the Court emphasized that even though 2 Live Crew's copying of the original's first line of lyrics and opening bass riff went to the original's "heart," that heart was what conjured up the song for parody. Moreover, 2 Live Crew thereafter departed markedly from the lyrics and produced distinctive music. The copying was not excessive in relation to the parodic purpose. Writing for the Court, Justice David Souter noted:

> Once enough has been taken to assure identification, how much more is reasonable will depend, say, on the extent to which the song's overriding purpose and character is to parody the original or, in contrast, the likelihood that the parody may serve as a market substitute for the original. But using some characteristic features cannot be avoided.

Under the fourth criterion, the effect of the use upon the potential market, Souter noted that it was unlikely that the work would seek to substitute for the original since the two works served different market functions. It seems fairly clear that the language of Souter's opinion supports the idea that parody may constitute a fair use. Nonetheless, the Supreme Court sent the case back for trial to determine whether the parody was a fair use. The trial court was better suited to deciding exactly how much of the original was taken and whether the parody version would hurt the sale of the original recording.

ACCESS

In some cases, a key issue was access — whether the defendant had an opportunity to copy the work. In MacDonald v. DuMaurier, 75 F.Supp. 655 (1948), the court relied heavily upon the author's "reputation" in finding lack of access. The court determined that Daphne DuMaurier, in writing Rebecca, did not have access to either of two works written by Edwina MacDonald.

> The circumstances do not inevitably lead to the conclusion of access.... The denial of access made by the defendant, her proven reputation as a writer, and a reading of the three stories, have convinced me that she never saw or heard of "I Planned to Murder My Husband" or "Blind Windows" prior to the writing or publication of "Rebecca."

In Doran v. Sunset House Distributing, 197 F.Supp. 940 (1961), the court found that the defendant had access to the plaintiff's Santa Claus plastic figure, had copied it, and therefore committed copyright infringement. The court explained a function of the access criterion: "Infringer's access to copyrighted article is but a means of eliminating coincidence or independent effort as an explanation for likeness between copyrighted articles and infringing articles."

The Sid & Marty Krofft Television v. McDonald's Corporation, 562 F.2d 1157 (1977), case involved commercials which copied the H. R. PufnStuf series. The court discussed the relationship of the access criterion to the copying and substantiality criteria.

> No amount of proof of access will suffice to show copying if there are no similarities. This is not to say, however, that where clear and convincing evidence of access is presented, the quantum of proof required to show substantial similarity may not be lower than when access is shown merely by a preponderance of the evidence.

The court, in finding for the plaintiff, emphasized that a high "degree of access justifies a lower standard of proof to show substantial similarity."

Jason v. Fonda, 526 F. Supp. 774 (1981), a related case, centered around the claim that makers of the film "Coming Home" had copied extensively from Sonya Jason's book Concomitant Soldier — Woman and War. The court determined that Jason could not establish access in either of two ways: There was no proof of actual reading or knowledge of the plaintiff's work, and the level of opportunity to view the work created no more than a "bare possibility" that defendants had access.   The court noted that Jason could establish infringement by showing circumstantial evidence of access, along with a substantial similarity of ideas and expression between the copyrighted work and the allegedly infringing work.   In this case, the court found that the works contained similar but unprotected ideas (morality, effects of war on women, injured soldiers, historical chronology).   The court also found substantial differences in the use of contexts, characters, and language.   The court concluded that the failure to show access, along with the substantial dissimilarities between the works, justified dismissal of the infringement claim.   The Jason decision, as with MacDonald, Doran, and Sid & Marty Krofft Television, demonstrates that the access element may be compelling in a copyright infringement case.

GUIDELINES FOR FAIR USE

The 1976 Copyright Act represents the first legislative statement of the fair-use doctrine.   According to the Act, determining fair use involves consideration of 1) the purpose and character of the use, 2) the nature of the copyrighted work, 3) the amount used, and 4) the effect of the use upon the value of the copyrighted work.   If a preponderance of these criteria are met, a fair use exists and there is no infringement.

PURPOSE AND CHARACTER OF USE

Generally, the courts have been more lenient toward copying that occurred in scholarly works than toward the use of copyrighted materials for commercial gain.   This point is illustrated by companion cases involving copyrighted musical compositions which were performed in restaurants.   In the first case, Herbert v. Shanley, 37 S.Ct. 232 (1917), Victor Herbert's "Sweethearts" was performed by musicians who were employed to play at mealtimes.   In the second case, John Church Company v. Hilliard Hotel, 37 S.Ct. 232 (1917), John Church's "From Maine to Georgia" was performed in order to entertain guests during their meals.   In both cases, the restaurant owners claimed that they had not violated copyright because no profit came from the music that was played to provide atmosphere in the restaurant.   The Supreme Court noted that "if the rights under the copyright are infringed only by a performance where money is taken at the door, they are very imperfectly protected."   The restaurants benefitted financially by playing the music; it provided "a luxurious pleasure not to be had from eating a silent meal." According to the Court: "If music did not pay, it would be given up. If it pays it pays out of the public's pocket. Whether it pays or not, the purpose of employing it is profit, and that is enough." In Herbert and John Church Company, the Court was unsympathetic to the restaurants — the use constituted copyright infringement.

In Thompson v. Gernsback, 94 F.Supp. 453 (1950), the court indicated that copying for scholarly purposes is entitled to lenient fair-use guidelines. The case involved an infringement suit initiated by psychiatrist Clara Thompson, author of an article titled "Changing Concepts of Homosexuality in Psychoanalysis," which appeared in Psychiatry magazine. Thompson sued Hugo Gernsback, who published Sexology, a magazine advertised as a "Sex Science Magazine-Illustrated." The court noted that the doctrine of fair use "permits a writer of scientific, legal, medical and similar books or articles of learning to use even the identical words of earlier books or writings dealing with the same subject matter." In this case, Gernsback's magazine did not qualify "as a work of science." The court decided for Thompson.

In Meeropol v. Nizer, 560 F.2d 1061 (1977), the court again upheld the scholarly-use standard. The case involved Louis Nizer's book, The Implosion Conspiracy, an account of the events surrounding the trial of Julius and Ethel Rosenberg, spies who were convicted and executed for conspiring to give national defense secrets to the Soviet Union. Michael and Robert Meeropol, sons of the Rosenbergs, alleged that Nizer incorporated in his book substantial portions of copyrighted letters written by the Rosenbergs. The court set forth the following standard for assessing fair use: "For a determination whether the fair use defense is applicable on the facts of this case...it is relevant whether or not the Rosenberg letters were used primarily for scholarly, historical reasons, or predominantly for commercial exploitation." The Meeropol decision, like Herbert, John Church Company, and Thompson, demonstrates that the courts are more lenient about copying for scholarly use than for commercial gain.

NATURE OF THE WORK

The courts have applied the fair use doctrine to works in various media. In so doing, the courts have determined guidelines which affect different types of copyrighted works. Some of the relevant cases are considered in this section.

Biography

The Rosemont Enterprises v. Random House, 366 F.2d 303 (1966), case involved Howard Hughes, the famous recluse who desired to remain out of the public eye. In 1954, Look magazine published a series, "The Howard Hughes Story," and in 1962, Random House published Howard Hughes — A Biography, by John Keats. In 1965, Rosemont Enterprises, a Hughes-owned company, purchased the copyright to the Look articles. Rosemont then started a copyright infringement suit against Random House, claiming that Keats copied several sentences from the Look articles. The Rosemont court, in deciding that John Keats' biography was an instance of fair use, rejected any dichotomy based on whether the use was commercial or scholarly. Such a consideration was "irrelevant to a determination of whether a particular use of copyrighted materials in a work which offers some benefit to the public constitutes a fair use." In this case, the public was entitled to learn about the life of an extraordinary man; publication of this interesting biographical information constituted a fair use. It contradicted the public interest to allow anybody "to buy up the copyright ownership to restrain others from publishing biographical material concerning him."

Characters

In Warner Brothers v. Columbia Broadcasting System, 216 F.2d 945 (1954), the court considered whether a writer's characters are copyrightable, and whether the characters pass with the transfer of a copyright. In 1930, Dashiell Hammett sold rights to his detective story, The Maltese Falcon, to Warner Brothers Pictures. When Hammett continued to use one of his characters, Sam Spade, in other stories, Warner Brothers claimed infringement of copyright. The court concluded that even if Hammett sold the copyright to Warner Brothers, the transfer did not prevent Hammett "from using the characters...in other stories. The characters were vehicles for the story told, and the vehicles did not go with the sale of the story." Furthermore, the court found that since the use of character names was not mentioned in the agreements, "the character rights with the names cannot be held to be within the grants." In Warner Brothers, the court concluded that Hammett retained the right to use his characters.

Walt Disney v. The Air Pirates, 345 F.Supp. 108 (1972), is another case involving copyright protection for characters. Walt Disney Productions held copyrights for several animal cartoon characters. Another company, The Air Pirates, published cartoon magazines with characters that looked similar to and used the same names as those created by Disney. The theme and plot of the publications differed markedly from Disney's cartoons. Nonetheless, Walt Disney Productions claimed infringement of copyright. In court, Air Pirates cited <u>Warner Brothers</u>, in which the court ruled that "the characters were vehicles for the story told, and the vehicles did not go with the sale of the story." The <u>Walt Disney</u> court concluded that Disney's works were different; the characters tended to constitute the story.

> The facial expressions, position and movement represented may convey far more than the words set out as dialogue in the "balloon" hovering over the character's head, or the explanatory material appended. It is not simply one particular drawing, in one isolated cartoon "panel" for which the plaintiff seeks protection, but rather it is the common features of all the drawings of that character appearing in the copyrighted work.

The main appeal of Disney's cartoons was to children, primarily through the use of "the characters and nothing else." Disney's characters were copyrightable and Air Pirates had infringed on the copyright. The decisions in <u>Warner Brothers</u> and <u>Walt Disney</u> are consistent, — a character that constitutes the story being told is entitled to copyright protection. Under such conditions, use of another writer's characters is restricted.

Speeches

During 1955 to 1958, Vice-Admiral Hyman Rickover delivered several public addresses on a variety of subjects. For most of them, he distributed advance copies to the press and sent copies to people who requested them. In 1958, Rickover began to compile texts of his speeches for publication. From that point on, he obtained copyright protection for his speeches. At the same time, a publisher asked Rickover for permission to publish some of his past speeches. Rickover refused. The publisher brought suit, seeking declaration that Rickover's previous speeches were in "the public domain." The court sided with the publisher for two reasons. First, Rickover had forfeited protection by distributing the speeches without copyright — an act that equals publication. Second, the use of government equipment and materials made the speeches uncopyrightable "government publications." In <u>Public Affairs Associates v. Rickover</u>, 82 S.Ct. 580 (1962), the U.S. Supreme Court vacated this judgment on a technicality and returned the case to the lower court

No further proceedings were held, probably because the district court was deciding the <u>King v. Mister Maestro</u>, 224 F.Supp. 101 (1963), case. On August 28, 1963, Dr. Martin Luther King delivered a speech in which he repeatedly used the phrase "I have a dream," during a march for civil rights in Washington, D.C.   Prior to delivery, King presented copies of the speech to the press. King did not want the speech to be distributed to the public; he specifically limited it to members of the press who were covering the march. King's speech impressed the crowd and subsequently received wide coverage by the press. Shortly thereafter, Mister Maestro Company, without King's consent, prepared and sold a record entitled "The March on Washington." The record contained King's "I Have A Dream" speech. At about the same time, a record of some of King's speeches, including an abbreviated version of "I Have A Dream," was sold with King's consent by Motown Record Company. Subsequently, King charged the Mister Maestro Company with violation of his copyright. Mister Maestro argued that King's speech had been published. The court decided that King's delivering the speech did not constitute a general publication so as to place it in the public domain.

> The word "general" with respect to publication in this sense is of
> greatest significance. There can be a limited publication, which is a
> communication of the work to others under circumstances showing
> no dedication of the work to the public. A general publication is
> one which shows a dedication to the public so as to lose copyright.

The delivery of this speech, no matter how vast the audience, did not amount to general publication.   The court then compared King with Rickover. Rickover made a general distribution, not only to the press, but also to members of the public. King made his speech available only to the press. The court banned further use of King's speech without permission.

Unpublished Presidential memoirs

In 1977, former President Gerald Ford granted Harper and Row Publishers the exclusive right to publish his memoirs. Shortly before the scheduled release of the work, reporters for Nation obtained a copy of the memoirs and published an article that contained at least 300 words taken verbatim from the manuscript. Harper and Row introduced a suit, alleging violation of the Copyright Act. Nation argued that the article constituted "fair use" because the article was published for purpose of commentary and news reporting. The Supreme Court, per Justice Sandra Day O'Connor, determined that the article violated the Copyright Law. According to O'Connor, "under ordinary circumstances, the author's right to control the first public appearance of his undisseminated expression will outweigh a claim of fair use." Furthermore, "the fact that the publication was commercial as opposed to nonprofit is a separate factor tending to weigh against a finding of fair use."

> The Nation's unauthorized use of the undisseminated manuscript had not merely the incidental effect but the intended purpose of supplanting the copyright holder's commercially valuable right of first publication. While there may be a greater need to disseminate works of fact than works of fiction, the Nation's taking of copyrighted expression exceeded that necessary to disseminate the facts and infringed the copyright holder's interests in confidentiality and creative control over the first public appearance of the work.

In Harper and Row v. Nation, 105 S.Ct. 2218 (1985), the copying of unpublished Presidential memoirs was not recognized as a "fair use."

Derivative works

Cornell Woolrich authored "It Had to Be Murder," which was published in 1942 in Dime Detective Magazine, the publishers of which obtained the copyright to the story. In 1945, Woolrich assigned the rights to make a motion picture version of the story to B. G. De Sylva Productions. Woolrich agreed to renew the copyright at the appropriate time, under the provisions of the 1909 Copyright Act. In 1953, actor Jimmy Stewart and director Alfred Hitchcock formed a production company, Patron Incorporated, and obtained the motion picture rights to the story from De Sylva. In 1954, the Patron Company produced and distributed "Rear Window," the movie version of Woolrich's work. Woolrich died in 1968 without a surviving spouse or child, and before he could obtain renewal of the copyright. He left his property to a trust, under which the rights to the story were granted to Sheldon Abend. When the Patron Company re-released "Rear Window" in videocassette form, and for exhibition in theatres and on cable television, Abend initiated court action. He claimed that copyright infringement had occurred because Patron's right to use the story under copyright renewal terms lapsed when Woolrich died. In Stewart v. Abend, 110 S.Ct. 1750 (1990), the Supreme Court agreed.

> The distribution and publication of a derivative work during the copyright renewal term of a pre-existing work incorporated into the derivative work infringes the rights of the owner of the pre-existing work where the author of that work agreed to assign the rights in the renewal term to the derivative work's owner but died before the commencement of the renewal period and the statutory successor does not assign the right to use the pre-existing work to the owner of the derivative work.

The Court determined that the unauthorized use of Woolrich's story in "Rear Window" did "not constitute a noninfringing 'fair use'." The film failed to qualify under the relevant criteria. First, the use was commercial rather than educational. Second, the nature of the copyrighted work was fictional and creative rather than factual. Third, the story was a substantial portion of the film, which used its setting, characters, plot, and sequence of events. Fourth, re-release of the film impinged on Abend's ability to market new versions of the story.

Cable television

Fortnightly Corporation operated a cable television service in the area around Clarksburg and Fairmont, West Virginia. There were two local television stations in the vicinity, but because of hilly terrain most residents could not receive the broadcasts of any additional stations through ordinary rooftop antennae. Fortnightly's system provided customers with signals from five television stations, ranging in distance from 52 to 82 miles away. United Artists held copyrights on some motion pictures that were shown on the five television stations carried by Fortnightly. United sued Fortnightly for copyright infringement, arguing that Fortnightly's cable system infringed United's exclusive right to "perform...in public for profit." Fortnightly maintained that the cable television system did not "perform" the copyrighted works. In Fortnightly Corporation v. United Artists Television, 88 S.Ct. 2084 (1968), the Supreme Court, per Justice Potter Stewart, agreed.

> Essentially, a CATV system no more than enhances the viewer's capacity to receive the broadcaster's signals; it provides a well-located antenna with an efficient connection to the viewer's television set.... If an individual erected an antenna on a hill, strung a cable to his house, and installed the necessary amplifying equipment, he would not be "performing" the programs he received on his television set. The result would be no different if several people combined to erect a cooperative antenna for the same purpose. The only difference in the case of CATV is that the antenna system is erected and owned not by its users but by an entrepreneur.

Six years later, in Teleprompter Corporation v. Columbia Broadcasting System, 94 S.Ct. 1129 (1974), the lower court distinguished between two functions of cable systems, and then compared Fortnightly with Teleprompter.

> CATV systems perform either or both of two functions. First, they may supplement broadcasting by facilitating satisfactory reception of local stations in adjacent areas in which such reception would not otherwise be possible; and second, they may transmit to subscribers the signals of distant stations entirely beyond the range of local antennae.

According to the court, Fortnightly performed the first function; it brought television signals to viewers who could not otherwise receive them. The signals were already in the community, but because of topographical conditions, residents could not receive the signals by usual methods. The court also noted that Teleprompter performed the second function, distributing signals beyond the range of local antennae. The system did not merely enhance the customers' chances of receiving signals that were in the area; it brought new signals into the area. Accordingly, the Teleprompter system violated copyright law. The Supreme Court disagreed. Importation of distant programs did not constitute a "performance" under the Copyright Act.

> Importation of "distant signals" from one community into another does not constitute a "performance" under the Copyright Act; thus, a community antenna television system does not lose its status as a nonbroadcaster and thus a non "performer" for copyright purposes when the signals it carries are those from distant rather than local sources.

Such activity was "essentially a viewer function, irrespective of the distance between the broadcasting station and the ultimate viewer." Teleprompter, like Fortnightly, had not violated copyright protection.

Radio

One year later, the question of what constitutes a "performance" reached the Supreme Court again, this time in relation to the radio medium. George Aiken, owner of a small, fast-service, food shop, which caters to "carry-out" customers who are in the restaurant for less than five minutes, had various radio stations turned on so that musical selections could be enjoyed by his employees and customers. A copyright infringement suit was initiated by Twentieth Century Music Corporation. The complaint alleged that the radio reception in Aiken's restaurant infringed the composers' exclusive rights to "perform" their copyrighted works in public for profit. The Supreme Court cited Fortnightly and Teleprompter in noting that if, in those cable television cases, such sophisticated technological facilities "were not performing, then logic dictates that no 'performance' resulted when...[Aiken] merely activated his restaurant radio." The Court pointed to the impracticality of enforcement.

> The practical unenforceability of a ruling that all of those in Aiken's position are copyright infringers is self-evident. One has only to consider the countless business establishments in this country with radio or television sets on their premises — bars, beauty shops, cafeterias, car washes, dentists' offices, and drive-ins — to realize the total futility of any evenhanded effort on the part of copyright holders to license even a substantial percentage of them.

The opinion of Justice Stewart concluded that a finding of infringement in this case would be inequitable for two reasons. First, a person like Aiken could guarantee freedom from liability only by keeping his radio turned off. Second, to hold that a person like Aiken "performed" these musical compositions would "authorize the sale of an untold number of licenses for what is basically a single public rendition of a copyrighted work." In <u>Twentieth Century Music Corporation v. Aiken</u>, 95 S.Ct. 2040 (1975), Justice Stewart held that such a policy "would go far beyond what is required for the economic protection of copyright owners."

Sound recordings

In 1972, Congress amended the copyright law to provide protection against unauthorized duplication of sound recordings. Prior to this legislation, a sound recording was presumed to fall into the public domain as soon as it was published. In 1973, the Supreme Court heard <u>Goldstein v. California</u>, 93 S.Ct. 2303 (1973), a case that challenged the constitutionality of a state ban on sound-recording duplication. This case was initiated prior to, but decided after, the 1972 congressional amendment. The State of California charged Goldstein with violating the portion of the California Penal Code that bans "record piracy" or "tape piracy" — the unauthorized duplication of sound recordings of performances by musical artists. Goldstein had duplicated tapes of popular musical performances and then sold the copies to the public in competition with the original tapes. Goldstein argued that the California law was unconstitutional because it prohibited the copying of works that were not entitled to federal protection. The Supreme Court disagreed.

> The Constitution neither explicitly precludes the States from granting copyrights nor grants such authority exclusively to the Federal Government. The subject matter to which the Copyright Clause is addressed may at times be of purely local concern. No conflict will necessarily arise from a lack of uniform state regulation, nor will the interest of one State be significantly prejudiced by the actions of another. No reason exists why Congress must take affirmative action either to authorize protection of all categories of writings or to free them from all restraint. We therefore conclude that, under the Constitution, the States have not relinquished all power to grant to authors "the exclusive right to their respective writings."

In <u>Goldstein</u>, the Court upheld the California statute; California had "exercised a power which it retained under the Constitution." A few years later, Congress included national protection for sound recordings in the 1976 Copyright Act.

Photocopying

During the twentieth century, technology placed great strains on the Copyright Act of 1909. One strain involved photocopy machines, which by 1970 were commonly used in almost every library. About this time, the National Institute of Health and the National Library of Medicine decided to provide photocopies of articles from medical and scientific periodicals, free of charge, to medical and scientific researchers. The Williams & Wilkins Company, publisher of several medical journals, initiated court action for copyright infringement. The suit complained of illegal massive photocopying. The lower court found that the "wholesale copying" was not a fair use because the photocopies were exact duplicates of the originals, they served as substitutes for the originals, and they diminished the publisher's economic gain. The court of claims reversed, noting that the belief that copying an entire work could never be a "fair use" was "an overbroad generalization, unsupported by the decisions and rejected by years of accepted practice." The court suggested three reasons why photocopying did not constitute infringement. First, the William & Wilkins Company had not shown that it was harmed economically. On the other hand, the libraries were nonprofit institutions. Second, medical research would be injured by holding these practices to be an infringement. Scientists would not use the articles needed in their work. Third, the problem called for legislative guidance and the court should not, during this period of anticipated congressional action, impose upon science and medicine a risk of harm. The court stressed that no question of "vending" arose; the purpose of the copying was "scientific progress, untainted by any commercial gain." In Williams & Wilkins v. United States, 95 S.Ct. 1344 (1975), an equally-divided Supreme Court affirmed the findings of the court of claims.

Section 108 of the 1976 Copyright Act provided some clarity to the photocopy issue. Under the law, a library may reproduce and distribute a copy of specified types of works without the permission of the copyright owner. Under certain conditions, a library may copy an entire work. The law did not, however, approve of mass photocopying, and the rights provided in Section 108 apply only to copies prepared "without any purpose of direct or indirect commercial advantage."

Basic Books v. Kinko Graphics Corporation, 758 F.Supp 1522 (1991), is a related case which involved copying by a business rather than by a library. Several book publishers brought suit against a duplication business which copied excerpts from books without permission, compiled them into university course packets, and sold them to college students. The business argued fair use. The court noted that though the packets in the hands of students were no doubt educational, in the hands of employees they were clearly commercial. The claim that copying was done with altruistic motives was not persuasive; the clearer motive was financial gain. The court noted that copying was extensive, covering key segments of the works, with excerpts varying in length from 14 to 110 pages. Clearly, the copying unfortunately impacted on sales of books. The business had 200 stores nationwide, serving hundreds of colleges and universities which enroll thousands of students. The court concluded that the infringement was not a fair use. The company had created a nationwide business allied to the publishing industry by usurping authors' and publishers' copyrights and profits.

Videotaping

In 1984, the Supreme Court heard a case involving alleged copyright infringement by the manufacturer of home videotape recorders. The case involved Sony Corporation, which manufactures videotape recorders, and Universal City Studios, which owned copyrights on several television programs aired on commercial networks. Universal Studios maintained that VTR owners had recorded copyrighted works, and that Sony contributed to copyright infringement by marketing the VTRs. Universal sought money damages, an accounting of profits, and an injunction against the manufacture and marketing of videotape recorders. When the case reached the Supreme Court, Justice John Stevens, writing for the majority, held that Sony's sale of VTRs to the general public did not constitute contributory infringement of Universal's copyright. The Court based its decision on two reasons. First, Sony did not control the use of the copyrighted works.

> Here, the only contact between petitioners and the users of the VTRs occurred at the moment of sale. And there is no precedent for imposing vicarious liability on the theory that petitioner sold the VTRs with constructive knowledge that their customers might use the equipment to make unauthorized copies of copyrighted material. The sale of copying equipment, like the sale of other articles of commerce, does not constitute contributory infringement if the product is widely used for legitimate, unobjectionable purposes, or, indeed, is merely capable of substantial non-infringing uses.

Second, VTRs are put to numerous noninfringing uses, including time shifting of programs by private viewers. The Sony Corporation v. Universal City Studios, 104 S.Ct. 774 (1984), Court, in a five-to-four decision, recognized that "even the unauthorized home time shifting of...programs is legitimate fair use." Justice Stevens urged Congress to "take a fresh look at this new technology" in order to revise the law to compensate television producers and performers for any losses resulting from videotaping. To date, congressional action has not been undertaken.

Computer programs

Computer programs may be classified as either applications or operating systems. Applications perform a certain task (play a game, balance checkbooks, word processing) while operating systems manage internal functions. In Apple Computer v. Franklin Computer Corporation, 714 F.2d 1240 (1983), the court determined that both program types are copyrightable. In this case, Franklin Computer Corporation argued that operating systems were "methods" or "processes" and were hence uncopyrightable. The court, however, saw no significant distinction in the two types of programs; both "instruct the computer to do something."

> Since it is only the instructions which are protected, a "process" is no more involved because the instructions in an operating system program may be used to activate the operation of the computer than it would be if instructions were written in ordinary English in a manual which described the necessary steps to activate an intricate complicated machine. There is, therefore, no reason to afford any less copyright protection to the instructions in an operating system program than to the instructions in an application program.

The court also awarded copyright protection to computer programming in Whelan Associates v. Jaslow Dental Laboratory, 797 F.2d 1222 (1986). The decision upheld the claim of Elaine Whelan, who developed a program for dental laboratory administrative record keeping. She argued that a dental lab relied heavily on her work in creating another program with more wide-spread capability. The court determined that "copyright principles derived in other areas are applicable in the field of computer programs." The court noted that the "structure" of a computer program for record keeping is not the "idea" of efficient record keeping, but rather the "expression" of that idea. Accordingly, the structure of the program enjoyed copyright protection. The court found substantial similarity in the "structure" of the programs.

> Computer program expert's testimony in comparing computer programs for dental laboratory record keeping, that most of file structures and screen outputs of programs were virtually identical, and that five particularly important subroutines within both programs performed almost identically, was sufficient to support finding that programs were substantially similar, for purposes of

copyright infringement analysis.

The court reached a different decision regarding computer command structures. In an early case, <u>Lotus Development Corporation v. Paperback Software International</u>, 740 F.Supp 37 (1990), the judges emphasized that copyright protection extends to expressive elements of computer programs, but not to the ideas. The menu command structure of a spreadsheet program, including the choice of command terms, order of those terms, their presentation on the screen, and the length of prompts, was copyrightable because that "structure was capable of being expressed in many if not an unlimited number of ways." It was the means of expressing an idea. In a later case, <u>Lotus Development Corporation v. Borland International</u>, 49 F.3d 807 (1995), the court ruled that Lotus could not copyright its command structure. The decision held that words and commands used to operate a spreadsheet are an uncopyrightable "method of operation." The court likened the command structure to a typewriter keyboard or a VCR control panel, which are not creative components. The U.S. Supreme Court deadlocked four to four on this case, 116 S.Ct. 804 (1996), thereby affirming the lower court decision but denying it precedent-setting power.

During the 1990s, the courts were asked to decide whether cyberspace service providers share in the liability for copyright infringement by its subscribers. In <u>Playboy Enterprises v. Frena</u>, 839 F.Supp 1552 (1993), the court held that the operator of a computer network could be held liable for acts of copyright infringement by users of the network, even when the operator did not participate in the infringement. In this case, the operator of a subscription computer bulletin board service, accessible via telephone modem to customers, included unauthorized copies of numerous photographs uploaded by customers from their home computers. Customers of the service could browse, down load, and even store the copied images in their home computers. Playboy Enterprises, the holder of the copyright on the photos, brought suit. Although the operator never uploaded or downloaded the copyrighted photographs, and removed the unauthorized copies as soon as he was sued, the court held him liable for copyright infringement. The display of the images constituted "public distribution" and therefore an infringement on Playboy's exclusive right to distribution. The fact that the operator did not make copies personally had no bearing on the determination of infringement.

The court reached a similar decision in <u>Sega Enterprises v. MAPHIA</u>, 857 F.Supp 679 (1994), a case which involved the unauthorized copying of copyrighted video games. The court ruled against a bulletin board service operator who encouraged subscribers to download the games into their computers after an anonymous member made the games available. Furthermore, the service also offered to sell subscribers an alternative form of the video games. The court concluded that the service operator contributed to copyright infringement although the member rather than the operator originally uploaded the video games.

Another court ruled that a cyberspace service provider does not share in the liability when the operator has not taken any affirmative action that directly relates to the copying. In Religious Technology Center v. Netcom On-Line Communications Services, Inc., 907 F.Supp 1361 (1995), the court noted that "although copyright is a strict liability statute, there should still be some element of violation or causation which is lacking where a defendant's system is merely used to create a copy by a third party."

AMOUNT OF WORK THAT IS USED

Encyclopedia Britannica brought suit against the Board of Cooperative Educational Services, a nonprofit corporation that provides educational services to public schools in Erie County, New York. The complaint alleged that the Board videotaped several films and television programs and distributed copies to the school districts. Records indicated that the volume of copying was substantial. For example, the Board duplicated approximately 10,000 tapes during a single year. The Board admitted that it videotaped copyrighted films without paying fees or obtaining permission. The Board justified the action in terms of the fair-use doctrine, claiming that noncommercial videotaping of programs for classroom viewing was not a copyright infringement. The district court admitted that the problem of accommodating the competing interests of educators and film producers raised questions which the legislature was better equipped to resolve than the judiciary. Congress, however, had left the issue to the courts. Accordingly, the judges found the Board's activities

> ...difficult to reconcile with its claim of fair use. This case does not involve an isolated instance of a teacher copying copyrighted material for classroom use but concerns a highly organized and systematic program for reproducing videotapes on a massive scale.

In Encyclopedia Britannica v. Crooks, 447 F.Supp. 243 (1978), the court directed the Board to stop videotaping educational films or television programs off the public airwaves.

Quinto v. Legal Times of Washington, 506 F.Supp. 554 (1981), involved another instance in which the amount of the work that was used mitigated against a claim of fair use. In 1979, second-year law student David Quinto wrote an article describing the experiences

Harvard Law students had while employed by law firms during the summer. The article was published in the Harvard Law Record. Shortly thereafter, the Legal Times published a verbatim copy of Quinto's article; the only difference was that the Legal Times deleted two of the seventeen paragraphs, apparently so that the article would fit on a specific number of pages. The court ruled:

> The admitted reprinting of approximately 92% of plaintiff's story precludes the fair use defense under prior law. It is well settled that the fair use defense is based on a concept of reasonableness and that it is unavailable where there has been extensive verbatim copying or paraphrasing such as in this case.

In Iowa State University Research Foundation v. American Broadcasting Company, 621 F.2d 57 (1980), the court cited a considerably smaller percentage of a work in defining "substantial amount." The case involved ABC Sports' use of a portion of the 28-minute student-produced film titled "Champion," a biography of Olympic champion wrestler Dan Gable. ABC stressed that it used only two and one-half minutes of the film, suggesting that such limited copying is insignificant.   The court disagreed: "ABC actually broadcast approximately eight percent of "Champion," some of it on three separate occasions. Obviously, ABC found this footage essential, or at least of some importance." The court concluded that the fair use defense was not available to ABC.

> Though television network possessed an unfettered right to use any factual information revealed in film biography of champion wrestler for the purpose of enlightening its audience, the network could claim no need to bodily appropriate plaintiff's expression of that information by utilizing portions of the actual film without consent of the copyright owner.

Cases cited in this section demonstrate that two distinct criteria may be used to determine whether the amount of the work used constitutes infringement. In Encyclopedia Britannica and Quinto, the fair use defense was denied on the basis of quantity of amount used. In Iowa State University Research Foundation, the fair use defense was rejected because of the quality of the amount used.

EFFECT OF USE UPON VALUE OF WORK

Time v. Bernard Geis Associates, 293 F.Supp. 130 (1968), provided an instance where a publisher's willingness to compensate the copyright owner contributed to a determination of fair use. When President John F. Kennedy was killed, Abraham Zapruder was at the scene filming the event. His film, the most important photographic evidence concerning the fatal shots, was purchased and eventually appeared in several issues of Life. When Josiah Thompson wrote Six Seconds in Dallas, a book that analyzed the assassination, he included copies of parts of Zapruder's film. Life had refused an offer by Bernard Geis Associates, Thompson's publisher, to pay a royalty equal to the entire profits from publication of the book in return for permission to use the film. Life sued, charging that certain frames of the Zapruder film were "stolen surreptitiously" by Thompson. The court was impressed by the offer Geis Associates had made to pay all of its profits for permission to use the film. The court applied the criteria for determining fair use and found that the balance was in favor of Thompson. There was public interest in having the fullest information available about the Kennedy assassination. Thompson engaged in serious work and had a theory entitled to public consideration. While the theory could be explained with sketches, an explanation with photographic copies was easier to understand. The court stressed that Thompson's book was not purchased because it contained the Zapruder pictures; it was purchased because of Thompson's theory, illustrated by Zapruder's pictures. Also, there seemed to be little injury to Life. This was a case of fair use.

In Italian Book Corporation v. American Broadcasting Companies, 458 F.Supp. 65 (1978), a company brought action against ABC for infringement of a song titled "Dova sta Zaza." The alleged infringement occurred when an ABC television crew, covering the annual San Gennaro Festival in the Little Italy section of Manhattan, filmed portions of a band playing music and then played the strip on the evening news. In sustaining the fair-use defense, the court held:

> The use which defendant made of the song in question is not competitive with the commercial use plaintiff seeks to make of the song. No loss of profit or lessening of the song's value as the result of defendant's use was demonstrated; on the contrary, plaintiff has stipulated that the use complained of "did not result in any actual damage to the plaintiff, or to the market for said work."

Salinger v. Random House, 811 F.2d 90 (1987), involved an infringement suit brought by author J.D. Salinger against Ian Hamilton, a biographer who had quoted and paraphrased substantial portions of Salinger's personal, copyrighted, unpublished letters, which had considerable "potential market value." In its decision for Salinger, the court cited effect on the market as a contributing factor. Even though Hamilton's biography would not displace the market for the letters, "some impairment...seems likely" because Hamilton copied "virtually all of the most interesting passages of the letters, including several highly expressive insights about writing and literary criticism."

In Rogers v. Koons, 960 F.2d 301 (1992), a photographer sued a sculptor for infringing one of his photographs. The court decided that the photographer had established a valid ownership of copyright in his original work of art and that the sculptor copied the work without authorization. In addressing the fourth criterion for fair use, the court noted that the act of copying in a different medium was an irrelevant concern. In this case there was nothing in the record to support a claim that the sculptor produced the copy "for anything other than sale as high-priced art." Accordingly the likelihood of future harm to the original work is "presumed" because the photographer's "market for his work has been prejudiced."

Though all four criteria for determining fair use are vital, the Supreme Court, per Justice O'Connor, has referred to criterion four as "undoubtedly the single most important element of fair use" (Harper & Row v. Nation, 105 S. Ct. 2233, 1985). The reasoning is based on pure economics — permitting "fair use" to displace normal copyright channels disrupts the copyright market without commensurate public benefit. Accordingly, the fourth criterion — effect of use upon value of work — may be the principal determiner of infringement or fair use.

CONCLUSION

The following principles regulate communication law regarding COPYRIGHT:

1. Copyright law enables an author to protect his or her work against plagiarism. To secure a copyright, an author should place a proper notice in a prominent place in the work, and file appropriate forms with the Register of Copyright.

2. Tests of copyright infringement include:
   a. originality — is the copied material the original work of the plaintiff?
   b. copying — did defendant copy plaintiff's work?
   c. substantiality — did defendant appropriate a sufficient amount of plaintiff's work?
   d. access — did defendant have the opportunity to copy the work?

3. The criteria for determining "fair use" of a copyrighted work are:
   a. purpose and character of the use,
   b. nature of copyrighted work,
   c. amount of work used,
   d. effect of use on value of the work.

KEY DECISIONS

1918 — INTERNATIONAL NEWS SERVICE — held that while facts cannot be copyrighted, the style and manner in which the facts are presented can be protected

1968 — GEIS — set forth guidelines for fair use

1968 — FORTNIGHTLY — maintained that a cable television system does not "perform" copyrighted works

1974 — TELEPROMPTER — held that importation of distant signals did not constitute a "performance" under copyright law

1975 — AIKEN — cautioned against awarding too much economic protection for copyright owners

1984 — SONY — held that copyright law does not forbid the video recording of television programs for personal use

1991 — FEIST — held that "originality" rather than "hard work" was the determining criterion of copyrightability

1996 — LOTUS — held that computer command structures are an uncopyrightable "method of operation," not a copyrightable creative aspect

RECOMMENDED READING

Goldwag, Celia, "Copyright Infringement and the First Amendment," Columbia Law Review 79 (March, 1979), 320-40.

Helm, Virginia M., What Educators Should Know About Copyright Bloomington: Phi Delta Kappa, 1986.

Jacobson, Jeffrey E., "Fair Use: Considerations in Written Works," Communications and the Law 2 (Fall, 1980), 17-38.

Patterson, L. R., "Free Speech, Copyright, and Fair Use," Vanderbilt Law Review 40 (January 1987), 1-66.

Patterson, L. R., "Understanding Fair Use," Law and Contemporary Problems 55 (Spring, 1992), 249-66.

CHAPTER 10

NEWS

In 1643, the English Parliament enacted a law that required licensing of the press. All printed material had to be registered with the Stationers' Company prior to publication. The Company had power to search for unlicensed presses, and to seize illegal publications. Numerous individuals defied the law. Some were brought before the courts of the Star Chamber and the High Commission, where illegal printers were sentenced to mutilation, life imprisonment, or hanging. In 1695, the licensing system was terminated.

Censorship took a different form in the American colonies. Prosecution for libel replaced licensing as the method through which the government restrained the press. The most memorable case involved John Peter Zenger, editor of the New York Weekly Journal. Politicians frequently used Zenger's paper to criticize the governor of New York. In 1734, Zenger was charged with publishing seditious libel, and was jailed for eight months prior to trial. When Zenger finally came to trial, the jury ignored the judge's instructions and decided that Zenger was not guilty. The jury deviated from accepted procedure. Under common law, truth was an irrelevant defense. And, the judge, not the jury, determined whether the publication contained seditious libel. The jury simply ascertained whether the defendant had published the material. During Zenger's trial, the jury recognized truth as a valid defense, and the jury decided both issues — the fact of the printing, and the libelousness of the words. The Zenger verdict marked a tremendous achievement for free expression in the American colonies.

The Sedition Act, which Congress passed in 1798, established as a misdemeanor the publishing of any false or scandalous writings designed to bring the government into disrepute, or incite resistance to the law. Under this statute, leading Republican journalists were punished because of their criticism of the Federalist Administration. The unpopularity of the Act led to the defeat of President John Adams and the Federalist Party in their bid for reelection. Under President Thomas Jefferson, the Sedition Act expired on March 3, 1801.[1] The Sedition Act represented an early legislative effort at managing information. Through the years, other attempts to regulate the gathering and publication of news have persisted.

NEWS GATHERING

One responsibility of the news media is to inform citizens about their government. Principal concerns include the efficiency level at which the government is operating and whether public officials are behaving honestly and responsibly. The gathering of information is essential to accomplishing such functions. Yet, news media cannot publish information if reporters lack access to it. In several cases, the courts have considered various rights associated with news gathering.

NEWS REPORTER'S PRIVILEGE

News reporters claim a privilege to refuse to testify before grand juries, and in courts. They argue that if reporters are required to identify confidential sources of information, the ability to use such sources in the future diminishes. Such a requirement impedes the ability to gather news. In Branzburg v. Hayes, 92 S.Ct. 2646 (1972), the Supreme Court handed down an important ruling on the matter of news reporter's privilege. The decision arose out of three separate cases.

In November, 1969, the Louisville Courier-Journal carried an article under reporter Paul Branzburg's by-line, describing two young people synthesizing hashish from marijuana. A grand jury subpoenaed Branzburg but he refused to reveal the identities of any individuals he had seen making hashish. Branzburg argued that the Kentucky reporters' privilege statute authorized his refusal to answer. In January, 1971, Branzburg wrote a story that described drug use in Frankfurt, Kentucky. The article claimed that in order to obtain a comprehensive view of the "drug scene," Branzburg had spent two weeks interviewing and observing drug users. Branzburg was subpoenaed to appear before a grand jury; he objected. An order was then issued that protected Branzburg from revealing confidential sources of information, but required that he answer any questions that concerned criminal acts he actually saw committed. Branzburg argued that if he were required to reveal information given to him in confidence, his effectiveness as a reporter would be severely damaged.

In July, 1970, Paul Pappas, a television newsperson-photographer, covered a Black Panther news conference in New Bedford, Massachusetts. Pappas recorded and photographed a statement presented by a Black Panther leader. Later that evening, Pappas was allowed to remain inside Panther headquarters when he agreed not to disclose anything that transpired inside the building, except an anticipated police raid. Pappas remained inside the headquarters for about three hours but there was no police raid and Pappas wrote no story concerning the incident. Two months later, Pappas appeared before a grand jury and refused to answer questions about what had occurred inside the headquarters. He claimed that the First Amendment afforded him a privilege to protect confidential informants and their information.

In February, 1970, Earl Caldwell, a reporter for the New York Times assigned to cover black militant groups, was ordered to appear before a grand jury to testify regarding interviews given him by leaders of the Black Panther Party, regarding the organization's aims, purposes, and activities. Caldwell objected on the ground that if he were required to appear in secret before the grand jury, it would "suppress vital First Amendment freedoms...by driving a wedge of distrust and silence between the news media and the militants." Caldwell argued that "so drastic an incursion upon First Amendment freedoms" should not be permitted "in the absence of a compelling governmental interest." In response, the government pointed out that the grand jury was investigating possible criminal activities. When Caldwell refused to appear before the grand jury, he was jailed for contempt.

Eventually, these cases reached the Supreme Court. The argument presented by the newsmen was:

> ...to gather news it is often necessary to agree either not to identify the source of information published or to publish only part of the facts revealed, or both; that if the reporter is nevertheless forced to reveal these confidences to a grand jury, the source so identified and other confidential sources of other reporters will be measurably deterred from furnishing publishable information, all to the detriment of the free flow of information protected by the First Amendment.

The majority opinion of the Court went against the reporters. The opinion, prepared by Justice Byron White, noted that requiring newsmen to testify before grand juries did not abridge First Amendment guarantees. White observed that news reporter's privilege enjoyed no constitutional safeguard. White acknowledged, however, that state legislatures were free to fashion shield laws to protect reporter's privilege in individual states. White claimed that the Court was "powerless to erect any bar to state courts responding in their own way and construing their own constitutions so as to recognize a newsman's privilege, either qualified or absolute."

The minority opinion, written by Justice Potter Stewart, set forth a three-prong test which should apply when a reporter is asked to appear before a grand jury to reveal confidences. According to Stewart, the government should: 1) demonstrate that the reporter has information that is clearly relevant to the probable violation of law, 2) demonstrate that the information cannot be obtained by alternative means, and 3) demonstrate a compelling interest in the information. Justice Stewart, fearing a "chilling effect," cautioned:

> ...the sad paradox of the Court's position is that when a grand jury may exercise an unbridled subpoena power, and sources involved in sensitive matters become fearful of disclosing information, the newsman will not only cease to be a useful grand jury witness; he will cease to investigate and publish information about issues of public import.

By the time the Supreme Court heard these cases, the Massachusetts and California grand juries had been dismissed; Pappas and Caldwell were already free. Branzburg had moved to Detroit, and Michigan refused to extradite him to Kentucky.

The Branzburg Court was deeply divided about news reporter's privilege. The division has also been evident in the lower courts. Following Branzburg, some courts upheld, while others denied the privilege. In several of the cases, Justice Stewart's three criteria were employed in rendering a decision. For example, the Baker v. F. & F. Investment, 470 F.2d 778 (1972), court held that "federal law on the question of compelled disclosure by journalists of their confidential sources is at best ambiguous." The judge analyzed Branzburg and noted that while federal law did not recognize journalist's privilege, neither did it require disclosure of confidential sources in every case. The judge noted that there were other sources of information that had not been exhausted. The judge also claimed that forced disclosure of confidential sources has a deterrent effect on investigative reporting and ultimately "threatens freedom of the press and the public's need to be informed."

In Democratic National Committee v. McCord, 356 F.Supp 1394 (1973), the court could not "blind itself to the possible 'chilling effect' the enforcement of these broad subpoenas would have on the flow of information to the press, and so to the public." According to the court, there had been no showing that alternative sources of evidence had been exhausted, nor had there been any showing of the materiality of the documents sought by the subpoenas.

In Morgan v. State, 337 So.2d 951 (1976), the court noted that the law enforcement agencies had not demonstrated a compelling need:

> These contempt proceedings were not brought to punish violation of a criminal statute and were not part of an effort to obtain information needed in a criminal investigation. Their purpose was to force a newspaper reporter to disclose the source of published information, so that the authorities could silence the source. The present case falls squarely within this language in the Branzburg plurality opinion: "Official harassment of the press undertaken not for purposes of law enforcement but to disrupt a reporter's relationship with his news sources would have no justification."

In Riley v. City of Chester, 612 F.2d 708 (1979), the court ruled that a reporter enjoys a "qualified" privilege when the "availability of the information from other sources" is not adequately pursued, and when the information sought "appears to have only marginal relevance to the case." In Riley, as in Baker, McCord, and Morgan, the courts ignored the thrust of Branzburg and recognized newsreporter's privilege.

In other cases, the courts rejected claims of news reporter's privilege. Bursey v. United States, 446 F.2d 1059 (1972), involved a speech in which David Hilliard, Chief-of-Staff of the militant Black Panther Party, claimed, "We will kill Richard Nixon." Hilliard's speech was printed in The Black Panther. Reporters for the newspaper were called before a grand jury, but refused to answer questions. They were held in contempt, and appealed. The court maintained that freedom of the press was not guaranteed solely to shield reporters "from unwarranted governmental harassment"; the "larger purpose was to protect public access to information." The reporters had to answer questions about threats against the life of the President. These questions were vital to the government's investigation, and the impact of such questions "on lawful association and protected expression" was "so slight that governmental interests would prevail."

The court also refused to recognize journalist's privilege in United States v. Liddy, 354 F.Supp 208 (1972). The Los Angeles Times printed four articles concerning the Watergate break-in. The stories contained information obtained from Alfred Baldwin, "in more than five hours of tape-recorded interviews with the Times." George Gordon Liddy, one of the Watergate defendants, sought a subpoena to order reporters to produce all documents related to their interviews with Baldwin. The reporters objected. The court noted that the First Amendment right to gather news afforded "no absolute privilege against the compelled revelation of news sources." Even though the public had an interest in the investigation of criminal activity, it had "an even deeper interest in assuring that every defendant receives a fair trial." The court emphasized that Liddy's right to secure evidence to counter Baldwin's testimony outweighed any First Amendment considerations. The reporters were required to produce the tapes.

The court also denied news reporter's privilege in Caldero v. Tribune Publishing Company, 562 P.2d 791 (1977). The case involved an article that described a police shooting incident, and which attributed certain statements to an undisclosed "police expert." The reporter was held in contempt when he refused to disclose the identity of the source. He appealed. The court, citing Branzburg, ruled that no "constitutional provisions in regard to freedom of speech and press afforded newsmen a privilege against such disclosure."

Scarce v. United States, 5 F.3d 397 (1993), provides another example in which the court denied reporter's privilege. The case originated when a group of vandals broke into the animal research facility at a west coast university and stole or set free several animals. The Animal Liberation Front claimed responsibility for the acts. A graduate student in the Department of Sociology, who had conducted extensive interviews and then authored several publications on animal rights groups, refused to answer questions of a federal grand jury on the ground that he was entitled to a "scholar's privilege" under the First Amendment. The court held that the student was required to disclose data related to his research even though he had received that information in confidence. He had to respond to relevant questions posed by the grand jury or face a contempt ruling. In Scarce, as in Bursey, Liddy, and Caldero, the courts denied reporter's privilege.

Following Branzburg, the courts have been somewhat inconsistent in deciding the matter of reporter's privilege. Nonetheless, courts have been guided by the three part test enunciated in Justice Stewart's minority opinion in Branzburg. Most judges acknowledge a "qualified" privilege unless the plaintiff demonstrates that 1) the reporter's source has relevant information, 2) alternative sources of information have been exhausted, and 3) a compelling need dictates surrender of the information.

A related issue appeared in Cohen v. Cowles Media Company, 111 S.Ct. 2513 (1991). During the 1982 Minnesota gubernatorial race, Dan Cohen, who was associated with one political party's campaign, gave court records concerning another party's candidate to the publisher for the Minneapolis Star and Tribune after he received a promise of confidentiality. Nonetheless, the paper identified him in their story and he was fired from his job. Cohen sued, alleging breach of contract. A jury returned a verdict in Cohen's favor, awarding him $200,000 in compensatory damages and $500,000 in punitive damages. Upon appeal, the Supreme Court sided with Cohen. Justice White noted that "Minnesota law simply requires those making promises to keep them.

The parties themselves, as in this case, determine the scope of their legal obligations, and any restrictions that may be placed on the publication of truthful information are self-imposed." According to White, it was "beyond dispute" that "a newspaper has no special immunity from the application of general laws" and "has no special privilege to invade the rights and liberties of others." The newspaper publisher should have kept his promise and Cohen should have remained a confidential source of information.

SHIELD LAWS

More than half the state legislatures have passed "shield laws" which set forth the conditions under which a news reporter's privilege applies.   Some states — for example, New York, Alabama, and Nevada — have almost absolute laws. Other state laws are qualified and forbid use of the privilege in specific situations. In New Mexico, a reporter may be compelled to reveal a source if disclosure is "essential to prevent injustice." The Indiana law restricts protection to news reporters connected with a paper that has been published for five consecutive years in the same city and has a paid circulation of two percent of the population of the county in which it is published. In Arkansas, the law provides that a reporter may be forced to disclose a source of information if it can be demonstrated that the story was written or published with malice. Overall, shield laws from state to state are inconsistent regarding the information, personnel, and media protected, as well as the procedures under which the privilege may be invoked. Several shield laws have been subject to court interpretation, and in such cases the interpretation has been narrow — tending to favor disclosure.

Newspaperman David Lightman, while investigating drug use in Maryland, learned that a store proprietor allowed customers to smoke some marijuana before making a purchase. Lightman indicated in a news story that he had observed a "customer" conversing with the storekeeper. Lightman was summoned by a grand jury, but he refused to disclose any information. The court found Lightman in contempt, noting that not all information published by news reporters has as its origin a "source" protected by Maryland's shield law. When a reporter, because of his or her own investigative efforts personally observes illegal activity,

> ...the newsman, and not the persons observed, is the "source" of the news or information in the sense contemplated by the statute. To conclude other-wise in such circumstances would be to insulate the news itself from disclosure and not merely the source, a result plainly at odds with the Maryland law.

If Lightman's information had been learned, not by personal observation, but through an informant, the identity of that informant would be protected. In Lightman v. Maryland, 294 A.2d 149 (1972), the court concluded that Lightman could be required to reveal the location of the shop and the identity of any persons who had engaged in illegal activities.

People v. Dan, 41 App.Div.2d 687 (1973), involved a court interpretation of the New York shield law. Television newscaster Stewart Dan was assigned to cover the Attica prison riots. He was subsequently called before a grand jury and asked to testify concerning what he had observed. He refused, citing the shield law as a defense. The court noted that the questions posed by the grand jury did not require disclosure of news or the sources of news, but merely requested testimony about events Dan had personally observed. The shield law allowed reporters to refuse to disclose the identity of any source who had supplied information, but the law "does not permit them to refuse to testify about events which they observed personally, including the identities of the persons whom they observed."

In WBAI-FM v. Proskin, 42 App.Div.2d 5 (1973), the court heard another New York case. Radio station WBAI-FM received an anonymous telephone call, claiming that a letter, describing an imminent bomb threat, had been placed in a nearby phone booth. A newscaster from the station found the letter, which stated that the "Weather Underground" was about to bomb certain offices in Albany. The newscaster immediately notified the police. An explosion occurred as threatened, causing considerable property damage. A month later, the station was subpoenaed to produce the letter. The station refused, claiming the shield law as a defense. According to the court, the statute protected a newscaster only when "the information was received under a cloak of confidentiality."

> The author of the letter took pains to conceal his identity by signing the letter "Weather Underground," and to insure that appellant would obtain the letter without learning its author's identity. Clearly, he was not willing to rely upon appellant to shield his identity from the authorities. He refused to establish a confidential relationship with appellant but preferred to talk with anyone who answered the phone. Moreover, since the letter was left in a public telephone booth where it might have been found by anyone and turned over to the police, it is clear that the author could not have been relying upon appellant to withhold the letter itself.

In re Farr, 111 Cal.Rptr. 649 (1974), involved the California shield law. It began with the refusal by William Farr, a reporter for the Los Angeles Herald Examiner, to identify the source of information regarding murders already committed and those planned by the Charles

Manson group. The court held Farr in contempt. It ordered him incarcerated in the county jail until he answered the questions. He appealed. The court of appeals noted that the California shield law provided a newsreporter's privilege to "a publisher, editor, reporter, or other person connected with or employed upon a newspaper, or by a press association." Even though Farr had been employed by a newspaper when he obtained the statement, he was no longer a newsman when questioned by the court. He was no longer entitled to protection under the law.

In re Investigative File, 4 M.L.Rptr. 1865 (1978), provides another example of restrictive interpretation of a shield law. The case involved the work of Associated Press investigative reporter Steve Moore, who, after a highway patrolman was fatally wounded, recorded a conversation with a man who identified himself as the killer. Shortly thereafter, the Montana Attorney General demanded that the AP release the tape. The AP refused on the ground that the information was protected under the Montana shield law. The court upheld the subpoena, noting that while the law protected the reporter who gathered the information, it did not protect his employer. A news service could not assert reporter's privilege.

People v. Korkala, 472 N.Y.S.2d 310 (1984), involved criminal charges that were issued against George Korkala for selling arms to police officers who posed as terrorists. Korkala fled the country. While a fugitive in Lebanon, Korkala gave an extensive interview to Mike Wallace, who broadcast part of it on the "60 Minutes" television program. Subsequently, Korkala was apprehended and brought to trial. The prosecution contended that since the interview lasted several hours, but only 22 minutes of it was broadcast, the entire tape should be provided so that the content could be considered in its exact context. CBS claimed that the material was protected under the New York shield law. The court disagreed, noting that "obviously there was no understanding...of confidentiality in respect to the...interview. Indeed, the clear expectation was that the interview would be broadcast on '60 minutes' thus exposing both the material and its source." The shield law did not apply because the interview was given "without any expectation of confidentiality."

Matera v. Superior Court, 825 P.2d 971 (1992), involved a state legislator who became a defendant in a criminal prosecution after she was caught in an undercover sting operation. When the legislator learned about an author who was writing a book about the investigation, she subpoenaed the author's notes and other documents. The author refused to submit the materials, claiming a privilege under the Arizona Media Subpoena Law. The court rejected this claim. It held that the law's application was "limited to persons engaged in the gathering and dissemination of news to the public on a regular basis." Furthermore, the court noted that there was no proof that compliance with the subpoena would cause the author to reveal confidential sources, nor would it impede the author in the information gathering process. The author was required to testify.

In Matera, as in Investigative File, Lightman, Dan, Proskin, Farr, and Korkala, the court required the news reporter or writer to reveal the requested information. In these cases, shield laws did not protect the journalist or author. The laws provided an illusion of protection rather than actual protection for the news gatherer.

EXECUTIVE PRIVILEGE

The Supreme Court recognized the concept of "Executive Privilege" in Marbury v. Madison, 55 S.Ct. 60 (1803). Chief Justice John Marshall held that a U.S. President was not required to reveal matters communicated in confidence.

> By the Constitution of the U.S., the President is invested with certain important political powers, in the exercise of which he is to use his own discretion, and is accountable only to the country in his political character and to his own conscience.

Throughout history, Executive Privilege has been invoked by various Presidents. During the 1970s, the concept was examined by the courts in several cases involving taperecorded conversations between President Richard Nixon and his advisors.

In 1973, Judge John Sirica subpoenaed President Nixon to produce tape recordings of particular meetings and telephone conversations between himself and his advisors. Nixon declined; he argued that Sirica lacked jurisdiction because Executive Privilege was absolute regarding Presidential communications. The court of appeals rejected Nixon's argument; the President was not above the law. Interference with the President's privilege depended, however, on the grand jury's ability to demonstrate the relevancy of the evidence to its investigation. The court felt that *in camera* judicial inspection constituted an appropriate method of protecting both the grand jury's purpose of obtaining relevant evidence and the President's privilege. During an *in camera* hearing, "privileged" material could be deleted, so that only "unprivileged" matter would go to the grand jury. In Nixon v. Sirica, 487 F.2d 700 (1973), the court protected the concept of Executive Privilege, while at the same time ruling that the privilege was not absolute.

A year later, the Supreme Court reached the same conclusion. In 1974, a federal grand jury named President Nixon as an unindicted co-

conspirator in the Watergate incident and subpoenaed him to produce tape recordings of conversations he had held with advisors. Nixon released edited transcripts of some conversations but refused to release other tapes. He asserted that the material was protected by Executive Privilege. When the case came to the Supreme Court, the justices ruled against Nixon. In United States v. Nixon, 94 S.Ct. 309 (1974), the Court concluded:

> ...when the ground for asserting privilege as to subpoenaed materials sought for use in a criminal trial is based only on the generalized interest in confidentiality, it cannot prevail over the fundamental demands of due process of law in the fair administration of criminal justice. The generalized assertion of privilege must yield to the demonstrated, specific need for evidence in a pending criminal trial.

The Court ordered that the subpoenaed materials be submitted to the district court to determine by *in camera* examination what evidence might be relevant.

After Richard Nixon resigned as President, he made an agreement with the General Services Administration for the storage of documents and tape recordings accumulated during his tenure in office. Three months later, Congress passed the Presidential Recordings and Materials Preservation Act which directed the Administrator of the General Services Administration to screen the materials, return to Nixon those that were personal, preserve materials of historical value, and make available any materials that might be relevant in judicial proceedings. The Administrator was also directed to formulate regulations regarding public access to the materials. Nixon initiated court action, alleging that the Act violated Executive Privilege. The Court noted that the screening and cataloguing of materials was performed by professional archivists. According to Justice William Brennan,

> ...the screening constitutes a very limited intrusion by personnel in the Executive Branch sensitive to executive concerns. These very personnel have performed the identical task in each of the Presidential libraries without any suggestion such activity has in any way interfered with executive confidentiality.

The Court concluded that the screening process contemplated by the Act would not constitute a more severe intrusion into Presidential confidentiality than the *in camera* inspection approved in United States v. Nixon. In Nixon v. Administrator of General Services, 97 S.Ct. 2777 (1977), the Court upheld the constitutionality of the Presidential Recordings and Materials Preservation Act. In this case, the Court reaffirmed that Executive Privilege was not absolute.

Nixon v. Warner Communications, 98 S.Ct. 1306 (1978), involved several tapes that were played during trials stemming from the

Watergate break-in. After the trial had begun, Warner Communications sought permission to copy, broadcast, and sell to the public the portions of the tapes played during trial. President Nixon objected on the ground that there were no safeguards against distortion through cutting, erasing, and splicing of tapes. Nixon expressed concern that such a procedure could result in personal embarrassment and anguish. Judge Sirica denied Warner Communications' request for access to the tapes. According to Sirica, such access might

> ...result in the manufacture of permanent phonograph records and tape recordings, perhaps with commentary by entertainers; marketing of the tapes would probably involve mass merchandising techniques designed to generate excitement in an air of ridicule to stimulate sales.

The Supreme Court agreed with Sirica. The Court stressed that the content of the tapes was given wide publicity by the media. So, the issue was not whether the press had been denied access to information that the public had a right to know, "but whether copies of the tapes — to which the public had never had physical access — must be made available for copying." The Court concluded that the First Amendment "generally grants the press no right to information about a trial superior to that of the general public." In Warner Communications, the Court sided with Nixon.

FREEDOM OF INFORMATION

Governmental secrecy has been a frequent barrier to information gathering by both news reporters and the general public. An instance occurred in United States v. Reynolds, 73 S.Ct. 528 (1953), a case which involved conflicting rights — the right of the public to know versus the right of the government to maintain secrecy in the interest of national security. The case began with the crash of a U.S. Air Force plane that was testing secret electronic equipment. The widows of government employees who were killed in the accident suspected negligence on the part of the Air Force. They wanted to examine the investigatory report of the crash. The Secretary of the Air Force refused to release the information on the ground that military secrets were involved. The case reached the Supreme Court. Chief Justice Frederick Vinson noted that air power was a potent weapon in the U.S. defense arsenal and that newly developed electronic devices had greatly enhanced the capabilities of air power. Such devices had to be kept secret if their military advantage was to benefit the national interest. The Court upheld the Air Force's claim of privilege, thereby protecting the interests of governmental secrecy.

Such interests were challenged in 1966, with the passage of the

Freedom of Information Act (FOIA). This measure was designed to make available to newsmen and other members of the public various types of information long closed to public inspection. The statute stated that all persons had access to "federal agency records," except those that fell into nine categories of exemption:

1. material concerning national defense or foreign policy,
2. information related to internal personnel rules,
3. matters exempted from disclosure by another statute,
4. confidential trade secrets and financial data,
5. interagency and intraagency memorandums,
6. personnel and medical files,
7. investigatory records compiled for law enforcement purposes,
8. information regarding the regulation of financial institutions, and
9. geological and geophysical data.

Initially, the act did not provide much improvement in obtaining information. When requests were made for records, federal agencies stalled in releasing requested information. Court action moved slowly, and often the information was no longer "news" or "relevant" by the time it was released. In 1974, and again in 1976, Congress amended FOIA in an effort to facilitate access to information. Procedural changes made records considerably more accessible. Under the amendments, federal agencies must answer requests for records within ten days. If an appeal is filed after a denial, the agency has 20 days to respond to the appeal. Each agency is required to publish a quarterly index of records. Agencies must file annual reports of all records to which access was granted. Any agency employee who denies access in an arbitrary manner can be disciplined by the Civil Service Commission. In 1976, Congress enacted the Government in Sunshine Act, which requires numerous agencies to conduct meetings in public. These statutes facilitate access to government records. Nonetheless, several tests of the Freedom of Information Act have reached the courts. The cases fall into two classifications: defining "agency records," and clarifying specific exemptions.

Defining "agency records"

The Freedom of Information Act defines an agency as "any executive department, military department, government corporation, government-controlled corporation or other establishment in the executive branch of government (including the Executive Office of the President), or any independent regulatory agency." In three cases, the courts were asked to clarify the definition. Long v. United States Internal Revenue Service, 596 F.2d 362 (1979), involved a request for the information the Internal Revenue Service had compiled in the

Taxpayer Compliance Measurement Program. The program involves a continuing series of statistical studies which measure the level of compliance with federal tax laws. The requested data were in the form of check sheets and data tapes. The Court determined that computer tapes are "agency records" and that the deletion of identifying information (names, addresses, social security numbers) does not create a new record. The tapes were accessible under FOIA.

Kissinger v. Reporters Committee For Freedom of the Press, 100 S.Ct. 960 (1980), centered around taped telephone conversations Henry Kissinger had compiled when he served in the Nixon and Ford administrations. Kissinger donated the materials to the Library of Congress, subject to an agreement restricting public access for a specified period. Shortly thereafter, a group of news reporters requested that the State Department release the transcripts. The request was denied on the ground that the transcripts were not "agency records" because their deposit with the Library of Congress terminated State Department control. The Supreme Court, per Justice William Rehnquist, agreed. Rehnquist noted that "the FOIA is only directed at requiring agencies to disclose those 'agency records' for which they have chosen to retain possession or control." Since the State Department no longer controlled the transcripts, they were no longer considered as "agency records" under the FOIA.

Forsham v. Harris, 100 S.Ct. 978 (1980), concerned a group of private physicians and scientists who, in 1959, had formed the University Group Diabetes Program. The group conducted a long-term study of the effectiveness of diabetes treatment. The study was funded by Department of Health, Education, and Welfare grants. The study generated more than 55 million records documenting the treatment of over 1,000 diabetic patients. A national association of physicians involved in the treatment of diabetes patients requested access to the data in order to review the findings. The Supreme Court, per Justice Rehnquist, concluded that data generated by a private organization that had received funds from a federal agency, "but which data has not at any time been obtained by the agency, are not 'agency records' accessible under the FOIA."

Clarifying specific exemptions

Several cases have reached the courts after federal agencies invoked specific exemptions. The Epstein v. Resor, 421 F.2d 930 (1970), case involved Exemption 1 — material kept secret in the interest of national security. The case involved a historian who was preparing a book on forced repatriation of anticommunist Russians following World War II.

He sought to examine an Army file on the topic. The army contended that the information fell within Exemption 1. The historian initiated court action, arguing that the justices should examine the file *in camera* to determine whether the file should still be classified as top secret. The court noted that "the function of determining whether secrecy is required in the national interest is expressively assigned to the executive." The court claimed that "the judiciary has neither the 'aptitude, facilities, nor responsibility' to review these essentially political decisions." The court concluded that, under Exemption 1, the Army had justified withholding the information.

Environmental Protection Agency v. Mink, 935 S.Ct. 827 (1973), offered another challenge to Exemption 1. The case involved a news article which indicated that President Richard Nixon had received conflicting reports on the advisability of the underground nuclear test scheduled for that coming fall. Congresswoman Patsy Mink and 32 of her colleagues in the House of Representatives initiated court action. They contended that the court should examine the reports in private to determine whether they were classified properly or whether the government was simply trying to keep controversial information from the public. The EPA claimed that the documents involved highly sensitive matter vital to the national defense which had been classified "top secret." The Supreme Court indicated that Exemption 1 stated "with the utmost directness" that the Act exempted matters "specifically required by Executive order to be kept secret." This made "wholly untenable any claim that the Act intended to subject the soundness of executive security classifications to judicial review at the insistence of any objecting citizen." Furthermore, it negated the idea that Exemption 1 authorized *in camera* inspection of a document so that the court could "separate the secret from the supposedly nonsecret, and order disclosure of the latter." In the Court's opinion, once information was classified, that classification could not be challenged.

The Mink decision facilitated governmental abuse of power under Exemption 1. During the Watergate investigation, the Nixon Administration classified numerous documents under the national security label, thereby precluding the information from public inspection. The 1974 FOIA amendments, however, went a long way toward curbing such abuse. Under the changes, courts were able to review governmental decisions to withhold documents. Courts had the power to inspect documents *in camera* to determine if they were classified properly. And, the Executive branch had to specify the criteria used to justify a particular classification. The courts were thus able to determine whether the documents actually met the criteria.

Though the FOIA amendments specify actions courts may take,

those actions are not mandatory. In <u>Knopf v. Colby</u>, 509 F.2d 1362 (1975), the court refused to take such action on the ground that it lacked the expertise required to make the necessary judgments. The <u>Knopf</u> case involved a former employee of the state department who had agreed not to disclose classified information acquired during his employment. When the employee prepared a manuscript for publication, the CIA objected, contending that the material was classified. The publisher pointed out that the FOIA amendments provided that a judge could examine the contents of agency records *in camera* to determine whether such records could be withheld under the FOIA exemptions. However, the court noted:

> There is a presumption of regularity in the performance by a public official of his public duty. The presumption of regularity supports the official acts of public officers, and, in the absence of clear evidence to the contrary, courts presume that they have properly discharged their official duties.

In <u>Knopf</u>, the court refused to exercise power provided to it by the FOIA amendments. Such practice by the courts tends to impede the intent of the FOIA because information becomes accessible only when judges assume responsibility for assuring access.

<u>Vaughn v. Rosen</u>, 484 F.2d 820 (1973), provided a test of Exemption 2 — information related to internal personnel rules. The case arose when a law professor who was researching the Civil Service Commission sought disclosure of evaluations of personnel management programs. The Executive Director of the Commission refused disclosure. In <u>Vaughn</u>, the district court noted that enforcement of the FOIA was hampered by two barriers. First, the method of resolving disputes actually encouraged the government to contend that large amounts of information were exempt. There were no inherent incentives that would spur government agencies to disclose information. Second, since the burden of determining the justification of a government claim of exemption ultimately fell on the court system, there was "an innate impetus that encourages agencies automatically to claim the broadest possible grounds for exemption for the greatest amount of information." In an effort to remedy these shortcomings, the court established the following standards:

1. detailed justification — courts would no longer accept conclusionary and generalized allegations of exemptions, but would require a relatively detailed analysis of the situation,
2. specificity, separation, and indexing — in a large document, the agency had to specify in detail which portions of the document were considered disclosable and which were allegedly exempt,
3. adequate adversary testing — a trial court could designate a special master to examine documents and evaluate claims of

exemption. This person would assume the burden of examining and
evaluating documents that currently fell on the trial judge.

The <u>Vaughn</u> decision sought to eliminate barriers to the effective
operation of the FOIA.

In 1975, a test of Exemption 3 — matters specifically exempted by
another statute — reached the Supreme Court. The case,
<u>Administrator, Federal Aviation Administration v. Robertson</u>, 95
S.Ct. 2140 (1975), involved a request of the Federal Aviation
Administration to make available analyses of the operation of
commercial airlines. The Federal Aviation Act permitted the FAA
Administrator to withhold disclosure if it was judged to be unnecessary
for the public interest. The Administrator declined to make the reports
available on the ground that confidentiality was necessary for the
effectiveness of the program. The Supreme Court, in an opinion
prepared by Chief Justice Warren Burger, noted that Exemption 3 was
ambiguously worded and lacked clear standards for application. If
"specifically" applied only to documents specified — either by naming
them precisely or by identifying the category into which they fell —
such an interpretation required Congress to perform a virtually
impossible task. The Court upheld the FAA's decision to withhold
the information. Subsequently, in 1976, Congress amended
Exemption 3, stipulating that material could be exempted from
disclosure when a statute required the matter to be withheld from the
public, established particular criteria for withholding the matter, or
referred to particular types of information to be withheld. The Court
can no longer give Exemption 3 as broad an interpretation as it did in
<u>Robertson</u>.

<u>Sims v. Central Intelligence Agency</u>, 105 S.Ct. 1881 (1985), also
tested Exemption 3. Between 1953 and 1966, the Central Intelligence
Agency financed a research project, code-named MKULTRA, that was
established to counter Russian and Chinese advances in brainwashing
and interrogation techniques. In 1977, two concerned individuals
requested the names of the institutions and individuals who had
performed the research. The CIA declined to disclose the information,
citing as the exempting statute the National Security Act of 1947,
which identifies the Director of the CIA as "responsible for protecting
intelligence sources and methods from unauthorized disclosure." The
Court, per Chief Justice Burger, ruled that the National Security Act
qualified as a withholding statute. According to Burger, the statutes'
language "vested in the Director of Central Intelligence broad authority
to protect all sources of intelligence information from disclosure."

Several cases involved challenges to Exemption 5, which covers
interagency and intraagency memoranda. The <u>National Labor Relations</u>

Board v. Sears, 95 S.Ct. 1504 (1975), case provides an example. In July, 1971, Sears-Roebuck and Company requested that the general counsel of the National Labor Relations Board release certain memoranda that dealt with employer/union bargaining disputes. When the case reached the Supreme Court, Justice White held that some of the requested memoranda were subject to disclosure, while others were not. White distinguished between predecisional communications, which are privileged, and communications made after the decision and designed to explain it, which are not. In Sears, the Court held that memoranda that are an "expression of a point of view" are not subject to disclosure, while those that are "final opinions" and "dispositions of a charge" are not protected under Exemption 5. This opinion was reinforced in Renegotiation Board v. Grumman AirCraft Engineering Corporation, 95 S.Ct. 1491 (1975).

United States v. Weber Aircraft Corporation, 104 S.Ct. 1488 (1984), involved an incident in which the engine of an Air Force plane failed in flight. The pilot was seriously injured when he ejected from the aircraft. The incident was a significant air crash, which, under Air Force regulations, required a "safety investigation." When the pilot filed a damages suit against Weber Aircraft Corporation, the designer and manufacturer of the plane's ejection equipment, Weber sought release of the investigation reports. The Air Force refused. In Weber, the Court held that the requested documents were intraagency memoranda within the meaning of Exemption 5. The opinion, prepared by Justice John Stevens, noted that "the legislative history of Exemption 5...recognizes a need for claims of privilege when confidentiality is necessary to ensure frank and open discussion and hence efficient governmental operations."

Department of Air Force v. Rose, 96 S.Ct. 1592 (1976), involved an agency's attempt to refuse access to records by invoking Exemption 6, which protects personnel files. Student editors of the New York University Law Review, while researching for an article about disciplinary systems at the military service academies, were denied access to case summaries of honor and ethics hearings. Even though the students requested that all personal references or other identifying information be deleted, the U.S. Air Force Academy refused the request. The Court opinion, written by Justice Brennan, maintained that Exemption 6 did not create "a blanket exemption for personnel files." Since the case summaries contained only limited amounts of personal information, and because the files are widely disseminated for examination by fellow cadets, the documents could not be classified as a "personnel file" under Exemption 6. The Court decided that access to the case summaries with personal, identifying references deleted met the confidentiality interests embodied in Exemption 6. The Rose decision marked a rare instance in which the Supreme Court assured access to requested information.

U.S. Department of State v. Ray, 112 S.Ct. 541 (1991), also involved application of Exemption 6. The case began in the 1970s when severe economic depression and a dictatorial government motivated large numbers of Haitians to emigrate to Florida without obtaining permission from either the Haitian or United States' governments. A small number were eligible for asylum as political refugees, but most were subject to deportation. In response to this burgeoning illegal migration, President Reagan ordered that those who failed to qualify for refugee status be returned to their point of origin. Following this directive, the Secretary of State obtained assurance from the Haitian government that the returnees would not be subjected to harassment or prosecution for illegal departure. In order to monitor compliance with that assurance, the State Department conducted confidential interviews with a "representative sample" of unsuccessful emigrants about six months after their return. All but two of the emigrants reported that they had not been harassed or prosecuted since their return to Haiti. Michael Ray, a lawyer who represented Haitians, made an FOIA request for copies of reports of the interviews. The Department produced 25 documents which describe interviews with returnees, but in 17 of the documents, the names and other identifying information had been removed. Ray initiated court action, seeking release of the names. The Supreme Court held that the documents were "personnel and medical files" within the meaning of Exemption 6. According to the Court, "an individual's right to privacy must be balanced against the FOIA's basic policy of opening agency action to the light of public scrutiny." In this case, disclosure of the names would constitute an unwarranted invasion of the returnee's privacy.

United States Department of Defense v. Federal Labor Relations Authority, 114 S.Ct. 1006 (1994), also involved consideration of exemption 6. The controversy arose when two unions requested federal agencies to provide the names and home addresses of the agency employees represented by the unions. The agencies supplied the unions with the employees names and work stations, but refused to release home addresses. The unions filed unfair labor practice charges and the case eventually reached the Supreme Court. The opinion was prepared by Justice Clarence Thomas. He looked to the public interest and concluded that disclosure of the addresses would not appreciably further the citizens' understanding of the Government or the activities of the employing agencies. Looking at the private interests of the employees, Thomas noted:

Perhaps some of these individuals have failed to join the union that represents them due to the lack of familiarity with the union or its services. Others may be opposed to their union or to unionism in general on practical or ideological grounds. Whatever the reason that these employees have chosen not to become members of the union or to provide the union with their addresses, however, it is clear that they have *some* nontrivial privacy interest in nondisclosure, and in avoiding the influx of union-related mail, and, perhaps, union-related telephone calls or visits, that would follow disclosure.

Because the privacy intent substantially outweighed the public interest in disclosure, the Court concluded that disclosure would constitute a "clearly unwarranted invasion of personal privacy."

Bibles v. Oregon National Desert Association, 117 S.Ct. 795 (1997), involved an environmental group that filed suit under FOIA, seeking names and addresses of all persons receiving the Bureau of Land Management newsletter. The environmental group was concerned that those people should receive information from alternative sources that do not share the Bureau's "self-interest in presenting government activities in the most favorable light." The Supreme Court rejected the suit, holding that an asserted public interest in providing persons on the mailing list with additional information was insufficient to warrant disclosure. The court held that such disclosure would be inconsistent with the recent Department of Defense v. Federal Labor Relations Authority decision which held that "the *only* relevant public interest in the FOIA balancing analysis" is "the extent to which disclosure of information...would shed light on the agency's performance of it's statutory duties." Since that was not the purpose of the environmental group's request, disclosure was denied under Exemption 6.

Five cases involved Exemption 7 — records compiled for law-enforcement purposes. The first case was National Labor Relations Board v. Robbins Tire and Rubber Company, 98 S.Ct. 2311 (1978). Following a contested election involving employees of the Robbins Tire and Rubber Company, the National Labor Relations Board issued an unfair labor practice complaint. Prior to a hearing on the complaint, the company sought release of copies of all witnesses' statements collected during the NLRB investigation. The Supreme Court, in an opinion prepared by Justice Marshall, decided that Exemption 7 allows nondisclosure of "investigatory records compiled for law enforcement purposes," when producing such records would "interfere with enforcement proceedings." The Court noted the presence of such "interference."

The most obvious risk of "interference" with enforcement proceedings in this context is that employers or, in some cases, unions will coerce or intimidate employees and others who have given statements, in an effort to make them change their testimony or not testify at all.... Not only can the employer fire the employee, but job assignments can be switched, hours can be adjusted, wage and salary increases held up, and other more subtle forms of influence exerted. A union can often exercise similar authority over its members and officers.

In Robbins, the Court concluded that prehearing disclosure of witnesses' statements constituted the potential level of "interference" that Exemption 7 was designed to offset. In this instance, nondisclosure was justified to ensure effective law enforcement.

Federal Bureau of Investigation v. Abramson, 102 S.Ct. 2054 (1982), is the second case. In 1976, journalist Howard Abramson sought to obtain FBI documents that were transmitted to the White House, which concerned individuals who had criticized the Nixon administration. Abramson was preparing an article on possible misuse of governmental information for partisan political activity. The FBI refused to release the information, citing Exemption 7. In Abramson, the Supreme Court sided with the FBI. The opinion acknowledged that information that is originally compiled for law-enforcement purposes retains Exemption 7 status when such information is reproduced in a new document prepared for a non-law-enforcement purpose.

The third case, John Doe Agency v. John Doe Corporation, 110 S.Ct. 471 (1989), began in 1978 when a defense contractor and a federal auditing agency corresponded concerning accounting procedures and findings. Eight years later, a grand jury investigating possible fraudulent practices by the contractor issued a subpoena requesting all documents relating to the 1978 correspondence. The agency denied the request, citing Exemption 7. In court, lawyers argued that the request should be honored because the materials were not investigatory records when originally prepared. The Supreme Court, per Justice Harry Blackmun, disagreed:

Exemption 7 may be invoked to prevent the disclosure of documents not originally created for, but later gathered for, law enforcement purposes. The plain words of the statute contain no requirements that compilation be effected at a specific time, but merely require that the objects sought be compiled when the Government invokes the Exemption.

A fourth case involved the Federal Bureau of Investigation, an agency charged with responsibility for maintaining criminal identification records or "rap sheets" on millions of persons. The United States Department of Justice v. Reporters Committee for Freedom of the Press, 109 S.Ct. 1468 (1989), case began when a group of news correspondents requested the "rap sheet" of an individual who had ties with a legitimate business that was allegedly dominated by organized crime figures and which allegedly had obtained a number of defense contracts as a result of an improper arrangement with a corrupt congressman. The news reporters maintained that the information involved a matter of public interest. The FBI denied the request, claiming that the rap sheet was protected by Exemption 7 of the FIOA. Writing for the Supreme Court, Justice Stevens pointed out that Exemption 7, by its terms, permits an agency to withhold a document only when revelation "could be reasonably expected to constitute an *unwarranted* invasion of personal privacy." Stevens applied the balancing test and supported the FBI's position.

> Where, as here, the subject of a rap sheet is a private citizen and the information is in the Government's control as a compilation, rather than as a record of what the government is up to, the privacy interest in maintaining the rap sheets "practical obscurity" is always at its apex while the FOIA-based public interest in disclosure is at its nadir. Thus, as a categorical matter, rap sheets are excluded from disclosure by the Exemption in such circumstances.

The fifth case, United States Department of Justice v. Landano, 113 S.Ct. 2014 (1993), involved clarification of "confidential source," a term that is not defined in the FOIA. The case began when a convicted murderer, in an effort to support his claim that the prosecution had withheld material exculpatory evidence, filed Freedom of Information Act requests with the Federal Bureau of Investigation. The FBI declined to release information under Exemption 7 on the ground that the records' release "could reasonably be expected to disclose" the identity of a "confidential source." The FBI contended that all sources should be presumed confidential. The convicted murderer argued that a source is "confidential" only if the source is assured, explicitly or implicitly, that the sources cooperation will be disclosed to no one. The Supreme Court disagreed with both positions. The Court maintained that the FBI is not entitled to presume that all sources are confidential. The Court suggested guidelines for determining when a source can be considered "confidential" under Exemption 7.

> Some narrowly defined circumstances can provide a basis for inferring confidentiality. For example, it is reasonable to infer that paid informants normally expect their cooperation with the FBI to be kept confidential. Similarly, the character of the crime at issue and the source's relation to the crime may be relevant to determining whether a source cooperated with the FBI with an implied insurance of confidentiality.... To the extent that the Government's proof may compromise legitimate interests, the Government still can attempt to meet its burden with *in camera* affidavits.

The cases cited in this section involved efforts to define the nature of FOIA exemptions, as well as to clarify the scope of access to information under the FOIA. In most of the cases — Epstein, Mink, Robertson, Sims, Sears, Grumman, Weber, Ray, Federal Labor Relations Authority, Bibles, Robbins, Abramson, John Doe Agency, and Reporters Committee for Freedom of the Press — the Supreme Court sided with governmental agencies and approved the exemption from disclosure.

NEWS REPORTER BANS

In recent years, court actions have arisen when news reporters were banned from specific sources of news. These cases involved such issues as interviewing prisoners, access to judicial proceedings, admission to press conferences, third party privacy, and currency reproduction.

Prisoners

A regulation of the Bureau of Prisons states: "Press representatives will not be permitted to interview inmates. This rule shall apply even where the inmate requests or seeks an interview." In Pell v. Procunier, 94 S.Ct. 2800 (1974), and Saxbe v. Washington Post Company, 94 S.Ct. 2811 (1974), the Supreme Court heard challenges to this regulation.   Pell involved a California regulation that prohibited members of the press from conducting interviews with inmates. The policy had been established after face-to-face interviews with reporters resulted in some inmates receiving considerable notoriety. Journalist Eve Pell brought suit to prevent prison officials from enforcing the regulation. The Saxbe case occurred about the same time. Reporters from the Washington Post were denied interviews with inmates at federal prisons in Connecticut. The bans were challenged in court. In Pell and Saxbe, prisoners argued that the regulations curtailed their right to free speech. Journalists contended that the rules constituted an unconstitutional obstacle to news gathering. Both cases reached the Supreme Court, where the regulations were upheld. First of all, the Court rejected the prisoners' argument. The majority believed that prisoners' free-speech rights must be balanced against government interests in deterring crime and protecting internal security. Since alternative methods of communication were open to inmates, their free-speech rights had not been violated. The opinion noted that "the medium of written correspondence affords inmates an open and substantially unimpeded channel for communication with persons outside the prison, including representatives of the news media." Another alternative was visitation policy, which allowed prisoners to visit with their families, friends, clergy, and attorneys. Second, the Court denied the claim of the journalists. Freedom of the press was not violated because reporters retained access to information that was available to the general public. The First Amendment did not guarantee news reporters special access to information.

The Court reaffirmed the Pell and Saxbe decisions in Houchins v. KQED, 98 S.Ct. 2588 (1978). The case began when television station KQED carried a news report about the suicide of a prisoner at the jail in Santa Rita, California. The report contained a statement by a psychiatrist that the conditions at the jail were responsible for the ill health of prisoners, and a statement from a local sheriff which denied that prison conditions were responsible for prisoner illnesses. KQED asked permission to inspect and take pictures within the jail. After the request was refused, KQED filed suit, alleging that refusal violated the First Amendment right of media access. In an opinion prepared by Chief Justice Burger, the Court noted:

> Inmates in jails, prisons or mental institutions retain certain fundamental rights of privacy; they are not like animals in a zoo to be filmed and photographed at will by the public or by media reporters, however "educational" the process may be for others.

The Court cited Pell and Saxbe in concluding that the "news media have no constitutional right of access to a county jail, over and above that of other persons."

Judicial proceedings

Several decisions upheld the right of news-reporter access to judicial proceedings. Landmark Communications v. Virginia, 98 S.Ct. 1535 (1978), involved the question of news-reporter access to the investigation of a judge. On October 4, 1975, the Virginia Pilot, a Landmark newspaper, published an article that reported on a pending investigation of a judge who was identified in the account. A grand jury indicted the Landmark Company for violating a Virginia law that prohibited such divulgence. Landmark was tried, found guilty, and fined $500 plus the costs of prosecution. On appeal, the Supreme Court sided with the press.

> The operation of the Virginia Commission, no less than the operation of the judicial system itself, is a matter of public interest, necessarily engaging the attention of the news media. The article published by Landmark provided accurate factual information about a legislatively authorized inquiry pending before the Judicial Inquiry and Review Commission, and in doing so clearly served those interests in public scrutiny and discussion of governmental affairs which the First Amendment was adopted to protect.

Smith v. Daily Mail Publishing Company, 99 S.Ct. 2667 (1979), concerned the access of reporters to juvenile proceedings. In February, 1978, a 15-year old student was shot and killed at a junior high school in West Virginia. The assailant, a 14-year old classmate, was identified by seven eyewitnesses and was arrested by the police. The Charleston Daily Mail learned of the shooting by monitoring the police-band radio frequency. Reporters were immediately dispatched to the school and obtained the name of the assailant. The Daily Mail included the juvenile's name in an article in its afternoon paper. The newspaper company was subsequently indicted for violating a law that prohibited publication of the name of a youth involved in a juvenile proceeding. The case reached the Supreme Court. A unanimous decision noted that if a newspaper lawfully obtains information about a matter of public significance, state officials may not punish publication of the information without furthering an interest of the highest order. In Daily Mail, a "substantial interest" was lacking. The only interest cited by officials was to protect the anonymity of juvenile offenders. That interest could not justify criminal sanctions against this type of publication.

Several cases involved attempts by news gatherers to obtain access to trials. In Gannett v. DePasquale, 99 S.Ct. 2898 (1979), the Supreme Court considered whether members of the public have a constitutional right of access to a pretrial judicial proceeding, even though the accused, the prosecutor, and the judge all agreed to close the proceedings in order to assure a fair trial. In Gannett, two suspected murderers argued that adverse publicity had jeopardized their ability to receive a fair trial. The judge granted an exclusionary order. Shortly thereafter, a reporter sought to have the order set aside. The case reached the Supreme Court, which concluded that any First Amendment right of the press to attend trials was not violated by orders excluding members of the public and the press from a pretrial hearing in order to insure the defendants' right to a fair trial.

The Richmond Newspapers v. Virginia, 100 S.Ct. 2814 (1980), case involved a series of trials for a murder suspect. The first trial ended in a conviction which was eventually reversed. The second and third trials ended in mistrials. When the fourth trial began, the defendant moved that it be closed to the public. When the prosecution offered no objection, the judge ordered the proceedings closed. A group of news reporters appealed the order. When the case reached the Supreme Court, Chief Justice Burger distinguished Richmond Newspapers from Gannett — the former treats access to trials, while the latter concerned access to pretrial hearings. Burger then discussed the historical significance of public trials, noting that "the Bill of Rights was enacted against the backdrop of the long history of trials being presumptively open." Burger argued:

> What this means in the context of trials is that the First Amendment guarantees of speech and press, standing alone, prohibit government from summarily closing courtroom doors which had long been open to the public at the time that Amendment was adopted.... The explicit, guaranteed rights to speak and to publish concerning what takes place at a trial would lose much meaning if access to observe the trial could, as it was here, be foreclosed arbitrarily.

Accordingly, the Supreme Court decided that "the right to attend criminal trials is implicit in the guarantees of the First Amendment." The right to such access was reaffirmed in Globe Newspaper Company v. Superior Court for the County of Norfolk, 102 S.Ct. 2613 (1982).

Press-Enterprise Company v. Superior Court of California, 104 S.Ct. 819 (1984), concerned access to the *voir dire* examination of prospective jurors. In this case, which involved the rape and murder of a teenage girl, news reporters argued that the public had a right to attend the trial, and the trial commenced with the *voir dire* proceedings. California argued that if the press were present, juror responses would lack the candor necessary to assure a fair trial. When the case reached the Supreme Court, Chief Justice Burger upheld the value of an open trial. Burger noted:

> The value of openness lies in the fact that people not actually attending trials can have confidence that standards of fairness are being observed; the sure knowledge that *anyone* is free to attend gives assurance that established procedures are being followed and that deviations will become known. Openness thus enhances both the basic fairness of the criminal trial and the appearance of fairness so essential to public confidence in the system.

Burger concluded that the guarantees of open criminal proceedings apply to voir dire examinations.

A related case involved the same newspaper. In Press-Enterprise Company v. Superior Court of California, 106 S.Ct. 2735 (1986), a judge closed a preliminary hearing of a murder trial to the press and public "to protect the defendants' right to a fair and impartial trial." The Supreme Court noted that "a qualified First Amendment right of access attaches to preliminary hearings." As a result, the proceedings could not be closed unless "closure is essential to preserve higher values and is narrowly tailored to serve that interest." The Court found no justification for closure in this case.

El Vocero De Puerto Rico v. Puerto Rico, 113 S.Ct. 2004 (1993), is another case that involved access to a preliminary hearing. Under the Puerto Rico Rules of Criminal Procedure, an accused felon is entitled to a hearing to determine if he or she should be held for trial. The hearing is held privately unless the defendant requests otherwise. When a reporter for the largest newspaper in the commonwealth was denied admission to preliminary hearings, he initiated court action. The Supreme Court of Puerto Rico held that

> ...closed hearings are compatible with the unique history and traditions of the Commonwealth, which display a special concern for the honor and reputation of the citizenry, and that open hearings would prejudice defendants' ability to obtain fair trials because of Puerto Rico's small size and dense population.

The U.S. Supreme Court disagreed, noting that the widespread tradition of open hearings had been established in Press-Enterprise and was the controlling principle in this case.

Another relevant case is Butterworth v. Smith, 110 S.Ct. 1376 (1990). When a news reporter testified before a Florida grand jury about alleged improprieties committed by public officials, he was warned that if he revealed his testimony he would be subject to criminal prosecution under Florida law. After the grand jury terminated its investigation, the reporter wanted to write about the investigation. He initiated court action, seeking to have the law declared unconstitutional. The Supreme Court, per Justice Rehnquist, held that the law was unconstitutional to the extent that it applied to witnesses who wanted to communicate about their own testimony after the investigation had ended. Rehnquist noted that Florida's interests in preserving grand jury secrecy was not compelling. Once the investigation had ended, there was "no need to keep information from the targeted individual to prevent his escape, since he will have either been exonerated or charged."

The cases discussed in this section focused on the right of news gatherers to witness and report about judicial proceedings. In all of these cases — Landmark Communications, Daily Mail, Richmond Newspapers, Globe Newspaper, Press Enterprise Company I, Press Enterprise Company II, El Vocero De Puerto Rico, Butterworth — the Court overturned regulations that banned news gatherers from access to judicial proceedings.

Press conferences

A government official can control publicity by banning unfavorable reporters from a press conference. In the three cases cited in this section, the courts had to decide the constitutionality of such bans. The first case was Borreca v. Fasi, 369 F.Supp. 906 (1974). Richard Borreca, a news reporter for the Honolulu Star-Bulletin, was assigned to cover press conferences at City Hall. During 1973, the mayor decided that Borreca was "irresponsible, inaccurate, biased, and malicious in reporting on the Mayor and the city administration." The Mayor instructed his staff to keep Borreca out of the Mayor's office. When Borreca appeared at the next Mayor's news conference as the representative of the Star Bulletin, he was not admitted. Borreca and the newspaper initiated court proceedings. The court noted that First Amendment freedom of the press "includes a limited right of reasonable access to news." The right includes access to public galleries, press rooms, and press conferences dealing with government. The court stressed that any limitations on this right to access must be determined "by a balancing process in which the importance of the news gathering activity and the degree and type of the restraint sought to be imposed are balanced against the state interest to be served." The court noted that newspapers take sides, reporters are not always accurate and objective, and the press is always subject to criticism.

> But when criticism transforms into an attempt to use the powers of governmental office to intimidate or to discipline the press or one of its members because of what appears in print, a compelling governmental interest that cannot be served by less restrictive means must be shown for such use to meet Constitutional standards. No compelling governmental interest has been shown or even claimed here.

The second case, Forcade v. Knight, 416 F.Supp. 1025 (1976), involved a similar situation. Thomas Forcade was a news reporter for the Alternate Press Syndicate, an international news service that represented more than 200 subscribing newspapers. Robert Sherrill was the Washington correspondent for Nation. On their arrival in Washington, Forcade and Sherrill applied for passes to attend White House press conferences and briefings. The passes were denied "for reasons of security." The reporters could obtain no more specific information for the denial and were offered no opportunity to present evidence on their own behalf. They initiated court action. When the case reached the district court, FBI secret-service files were offered as evidence for the denials. The files showed that Forcade had been active in leftist student groups and that Sherrill had been involved in two cases of assault which gave rise to charges that he was "mentally unbalanced." It was because of these activities that Forcade and Sherrill had been barred entry to the White House. The court sided with the reporters and cited two reasons for its decision. First, the White House's failure to devise specific standards for issuance or denial of press passes infringed on Forcade's and Sherrill's First Amendment right to freedom of the press. Second, the White House's failure to inform the reporters of the grounds for the denial of the pass, or to permit them an opportunity to respond, violated their Fifth Amendment right to procedural due process. The court directed the

Secret Service to devise and publicize specific standards for the issuance and denial of press-pass applications, and then consider Forcade's and Sherrill's applications within the context of those standards.

In the third case, WJW-TV v. City of Cleveland, 686 F. Supp 177 (1988), a television station initiated court action when members of the news media were refused access to a meeting of the city council. The city did not argue that any privileged or confidential matters were on the agenda, but rather that government agencies enjoy the prerogative to close a meeting to the public and the press. The court disagreed, noting that the First Amendment requires such meetings to be open to the public unless "specific findings supporting confidentiality have been made on the record." In WJW-TV, as in Borreca and Forcade, the court specified that a governmental official could not, without good reasons, ban a news gatherer from access to press conferences.

Locker rooms

A female reporter for Sports Illustrated initiated court action to challenge a policy of the New York Yankees baseball team, approved by the American League, which required that accredited female reporters be excluded from the team's locker room. The reporter argued that the policy was discriminatory because male reporters were allowed access to the locker room. She also argued that fresh-off-the-field interviews were important to the work of sports reporters; thus, she was hampered in the pursuit of her professional goals. The team argued that such a policy was necessary to maintain the privacy of players. In Ludtke v. Kuhn, 461 F. Supp 86 (1978), the court sided with the reporter. The decision noted that the team's "intent in protecting ballplayer privacy may be fully served by much less sweeping means." In addition, the court balanced competing claims:

> The other two interests asserted by defendants, maintaining the status of baseball as a family sport and conforming to traditional notions of decency and propriety, are clearly too insubstantial to merit serious consideration. Weighed against plaintiff's right to be free of discrimination based upon her sex, and her fundamental right to pursue her profession, such objectives cannot justify the defendant's policy.

Third-party privacy

In Zurcher v. Stanford Daily, 98 S.Ct. 1970 (1978), the Court considered the issue of "third-party privacy." The case began when police officers responded to a call from the Director of the Stanford University Hospital, requesting the removal of a group of demonstrators who had seized the hospital's administrative offices. During the next few hours, physical violence occurred involving the officers and demonstrators. Several officers were injured in the melee, but were unable to identify their assailants. Two days later, a special edition of the Stanford Daily, a student newspaper, printed articles and photographs about the clash. The next day the District Attorney obtained a warrant for an immediate search of the Daily's offices. The Daily initiated court action. The Supreme Court, per Justice White, upheld the issuance of a warrant.

> Properly administered, the preconditions for a warrant — probable cause, specificity with respect to the place to be searched and the things to be seized, and overall reasonableness — should afford sufficient protection against the harms that are assertedly threatened by warrants for searching newspaper offices.

In Stanford Daily, the Court upheld the criminal investigation procedures over the free-press interests of the First Amendment. In fact, the Court approved the search of a newspaper's premises, even though no one on the paper's staff was suspected of any crime. By allowing such an invasion of innocent third-party privacy, the Court dealt a potentially chilling blow to the newsgathering process.

Currency reproduction

A federal code, enacted during the Civil War to combat the surge in counterfeiting, placed a ban on the use of photographic reproductions of currency. About a century later, Congress amended that law to allow an individual to make photographic reproductions if they conformed to specific guidelines of purpose, publication, color, and size. During the 1970s, the publishers of Time were advised that certain reproductions of currency depicted in their magazine violated the law. Time sought a declaratory judgement that the law was unconstitutional. In Regan v. Time, 104 S.Ct. 3262 (1984), the Supreme Court found part of the law to be unconstitutional. The purpose provision was not a valid time, place, and manner regulation because it discriminated on the basis of content: "A determination as to the newsworthiness or educational value of a photograph cannot help but be based on the content of the photograph and the message it delivers." However, the fact that the purpose provision was unconstitutional did not render the entire regulatory scheme invalid. The size and color provisions did not discriminate on the basis of content. Complying with these requirements would not prevent Time from expressing any idea on any subject or from using illustrations of currency in expressing those ideas. Further, the size and color limitations served a valid government interest in the prevention of counterfeiting.

PUBLISHING NEWS

The Supreme Court has dealt with numerous issues that have a direct impact on the publication of news. Some of the most important include prior restraint, taxation, victim compensation, post-office control, antitrust laws, failing company doctrine, politically oriented information, right of reply, and prepublication review.

PRIOR RESTRAINT

The second-class mail privilege encourages the dissemination of information by affording publishers low postal rates. In order to obtain the privilege, a publisher must obtain permission from the Postmaster General. The privilege may be revoked when the publication prints other than "mailable matter." In 1917, the second-class privilege for the Milwaukee Leader was revoked because the paper had become "non-mailable" under the provisions of the National Defense Law. According to the Postmaster General, editorial comments appearing in the Milwaukee Leader during the first five months of U.S. involvement in World War I constituted the basis for the revocation. The articles claimed that it was a capitalistic war, denounced the draft law as unconstitutional and oppressive, and implied that the law should not be obeyed. Justice John Clarke, in Milwaukee Social Democrat Publishing Company v. Burleson, 41 S.Ct. 352 (1921), claimed that the articles encouraged violation of the law, thus rendering the material "non-mailable." It was reasonable to conclude that the paper would continue its unpatriotic editorial policy. It was within the power of the Postmaster General to suspend the privilege until the paper corrected its editorial policy and published material that conformed to the law. When it did so, the secondclass privilege could be restored. The Court upheld prior restraint.

This view was overturned by the Court in Near v. Minnesota, 51 S.Ct. 625 (1931). The Saturday Press [Minneapolis] published articles that charged law enforcement officers and other public figures with gross neglect of duty, illicit relations with gangsters, and participation in graft. Under the Session Laws of Minnesota, the County Attorney secured a temporary order restraining publication of the periodical. The publisher appealed. The Supreme Court, per Chief Justice Charles Hughes, noted that public officers whose behavior remained open to free discussion in the media had remedies available for dealing with false accusations under libel laws. The Court decided that the First Amendment provided immunity from prior restraints. According to the Court:

The fact that the public officers named in this case, and those associated with the charges of official dereliction, may be deemed to be impeccable, cannot affect the conclusion that the statute imposes an unconstitutional restraint upon publication.

In New York Times Company v. United States, 91 S.Ct. 2140 (1971), a sharply divided Supreme Court again considered the issue of prior restraint. In June, 1971, the New York Times published articles dealing with the previously secret "Pentagon Papers," a study of the origins and conduct of the Vietnam War. The U.S. Government sought a court injunction to prevent further publication. Before the Supreme Court, the government argued that releasing this information posed a threat to national security; the paper said the people had a right to know about the war and that the government simply wanted to save the Pentagon from embarrassment. The Court banned the newspaper from further publication of the "Pentagon Papers" until a hearing on the matter could be held. Eventually, the Court wrote a decision that lifted the restraint on publication. Each of the justices wrote a separate opinion. Three were identified as dissents, based on acceptance of the government's claim that publication would cause national harm. The majority supported the newspaper's right to publish. Justice William Douglas cited the absolutist position. The First Amendment provided that "Congress should make no law...abridging the freedom of speech, or of the press." In his opinion, that left "no room for governmental restraint on the press." Justice William Brennan agreed that the Court had no right to levy prior restraint; in fact, the temporary restraint, which had been issued on the ground that it was necessary to give the Court an opportunity to examine the claim more thoroughly, should not have been issued. According to Brennan, the Constitution precluded any injunction from being issued until the government had clearly made its case. The opinion stressed that the government had a heavy burden to justify the imposition of a prior restraint. In New York Times, as in Near, the government had not met that burden.

The Supreme Court overturned another prior restraint in CBS v. Davis, 114 S.Ct. 912 (1994). As part of an ongoing investigation into unsanitary practices in the meat industry, CBS obtained video footage of a company's meat packing operations. The company obtained an injunction which prohibited CBS from airing the tape on its already scheduled 48 Hours investigative news program. CBS applied for an emergency stay of the injunction on the ground that it constituted a prior restraint. Justice Blackmun agreed. He claimed that the injunction conflicts with prior decisions of the Court and the "indefinite delay of the broadcast will cause irreparable harm to the news media that is intolerable to the First Amendment." Blackmun also noted that if CBS had violated any laws in obtaining the video, the First Amendment requires that the company remedy the harm trough a damages proceeding rather than through suppression of protected expression.

United States v. Progressive, 467 F.Supp 990 (1979), provides an example of a lower court's willingness to uphold prior restraint. On March 9, 1979, the government obtained a temporary restraining order enjoining Progressive magazine from publishing an article about the construction of a hydrogen bomb. Shortly thereafter a court hearing was held, at which both sides — government and press — aired their arguments. The government argued that national security permits the retention and classification of government secrets. It contended that publication of such information presented "immediate, direct, and irreparable harm to the interests of the United States." The Progressive staff argued that freedom of expression "is so central to the heart of liberty that prior restraint in any form becomes anathema." They contended that the article contained data that were already in the public domain. Thus, it did not pose a harm to national security. In the Progressive case, the district court sided with the government.

> Publication of the technical information on the hydrogen bomb contained in the article is analogous to publication of troop movements or locations in time of war and falls...within the narrow area recognized by the Court in Near v. Minnesota in which a prior restraint on publication is appropriate.

In the Progressive case, a lower court upheld prior restraint. That decision differed from the Supreme Court rulings in Near, New York Times, and Davis — cases in which the Court viewed prior restraint as an unconstitutional method of censorship.

TAXATION

In three cases, the Supreme Court turned back legislative attempts to control newspaper and magazine publication and circulation through unfair taxation. The first case began in 1934 when the Louisiana legislature passed a law that required any newspaper that sold advertising and had a weekly circulation in excess of 20,000 to pay a license tax of two percent on its gross receipts. Only thirteen out of 163 state newspapers qualified for the tax, but twelve of the thirteen were outspoken critics of Governor Huey Long — at whose request the law had been enacted. Nine publishers sued to stop enforcement of the statute. In Grosjean v. American Press Company, 56 S.Ct. 444 (1936), the Supreme Court determined that the Louisiana law operated as a prior restraint in two ways. First, it curtailed the amount of revenue obtained through advertising. Second, it restricted circulation. Justice George Sutherland wrote:

The form in which the tax is imposed is in itself suspicious. It is not measured or limited by the volume of advertisements. It is measured alone by the extent of the circulation of the publication in which the advertisements are carried, with the plain purpose of penalizing the publishers and curtailing the circulation of a selected group of newspapers.

Minneapolis Star and Tribune Company v. Minnesota Commissioner of Revenue, 103 S.Ct. 1365 (1983), is a related case. Minnesota law imposed a "use tax" on the cost of paper and ink products consumed in the production of periodical publications, but exempted the first $100,000 worth of paper and ink consumed in any year. The Minneapolis Star and Tribune Company instituted court action. The Supreme Court, per Justice Sandra O'Connor, noted:

> Minnesota's ink and paper tax violates the First Amendment not only because it singles out the press, but also because it targets a small group of newspapers. The effect of the $100,000 exemption...is that only a handful of publishers pay any tax at all, and even fewer pay any significant amount of tax.

In Minneapolis Star and Tribune Company, the Court concluded that the use tax resembled "more a penalty for a few of the largest newspapers than an attempt to favor struggling smaller enterprises." The practice was unconstitutional.

The third case, Arkansas Writers' Project v. Ragland, 107 S.Ct. 1722 (1987), involved a tax on sales of tangible personal property. Numerous items, including newspapers, and religious, professional, trade, and sports journals, were exempt from the tax. Arkansas Times, a general interest monthly magazine with a circulation of 28,000, was subject to the tax. The publisher initiated court action. Before the Supreme Court, the Arkansas Commissioner of Revenue justified the tax on the ground that it encouraged "fledgling" publishers who have only limited audiences and do not have access to the same volume of advertising revenues as general interest magazines. The Supreme Court found flaws in the tax:

> ...the exclusion is both overinclusive and underinclusive. The types of magazines enumerated in [the law] are exempt, regardless of whether they are "fledgling"; even the most lucrative and well-established religious, professional, trade and sports journals do not pay sales tax. By contrast, struggling general interest magazines on subjects other than those specified in [the law] are ineligible for favorable tax treatment.

Arkansas had failed to advance a compelling justification for selective, content-based taxation of certain magazines. The tax was invalid under the First Amendment.

In a fourth case, Leathers v. Medlock, 111 S.Ct. 1438 (1991), the Court held that the application of the Arkansas' sales tax to cable television services, while exempting print media, does not violate the First Amendment. Writing for the Court, Justice O'Connor noted that the Constitution "does not prohibit the differential taxation of different media." Furthermore, this case presented none of the violations found in Grosjean, Minneapolis Star and Tribune Company, and Arkansas Writers' Project. O'Connor offered two reasons. First, the tax has general applicability to a broad range of property and services and, thus, "does not single out the press and...threaten to hinder it as a watchdog of government activity." Second, the tax is not content-based; the variety of programming cable television offers to subscribers does not differ in its message from that communicated by other media. The tax was acceptable; it did not threaten to suppress the expression of particular ideas or viewpoints.

VICTIM COMPENSATION

In Simon & Schuster v. Members of the New York State Crime Victims Board, 112 S.Ct. 501 (1991), the Supreme Court rejected the "Son of Sam" law which required that a criminal's income, which was derived from works describing the crime, be made available to the victims. The case centered around a book contract between a publisher and organized-crime-figure Henry Hill. The publisher argued that the law violated the First Amendment. The Court agreed, holding that the law "imposes a financial burden on speakers because of the content of their speech."

> The Son of Sam law is...a content-based statute. It singles out income derived from expressive activity for a burden the State places on no other income and it is directed only at works with a specified content.

Furthermore, the law was discriminatory; the government could not justify compensating victims of crimes with the proceeds of such "storytelling" and ignore any or all of the criminal's other assets. The Court recognized that a State's interest in compensating victims of crime is a compelling one, but the law was "not narrowly tailored to advance that objective." As written, the law was "inconsistent with the First Amendment."

POST-OFFICE CONTROL

The Postal Service has a unique policy that pertains to the dissemination of news — it distributes newspapers and other materials at a reduced cost. As a feature of this policy, the Postmaster General possesses considerable control over the dissemination of news through regulation of the second-class mailing privilege. When the privilege is denied, a periodical operates at a serious economic disadvantage with competitors. The question of post office control was central in Lewis Publishing Company v. Morgan, 33 S.Ct. 867 (1913). The case involved the 1912 Newspaper Publicity Law, which required the manager of newspapers and magazines to file twice annually the names of the editor, managing editor, publisher, and stockholders of the publication. In addition, all advertising material had to be plainly marked. Failure to comply with the provisions of the Act could result in denial of the second-class privilege. The Lewis Publishing Company brought suit, complaining that the law abridged freedom of the press. The Supreme Court upheld the requirement; placing these conditions upon the right to use the mail system was not antithetical to freedom of the press.

In Hannegan v. Esquire, 66 S.Ct. 456 (1946), the Supreme Court restricted the power of the postal service. Based on his judgment that the contents of some issues of Esquire did not contribute to the public good, the Postmaster General revoked the magazine's second-class privilege. Esquire appealed, and the case reached the Supreme Court. In a unanimous opinion, the Court noted that the postal laws granted second-class rates to periodicals so that the public good might be served through a "dissemination of information." Congress did not intend that each applicant for the second-class rate had to convince the Postmaster General that the publication contributed to the public good. Only through uncensored distribution of literature could the public use individual tastes to choose from the multitude of competing offerings. Justice Douglas noted: "Congress has left the Postmaster General with no power to prescribe standards for the literature or the art which a mailable periodical disseminates."

In Lamont v. Postmaster General, 85 S.Ct. 1493 (1965), the Court further restricted the Postal Service, this time forbidding the Department to screen political mail from abroad. The case involved a challenge to the Postal Service and Federal Employees Salary Act of 1962, which provided that unsealed mail from a foreign country that was determined by the Secretary of the Treasury to be "Communist political propaganda" would be detained by the Postmaster General and the addressee would be notified that the mail would be delivered only upon request. In 1963, the Post Office detained a copy of the Peking Review #12, which was addressed to Dr. Corliss Lamont, a publisher and distributor of pamphlets. The case reached the Supreme Court. The Court concluded that the law was unconstitutional because it required an official act — returning the reply card — as a restriction on a person's constitutional right to obtain information. Any person was likely to feel some inhibition in sending for material that federal officials had condemned as Communist propaganda. The law violated the concept of "uninhibited, robust, and wide-open" debate that characterized the First Amendment.

ANTITRUST LAWS

In 1890, Congress enacted the Sherman Antitrust Act. The law declared illegal all monopolistic combinations in restraint of trade. Subsequently, the Supreme Court heard several cases involving combinations that allegedly restrained trade in the news industry. Associated Press v. United States, 65 S.Ct. 1416 (1945), is an example. The Associated Press, a nonprofit cooperative association of newspaper publishers, collects and distributes news to the members of the association, who pay for it under an assessment plan. The United States charged that the AP had violated antitrust laws by restraining trade in news and attempting to monopolize that trade. The major charge was that AP had established a system that prohibited AP members from selling news to nonmembers and granted members power to block nonmember competitors from membership. Another charge concerned a contract between AP and the Canadian Press Agency, which obligated both organizations to furnish news exclusively to each other. The Supreme Court noted:

...inability to buy news from the largest news agency, or any one of its multitude of members, can have most serious effects on the publication of competitive newspapers, both those presently published and those which but for these restrictions, might be published in the future.

The Court emphasized that freedom to publish is a constitutional guarantee, but freedom to combine to prevent others from publishing is not. The Court emphasized that the decision did not restrict the AP as to what could be printed, but rather compelled AP to make the dispatches accessible to others. With more outlets, there would be more varied coverage of news events. In Associated Press, the Court held newspapers subject to antitrust legislation.

Lorain Journal v. United States, 72 S.Ct. 181 (1951), involved another antitrust violation. In 1932, the Lorain Journal Company, an Ohio corporation that published the Journal, purchased the Times-Herald, the only competing paper published in the city. After 1933, the Journal held a commanding position regarding news dissemination in Lorain. The paper had a daily circulation that reached 99 percent of the families in the city. In 1948, the Elyria-Lorain Broadcasting Company was licensed by the FCC to operate radio station WEOL in Elyria, eight miles south of Lorian. With the arrival of a competing medium, the Lorain Journal Company devised a plan to eliminate the threat of competition from the radio station. Under the plan, the newspaper refused to accept any advertisement for the Journal from any Lorian County advertiser who also advertised over WEOL. The Supreme Court held that the newspaper publisher's conduct was an attempt to monopolize interstate commerce and bring about the elimination of the radio station. The Lorain Journal Company's attempt to force advertisers to boycott a competitor violated antitrust laws.

Two years later, the Court heard another antitrust challenge in the Times Picayune v. United States, 73 S.Ct. 872 (1953), case. In 1950, three major daily newspapers served the New Orleans area. The Item Company published the evening Item. The Times-Picayune Publishing Company distributed the morning Times-Picayune and the evening States. The Times-Picayune Company instituted a unit plan for selling advertising. As a result, advertisers could not buy space in either the Times-Picayune or the States alone; parties who purchased advertising in the publications could purchase only combined insertions which appeared in both papers, and not in either separately. The United States filed suit under the Sherman Act, challenging these "unit" contracts as unreasonable restraints of trade. The Supreme Court rejected the government's case. The unit plan had not enabled the company to enjoy a dominant position. The Times-Picayune's sale of advertising over the years was about 40 percent, slightly more than an equal share of the market. Furthermore, the year 1950 was the Item's peak year for total advertising as well as circulation. The newspaper appeared "to be doing well." The Court concluded that although the unit rule benefitted the Times-Picayune because it expanded advertising sales, it did not disadvantage the Item. Since the government's case was based primarily on that supposition, the Court's decision was awarded to the Times-Picayune Company.

In Times-Mirror v. United States, 88 S.Ct. 1411 (1968), a combination was broken up because of its adverse effect on independent newspaper publishing. In 1964, the Sun Company, the largest independent publishing company in southern California, was in sound financial condition. With three newspapers — the morning Sun, the evening Telegram, and the Sunday Sun-Telegram — the company dominated the newspaper business in San Bernardino County. These were the only news-papers, other than Los Angeles papers, that were home delivered throughout the county. The Times-Mirror company, publisher of the Los Angeles Times, the largest daily newspaper in southern California, purchased the Sun Company. The government filed a complaint, alleging that the acquisition violated antitrust laws. The court observed that the acquisition was especially anticompetitive because it eliminated one of the few independent papers that had been able to function successfully in the morning and Sunday fields. The court observed that

> ...the acquisition has raised a barrier to entry of newspapers in the San Bernardino County market that is almost impossible to overcome. The evidence discloses the market has now been closed tight and no publisher will risk the expense of unilaterally starting a new daily newspaper there.

The court decided that "acquisition which enhances existing barriers to entry in the market or increases the difficulties of smaller firms already in the market is particularly anticompetitive." The court concluded that the acquisition violated the Clayton Act and directed the Times-Mirror Company to divest itself of all forms of control of the Sun Company. On appeal, this judgment was unanimously affirmed by the Supreme Court. Times-Mirror, as well as other cases cited in this section, suggest that the Court is willing to break up monopolistic combinations in order to protect freedom of the press.

FAILING COMPANY DOCTRINE

In 1940, the Citizen Publishing Company, the publisher of the only evening daily newspaper in Tucson, Arizona, formed a joint operating agreement with the Star Publishing Company, publisher of the only morning daily newspaper and the only Sunday newspaper in Tucson. Since 1932, the Citizen Publishing Company had operated at a substantial financial loss. Under the provisions of the agreement, the news and editorial departments of the two newspapers remained separate, but a new corporation operated all other departments as a joint project. Profits were pooled and all competition between the companies ceased. Under this agreement, combined profits rose from $27,531 in 1940 to $1,727,217 in 1964. In 1965, an out-of-state publisher offered to purchase the Star Company for $10 million, provided that the joint operating agreement remained in operation. According to prior agreement, the Citizen Company had the opportunity to purchase the Star at this price, which it did. The sale resulted in a merger, with the news and editorial staffs of the Star under the direction of the Citizen. The United States initiated suit, charging that the agreement constituted an unreasonable restraint of trade. The case reached the Supreme Court. Lawyers representing the Citizen Publishing Company argued the "failing company" defense as justification for the merger. Justice Douglas, writing for the Court, explained why the "failing company" doctrine did not apply in this case. First, at the time the companies entered into the agreement, the Citizen Publishing Company was not on the verge of going out of business, nor was there a strong likelihood that the company would terminate its business if the agreement were not reached. In fact, there was "no evidence that the joint operating agreement was the last straw at which Citizen grasped. Indeed, the Citizen continued to be a significant threat to the Star." Second, the failing company doctrine could not be applied in a merger unless it was established that the company that acquired it was the only available purchaser; for, if another possible purchaser expressed interest, "a unit in the competitive system could be preserved and not lost to monopoly power." In Citizen Publishing Company v. United States, 89 S.Ct. 927 (1969), the Court established two prerequisites to the "failing company" defense: the company must be on the verge of liquidation, and there must be no prospective buyer of the failing company other than its competitor.

The Citizen Publishing decision caused concern among newspaper publishers. When that case was decided, 44 daily newspapers in 22 cities operated under the terms of joint agreements similar to the Citizen-Star arrangement. In 1970, in an effort to protect such combinations, Congress passed the Newspaper Preservation Act. The statute provided an exemption from antitrust laws to newspapers in the same city that had pre-existing joint operating agreements. As a result, the 44 newspapers were allowed to maintain joint advertising and subscription rates, which might otherwise have been found in violation of the antitrust laws.

The Bay Guardian Company v. Chronicle Publishing Company, 344 F.Supp. 1155 (1972), case provided a test of the new law. The case originated when Bruce Brugmann, publisher of the San Francisco Bay Guardian, a monthly newspaper with a circulation of 17,000, complained that the Newspaper Preservation Act had legitimized the joint advertiser and subscription rates charged by the two San Francisco daily newspapers, the Morning Chronicle and the evening San Francisco Examiner. Under the rate policy, advertisers were required to advertise in both dailies. Profits were shared by the companies on a 50-50 basis. According to Brugmann, the Chronicle and Examiner had achieved a monopoly position in the San Francisco newspaper market. Many advertisers were unable to afford to advertise in other newspapers. The result was that the Bay Guardian had been crippled in efforts to obtain advertisers. Brugmann initiated court action against the Examiner and Chronicle, contending that the Newspaper Preservation Act violated freedom of the press. The court held that

> ...the Act was designed to preserve independent editorial voices. Regardless of the economic or social wisdom of such a course, it does not violate freedom of the press.... The Act in question does not

regulate or restrict publishing, rather it merely permits newspapers to merge when they might not otherwise have been able to do so because of the antitrust laws.

According to the court, the Newspaper Preservation Act did not offend First Amendment freedoms.

Michigan Citizens For An Independent Press v. Thornburgh, 868 F.2d 1285 (1989), provided another test for the Newspaper Preservation Act. The case involved the challenge of various individuals, advertisers, and newspaper employees who objected to the Attorney General's approval of a joint operating arrangement between two competing Detroit newspapers. In arriving at their decision, the judges noted that, under the law, the Attorney General had a difficult task — "to balance two legislative policies in tension." One concern involved the pro-consumer direction of the antitrust laws. The other concern was "congressional desire embodied in the Newspaper Preservation Act that diverse editorial voices be preserved despite the unique economics of the newspaper industry." The court acknowledged the vagueness of the statute before concluding:

> Congress...delegated to the Attorney General...the delicate and troubling responsibility of putting content into the ambiguous phrase "probable danger of financial favor." We cannot therefore say that his interpretation of that phrase as applied to this case, with all its obvious policy implications, was unreasonable.

The joint operating agreement between the two newspapers was affirmed.

POLITICALLY-ORIENTED INFORMATION

Occasionally, legislation has been directed at controlling the publication of politically-oriented information. In Mills v. Alabama, 86 S.Ct. 1434 (1966), the constitutionality of such legislation was left to the Supreme Court. At issue was an Alabama law that controlled election-day editorials. In 1962, the city of Birmingham held an election to determine whether the citizens preferred to keep their city-commission form of government or replace it with a mayor-council system. On election day, the Post-Herald carried an editorial that strongly urged the voters to adopt the mayor-council form. The editor was arrested for violating the Alabama Corrupt Practices Act, which made it a crime to solicit votes in support of any candidates or propositions "on the day on which the election affecting such candidates or propositions is being held." The Supreme Court noted that a primary purpose of the First Amendment was to protect the free discussion of governmental affairs which "of course includes discussion of candidates, structures, and forms of government, the manner in which government is operated or should be operated, and all such matters relating to political processes." The Alabama law tended to silence the press at a time when it could be most effective. The Court concluded that the law was an "obvious and flagrant abridgement of the constitutionally guaranteed freedom of the press."

RIGHT TO REPLY

The 1913 Florida Election Code provided that a political candidate had the right to publish, free of charge, a reply to a newspaper article that assailed his/her personal character or charged malfeasance in office. In Miami Herald Publishing Company v. Tornillo, 94 S.Ct. 2831 (1974), the Supreme Court heard a claim for the "right to reply." In 1972, Pat Tornillo, Executive Director of the Classroom Teacher's Association, was a candidate for the Florida House of Representatives. The Miami Herald printed editorials critical of Tornillo's candidacy. The articles claimed that it would be "inexcusable of the voters" if they elected Tornillo to the legislature. The paper's opposition to Tornillo stemmed from an illegal strike by Miami public-school teachers, which Tornillo had led. In light of the editorial comments, Tornillo asked for the right to reply. When the Herald refused to print a reply, Tornillo initiated court action. The Supreme Court of Florida made two points in upholding the right to reply. First, the public "need to know" was critical during an election campaign. In order to assure fairness in campaigns, assailed candidates were entitled to an opportunity to respond. Second, the Florida law promoted the flow of ideas and did not infringe upon First Amendment rights against prior restraint, since no specified newspaper content was excluded. The U.S. Supreme Court reversed, disagreeing on both points. First, faced with the penalties that would accrue to any newspaper that published commentary that might warrant the "right of reply," editors might conclude that the safe course was to avoid controversy. In such instances, political coverage would be reduced. According to the Court, "government enforced right of access inescapably dampened the vigor and limits and variety of public debate." Second, the Florida statute required publishers to publish that which "reason" told them should not be published. The law operated as a command in the same sense as a law forbidding a publisher from publishing specified matter. According to the Court, "governmental restraint on publishing need not fall into familiar or traditional patterns to be subject to constitutional limitations on governmental powers." The Supreme Court concluded that the statute violated the First Amendment; the Court rejected the "right of reply."

PREPUBLICATION REVIEW

In <u>Snepp v. United States</u>, 100 S.Ct. 763 (1980), the Supreme Court approved the concept of prepublication review. The case involved Frank Snepp, who had been employed with the Central Intelligence Agency. Snepp published a book about CIA activities in South Vietnam, based on his experiences as an agent. He published the information without submitting it to the CIA for prepublication review. As a condition of his employment with the CIA, Snepp had agreed not to publish any information relating to the CIA "without specific prior approval by the Agency." The CIA initiated court action. The district court found that Snepp had deliberately misled CIA officials into believing that he would submit the book for prepublication clearance. The court also determined that publication of the information had "caused the United States irreparable harm and loss." The court therefore imposed a constructive trust on Snepp's profits. The Supreme Court approved the trust as a remedy that "deals fairly with both parties."

> If the agent secures prepublication clearance, he can publish with no fear of liability. If the agent publishes unreviewed material in violation of his fiduciary and contractual obligation, the trust remedy simply requires him to disgorge the benefits of his faithlessness. Since the remedy is swift and sure, it is tailored to deter those who would place sensitive information at risk.

In a dissenting opinion, Justice Stevens argued that the remedy constituted "a species of prior restraint on a citizen's right to criticize his government." Stevens noted:

> Inherent in this prior restraint is the risk that the reviewing agency will misuse its authority to delay the publication of a critical work or to persuade an author to modify the contents of his work beyond the demands of secrecy.

Nonetheless, in <u>Snepp</u>, the majority supported the government's right of prepublication review.

CONCLUSION

The following principles regulate communication law regarding NEWS:

1. The government may ban access to news under certain conditions:
   a. there is no absolute national privilege protecting reporters while keeping a news source's identity confidential,
   b. the Freedom of Information Act specifies federal records for which access may be denied,

    c. news reporters usually do not enjoy any "special" access to information, that is, beyond the rights enjoyed by the general public.

2. News reporters and publishers are aided by the following doctrines:
    a. reporter's privilege has been recognized in states that have enacted shield laws, though most laws have numerous exceptions and thus provide limited protection for the reporter,
    b. courts have generally turned back practices of prior restraint.

NOTES

1. Hentoff, Nat, The First Freedom: The Tumultuous History of Free Speech in America New York: Dell Publishing, 1981, pp. 79-85. See also Emerson, Thomas I., The System of Freedom of Expression New York: Vintage Books, 1970, pp. 98-101; and Chafee, Zechariah, Jr., Free Speech in the United States Cambridge: Harvard University Press, 1941, pp. 497-516.

KEY DECISIONS

1931 — NEAR — acknowledged that First Amendment provides immunity from prior restraint

1946 — HANNEGAN — restricted post-office control of the mails; protected publisher's right to send material through the mails

1965 — LAMONT — affirmed individual's right to receive information without post office infringement

1971 — NEW YORK TIMES — stressed that government has a heavy responsibility to justify the imposition of a prior restraint

1972 — BRANZBURG — rejected the idea of a national news reporter's privilege

1974 — NIXON — determined that executive privilege is not absolute

1974 — TORNILLO — rejected the "right to reply," because of potential chilling effect on publishing news

1974   —   <u>PELL</u> — held that the First Amendment does not guarantee news reporters any special access to information

1975   —   <u>SEARS</u> — determined that final opinions are subject to disclosure under the Freedom of Information Act, while predecisional opinions are protected under exemption five

1978   —   <u>STANFORD DAILY</u> — approved the search of a newspaper's premises even though no one on the paper's staff was suspected of any crime

1980   —   <u>RICHMOND NEWSPAPERS</u> — held that the public's right to attend criminal trials is protected by the First Amendment

1980   —   <u>SNEPP</u> — approved governmental prepublication review

1991   —   <u>RAY</u> — continued decade-long Supreme Court policy of siding with governmental agencies and approving FOIA exemption from disclosure

RECOMMENDED READING

Barnett, Stephen R., "Newspaper Monopoly and the Law," <u>Journal of Communication</u> 30 (Spring, 1980), 72-80.

Berman, Jerry J., "National Security vs. Access to Computer Databases: A New Threat to Freedom of Information." <u>Software Law Journal</u> 2 (1987), 1-15.

Birkinshaw, Patrick, <u>Freedom of Information: The Law, the Practice, and the Ideal</u>. London: Weidenfeld and Nicolson, 1988.

Bosmajian, Haig A., ed., <u>The Freedom to Publish</u>. New York: Neal-Schuman, 1989.

Carter, T. Barton, Marc A. Franklin, and Jay B. Wright, <u>The First Amendment and the Fourth Estate: The Dynamics of Communication Law</u>. Westbury, New York: Foundation Press, 4th. Ed., 1990.

Dyk, Timothy B., "Newsgathering, Press Access, and the First Amendment," <u>Stanford Law Review</u> 44 (May, 1992), 927-960.

Frenznick, David A., "The First Amendment on the Battlefield: A Constitutional Analysis of Press Access to Military Operations in Grenada Panama, and the Persian Gulf," Pacific Law Journal 23 (January, 1992), 315-59.

Grodsky, Jamie A., "The Freedom of Information Act in the Electronic Age: the Statute is not User Friendly," Jurimetrics Journal 31 (Fall, 1990), 17-51.

Higdon, Philip R., "The Burger Court and the Media: A Ten-Year Perspective," Western New England Law Review 2 (Spring, 1980), 593-680.

Levy, Leonard W., The Emergency of a Free Press. New York: Oxford University Press, 1985.

Pinkerton, Barbara F., "Press and a Reporter's Ability to Gather News," Wayne Law Review 26 (1979), 79-95.

Simmons, Charles E., "United States Foreign Policy v. The Press and the American Information Consumer: The Embattled First Amendment," Howard Law Journal 30 (1987), 1141-50.

Venkataramiah, E. S., Freedom of Press: Some Recent Trends Apt. Books, 1988.

CHAPTER 11

FAIR TRIAL

Two constitutional guarantees — freedom of expression and the right to a fair trial — come into conflict when the public clamors to know the facts of a case, but the discussion of those facts might jeopardize the defendant's right to a fair trial. In <u>Times-Picayune Publishing Company v. Schulingkamp</u>, 95 S.Ct. 1 (1974), Justice Lewis Powell acknowledged that "the task of reconciling First Amendment rights with the defendant's right to a fair trial before an impartial jury is not an easy one." In several instances, the Supreme Court has been asked to balance those conflicting rights. Relevant cases may be considered under two headings — contempt and pretrial publicity.

CONTEMPT

In 1831, federal judge James Peck suspended from legal practice an attorney who had criticized Peck's handling of some cases. A political dispute followed; Peck was impeached and tried in the U.S. Senate. The impeachment attempt failed by a one-vote margin, but the event furthered wide-spread resentment of the common-law method of dealing with contempt that was currently practiced. Within nine days, Congress passed the Federal Contempt Act, which limited punishable contempt to disobedience of any judicial procedure in the presence of the court "or so near thereto as to obstruct the administration of justice." In two subsequent cases, the Supreme Court interpreted the phrase "so near thereto."

"SO NEAR THERETO"

In Toledo Newspaper Company v. United States, 38 S.Ct. 560 (1918), the Court offered a causal interpretation of the phrase. The case involved a dispute between the city of Toledo and a local street-railway company. When the Toledo NewsBee published editorials that defended the city's right to enact an ordinance, and challenged any power of the courts to grant relief to the company, a contempt order was issued against the editor of the newspaper. On appeal, the Supreme Court noted:

> Newspaper articles, referring to a suit in the federal court to enjoin municipal ordinances regulating street car fares, which held the federal judge up to ridicule and hatred in case he should grant an injunction, and in advance impeached his motives in so doing, and practically urged noncompliance with any such order, must be deemed acts tending to obstruct the administration of justice.

The Court interpreted the Federal Contempt Act as granting power to the judiciary to punish behavior that showed a "reasonable tendency" to obstruct justice. In Toledo Newspaper, the phrase "so near thereto" received a causal construction.

In Nye v. United States, 61 S.Ct. 810 (1941), the Court reversed the causative interpretation of the phrase, and set forth a geographical construction. The case began with a wrongful-death action brought by W. H. Elmore against a medical company concerning the death of Elmore's son. Shortly thereafter, attorney R. H. Nye used alcoholic beverages and persuasive tactics to coax Elmore, a feeble, illiterate, elderly man, to drop the suit. These events took place more than 100 miles from where the court hearing the suit was located. Nye was held in contempt for obstructing justice. He appealed. The Supreme Court interpreted the phrase, "so near thereto," to mean physical proximity. According to Justice William Douglas, the phrase connoted that the misbehavior must be in the vicinity of the court. Nye's influence on Elmore had not been perpetrated in the "presence" of the court or "near thereto." According to Douglas, the causal interpretation applied in Toledo Newspaper contradicted the intention of the Contempt Act. The Court reversed Nye's conviction and by overturning Toledo Newspaper, limited the power of judges to punish contempt that occurred outside of the courtroom.

BRIDGES PRINCIPLE

In companion cases, the Supreme Court expanded the power of the press to comment on cases and judges. In the first case, Bridges v. California, 62 S.Ct. 190 (1941), a motion for a new trial was pending in a legal dispute between two labor unions. Harry Bridges, the President of one of the unions, sent a telegram to the Secretary of Labor which described the judge's decision in the case as "outrageous," threatened a strike by the longshoremen that would have tied up the port of Los Angeles if the decision were enforced, and announced that the union did "not intend to allow state courts to override the majority vote of members." The telegram was published in Los Angeles and San Francisco newspapers. Bridges was found guilty of contempt. He appealed. In the second case, Times-Mirror Company v. Superior Court of California, 62 S.Ct. 190 (1941), the Times-Mirror Company was cited for contempt for publishing editorials while the outcome of a court case was still pending. An editorial that approved of the convictions of 22 sit-down strikers appeared in the Los Angeles Times after the verdict was rendered, but prior to sentencing. Another editorial approved of the convictions of two labor leaders who had previously been found guilty of assaulting nonunion truck drivers. The article urged the judge to give stiff sentences to the labor officials. The Times-Mirror Company appealed the conviction. In these cases, the Supreme Court applied the "clear and present danger" test. Justice Hugo Black claimed,

> ...what finally emerges from the "clear and present danger" cases is a working principle that the substantive evil must be extremely serious and the degree of imminence extremely high before the utterances can be punished.

In Bridges, as in Times-Mirror, the Court acknowledged that there were greater benefits to be derived from public discussion of pending court cases than from forced silence. The convictions were overturned.

In several ensuing cases, the Supreme Court affirmed the Bridges principle. Pennekamp v. Florida, 66 S.Ct. 1029 (1946), involved a newspaper that published two editorials and a cartoon accusing judges of leniency toward criminals. The newspaper's associate editor was convicted of contempt. The Court held that the editorials and cartoon did not constitute a "clear and present danger to fair administration of justice" because the effect on juries that might eventually try alleged offenders was very remote, and the editorials criticized only court action already taken. Justice Stanley Reed noted that "the danger under this record to fair judicial administration had not the clearness and immediacy necessary to close the door of permissible public comment." The Court reversed the conviction.

One year later, in Craig v. Harney, 67 S.Ct. 1249 (1947), the Court again applied the Bridges principle. At the close of testimony in a civil jury trial, each side moved for an instructed verdict. The judge instructed the jury to return a verdict for the plaintiff, but the jury decided in favor of the defendant. The judge refused to accept the verdict. Eventually, the jury complied, noting that it acted under coercion and against its conscience. The Caller-Times (Corpus Christi) criticized the judge for taking the case away from the jury. The ruling was called "arbitrary action" and a "travesty on justice." A trial court ruled that the editorials falsely represented the proceedings. The court found the paper to be in contempt. The case was appealed. Writing for the Supreme Court, Justice Douglas noted that the articles reflected inept reporting and constituted an unfair account of what transpired. According to Douglas, however, "it takes more imagination than we possess to find in this rather sketchy and one-sided report of a case any imminent or serious threat to a judge of reasonable fortitude." Douglas noted that "a judge may not hold in contempt one who ventures to publish anything that tends to make him unpopular or to belittle him." The vehemence of the language used does not, alone, constitute the measure of the power to punish for contempt. That language must spark an imminent threat to the administration of justice. The danger must not be remote or even probable; it must immediately imperil. In Craig, it did not.

In cases cited thus far, the Bridges principle was applied to the print and broadcast media. In Wood v. Georgia, 82 S.Ct. 1364 (1962), the Court upheld the right of a citizen to criticize a court. The case began when a judge instructed a grand jury to investigate whether black bloc voting was being stimulated by illegal payments by political candidates. On the next day, with the grand jury in session, Sheriff James Wood issued a news release criticizing the judge's action. Wood also sent an open letter to the grand jury, in which he implied that the County Democratic Executive Committee was behind the corrupt purchase of votes, and that the grand jury should investigate the committee. The Sheriff was convicted of contempt. On appeal, the Supreme Court supported Wood's right to engage in the public dialogue. At the time of Wood's criticism, no individual was under investigation. Wood merely contributed to the public discussion at a time when public interest in the matter was at its peak. The Court, in reversing Wood's conviction, noted:

> Particularly in matters of local political corruption and investigations it is important that freedom of communication be kept open and that the real issues not become obscured to the grand jury. It cannot effectively operate in a vacuum.

In a recent case, Pounders v. Watson, 117 S. Ct. 2359 (1997), the Court upheld a finding of contempt. The case involved a defense attorney who was found to be in contempt for discussing possible punishments for her client after the trial judge had "at least twice ordered counsel not to cover" that issue. Upon appeal, the Supreme Court maintained that the attorney's questions had "permanently prejudiced the jury in favor of her client" and that the prejudice "cannot be overcome." The opinion concluded:

> ...the conduct of counsel here was well within the range of contumacious conduct disruptive of judicial proceedings and damaging to the court's authority. Advocacy that is "fearless, vigorous, and effective," does not extend to disruptive conduct in the course of trial and in knowing violation of a clear and specific direction from the trial judge.

In Pounders, as in Pennekamp, Craig, and Wood, the Court affirmed the principle established in Bridges — representatives of the media, the legal profession, and the general public are allowed to discuss judicial matters, court actions, and the legal process so long as such discussion does not constitute a "clear and present danger" to the administration of justice.

GAG ORDERS

In order to control news coverage of court proceedings, judges may impose gag orders. For example, judges have banned news reporters from performing specific behaviors — taking photographs in Seymour v. United States, 373 F.2d 629 (1967), publishing jurors' names in Schuster v. Bowen, 347 F.Supp. 319 (1972), reporting a verdict in Wood v. Goodson, 485 S.W.2d 213 (1972), publishing any information about a case in Miami Herald v. Rose, 271 So.2d 483 (1972), printing names of witnesses in Sun Company v. Superior Court, 29 Cal.App.3d 815 (1973), making sketches of courtroom participants in United States v. Columbia Broadcasting System, 497 F.2d 102 (1974). When the media appealed such orders, the courts had to resolve conflicts between the First Amendment right of free speech and the Sixth Amendment right to a fair trial. In United States v. Dickinson, 465 F.2d 496 (1972), the court established a specific requirement that reporters must follow in dealing with a gag order. In this case, reporters were cited for contempt when they published testimony, in violation of a judicial order. The judge acknowledged that the press could report the fact that a hearing was being held, but he outlawed reporting details of any evidence presented during the proceeding. The reporters ignored the order and wrote articles summarizing the court's testimony. They were found guilty of contempt. The court of appeals noted that the trial judge had acted improperly; the public had a right to know the facts brought out in the hearing. Nonetheless, the court of appeals held:

> The conclusion that the...[judge's] order was constitutionally

> invalid does not necessarily end the matter of the validity of the
> contempt convictions. There remains the very formidable question of
> whether a person may with impunity violate an order which turns
> out to be invalid. We hold that in the circumstances of this case he
> may not.

The court held that even though the judge's order was
unconstitutional, the reporters should have respected the order until
they had exhausted all available court remedies. The Supreme Court
denied certiorari.

In Times-Picayune Publishing Corporation v. Schulingkamp, 95
S.Ct. 1 (1974), the Supreme Court rejected a gag order because the
situation did not constitute a "clear and present danger" to the
administration of justice. The case began with the rape of a young
nursing student. Two suspects were arrested and charged with the
crime. The case received thorough coverage. Eleven months after the
crime, when the case came to trial, the judge banned news personnel
from reporting any testimony after the selection of a jury. The Times-
Picayune Company sought to have the order overturned. The Supreme
Court agreed. Justice Powell noted that the judge's decision to
continue the order during all of the trial proceedings imposed
"significant prior restraints on media publication." In addition, the
record revealed "the absence of any showing of an imminent threat to
fair trial."

In Nebraska Press Association v. Stuart, 96 S.Ct. 2791 (1976), the
Court struck down another gag order. In October of that year, Erwin
Simants was charged with murdering six members of a family. In the
ensuing court proceedings, there was testimony that Simants confessed
to police officers. The judge ordered that the Nebraska Press
Association refrain from publishing or broadcasting accounts of the
confession until a jury was selected. The gag order also prohibited any
reporting of the contents of a note written by Simants on the night of
the crime, portions of medical testimony, the identity of the victims,
the nature of the assault, and the provisions of the gag order. The
judge said that "because of the nature of the crimes charged in the
complaint...there is a clear and present danger that pretrial publicity
could impinge upon the defendant's right to a fair trial." Several press
associations initiated court action, asking that the restrictive order be
vacated. The Supreme Court overturned the order. Writing for the
Court, Chief Justice Warren Burger argued that "prior restraints on
speech and publication are the most serious and least tolerable
infringements on First Amendment rights." Burger claimed that

> ...there was indeed a risk that pretrial news accounts, true or false,
> would have some adverse impact on the attitudes of those who might
> be called as jurors. But on the record now before us it is not clear

that further publicity, unchecked, would so distort the views of potential jurors that 12 could not be found who would, under proper instructions, fulfill their sworn duty to render a just verdict exclusively on the evidence presented in open court. We cannot say on this record that alternatives to a prior restraint on petitioners would not have sufficiently mitigated the adverse effects of pretrial publicity so as to make prior restraint unnecessary.

The Court acknowledged that it was a "heavy burden to demonstrate in advance of trial that without prior restraint a fair trial will be denied," but that kind of evidence was necessary in order to demonstrate a "threat to fair trial rights that would possess the requisite degree of certainty to justify restraint." Such evidence was not apparent in Nebraska Press Association, so the order was vacated.

The KPNX v. Arizona Superior Court, 103 S.Ct. 584 (1982), decision upheld a gag order. While presiding over a murder trial, the judge imposed two restrictions on the press. First, the judge ordered court personnel, counsel, witnesses, and jurors not to speak directly with the press. Instead, he appointed a court employee as "liaison with the media," to provide a "unified and singular source for the media concerning these proceedings." Second, he ordered that any drawings of jurors that were intended for broadcast on television had to be reviewed by the judge. The KPNX Broadcasting Company initiated court action that sought to overturn the judge's order. Justice William Rehnquist, writing for the Court, sided with the trial judge. Concerning the first order, Rehnquist noted that "unregulated communication between trial participants and the press at a heavily covered trial" posed a serious problem that warranted such a restriction. Though Rehnquist found the second order "more troubling" because it "smacks...of the notion of prior restraint," he upheld the restriction. Rehnquist decided that

...of all conceivable reportorial messages that could be conveyed by reporters or artists watching such trials, one of the least necessary to appreciate the significance of the trial would be individual juror sketches.

In KPNX, Justice Rehnquist sided with the trial judge and upheld the restrictions on the press. On balance, the fair-trial rights outweighed those of the court reporters.

The cases considered in this section suggest that in order for a judge to impose a gag order, there must be an imminent, not merely a potential, "clear and present" threat to the administration of justice. That level of harm was absent in Times-Picayune and Nebraska Press Association, but present in KPNX. The cases also indicate that reporters are subject to the Dickinson principle, which requires that news gatherers must exhaust all available court remedies before violating an unconstitutional gag order.

TRIAL BY MEDIA

In an age of sophisticated media techniques, the selection of impartial juries has become an extremely difficult task. Prior to jury selection, news reporters disseminate information about the crime, the victim, and the accused. News media publish the results of interviews held with police, lawyers, witnesses, even the accused. The public is bombarded with a vast amount of prejudicial data, some relevant and some irrelevant to the case. The problem of prejudicial information does not end with jury selection. News reports often are available to jurors after the trial has begun. Such occurrences place in conflict the right of the accused to a fair trial and the right of the public to be informed.

PRETRIAL PUBLICITY

Two black men were charged with the rape of a 17-year-old white girl in Florida. During the trial, a local newspaper reported that the men had confessed, and printed a cartoon that pictured electric chairs with the caption "No Compromise — Supreme Penalty." The suspects were sentenced to death, although their confessions were never introduced as evidence. On appeal, the Supreme Court found it

> ...hard to imagine a more prejudicial influence than a press release by the officer of the court charged with defendant's custody stating that they had confessed, and here just such a statement, unsworn to, unseen, uncrossexamined, and uncontradicted, was conveyed by the press to the jury.

The Court held that newspapers may not deprive the accused of the right to a fair trial. In Shepherd v. Florida, 71 S.Ct. 549 (1951), the crime had stirred deep feelings which were exploited to the limit by the press. The Court acknowledged that the publicity had made it impossible for the judge to provide the accused "any real protection against this out-of-court campaign to convict." The Court reversed the convictions.

The Marshall v. United States, 79 S.Ct. 1171 (1959), case involved pretrial publicity. Howard Marshall was convicted of illegally dispensing prescription drugs. During the trial, two newspapers published reports about Marshall's previous convictions for practicing medicine without a license. The defense asked for a mistrial. When questioned by the judge, seven jurors admitted reading the newspaper accounts. These jurors told the judge that they would not be influenced by the articles, that they could decide the case on the basis of the evidence presented, and that they felt no prejudice against Marshall as a result of the articles. When the judge denied the motion for mistrial, Marshall appealed. The Supreme Court noted that the jurors had been exposed to information which the trial judge had ruled to be so prejudicial that it could not be offered as evidence during the trial. Clearly, the prejudice to Marshall was almost certain to be as great when that evidence reached the jury through news accounts, as when it was a part of the prosecution's case. The Court held that a new trial should be granted.

In Irvin v. Dowd, 81 S.Ct. 1639 (1961), the Court reversed another conviction because of prejudicial pretrial publicity. The case involved Leslie Irvin, who had been arrested on suspicion of burglary and writing bad checks. Within a few days, police officials released reports announcing that "Mad Dog" Irvin had confessed to six killings. In the months preceding Irvin's trial, "a barrage of newspaper headlines, articles, cartoons and pictures were unleashed against him." When the trial began, the press observed that "strong feelings, often bitter and angry, rumbled to the surface," and noted the existence of "a pattern of deep and bitter prejudice against the former pipefitter." Headlines announced that "impartial jurors are hard to find." Irvin's attorney asked for and received a change of venue to a nearby county. The same media, however, were available in this location. Another request for change was denied. During *voir dire*, 370 of the 430 prospective jurors said they believed Irvin was guilty, but his lawyer had exhausted all peremptory challenges. When 12 jurors were selected, the defense attorney unsuccessfully challenged all of them for bias. The pretrial publicity appeared in newspapers that were delivered regularly to about 95 percent of the homes in the area, and local radio and television stations carried extensive newscasts covering the same incidents. Irvin was tried, found guilty, and sentenced to death. He appealed. The Supreme Court concluded that Irvin had not received a fair and impartial trial.

> With his life at stake, it is not requiring too much that petitioner be tried in an atmosphere undisturbed by so huge a wave of public passion and by a jury other than one in which two-thirds of the members admit, before hearing any testimony, to possessing a belief in his guilt.

Irvin was retried in a less emotional climate. He was found guilty, and sentenced to life in prison.

Two years later, in Rideau v. Louisiana, 83 S.Ct. 1417 (1963), the Court set aside another conviction because prejudicial pretrial publicity had precluded a fair trial. The case involved Wilbert Rideau, who had been arrested on suspicion of robbing a bank in Lake Charles,

Louisiana, while kidnapping three and killing one of the bank's employees. The morning after his arrest, a film was made of a 20-minute "interview" between Rideau and the Sheriff. Under interrogation, Rideau admitted that he had committed the crimes. The film was broadcast over television station KLPC in Lake Charles. A substantial portion of the population of 150,000 persons living in Calcasieu Parish saw the film. When Rideau was charged with armed robbery, kidnapping, and murder, his lawyers filed a motion for a change of venue on the ground that a fair trial was impossible in Calcasieu Parish. Three members of the jury admitted during *voir dire* that they had seen the television interview. The motion for a change of venue was denied. Rideau was convicted, and sentenced to death. The Supreme Court held that Rideau was denied due process when the court refused to grant a change of venue "after the people of Calcasieu Parish had been exposed repeatedly and in depth to the spectacle of Rideau personally confessing in detail to the crimes with which he was later to be charged." Writing for the court, Justice Potter Stewart noted:

> For anyone who has ever watched television the conclusion cannot be avoided that this spectacle, to the tens of thousands of people who saw and heard it, in a very real sense was Rideau's trial — at which he pleaded guilty to murder. Any subsequent court proceedings in a community so pervasively exposed to such a spectacle could be but a hollow formality.

The conviction was reversed. Rideau was later retried and convicted.

The classic case of pretrial publicity is Sheppard v. Maxwell, 86 S.Ct. 1507 (1966). On July 4, 1954, Marilyn Sheppard, wife of Dr. Sam Sheppard, was bludgeoned to death in the upstairs bedroom of their lake-shore home in a suburb of Cleveland. From the beginning, law-enforcement officials suspected Dr. Sheppard of the crime. Throughout the investigation, considerable press coverage surrounded the case. Headline stories constantly stressed Sheppard's unwillingness to cooperate with the police. Newspaper articles described Sheppard's extra-marital love affairs as a motive for the crime. The press sought Sheppard's arrest. A front-page editorial inquired, "Why Isn't Sam Sheppard in Jail?" It demanded, "Quit Stalling — Bring Him In." Shortly thereafter, Sheppard was arrested and charged with murder. A list of the names and addresses of prospective jurors was published in all three Cleveland newspapers. Anonymous correspondence concerning the trial was received by all the prospective jurors. All but one juror admitted at *voir dire* to being exposed to the case by the media. During the trial, the jurors were constantly exposed to news coverage, and pictures of the jury appeared more than 40 times in Cleveland newspapers. During the trial, anti-Sheppard news coverage continued. One headline claimed that Marilyn had told friends that Sam was a "Dr. Jekyll and Mr. Hyde character." No such testimony was presented at the trial. Broadcaster Walter Winchell reported that Carole Beasley, under arrest in New York for robbery, had claimed that she had borne Sheppard a child when she was his mistress. Two jurors admitted hearing the broadcast, but when they indicated it would have no effect on their verdict, the judge accepted their statement. Although he was not a witness at the trial, Captain Kerr of the Homicide Bureau issued a press statement denying Sheppard's claim that he had been abused by detectives after his arrest. Newspapers printed the detective's story under the headline "'Bare-faced Liar', Kerr says of Sam." Sheppard was convicted of second degree murder. The case came to the Supreme Court. Justice Tom Clark's opinion noted that the trial judge failed to protect Sheppard from the prejudicial publicity that saturated the community, and neglected to control the disruptive influences in the courtroom. Clark noted that "the carnival atmosphere at trial could easily have been avoided since the courtroom and courthouse premises are subject to the control of the court." He suggested ways in which the courtroom atmosphere could have been improved. First, the presence of the press at judicial proceedings could have been restricted when it was clear that Sheppard could be disadvantaged. Second, the judge should have "insulated the witnesses." The media interviewed prospective witnesses at will and on numerous occasions disclosed their testimony. Third, the judge should have controlled the release of information to the press. Much of the data thus disclosed "was inaccurate, leading to groundless rumors and confusion." The Court ordered that Sheppard be released unless Ohio tried him again within a reasonable time. Ohio tried Sheppard again; this time he was acquitted.

In cases discussed thus far — Shepherd, Marshall, Irvin, Rideau, Sheppard — the Supreme Court overturned convictions obtained in a trial atmosphere that was corrupted by media coverage. The decision in Murphy v. Florida, 95 S.Ct. 2031 (1975), upheld a conviction in which the jury had been exposed to press reports regarding prior convictions of the defendant. The case involved Jack Murphy, whose arrest in Dade County, Florida, for robbery and assault received extensive media coverage because he had frequently been in the news before. He had been involved in the 1964 theft of the Star of India sapphire from a museum in New York. In 1968, Murphy had been convicted of murder. In 1969, he had pleaded guilty to a federal indictment involving stolen securities. Each new case against Murphy was considered newsworthy; scores of articles reporting his activities were published during the decade. The defense moved to dismiss the jurors on the ground that they were aware of Murphy's prior convictions. The defense also requested a change of venue on the basis of alleged prejudicial pretrial publicity. Both motions were denied, and Murphy was convicted. He appealed. The Supreme Court noted that unlike Marshall, the *voir dire* in this case indicated no such hostility to Murphy by the jurors "as to suggest a partiality that could not be laid aside." Some of the jurors had some knowledge of Murphy's past crimes, but none indicated any belief in the relevance of the past to the present case. Furthermore, news coverage of Murphy's past experiences was largely factual in nature. The Court decided:

> ...we are unable to conclude, in the circumstances presented in this case, that petitioner did not receive a fair trial. Petitioner had failed to show that the setting of the trial was inherently prejudicial or that the jury selection process of which he complains permits an inference of actual prejudice.

In Murphy, the Court based its decision on the notion that jurors "need not...be totally ignorant of the acts and issues involved." It was sufficient that jurors be able to set aside their impressions and render a verdict based on the evidence presented in the case. The Court concluded that appropriate juror impartiality was evident. Nonetheless, as Shepherd, Marshall, Irvin, Rideau, and Sheppard indicate, the Court will reverse a conviction in order to offset prejudicial pretrial publicity.

Mu'min v. Virginia, 111 S. Ct. 1899 (1991), is a related case. It involved an inmate serving time for first degree murder who committed another murder while out of prison on work detail. The case engendered substantial publicity in local news media. At trial, the judge conducted a group *voir dire*, asking questions about the effect of pretrial publicity on potential jurors. At that time, several potential jurors were excused. Eight of the twelve people eventually sworn in as jurors admitted that they had heard or read some thing about the case, but none indicated that they had formed an opinion based on the publicity. They also maintained that they would not be biased in any way. The trial judge had denied the defendant's request for individual *voir dire* and refused to ask specific questions suggested by the defendant. After hearing the evidence, the jury found the defendant guilty of capital murder and the judge sentenced him to death. The case was appealed. Delivering the opinion of the Court, Justice Rehnquist noted that wide discretion is granted to trial courts in conducting *voir dire* in the area of pretrial publicity, and, in this instance, the examination "was by no means perfunctory and adequately covered the subject of possible bias by pretrial publicity."

Court decisions discussed in this section illustrate the potential damage pretrial publicity poses to the Sixth Amendment right to a fair trial. There are, however, remedies that might be imposed by a judge

to offset or mitigate negative influences. The list of suggestions
includes:

1. change of venue -- shifting location of trial
2. *voir dire* -- questioning jurors to detect bias
3. change of venire -- altering the jury pool
4. sequestration -- shielding jurors from information
5. admonition -- instructing jurors to render verdict based solely on the evidence
6. continuance -- postpone trial until publicity subsides
7. severance -- try two defendants separately to prevent publicity related to one trial from influencing the other
8. new trial -- used as a last resort

Even though invoking these remedies does not prevent the occurrence
of publicity, such action can reduce the impact of publicity on judicial
proceedings.

IMPLIED BIAS

In 1937, the American Bar Association endorsed Canon 35, a
judicial rule banning photographic and broadcast equipment in the
courtroom. This policy was adopted by most states. It seemed
appropriate during a period when photography was a disruptive process.
Beginning in the 1960s, journalists complained about the regulations,
arguing that modern photographic equipment rendered the ban obsolete.
They also asserted that broadcasting a trial was a First Amendment
freedom.

In 1962, the television ban was challenged in court. The case
involved Texas financier Billie Sol Estes, who was tried on charges of
theft and embezzlement. During the pretrial hearing, the courtroom was
crowded to overflowing. A defense motion to prevent telecasting, radio
broadcasting, and news photography was denied; so, several
broadcasters carried the proceedings live. Activities of the broadcast
crews often disrupted the hearing. The actual trial took place in a
different environment. Live telecasting was restricted; only the opening
and closing arguments of the prosecution and the return of the verdict to
the judge were carried live. Various portions of the trial were videotaped for broadcast on regularly scheduled newscasts later in the day.
News commentators used the tape as a backdrop for their reports
concerning the trial. After Estes was convicted, he appealed on the
ground that because of the way the pretrial hearing was conducted, he
had been denied a fair trial. When the case reached the Supreme Court,
the justices agreed that publicity in a pretrial hearing could hamper due
process in an ensuing criminal trial. Justice Clark argued the doctrine
of "implied bias" — that is, prejudice is inherent in a televised trial.

He offered four reasons. First, the potential impact of television on the jurors may be detrimental because "while it is practically impossible to assess the effect of television on jury attentiveness, those of us who know juries realize the problem of jury 'distraction.'"

> We are all self-conscious and uneasy when being televised. Human nature being what it is, not only will a juror's eyes be fixed on the camera, but also his mind will be preoccupied with the telecasting rather than with the testimony.

Second, the quality of the testimony could be impaired. The knowledge that he or she is being viewed by a vast audience may affect a witness. Some may be demoralized and frightened, while others become cocky and given to overstatement. Memories may falter, and accuracy of statement may be severely undermined. For some, "embarrassment may impede the search for the truth, as may a natural tendency toward overdramatization." Third, the presence of television places additional responsibilities on the judge. According to Clark, a judge's job is to ensure that the accused receives a fair trial, but "when television comes into the courtroom he must also supervise it." Fourth, the presence of television has an impact on the defendant; "its presence is a form of mental — if not physical — harassment, resembling a police line up or the third degree." The Court concluded that the presence of television could only have impressed the people in the courtroom, as well as those in the community, with the notorious character of Billie Sol Estes and the significance of the trial. Televising the proceedings impaired due process. As a result of Estes v. Texas, 85 S.Ct. 1628 (1965), cameras were prohibited in courtrooms, except in those states that did not subscribe to Canon 35. In a separate concurring opinion, Justice John Harlan envisioned the day "when television will have become so commonplace an affair in the daily life of the average person as to dissipate all reasonable likelihood that its use in courtrooms may disparage the judicial process." When that day comes, the opinions set forth in Estes will be "subject to re-examination." That reexamination and ultimate revision of Canon 35 took place in the late 1970s.

In February, 1978, the American Bar Association proposed permitting courtroom coverage by the electronic media "if such coverage was carried out unobtrusively and without affecting the conduct of the trial." Later that year, the Conference of State Chief Justices, by a vote of 44 to one, approved a resolution to allow the highest court of each state to establish standards regulating radio, television, and other photographic coverage of court proceedings. Subsequently, the Florida Supreme Court established a one-year pilot program, during which electronic media were allowed to cover judicial proceedings in Florida. The Court set forth guidelines detailing the kind of electronic equipment to be used, and the manner of its use.

Chandler v. Florida, 101 S.Ct. 802 (1981), a case that took place under the pilot program, involved the criminal trial of two former policemen who were charged with the burglary of a restaurant. A television camera recorded the testimony of the prosecution's chief witness, as well as the prosecution's closing statement. No camera was present during the presentation of any part of the case for the defense. When the jury returned a guilty verdict, the defense moved for a new trial, arguing that because of the television coverage they had been denied a fair and impartial trial. When Chandler reached the Supreme Court, the justices noted that several of the negative factors present in Estes — cumbersome equipment, distracting lighting, cables, numerous camera technicians — "are less substantial factors today than they were at that time." The justices then considered whether the presence of television cameras in the courtroom inescapably produces an adverse psychological impact on the participants in the trial. The Court concluded:

> Whatever may be the "mischievous potentialities [of broadcast coverage] for intruding upon the detached atmosphere which should always surround the judicial process," at present no one has been able to present empirical data sufficient to establish that the mere presence of broadcast media inherently has an adverse effect on that process.

In Chandler, the Supreme Court decided that Florida could permit electronic media to cover trials in its state courts. Since then, several states have adopted such a policy.

CONCLUSION

The following principles regulate communication law regarding FAIR TRIAL:

1. Judicial orders have been overturned because of
   a. unwarranted prior restraint,
   b. absence of showing of clear and present danger to the administration of justice.

2. Newsgatherers must exhaust all available court remedies before violating an unconstitutional judicial gag order.

3. Suspected criminals have been granted a change of venue, mistrial, or new trial in the event of potential
   a. prejudicial pretrial publicity,

b. bias created by the presence of television cameras.

KEY DECISIONS

1918 — TOLEDO   NEWSPAPER — offered a causal interpretation of the phrase "so near thereto" (Federal Contempt Act)

1941 — NYE — offered a geographical interpretation of the phrase "so near thereto"

1941 — BRIDGES — applied "clear and present danger" rather than "bad tendency" test to contempt-of-court cases, thus expanding the power of the press to comment on judges and proceedings

1965 — ESTES — established doctrine of "impled bias" regarding the televising of trials

1966 — SHEPPARD — overturned conviction obtained in a trial atmosphere that was corrupted by media coverage

1973 — DICKINSON — required reporters to exhaust all court remedies prior to violating an unconstitutional gag order

1975 — MURPHY — held that jurors need not be totally ignorant of background information regarding defendant, if they can set aside impressions and render impartial verdict

1976 — NEBRASKA PRESS ASSOCIATION — held that for a judge to impose a gag order there must be imminent, not merely potential, threat to the administration of justice

1981 — CHANDLER — challenged the doctrine of "implied bias"; noted absence of proof that television cameras in the courtroom inescapably produce an adverse impact of trial participants

RECOMMENDED READING

Jennings, James M., "Is *Chandler* a Final Rewrite of *Estes*?" Journalism Quarterly 59 (Spring, 1982), 66-73.

Kane, Peter E., <u>Murder, Courts, and the Press: Issues in Free Press/Fair Trial</u> Carbondale: Southern Illinois University Press, 1992.

Stephenson, D. Grier, Jr., "Fair Trial-Free Press: Rights in Continuing Conflict," <u>Brooklyn Law Review</u> 46 (Fall, 1979), 39-66.

CHAPTER 12

ELECTRONIC MEDIA

During the Twentieth Century, society has experienced a revolution in communication technology. This is evident in the media field — radio, television, cable TV, satellites, multi-channel distribution systems, public broadcasting, computer services — where each new advancement alters society's orientation toward information, entertainment, and promotion. Each change triggers reconsideration of the appropriate forms of regulation and deregulation. This chapter contains an examination of both the history of regulation, and significant doctrines affecting the licensing process.

HISTORY OF REGULATION

At the beginning of the twentieth century, the focus of media regulation was the telegraph. In 1910, Congress passed the Wireless Ship Act (P.L.262), which set forth guidelines for maritime communication. The Act required that ocean going vessels must carry telegraphic equipment, and exchange information with other ships. The United States had its first broadcast regulation. The revolution in communication technology that took place during the Twentieth Century spurred the passage of other forms of regulation. First, the Federal Radio Commission, and later, the Federal Communications Commission, were assigned the task of regulating electronic media.

FEDERAL RADIO COMMISSION

At the turn of the century not many people owned a radio, and only a few attempted broadcasting on their own. There was no need for government regulation. By 1912, electrical interference from stations using the same frequency necessitated some form of control. Congress passed the Radio Act of 1912 (P.L.264), which placed radio licensing under the authority of the Secretary of Commerce. The law contained several guidelines for broadcast regulation. First, in order to deal with problems resulting from electrical interference, each station was given a separate call number. Second, in applying for a license, a station had to identify its ownership, location, purpose, hours of operation, and authorized frequency. Third, in time of war or public peril, the President could close any station or authorize use of a station by the government with fair compensation of the owners. Fourth, the Act listed regulations concerning appropriate wavelengths, broadcasting of distress signals, division of time, uses of power, secrecy of messages, and control of vicinities.

One of the first court challenges to the Act occurred in the Hoover v. Intercity Radio Company, 286 F. 1008 (1923), case. Intercity Radio Company was granted a license in 1920. The following year, Secretary of Commerce Herbert Hoover refused to renew the license because he was unable to assign a wavelength that would not interfere with other stations. Furthermore, Hoover maintained that issuing or refusing a license was left solely to his discretion. The court disagreed. The duty of assigning a wavelength was "mandatory upon the Secretary." The only discretionary act left to the Secretary was to select a wavelength that would result in the "least possible interference." In Hoover, the court declined to grant the Secretary broad discretion in radio licensing.

Another challenge to the Secretary's authority occurred in United States v. Zenith Radio Corporation, 12 F.2d 614 (1926). The case arose when the Zenith Radio Corporation operated its station on a wavelength that was not authorized by the Secretary. This action, according to the Secretary, was punishable by a fine of up to $500 and forfeiture of the station's apparatus. The court ruled for Zenith Radio Corporation because there was "no express grant of power in the [Radio Act of 1912] to the Secretary of Commerce to establish regulations." The court again refused to grant power to the Secretary.

In 1927, Congress passed a new Radio Act (P.L.632). The Act retained many of the features of the 1912 law, and it also introduced new areas of station operation to government control. For example, the Act established an equal-time doctrine concerning political candidate broadcasts. The law also specified that any program for which money was paid had to be properly identified; the name of the sponsor had to be announced during the broadcast. Though the Act gave the government significant power to regulate radio communication, it banned any form of censorship or prior restraint by the licensing authority.

The 1927 Act created the Federal Radio Commission and defined its responsibilities and powers. The FRC was composed of five commissioners appointed for six-year terms by the President. Each commissioner represented a different geographical zone and not more than three could be from the same political party. The Commission was authorized to regulate broadcasting "as public convenience, interest or necessity requires." The Act also acknowledged some rights and responsibilities of applicants. All potential or incumbent licensees were afforded procedural safeguards, including the opportunity for a formal hearing. In all cases, the license was granted for no longer than three years. Licenses were to be automatically denied to any station attempting to monopolize radio communication. The FRC retained discretion to revoke licenses when a station made false statements, used profane language, or failed to operate within the limitations set forth by the license. Any station whose application was refused had the right to appeal to the Court of Appeals of the District of Columbia.

For the next few years, the Federal Radio Commission went about its work without incident. Its authority to license stations was generally unquestioned. During the 1930s, however, the authority of the FRC was tested in the courts. KFKB, a radio station located in Milford, Kansas, was first licensed by the Secretary of Commerce in 1923, in the name of the Brinkley-Jones Hospital Association. In 1926, it was relicensed to Dr. J. R. Brinkley. In early 1930, when the station filed for renewal of its license, the FRC decided that public interest, convenience, or necessity would not be served by granting the application. The evidence indicated that Dr. Brinkley controlled the programming of the station. Each day, Brinkley broadcast three half-hour programs entitled, "Medical Question Box." Without ever personally diagnosing the callers, Brinkley prescribed patent medicines produced by his drug company. The FRC noted that the practice "is inimical to the public health and safety, and for that reason is not in the public interest." According to the FRC:

> ...the testimony in this case shows conclusively that the operation of Station KFKB is conducted only in the personal interest of Dr. John R. Brinkley. While it is to be expected that a licensee of a radio broadcasting station will receive some remuneration for serving the public with radio programs, at the same time the interest of the listening public is paramount, and may not be subordinated to the interests of the station licensee.

The Court of Appeals, District of Columbia, unanimously affirmed the FRC's decision. In KFKB Broadcasting Association v. Federal Radio Commission, 47 F.2d 670 (1931), the court provided the first judicial support for the FRC's right to consider a station's programming with relation to the public interest, convenience, and necessity.

One year later, the court strengthened this position. The case involved Trinity Methodist Church, South, the lessee and operator of Los Angeles radio station KGEF. The FRC determined that, though in the name of a church, the station was actually owned and operated by Reverend Doctor Shuler. Numerous citizens protested when KGEF filed an application for renewal of its license. The FRC denied the application because the station had been used to attack the Roman Catholic Church, the broadcasts by Shuler were sensational rather than instructive, and on two occasions Shuler had been cited for using his radio talks to obstruct the administration of justice. In addition, Shuler made defamatory statements against the Board of Health, members of the judiciary, and officers in the Los Angeles Labor Temple. Appealing the decision, KGEF argued that the Commission's decision violated free speech. In <u>Trinity Methodist Church, South v. Federal Radio Commission</u>, 62 F.2d 850 (1932), the court affirmed the authority of the FRC to regulate broadcasting.

In <u>United States v. Gregg</u>, 5 F.Supp 848 (1934), the district court expanded FRC power by ruling that even unlicensed radio operators with an intrastate signal came under federal control. The case involved a complaint against Paul Gregg, owner and operator of a radio station in Houston, Texas, known as the "Voice of Labor." The station operated without a license. The FRC sought an injunction on the ground that the station caused interference with other duly licensed stations in the Houston area. In court, Gregg argued that his station was justified because of the nature of his programming. The station did not operate as a commercial venture, but for educational, religious, charitable, labor-related, and other such purposes. The court found the wording of the 1927 Radio Act explicitly clear — Gregg was prohibited from operating without a license from the FRC. In <u>Gregg</u>, as in <u>KFKB</u> and <u>Trinity Methodist</u>, the authority of the government to license radio broadcasting in the public interest was firmly established. As a result, Federal Radio Commission rulings attained authoritative validity.

FEDERAL COMMUNICATIONS COMMISSION

Faced with the complexities of new broadcast technology, especially the introduction of television, Congress enacted the Federal Communications Act of 1934 (P.L.416). The Radio Commission was replaced by a seven-member Federal Communications Commission. The Commission's chairman and members were appointed by the

President for seven-year terms. The Commission was granted exclusive authority to regulate the broadcasting industry. The FCC retained all of the responsibilities and powers enunciated in the 1927 Act and was, in addition, provided with more effective means of enforcement. Since its formation in 1934, the FCC has faced several problems concerning network broadcasting, cable television, and public broadcasting.

Network broadcasting

According to the Communications Act of 1934, chain (network) broadcasting consisted of the "simultaneous broadcasting of an identical program by two or more connected stations." In 1938, the FCC initiated a study to determine whether any special regulations were applicable to chain broadcasting. In 1941, the findings were published in the Commission's Report on Chain Broadcasting which concluded that network control over the industry was extensive. The FCC found that at the end of 1938 there were 660 commercial radio stations in the United States and that 341 of those were affiliated with national networks. The report noted that the stations affiliated with the national networks utilized more than 97 percent of the total night-time broadcasting power of all the stations in the country.

The FCC report argued that the networks controlled the stations, and precluded the formation of competing networks. Accordingly, the FCC adopted rules to prevent such network practices as exclusive affiliation of stations, required programming, ownership of stations, and control of station rates. According to the FCC, such practices were not in the "public interest, convenience, or necessity." The networks initiated court action in an attempt to prevent the enforcement of these rules on two grounds. First, the FCC had exceeded its authority. Second, the regulations violated the First Amendment. The case reached the Supreme Court. The opinion, written by Justice Felix Frankfurter, stressed that the FCC was empowered to provide effective use of radio in the public interest.

> ...with the number of radio channels limited by natural factors, the public interest demands that those who are entrusted with the available channels shall make the fullest and most effective use of them. If a licensee enters into a contract with a network organization which limits his ability to make the best use of the radio facility assigned him, he is not serving the public interest.

Frankfurter also rejected the First Amendment argument. He noted that broadcasting was a limited access medium; "unlike other modes of expression, radio inherently is not available to all. That is its unique characteristic." Frankfurter concluded that "since the spectrum is finite and the frequencies are not available to all who might like them, some regulation is necessary." The system established by the Federal Communications Act of 1934 placed the power to grant and supervise licenses in the hands of the FCC. In <u>National Broadcasting Company v. United States</u>, 63 S.Ct. 997 (1943), the Court upheld the FCC's authority to regulate network broadcasting.

Cable television

Cable television systems, initially called community antenna television (CATV), began in the late 1940s. Cable systems receive signals from television broadcasting stations, then amplify and distribute the signals to subscribers who pay for the service. Traditionally, cable systems perform two functions. First, they facilitate satisfactory reception of adjacent stations. Second, they transmit the signals of distant stations. Importation of distant signals has increasingly become the dominant function of cable television. Since the cable industry merely redistributes signals and does not produce its own programming, it is not subject to the same FCC regulation as conventional stations. Nonetheless, the FCC established its authority over cable television in a series of cases.

Carter Mountain Transmission Corporation applied to the FCC for permission to transmit signals received from television stations located in several distant cities to cable systems established in Riverton, Lander, and Thermopolie, Wyoming. The FCC denied the application. The FCC reasoned that to permit Carter Mountain to bring in outside programs would result in the "demise" of local television station KWRB-TV, and the loss of service to a substantial rural population not served by the cable system. According to the FCC, the need for the local outlet outweighed the improved service the proposed facilities would bring to those who subscribed. The FCC concluded that the cable system would not serve the public interest, convenience, and necessity. Carter Mountain brought the case before the court of appeals. In rejecting Carter Mountain's appeal, the court stressed that the FCC's exercise of power in this case was not arbitrary, nor did it exceed the FCC's statutory jurisdiction to regulate cable systems. The Supreme Court denied certiorari in the <u>Carter Mountain Transmission Corporation v. Federal Communications Commission</u>, 321 F.2d 359, 84 S.Ct. 442 (1963), case. In so doing, the Court expanded the scope of FCC regulation into the domain of cable television.

In <u>United States v. Southwestern Cable Company</u>, 88 S.Ct. 1994 (1968), the Court reaffirmed the FCC's power to regulate the cable industry. The case began when Midwestern Television Company claimed that Southwestern Cable Company had transmitted the signals of Los Angeles broadcasting stations into the San Diego area, and thereby had adversely affected Midwestern's San Diego market. Midwestern argued that Southwestern's action had fragmented the San Diego audience, reduced the advertising revenues of local stations, and that the station would have to eventually terminate or reduce its service. Shortly thereafter, the FCC restricted Southwestern's service area. On petition for review, the court of appeals held that the FCC lacked authority under the Communications Act of 1934 to issue such an order. In an important victory for the FCC, the Supreme Court unanimously overturned the decision and upheld FCC authority. The Court also expressed concern that the cable system conflicted with the emphasis the FCC had placed on local service programming. The Court stressed that "the ability of listeners to view channels far from their homes erodes the audience of the locally based channel and therefore shrinks its appeal to local advertisers." The Court guaranteed support for incumbent license holders who, by their past performance, demonstrated concern for the public interest. In Southwestern Cable, the Court upheld the authority of the FCC to regulate cable television and also approved the local programming requirement.

In United States v. Midwest Video Corporation, 92 S.Ct. 1860 (1972), the Court expanded the FCC's authority over cable television by supporting a program-origination rule which provided that

...no CATV system having 3,500 or more subscribers shall carry the signal of any television broadcast station unless the system also operates to a significant extent as a local outlet by cable casting and has available facilities for local production and presentation of programs other than automated services.

This ruling was designed to spur local participation in community affairs through cable television. Upon the challenge of Midwest Video Corporation, the court of appeals set aside the regulation on the ground that the FCC "is without authority to impose it." The Supreme Court decided that the rule was within the FCC's authority, and that the rule would promote the public interest. The Midwest Video I decision approved FCC authority that was more encompassing than that enunciated in Southwestern Cable.

In recent years, the courts decided several cases that examined the extent of authoritative control the FCC should hold over cable television. In City of New York v. Federal Communications Commission, 108 S.Ct. 1637 (1988), the Court upheld FCC authority to establish technical standards to govern the quality of television signals. Other decisions involved a variety of regulatory proposals, including pay cable rules, common carrier rules, and must carry provisions.

Pay cable rules. Home Box Office v. Federal Communications Commission, 98 S.Ct. 111 (1977), involved a successful challenge to the FCC's "pay cable" rules. The rules restricted cablecasters from presenting feature films and sports programs if a separate charge was made for the programs. In addition, the rules prohibited cablecasters from devoting more than 90 percent of their broadcast hours to movie and sports programs and also banned cablecasters from showing commercial advertising. According to the FCC, the rules served two ends. First, cable service is undesirable unless the programming is distinct from that on commercial television. Second, the revenue involved would be sufficient to allow cable operators to bid away the best programs, thus reducing the quality of conventional television. By limiting the cablecaster to material that is not otherwise shown on television, the FCC hoped to prevent such "siphoning" and to enhance the diversity of program offerings on broadcast television. In Home Box Office, the court of appeals found the "pay cable" rules to be in violation of the First Amendment for three reasons. First, the FCC failed to show that the 90 percent and the no-advertising rules served an "important or substantial government interest." Second, the FCC failed to demonstrate that the alleged siphoning phenomenon constitutes a real threat to those not served by cable. Third, the rules were overbroad — they applied to all films and sports programs regardless of their suitability for broadcast. For these reasons, the court overturned the FCC's "pay cable" rules.

Common carrier rules. Midwest Video Corporation challenged the FCC's "common carrier" rules. Under these rules, cable systems that have 3,500 or more subscribers were obliged to develop at least a 20-channel capacity, to make available channels for access by public educational and local governmental users, and to furnish equipment and facilities for access purposes. Cable operators were deprived of authority regarding who could use access channels and what could be transmitted over such channels. On petition for review, the court of appeals held that the rules imposed common carrier obligations on cable operators and thus ran counter to the command of the Federal Communications Act of 1934. The court stressed that Congress had limited the FCC's ability to provide "public access at the expense of the journalistic freedom of persons engaged in broadcasting." In Federal Communications Commission v. Midwest Video Corporation, 99 S.Ct. 1435 (1979), the Supreme Court agreed with the court of appeals. The rules exceeded the FCC's authority.

Must carry rules. In the Quincy Cable T.V. v. Federal

Communications Commission, 768 F.2d 1434 (1985), case, the court again restricted FCC regulatory power. The case involved a challenge of FCC regulations which required cable operators to transmit to their subscribers every television signal that was "significantly viewed in the community." These regulations, known as the "mandatory carriage" or "must carry" rules, required carriage of every local signal irrespective of the number of must-carry channels already being transmitted, the amount of programming duplicity, or the channel capacity of the cable system. These rules were established to guard against the destruction of free, community-oriented television. The court provided three reasons in overturning the regulations. First, cable and broadcast television are significantly different and should not be regulated in the same way.

> In sum, beyond the obvious parallel that both cable and broadcast television impinges on the senses via a video receiver, the two media differ in constitutionally significant ways. In light of cable's virtually unlimited channel capacity, the standard of First Amendment review reserved for occupants of the physically scarce airwaves is plainly inapplicable.

Second, the FCC failed to demonstrate that the regulations furthered a substantial governmental interest. According to the court, the rules "represent a 'fatally overbroad response' to the perceived fear that cable will displace free, local television." Third, the rules discriminate against viewer preferences; the rules prevent cable programmers from reaching their intended audience.

> This conscious disregard of subscribers' viewing preferences is difficult, if not impossible, to reconcile with the Supreme Court's repeated admonition that the interests of viewers should be considered "paramount" in the First Amendment calculus.

Based on these reasons, the court rejected the "must-carry" rules. However, the court invited the FCC to recraft some form of mandatory carriage rules "in a manner more sensitive to First Amendment concerns."

A year later, the FCC released a new set of "must carry" rules which offered more narrow justification and limited the sweep of their application. Nonetheless, in Century Communications Corporation v. Federal Communications Commission, 835 F.2d 292 (1987), the court invalidated the rules as "unjustified and unduly sweeping."

> We do not suggest that must-carry rules are *per se* unconstitutional, and we certainly do not mean to intimate that the FCC may not regulate the cable industry so as to advance substantial governmental interests. But when trenching on first amendment interests, even incidentally, the government must be able to adduce either empirical support or at least sound reasoning on behalf of its measures. As in Quincy Cable TV, we reluctantly conclude that the

> FCC has not done so in this case, but instead has failed to "put itself
> in a position to know" whether the problem that its regulations seek
> to solve "is a real or fanciful threat."

The issue was addressed by the Supreme Court in <u>Turner Broadcasting System v. Federal Communications Commission</u>, 114 S.Ct. 2445 (1994). Concerned that a competitive imbalance existed between cable television and network broadcasting, Congress passed the Cable Television Consumer Protection and Competition Act of 1992. Sections of the Act required cable systems to devote a portion of their channels to the transmission of local commercial and public broadcast stations. Numerous cable programmers challenged the constitutionality of the must-carry provisions. Writing for the Court, Justice Kennedy claimed that the appropriate criterion for evaluating these provisions was not a lenient nor a strict standard, but rather the intermediate level of scrutiny applicable to content-neutral restrictions. The less rigorous standard used for network broadcast regulation was not applicable to cable since the rationale for such analysis — the dual issues of spectrum scarcity and signal interference — did not apply to cable. According to Kennedy, the must-carry rules under review were content-neutral because they focused on the manner in which programmers transmitted their messages to viewers, not the messages they carried. A strict scrutiny standard was not applicable because congressional differential treatment showing preference for network over cable was based not on content but on the belief that network programming was in economic peril.

> Congress' acknowledgement that broadcast television stations
> make a valuable contribution to the Nation's communications
> structure does not indicate that Congress regarded broadcast
> programming to be more valuable than cable programming; rather, it
> reflects only the recognition that the services provided by broadcast
> television have some intrinsic value and are worth preserving
> against the threats posed by cable. It is also incorrect to suggest
> that Congress enacted must-carry in an effort to exercise content
> control over what subscribers view on cable television, given the
> minimal extent to which the Federal Communications Commission
> and Congress influence the programming offered by broadcast
> stations.

Kennedy applied the <u>O'Brien</u> test, under which a content-neutral regulation is sustained if it furthers an important governmental interest, and if any restrictions on First Amendment freedoms are no greater than necessary to further that interest. Kennedy acknowledged that the interests asserted in his case — preserving the benefits of free local broadcasting, disseminating information from multiple sources, and promoting fair competition — are important. However, in this case the government had not demonstrated that the must-carry provisions would further those interests in a "direct and material way." Furthermore, the government bore the burden of showing that the regulation did not place an unnecessary burden on free speech rights. The case was remanded for reconsideration. The Court suggested that the must-carry rules would be judged to be constitutional if they satisfied the provisions of the O'Brien test.

A few years later, following additional congressional factfinding, the Supreme Court reconsidered the case and voted to uphold the must-carry provisions. In Turner Broadcasting System v. Federal Communications Commission, 117 S.Ct. 1174 (1977), Justice Kennedy's majority opinion concluded that the provisions satisfied the O'Brien test. The promotion of widespread dissemination of information from a multiplicity of sources and the promotion of fair competition in the market for television programming constituted vital governmental interests. Congressional evidence demonstrated that significant numbers of broadcast stations would be refused carriage on cable systems and would be at serious financial disadvantage without must-carry rules. Finally, the provisions did not burden substantially more speech than was necessary to further the governmental interests. The Court concluded that the must-carry rules were consistent with the First Amendment. Following Turner Broadcasting II, the must-carry provisions of the 1992 Cable Act remained in effect.

Deregulation. During the 1980's, the FCC adopted a policy of deregulation, while at the same time encouraging new satellite and multi-channel distribution systems. The objective was to create a vast marketplace of viewing options, thereby reducing the need for governmental intervention in order to protect the public interest. This line of thinking was acknowledged by the Supreme Court. In Federal Communications Commission v. League of Women Voters of California, 104 S.Ct. 3106 (1984), Justice William Brennan noted: "The prevailing rationale for broadcast regulation based upon spectrum scarcity has come under increasing criticism in recent years. Critics... charge that with the advent of cable and satellite technology, communities now have access to such a wide variety of stations that the scarcity doctrine is obsolete."

In 1996, Congress passed the Telecommunications Act (P.L. 104-104), the most comprehensive piece of communications legislation since 1934. The 1996 law fostered new competition among network broadcasters, cable systems, telephone companies, and other corporations that offer communications services. The law freed the communications industry from some regulations and restrictions established by the 1992 law. For example, the law granted virtually perpetual licenses to broadcast stations; the basic term was extended to eight years with the guarantee that at renewal time the Commission must grant the application of the incumbent if the license "served the public interest" and committed "no serious violations." The law also made two changes in cable regulation; entry barriers were reduced and rate regulations were removed as of 1999. One facet of the law, the "communications decency" provision, which was designed to regulate indecency on the internet, was found to be unconstitutional in Reno v. American Civil Liberties Union, 117 S.Ct. 2329 (1997), a case that is discussed later in this chapter.

Public broadcasting

In 1967, the Carnegie Foundation suggested the formation of a nonprofit corporation to encourage the development of noncommercial television. The Carnegie report provided the impetus toward government-financed public broadcasting and helped to secure passage of the Public Broadcasting Act of 1967. The Act funded the development of noncommercial educational broadcasting, under the direction of the Corporation for Public Broadcasting. To become certified by the CPB, a station had to possess a FCC noncommercial education license, facilities for local program origination, and a schedule of local programming. Certification was generally limited to one station in an area. In 1970, the CPB formed the Public Broadcasting Service, a network for public programs. At the same time, the government began to reduce funding for public stations, as they became able to meet their own economic and programming needs.

Public broadcasting has been the focus of few court actions. One case, Maine v. University of Maine, 266 A.2d 863 (1970), involved a challenge to the University of Maine's public television station. In 1970, the University broadcast a program that contained comments by State Senator Robert Stuart, an active and legally-qualified candidate for the U.S. House of Representatives. The program, which lasted 40 minutes, consisted of Stuart answering questions telephoned in by the public. The station accepted the calls on a collect basis. The State of Maine initiated court action, seeking to stop the University from using its educational television system for interviews with political candidates. The State cited a law which prohibited the use of state-funded broadcast systems for political promotions. The University contended that the law conflicted with the Federal Communications Act of 1934. The Supreme Court of Maine agreed with the University; the "public interest" standard was as binding upon noncommercial stations as it was upon those that operated for profit.

In <u>Federal Communications Commission v. League of Women Voters of California</u>, 104 S.Ct. 3106 (1984), the Supreme Court heard a challenge to Section 399 of the Public Broadcasting Act of 1967, which forbade any noncommercial educational station that receives federal funding to "engage in editorializing." The FCC argued that Section 399 served "a compelling government interest in ensuring that funded non-commercial broadcasters do not become propaganda organs for the government." The Court acknowledged that the FCC holds "power to regulate the content, timing, or character of speech by noncommercial educational stations." However, because the breadth of Section 399 "extends so far beyond what is necessary to accomplish the goals identified by the Government, it fails to satisfy First Amendment standards." Application of Section 399 was unnecessary in this instance.

> ...the public's interest in preventing broadcasting stations from becoming forums for lopsided presentations of narrow partisan positions is already secured by a variety of other regulatory means that intrude far less drastically upon the "journalistic freedom" of noncommercial broadcasters.

In <u>League of Women Voters of California</u>, as in <u>University of Maine</u>, the Court acknowledged that the FCC has regulatory power over public broadcasting. At the same time, the Court served notice that any excessive regulatory efforts would be overturned.

LICENSE DECISION GUIDELINES

Under the regulatory scheme established by the Radio Act of 1927 and continued in the Communications Act of 1934, no radio or television station may operate without the approval of the Federal Communications Commission. The FCC regulates electronic media primarily through its power to grant, renew, and revoke licenses. Several guidelines, involving economic, programming, and procedural factors, are considered by the FCC when making a licensing decision.

ECONOMIC GUIDELINES

The licensing decision is influenced by two economic guidelines: the effect of competition on incumbent license holders, and the extent to which ownership of broadcasting facilities is diversified among different groups and individuals.

Incumbent license holders

The <u>Federal Communications Commission v. Sanders Brothers</u>

Radio Station, 60 S.Ct. 693 (1940), case began when the Telegraph Herald Company, owner of a newspaper published in Dubuque, Iowa, applied for a permit to build a broadcasting station. The incumbent license holder, Sanders Brothers radio station WKBB, sought to prevent the new station on the grounds that the loss in advertising revenue would harm WKBB and that the public interest was being adequately served. The FCC approved of the new station, noting that two stations were necessary and that no electrical interference would result. The court of appeals reversed the decision, holding that the FCC should have investigated possible economic injury to Sanders Brothers. On appeal to the Supreme Court, the Telegraph Herald Company argued that economic injury to a competitor was not a valid basis for refusal to grant a license. The Court, per Justice Owen Roberts, held

> ...that resulting economic injury to a rival station is not, in and of itself, and apart from considerations of public convenience, interest, or necessity, an element the petitioner must weigh, and as to which it must make findings, in passing on an application for a broadcasting license.

Roberts stressed that the incumbent licensee did not enjoy a vested property right to continue broadcasting. Roberts noted, however, that the question of incumbent economic well-being was a relevant concern if it affected the public interest, convenience, and necessity. In Sanders Brothers, the objection to the FCC ruling was not that the public interest was insufficiently protected, but that the financial interests of the incumbent had not been considered. Accordingly, the Supreme Court affirmed the FCC's decision to grant two licenses.

From 1940 to 1958, the FCC interpreted the Sanders Brothers decision to mean that potential economic injury to an incumbent was no basis for refusing to license a competitor. In 1958, the court of appeals rejected the FCC's interpretation of the Sanders Brothers decision. The case arose when Carroll Broadcasting Company, a radio station in Carrollton, Georgia, tried to prevent West Georgia Broadcasting Company from operating in the same area. The FCC granted a license to the West Georgia Company, noting that the issue of competition was not relevant. The court of appeals reversed the FCC ruling; competition was relevant if it adversely affected the public interest.

> We hold that, when an existing licensee offers to prove that the economic effect of another station would be detrimental to the public interest, the Commission should afford an opportunity for the presentation of such proof and, if the evidence is substantial (i.e. if the protestant does not fail entirely to meet his burden), should make a finding or findings.

According to the court, "the public interest is affected when service is affected." In Carroll Broadcasting Company v. Federal Communications Commission, 258 F.2d 440 (1958), the court instructed the FCC to give appropriate consideration to the issue of economic harm to an incumbent licensee, especially with an eye toward the economic impact on the public interest.

In 1988, after examining 80 relevant cases, the FCC issued a policy statement (3 FCC 678) which noted that the likelihood of a Carroll-type injury was "virtually nonexistent" because "the multiplicity of media voices that now exists makes the amount of harm that would result minimal." Accordingly, the FCC eliminated the Carroll doctrine.

Diversification of ownership

In setting licensing policies, the FCC has acted on the theory that diversification of media ownership serves the public interest by promoting diversity of program and service viewpoints, as well as by preventing undue concentration of economic power. This perception has been implemented over the years by a series of regulations imposing stringent restrictions on multiple ownership of broadcast stations. These regulations were at issue in several court cases.

In the early 1950s, the city of Mansfield, Ohio, enjoyed two forms of media, the Mansfield Journal and radio station WMAN. These media competed for local advertising. The Mansfield Journal Company attempted to coerce its advertisers to enter into exclusive contracts with the newspaper and to refrain from advertising on WMAN, by refusing to permit clients who advertised on the radio to advertise in the paper. In addition, the company refused to print WMAN's program log in the paper. When the Mansfield Journal Company applied for a radio broadcasting license, the FCC denied the application. The FCC ruled that the company's previous actions were designed to suppress competition and to achieve a monopoly of news dissemination and advertising. Such practices were likely to be intensified by the acquisition of a radio station. Granting a license would be inconsistent with the public interest. In Mansfield Journal Company v. Federal Communications Commission, 180 F.2d 28 (1950), the court of appeals affirmed the FCC ruling.

> This would not appear to be a consideration conceived in whimsy but rather a sound application of what has long been the general policy of the United States. Congress intended that there be competition in the radio broadcasting industry. It is certainly not in the public interest that a radio station be used to achieve monopoly.

Twenty years later, in Greater Boston Television Corporation v.

Federal Communications Commission, 444 F.2d 841 (1970), the court
again took a firm stand against concentrated ownership of broadcasting
facilities. The case involved WHDH Incorporated, which had broadcast
over Channel 5 in Boston since 1957. In 1969, the FCC granted the
license to the Boston Broadcasters Company because of potential
superior service due to its diversification of media control. WHDH, by
contrast, was licensee of two radio stations, owner of a daily newspaper,
and holder of a controlling interest in a cable television equipment
manufacturing company. The FCC noted: "Diversification is a factor of
first significance since it constitutes a primary objective in the
Commission's licensing scheme." According to the FCC, WHDH did
not deserve license renewal because it owned and controlled a
concentration of media. Approval of the Boston Broadcasters Company
application would provide a new voice for the community as well as
"the widest possible dissemination of information from diverse and
antagonistic sources."

In Federal Communications Commission v. National Citizens
Committee for Broadcasting, 98 S.Ct. 2096 (1978), the Supreme Court
heard a challenge to FCC regulations that prohibited "co-located
combinations." At issue was a FCC order that barred the licensing of
newspaper-broadcast combinations where there was common ownership
of a radio or television broadcast station and a daily newspaper located
in the same community. The FCC ordered divestiture of 16 existing
co-located combinations. Several petitions were filed, seeking review
of the FCC regulations. In an opinion prepared by Justice Thurgood
Marshall, the Court held that the regulations were "valid in their
entirety." The Court noted that 1) the regulations were properly based
on the "public interest" standard, and their promulgation falls within
the FCC's rule-making authority; 2) the regulations did not violate the
First Amendment rights of newspaper owners; 3) limiting divestiture to
16 cases of effective monopoly was not arbitrary or capricious; and 4)
disregarding media sources other than newspapers and broadcast
stations and differentiating between radio and television stations in
setting divestiture standards was not arbitrary.

The Mansfield Journal, Greater Boston, and National Citizens
Committee cases indicate that the concentration of media is looked
upon with disfavor by the courts. The greater the diversity, the better
the chance that the public interest will be served.

PROGRAMMING GUIDELINES

Although the Communications Act of 1934 prohibits the FCC from
"censoring" broadcasters, the Commission has adopted several

regulations governing broadcast programming. These regulations have been considered at the time of license renewal.

Local service

In 1947, the FCC denied Allen Simmons' application to increase the power of station WADC in Akron, Ohio, because the station intended "to broadcast all programs, commercial and sustaining, offered by the CBS network." The FCC noted that

> ...the application of WADC thus raises squarely the issue of whether the public interest, convenience and necessity would be served by a station which during by far the largest and most important part of the broadcast day 'plugs' into the network line and, thereafter, acts as a mere relay station of program material piped in from outside the community. We are of the opinion that such a program policy which makes no effort whatsoever to tailor the programs offered by the national network organization to the particular needs of the community served by the radio station does not meet the public service responsibilities of a radio broadcast licensee.

The FCC ruling stressed that a licensee was obliged to provide programming adapted to the interests of the local community. In Simmons v. Federal Communications Commission, 169 F.2d 670 (1948), the court of appeals agreed with the FCC's decision. The court rejected Simmons' contention that the policy amounted to censorship. According to the court, "censorship would be a curious term to apply to the requirement that licensees select their own programs by applying their own judgment to the conditions that arise...."

The importance of local-service programming was affirmed in Henry v. Federal Communications Commission, 302 F.2d 191 (1962). The case arose when Suburban Broadcasters filed an application for a permit to construct a station in Elizabeth, New Jersey. None of Suburban's owners were residents of Elizabeth, and they did not inquire into the programming needs of that community. Furthermore, Suburban's program proposals were identical with those contained in its application for stations in Illinois and California. The Commission found that the "program proposals were not 'designed' to serve the needs of Elizabeth" and that it was not known whether the proposals could be expected to serve those needs since no evidence was offered. In essence, the FCC refused to grant an application prepared by individuals who were without knowledge of the area they sought to serve. The court of appeals affirmed the decision, ruling that the FCC could require an applicant to demonstrate an earnest interest in serving the local community.

Quality service

A 1970 FCC policy statement made it difficult for applicants to demonstrate that an existing licensee had not performed in the public interest. According to the statement, when an applicant sought the license of an incumbent licensee, the incumbent was preferred if he or she could demonstrate "substantial" past performance not characterized by serious deficiencies. The criterion for renewal — substantial service to the public — rather than choosing the applicant most likely to render the best possible service, was justified on the basis of "considerations of predictability and stability." The FCC feared that if there were no stability in the broadcast industry, it would be difficult for a station to render "substantial" service. When citizen groups brought legal challenge, the court of appeals directed the FCC to stop applying the statement. In the opinion of the court, the statement had produced *rigor mortis* instead of stability. In <u>Citizens Communications Center v. Federal Communications Commission</u>, 447 F.2d 1201 (1971), the court sought to restore healthy competition "by repudiating a Commission policy which is unreasonably weighted in favor of the licensees it is meant to regulate, to the great detriment of the listening and viewing public." The court, nonetheless, recognized the value of a worthy incumbent and established a different criterion — the public would suffer if the incumbent licensees could not expect renewal when they render "superior" service. Given such an incentive, "an incumbent will naturally strive to achieve a level of performance which gives him a clear edge on challengers at renewal time." Thus, the court introduced competition into a system that previously tended merely to entrench existing broadcast ownership.

Following this decision, the FCC instituted a proceeding to determine whether it should attempt to quantify the concept of "substantial" service. After lengthy inquiry, the FCC declined to establish quantitative standards regarding such factors as the time that was devoted to local programming, news, public affairs, and the network affiliate. The FCC expressed concern that quantitative standards would restrict licensee discretion without any guarantee as to qualitative standards. The FCC concluded that "quantitative standards would not provide significantly greater certainty as to what constituted substantial service." The Commission indicated that in future comparative renewal proceedings, it would review all elements of an applicant's past performance with "particular emphasis on the incumbent's responsiveness to the recognized problems, needs, and interests of the community." Shortly thereafter, the National Black Media Coalition initiated court action, seeking review of the FCC policy. The court of appeals, in upholding the FCC's position, noted: "Nothing in the Communications Act imposes any requirement that the FCC promulgate quantitative programming standards." In National Black Media Coalition v. Federal Communications Commission, 589 F.2d 578 (1978), the court concluded that the FCC's "decision concerning quantitative program standards was reasonable and not arbitrary, capricious, or an abuse of discretion."

In a somewhat related case, Yale Broadcasting Company v. Federal Communications Commission, 478 F.2d 594 (1973), the court of appeals acknowledged the licensee's responsibility to provide quality programming consistent with the public interest. The controversy involved an order issued by the FCC regarding "drug-oriented music" which was played by some radio stations. The order required licensees to have knowledge of the content of their programming and to evaluate the desirability of airing such programs. The FCC set up guidelines whereby a broadcaster could obtain the required knowledge: prescreening by a responsible station employee, monitoring selections while they were being played, or considering and responding to complaints made by the public. In 1973, influenced by the claim that the licensee had failed to meet its responsibility, the FCC denied license renewal to the Yale Broadcasting Company. Yale argued that the FCC order was both unduly vague and an unconstitutional infringement of the right of free expression. The court of appeals rejected these arguments and affirmed the action of the FCC. The Yale case reflects the concern the courts have in guaranteeing quality programming. The presumption of substantial performance by incumbent license holders is no longer adequate. Licensees have a responsibility to provide programming of superior quality, which serves the public interest, convenience, and necessity.

Format

In several cases, the court evaluated guidelines designed to affect station programming formats. In these cases, the court has been somewhat inconsistent, but has preferred that format considerations be determined by market forces and competition. The Citizens Committee to Save WEFM v. Federal Communications Commission, 506 F.2d 246 (1974), case concerned an application for transfer of station ownership, which would result in a change in program format. Since it was first licensed in 1940, Chicago radio station WEFM had offered a classical music format. In 1972, WEFM was offered for sale to a corporation that proposed to broadcast contemporary music approximately 70 percent of the time. A citizens' committee contested the transfer. It argued that the classical-music format would be sorely missed by a sizable audience and that its loss would not be in the public interest. The FCC ruled that programming decisions had traditionally been left to the licensee's judgment, and competitive marketplace forces. In the FCC's view, abandonment of the classical format was "not a matter affected with the public interest but a business decision within the licensee's discretion." The Court of Appeals acknowledged that the committee had raised substantial questions concerning whether changes in program format should be left to competitive forces in the marketplace. According to the court, the FCC should have held a hearing to determine the community's needs.

A related case, Federal Communications Commission v. WNCN Listeners Guild, 101 S.Ct. 1266 (1981), arose when the FCC issued a policy statement concluding that the public interest is best served by promoting diversity in entertainment formats through market forces and competition among broadcasters. The statement maintained that a change in programming is not a material factor that should be considered by the FCC in ruling on an application for license renewal or transfer. Soon thereafter, several citizen groups interested in preserving specific formats petitioned for review of the policy. The case reached the Supreme Court. Writing for the majority, Justice Byron White held that the policy statement 1) was consistent with the FCC's traditional view that the public interest is best served by promoting diversity through market forces, and 2) did not conflict with the First Amendment since the FCC seeks to promote "the interests of the listening public as a whole and the First Amendment does not grant individual listeners the right to have the FCC review the abandonment of their favorite entertainment programs." In WNCN, the Court upheld the FCC policy statement, thereby leaving programming-format decisions largely to market forces and competition among broadcasters.

In companion cases, Metro Broadcasting v. Federal Communications Commission and Astroline Communications Company Limited Partnership v. Shurberg Broadcasting of Hartford, 110 S.Ct. 2997 (1990), the Supreme Court acknowledged that, in some areas, market forces are unable to provide sufficient program diversity. The Court considered the constitutionality of two minority preference policies adopted by the FCC. The first policy favored minority ownership in comparing applicants for licenses for new broadcast stations. The second policy, known as the "distress sale" policy, allowed a broadcaster whose qualifications to hold a license had come into question to transfer that license to a minority enterprise that meets certain requirements. The FCC adopted these policies in an attempt to promote diversification of programming. The broadcast companies brought court action on the ground that the policies violated equal protection rights of non-minorities. According to the Court, the policies are constitutional because they are related to the achievement of broadcast diversity.

> ...they [FCC] maintain simply that expanded minority ownership of broadcast outlets will, in the aggregate, result in greater broadcast diversity. This judgment is corroborated by a host of empirical evidence suggesting that an owner's minority status influences the selection of topics for news coverage and the presentation of editorial viewpoint, especially on matters of particular concern to minorities, and has a special impact on the way in which images of minorities are presented. In addition, studies show that a minority owner is more likely to employ minorities in managerial and other important roles where they can have an impact on station policies.

Five years later, in <u>Adarand Constructors Inc. v. Pena</u>, 115 S.Ct. 2097 (1995), the Court reversed this policy by ruling that federal affirmative action programs must be justified by proof that it is an appropriate remedy for a specific, provable instance of previous discrimination. Accordingly, any race preference program must be subjected to a strict judicial scrutiny test.

Lotteries

In 1868, Congress passed a postal regulation that prohibited the use of the mails to promote lotteries. The FCC applied this regulation to broadcast media. Violation could lead to loss of license, fines, and/or imprisonment. In 1953, the Post Office exempted some give-away lotteries from regulation. Soon thereafter, the three major networks began to broadcast give-away programs which were based on participation by viewers and listeners at home. The FCC sought to ban the programs on the ground that they were lotteries. The networks appealed. Speaking for the Supreme Court, Chief Justice Earl Warren defined the give-away show in a permissive way.

> To be eligible for a prize on the "give away" programs involved here, not a single home contestant is required to purchase anything or pay an admission price or leave his home to visit the promoter's place of business; the only effort required for participation is listening.

The Court believed "that it would be stretching the statute to the breaking point to give it an interpretation that would make such programs a crime." According to the <u>Federal Communications Commission v. American Broadcasting Company</u>, 74 S.Ct. 593 (1954), decision, the FCC had exceeded its rule-making power.

In 1967, the New York State Broadcasting Association challenged the FCC lottery regulations on First Amendment grounds. The issue concerned where to draw the line between lottery promotion and genuine news reporting. According to the Association, the specific terminology of Section 1304 of the lottery regulation punished the broadcasting of "any...information concerning any lottery." Broad interpretation of this language violated the First Amendment right of people to receive information. According to the FCC, which used a narrow construction of the terms, broadcasting of information about lotteries was prohibited, except for "ordinary news reports concerning legislation authorizing the institution of a state lottery, or of public debate on the course state policy should take." In New York State Broadcasters Association v. United States, 414 F.2d 990 (1969), the court sided with the FCC; broad construction was not warranted. Instead, the court interpreted the phrase "information concerning any lottery" to refer only to information that directly promoted an existing lottery. In 1970, Congress amended federal lottery law by indicating that Section 1304 did not apply to advertising or reporting of newsworthy information regarding a legally-conducted lottery. Both the ABC and New York Broadcasting cases illustrate that the broadcasting of lottery information is regulated, but not prohibited. Clearly, "newsworthy" lottery programming is outside the scope of FCC regulation.

Violence

Zamora v. Columbia Broadcasting System, 480 F.Supp 199 (1979), involved the claim that a young boy had become "involuntarily addicted to" and "completely subliminally intoxicated" by extensive viewing of television violence and that the boy developed a sociopathic personality and became desensitized to violent behavior. As a result, it was alleged, the boy shot and killed an elderly neighbor. The boy and his parents sought compensation from the television networks. The court rejected the claim as a violation of First Amendment principles.

> At the risk of overdeveloping the apparent...the liability sought by plaintiffs would place broadcasters in jeopardy for televising Hamlet, Julius Caesar, Grimm's Fairy Tales; more contemporary offerings such as All Quiet On The Western Front, and even The Holocaust, and indeed would render John Wayne a risk not acceptable to any but the boldest broadcasters.

A similar decision appeared in DeFilippo v. National Broadcasting Company, 446 A.2d 1036 (1982). Parents of a deceased minor sued the television network after their son hanged himself while imitating a hanging stunt he observed on television. The court held:

> ...allowing recovery under such an exception would inevitably lead to self-censorship on the part of broadcasters, thus depriving both

broadcasters and viewers of freedom and choice, for "above all else, the First Amendment means that government has no power to restrict expression because of its message, its ideas, its subject matter, or its content."

Indecency and obscenity

In re Palmetto Broadcasting Company, 33 FCC 250 (1962), the FCC refused to renew a license on the ground that indecent programming is not in the public interest. The case involved radio station WDKD, which devoted 25 percent of its programming to off-color jokes and statements that the FCC examiner concluded were "coarse, vulgar, suggestive, and susceptible of indecent, double meaning." The FCC denied renewal because such a large portion of broadcast time devoted to indecent material represented "an intolerable waste of the only operating broadcast facilities in the community."

Two years later, the FCC modified its position. In deciding whether to renew licenses of four stations owned by Pacifica Corporation, the FCC considered complaints against five programs which were considered "filthy" by a group of listeners. Pacifica Corporation argued that the programs served the interests of the listening public. The Commission upheld the programming.

> We recognize...such provocative programming as here involved may offend some listeners. But this does not mean that those offended have the right, through the Commission's licensing power, to rule such programming off the airwaves. Were this the case, only the wholly inoffensive, the bland, could gain access to the radio microphone or TV camera.

According to the FCC, "Pacifica's judgments as to the above programs clearly fall within the very great discretion which the act wisely grants to the licensee." The In re Pacifica Foundation, 36 FCC 147 (1964), decision signaled a philosophical shift by the FCC.

In 1970, the FCC reconsidered its philosophy once again. The case involved educational radio station WUHY-FM. On January 4, 1970, Jerry Garcia of the musical group "The Grateful Dead" was interviewed as part of a weekly program. His comments were frequently interspersed with the words "fuck" and "shit." The FCC fined WUHY $100. The FCC concluded that the language was obscene; it had "no redeeming social value" and was "patently offensive by contemporary community standards," having "very serious consequences to the 'public interest in the larger and more effective use of radio'." The FCC opinion also stressed an inherent distinction between radio and other communication media.

Unlike a book which requires the deliberate act of purchasing and reading (or a motion picture where admission to public exhibition must be actively sought), broadcasting is disseminated generally to the public under circumstances where reception requires no activity of this nature. Thus, it comes directly into the home and frequently without any advance warning of its content.

It should be noted that the In re WUHY-FM, Eastern Educational Radio, 24 FCC 2d 408 (1970), FCC definition of obscenity differed significantly from the prevailing Supreme Court definition, the Roth v. United States, 77 S.Ct. 1304 (1957), test. For example, the FCC banned specific words, rather than judging the expression in its entirety. Also, the FCC failed to determine whether the expression possessed any intrinsic value, as judged by contemporary community standards. According to WUHY, the broadcasting of obscenity was subject to a different standard than obscenity that was communicated through other media.

In Sonderling Broadcasting Corporation, WGLD-FM, 27 P.&F.Rad.Regs.2d 185 (1973), the FCC considered selected programming of radio station WGLD-FM of Oak Park, Illinois. The station aired a program in which an announcer accepted calls from the audience and discussed "sex-oriented" topics. On February 23, 1973, the topic was "oral sex." The program consisted of explicit comments in which female callers spoke of their oral-sexual experiences. The FCC found the station guilty of obscene and indecent programming and levied a fine of $2,000. The FCC distinguished the Sonderling decision from Pacifica: "We are not dealing with works of dramatic or literary art as we were in Pacifica." The FCC concluded that the program contained explicit material that was "patently offensive to contemporary standards for broadcast matter." Special importance was placed on the fact that minors compose a significant segment of a radio audience.

There are significant numbers of children in the audience during these afternoon hours — and not all of a pre-school age. Thus, there is always a significant percentage of school age children out of school on any given day. Many listen to radio; indeed it is almost the constant companion of the teenager.

The Sonderling decision reaffirmed FCC authority to ban not only obscene speech, but indecent speech as well.

In Federal Communications Commission v. Pacifica Foundation, 98 S.Ct. 3026 (1978), the Supreme Court rendered an opinion about the broadcasting of indecent material. The case examined the merits of a George Carlin record, aired by New York station WBAI as part of its general discussion of society's attitude toward language. The record devoted considerable time to a discussion of the use of seven "four-letter" words: shit, piss, fuck, cunt, cocksucker, motherfucker, tits.

The FCC received a complaint from a father, claiming that his young son had heard the broadcast. The FCC conducted an investigation, found the seven words to be indecent for children, and sought to channel the program to a time of the day when it would be less likely that children would be present. Pacifica Foundation, the license holder of station WBAI, challenged the ruling in court. In an opinion prepared by Justice John Stevens, the Court claimed that the content of Pacifica's broadcast was "vulgar," "offensive," and "shocking." Because content of that nature was not entitled to First Amendment protection under all circumstances, the justices had to consider its context. Stevens noted that

> ...patently offensive, indecent material presented over the airwaves confronts the citizen, not only in public, but also in the privacy of the home, where the individual's right to be let alone plainly outweighs the First Amendment rights of an intruder.... The concept requires consideration of a host of variables. The time of day was emphasized by the Commission. The content of the program in which the language is used will also affect the composition of the audience, and differences between radio, television, and perhaps closed circuit transmissions, may also be relevant.

In Pacifica, the Supreme Court acknowledged that the FCC may regulate "indecent" as well as "obscene" expression.

Shortly thereafter, broadcast industry executives sought clarification of the nature of "indecency" and the manner by which FCC policies would be implemented. In a series of cases titled Action For Children's Television v. Federal Communications Commission, 852 F.2d 1332 (1988), 932 F.2d 1504 (1991), 11 F.3d 170 (1993), 58 F.3d 654 (1995), 59 F.3d 1249 (1995), the U.S. Court of Appeals acknowledged that the FCC could implement its policy of regulating indecent material on the networks. Accordingly, the FCC forbade the airing of sexually explicit language and most nudity except during the "safe harbor" between 10 p.m. and 6 a.m.

Seven years after Pacifica, in Cruz v. Ferre, 755 F.2d 1415 (1985), the court of appeals considered an ordinance which banned the distribution of "obscene" and "indecent" material through cable television. According to the court, the section that regulated "indecent material" was overbroad. The court held that the Pacifica decision was not applicable because of differences between cable and broadcast media.

> A Cablevision subscriber must make the affirmative decision to bring Cablevision into his home. By using monthly program guides, the Cablevision subscriber may avoid the unpleasant surprises that sometimes occur in broadcast programming. Additionally, the ability to protect children is provided through the use of a free "lockbox" or "parental key" available from Cablevision.

The court recalled that Pacifica focused upon broadcasting's "pervasive presence," the fact that it is "uniquely accessible to children," and that it functions as an "intruder into the privacy of the home." The whole concept of a "nuisance rationale" is not relevant to cable. The Cruz decision limited the Pacifica principle to broadcast media.

Sable Communications of California v. Federal Communications Commission, 109 S.Ct. 2829 (1989), is a related case. A "dial-a-porn" service initiated court action against enforcement of Communications Act amendments which imposed blanket prohibition on indecent as well as obscene commercial telephone messages. The Supreme Court acknowledged that prohibition of obscene messages was constitutional, but denial of adult access to messages that were indecent but not obscene was overbroad — the amendment was not narrowly drawn to achieve the valid state interest of protecting children from exposure to indecent messages. The Court, per Justice White, distinguished Pacifica from Sable.

> Pacifica, which did not involve a total ban on broadcasting indecent material, relied on the "unique" attributes of broadcasting, which can intrude on the privacy of the home without prior warning of content and which is uniquely accessible to children. In contrast, the dial-it medium requires the listener to take affirmative steps to receive the communications. The Government's argument that nothing less than a total ban could prevent children from gaining access to the messages...is unpersuasive.

In another related case, Reno v. American Civil Liberties Union, 117 S.Ct. 2329 (1997), the Supreme Court examined the constitutionality of two provisions of the Communications Decency Act of 1996 (CDA). The provisions sought to protect minors from harmful expression on the Internet. One provision criminalized the "knowing" transmission of "obscene or indecent" messages to any recipient under 18 years of age. Another prohibited sending to persons under 18 any "patently offensive" messages, as "measured by contemporary community standards," which depict "sexual or excretory activities or organs." The Supreme Court, per Justice Stevens, found the provisions to be content-based blanket restrictions on speech; in addition, they were facially vague and overbroad. Stevens noted that the CDA resembled the ban on "dial-a-porn invalidated in Sable. In that case, the Court "rejected the argument that we defer to the congressional judgment that nothing less than a total ban would be effective in preventing enterprising youngsters from gaining access to indecent communications." Stevens accepted district court reasoning that the CDA imposed an unreasonable burden on adults.

> The District Court found that...existing technology did not include any effective method for a sender to prevent minors from obtaining

> access to its communications on the Internet without also denying access to adults. The Court found no effective way to determine the age of a user who is accessing material through e-mail, mail exploders, newsgroups, or chat rooms. As a practical matter, the Court also found that it would be prohibitively expensive for noncommercial — as well as some commercial — speakers who have Web sites to verify that their users are adults. These limitations must inevitably curtail a significant amount of adult communication on the Internet.

Stevens also noted that the CDA failed to define "indecency" or "patent offensiveness." In addition, the CDA went beyond the acceptable scope of constitutional bans. Based on previous Supreme Court decisions, a total ban on obscenity and child pornography is acceptable. But a similar restriction of indecent expression is not acceptable.

> We agree with the District Court's conclusion that the CDA places an unacceptably heavy burden on protected speech, and that the defenses do not constitute the sort of "narrow tailoring" that will save an otherwise patently invalid unconstitutional provision. In Sable, we remarked that the speech restriction at issue there amounted to "burning the house to roast the pig." The CDA, casting a far darker shadow over free speech, threatens to torch a large segment of the Internet community.

In Sable, Cruz, and Reno, the Court decided that circumstances which justify the restriction of "indecent" material on broadcast media are not applicable to either cable, dial-it media, or the Internet. These media are subject to a less restrictive standard.

Family viewing

As a result of FCC pressure, including threats of license denial, the television networks adopted a programming-format policy they did not wish to adopt. The "family viewing policy" held that

> ...entertainment programming inappropriate for viewing by a general family audience should not be broadcast during the first hour of network entertainment programming in prime time and in the immediately preceding hour. In the occasional case when an entertainment program is deemed to be inappropriate for such an audience, advisories should be used to alert viewers.

When the FCC imposed the family viewing policy, various directors, actors, writers, and producers of television programs challenged its validity. The court of appeals noted that the desirability or undesirability of the policy was not the issue. Rather, the question was "who should have the right to decide what shall and shall not be broadcast and how and on what basis should these decisions be made."

The court concluded that implementation of the family viewing policy violated the First Amendment because the FCC chairman had issued threats of government action should the industry refuse to adopt it. Furthermore, FCC enforcement of the policy through the licensing process would violate the First Amendment. In Writers Guild of America, West v. Federal Communications Commission, 423 F.Supp 1064 (1976), the court rejected FCC efforts to force a family viewing policy on television networks.

Public affairs

The FCC has exercised control over programming through application of several doctrines that relate to the coverage of public affairs. Chief among these are the equal-time, candidate-access, fairness, personal-attack, and limited-access doctrines. Three of these doctrines are still applicable to the licensing process; however, the fairness doctrine has been discontinued, and the limited-access doctrine never received strong support.

Equal-time rule. The equal-time rule, set forth in Section 315 of the Federal Communications Act of 1934, maintains that

> ...if any licensee shall permit any person who is a legally qualified candidate for any public office to use a broadcasting station, he shall afford equal opportunities to all other such candidates for that office in the use of such broadcasting station.

Such "opportunities" require equal time, equal facilities, and comparable costs for political candidates in the same election. Section 315 provides some "outs" for broadcasters. Though a station must provide equal "opportunities" if so requested by opposing candidates, it is under no obligation to solicit an appearance by every candidate. Furthermore, if they so choose, broadcasters do not have to allow any political candidates the use of their facilities. That would give all candidates equal time — none.

The equal-time rule contains a number of unclear and troublesome provisions. One problematic aspect concerns the meaning of the term "use." In 1959, Congress amended Section 315 to provide that an appearance by a candidate does not constitute a "use" when the program falls into the following categories: bona fide newscast; bona fide news interview; bona fide news documentary, if the appearance of the candidate is incidental to the presentation of the subject; and on-the-spot coverage of bona fide news events. In the years following that amendment, the FCC has been called upon to apply these exemptions to specific events to determine what constitutes a "use." One such case arose when President Jimmy Carter held a press conference which was carried live in prime time by the four major television networks. On the next day, the Kennedy for President Committee complained that the President had taken advantage of the occasion to promote his candidacy for reelection. The committee requested that Senator Edward Kennedy be given an "equal opportunity" to respond. The networks, and eventually the court in Kennedy For President Committee v. Federal Communications Commission, 636 F.2d 417 (1980), rejected the request. The court maintained that the network's unbiased live coverage of the press conference was "based upon good-faith determination of broadcasters that the conference was a *bona fide* news event" and that Section 315 did not apply.

Several rulings have been directed at determining whether political debates constitute a "use" under Section 315. In three cases, The Goodwill Stations, 40 FCC 362 (1962), National Broadcasting Company, 40 FCC 370 (1962), and Columbia Broadcasting System, 40 FCC 295 (1964), the FCC ruled that political debates fail to qualify for exemption under the four categories. In re Aspen Institute and CBS, 55 FCC2d 697 (1975), however, the FCC decreed that "nonstudio" debates between qualified political candidates are exempt from the equal-time requirements, provided that they are covered live and there is no broadcaster favoritism. This FCC policy was upheld in Chisholm v. Federal Communications Commission, 538 F.2d 349 (1976). In 1983, the FCC ruled that broadcasters could sponsor debates directly, instead of being limited to "nonstudio" presentations. The ruling was upheld by the court of appeals in League of Women Voters v. Federal Communications Commission, 731 F.2d 995 (1984). And, in Johnson v. Federal Communications Commission, 829 F.2d 157 (1987), the court ruled that minority candidates had no Communications Act or First Amendment right to be included in televised presidential debates.

The court of appeals has examined other types of "uses." In Paulsen v. F.C.C., 491 F.2d 887 (1974), the court held that entertainer and Presidential candidate Pat Paulsen's appearance in a television series constituted a "use" that obligated stations to provide "equal opportunities" to other qualified candidates. The court rejected Paulsen's contention that "non-political" uses of the media were free of Section 315 obligations. Likewise, in Branch v. F.C.C., 824 F.2d 37 (1987), the court determined that a station which employs a news reporter who runs for public office must provide "equal time" to his political opponents. The lesson of Paulsen and Branch is that Section 315 does not exempt entertainer and newscaster candidates from the equal time rule.

A second problematic term is "legally-qualified candidate." According to the FCC, a legally-qualified candidate is a person who publicly announces that he or she is a candidate for nomination, meets the qualifications for the office, qualifies for a place on the ballot, and was duly nominated by a political party or makes a substantial showing that he or she is a *bona fide* candidate. The McCarthy v. Federal Communications Commission, 390 F.2d 471 (1968), case dealt with the question of who is a legally-qualified candidate. On December 19, 1967, the three major television networks carried an hour-long interview of President Lyndon Johnson. Senator Eugene McCarthy, who had prior to the broadcast announced his candidacy for the Democratic nomination, requested "equal time," on the ground that President Johnson was a legally-qualified candidate. The FCC denied McCarthy's request because President Johnson had not announced his candidacy for the nomination and thus did not fulfill the requirements of the definition. McCarthy argued that the definition was unreasonable if a candidate deprived his opponents of the benefits of the equal-time rule simply by withholding an announcement of his own candidacy. The court of appeals upheld the FCC decision, and by so doing enabled incumbents to achieve the advantage of media exposure through *bona fide* news coverage, without allowing equal coverage of an opponent's campaign. By delaying formal announcement of candidacy, an incumbent may forestall operation of the equal-time rule.

A third problem with the equal-time rule concerns a provision that prohibits censorship. In establishing this provision, Congress recognized the necessity of free and open discussion of public issues, but did not fully take into account the question of libel. Could a broadcaster be sued for libel for merely presenting the message of a political candidate, in accord with the equal-time rule? The issue came before the Supreme Court in 1959. A libel suit arose regarding remarks made over station WDAY by A.C. Townley, a legally-qualified candidate in the 1956 U.S. Senate race in North Dakota. WDAY permitted Townley to broadcast a speech, uncensored in any respect, as a reply to previous speeches made by other senatorial candidates. Townley accused his opponents, together with the Farmers Educational and Cooperative Union, of conspiring to "establish a Communist Farmers Union Soviet right here in North Dakota." Farmers Union sued Townley and WDAY for libel. The case reached the Supreme Court. In Farmers Educational and Cooperative Union of America, North Dakota Division v. WDAY, 79 S.Ct. 1302 (1959), the justices decided that any system of broadcast censorship would undermine the purpose for which Section 315 was passed — providing unhindered discussion of political issues by legally-qualified candidates. The Court noted:

Quite possibly, if a station were held responsible for the broadcast of libelous material, all remarks even faintly objectionable would be excluded out of an excess of caution. Moreover, if any censorship were permissible, a station so inclined could intentionally inhibit a candidate's legitimate presentation under the guise of lawful censorship in libelous matter. Because of the time limitation inherent in a political campaign, erroneous decisions by a station could not be corrected by the courts promptly enough to permit the candidate to bring improperly excluded matter before the public. It follows from all this that allowing censorship...would almost inevitably force a candidate to avoid controversial issues during political debates over radio and television, and hence restrict the coverage of consideration relevant to intelligent political decision.

In WDAY, the Court granted broadcasters immunity from libel suits based on the remarks of political candidates presented in accordance with Section 315.

A fourth problem with the equal-time rule is that it operates only when a candidate uses the broadcasting facilities. A candidate has to appear in person before Section 315 may be invoked. If a spokesperson for the candidate broadcasts a campaign message, the equal-time rule is not applicable. In order to offset the impact of such a partisan campaign broadcast, the FCC developed the Zapple rule. The doctrine set forth in Letter to Nicholas Zapple, 23 FCC2d 707 (1970), holds that when, during a political campaign, a broadcaster sells air time to a candidate's spokespersons, who use that time to discuss issues in the campaign, spokespersons of the candidate's opponent are entitled to purchase comparable air time for a reply. Zapple does not require free reply time if the original broadcast was paid for. All Zapple stipulates is that the opposing candidate's supporters must be sold comparable time if they want it. Thus, Zapple applies the principles of the equal-time rule to a candidate's supporters and campaign committees.

A fifth problem involves "channeling" of offensive advertising. In recent years, some candidates who oppose abortions have included photographs of aborted fetuses in their campaign ads. Several stations, supported by a FCC declaratory order, refused to air such ads in prime time, even if an opposing candidate had advertised in prime time. Becker v. Federal Communications Commission, 95 F.3d 75 (1996), held that this practice violated the Equal Time Rule because politicians have a special right of access, even if their ads are offensive.

The Commissions Declaratory Ruling violates the "reasonable access" requirement of section 312 by permitting content-based channeling of non-indecent political advertisements, thus denying qualified candidates the access to the broadcast media envisioned by Congress. The ruling also permits licensees to review political advertisements and to discriminate against candidates on the basis of their content, in violation of both the "no censorship" and "equal opportunities" provisions of section 315.

Candidate-access rule. Section 312 of the Communications Act of 1934, as amended by the Federal Election Campaign Act of 1971, authorizes the FCC to revoke any broadcast-station license for failure to allow reasonable amounts of time for use by a legally-qualified candidate for federal elective office. In October, 1979, the Carter-Mondale Presidential Committee requested the three major television networks to provide time for a 30-minute program early in December. The Committee intended to present, in conjunction with President Carter's formal announcement of his candidacy, a documentary outlining the record of Carter's Administration. The networks refused to make the time available. In their refusal, the networks cited the large number of Presidential candidates and the potential disruption of regular programming to accommodate requests for equal treatment. The networks also noted that they had not yet determined when they would begin selling political time for the 1980 campaign. The Carter-Mondale Committee filed a complaint with the FCC, charging that the networks had violated their obligation to provide "reasonable access." The FCC agreed. The networks then initiated court action, arguing that no person has the right to command access to the broadcast media. The case reached the Supreme Court. The majority opinion, delivered by Chief Justice Warren Burger, noted that broadcasters may deny the sale of air time prior to the start of the campaign, but once a campaign begins they must give reasonable attention to access requests from legally-qualified candidates. Furthermore, such requests must be considered on an individual basis, and broadcasters are required to tailor their responses to accommodate a candidate's stated purposes in seeking air time. Burger noted that, in this case, the networks had employed "blanket rules concerning access." According to Burger, the FCC was justified in rejecting such a policy.

> While the adoption of uniform policies might well prove more convenient for broadcasters, such an approach would allow personal campaign strategies and the exigencies of the political process to be ignored. A broadcaster's "evenhanded" response of granting only time spots of a fixed duration to candidates may be "unreasonable" where a particular candidate desires less time for an advertisement or a longer format to discuss substantive issues. In essence, petitioners seek the unilateral right to determine in advance how much time to afford all candidates. Yet (Section 312) assures a right of reasonable access to individual candidates for federal elective office, and the Commissioner's requirement that their requests be considered on an individualized basis is consistent with that guarantee.

In Columbia Broadcasting System v. Federal Communications Commission, 101 S.Ct. 2813 (1981), the Court decided that a limited right of access to the media did not violate the First Amendment rights of broadcasters, but rather, properly balanced the rights of candidates, the public, and the media.

Fairness doctrine.   The fairness doctrine influenced licensing decisions during the period 1949 to 1988.   The doctrine was established by the FCC in 1949, but its provisions developed out of earlier cases.   The Mayflower, WHKC, and Scott decisions illustrate the evolution of the "fairness doctrine."

In 1938, the Yankee Network Corporation applied for renewal of its license for Boston radio station WAAB. The Mayflower Broadcasting Company challenged the renewal and applied for a construction permit. The FCC hearing revealed that Yankee Broadcasting had aired "editorials" urging the election of various candidates to public office. No pretense of impartiality was made by the station in announcing the choices. The FCC sharply condemned Yankee's partisan practices.

> Radio can serve as an instrument of democracy only when devoted to the communication of information and the exchange of ideas fairly and objectively presented. A truly free radio cannot be used to advocate the causes of the licensee. It cannot be used to support the candidacies of his friends. It cannot be devoted to the support of principles he happens to regard most favorably.   In brief, the broadcaster cannot be an advocate.

Nevertheless, the FCC denied Mayflower's application on the ground that the company was not financially qualified to construct and operate the proposed station. The real importance of the decision, however, is that broadcasters were discouraged from editorializing. The FCC noted in In the Matter of the Mayflower Broadcasting Corporation and the Yankee Network (WAAB), 8 FCC 333 (1941), that "freedom of speech on the radio must be broad enough to provide full and equal opportunity for the presentation to the public of all sides of public issues."

The In Re United Broadcasting Company (WHKC), 10 FCC 515 (1945), decision also recognized the importance of fairness.   In a petition to deny renewal of license for station WHKC, two labor unions cited a station policy not to sell time for programs that solicited union memberships or discussed controversial subjects.   While conceding that stations do not have to sell time to all who want it, the FCC noted that stations were not justified in establishing a policy of unfair coverage of controversial issues.

> The Commission recognizes that good program balance may not permit the sale or donation of time to all who may seek it for such purposes and that difficult problems calling for careful judgment on the part of station management may be involved in deciding among applicants for time when all cannot be accommodated. However,

competent management should be able to meet such problems in the public interest and with fairness to all concerned.

The In Re Petition of Robert Harold Scott, 11 FCC 372 (1946), decision also suggested the emerging doctrine of "fairness." Robert Scott filed a petition requesting that the FCC revoke the licenses of three radio stations because he had been denied air time to broadcast talks on the topic of atheism. Scott argued that the stations did not present contrasting sides of the issue and therefore did not operate in the public interest. Even though the FCC denied the petition because Scott's complaint was too broad, the Commission stressed that even though a majority of the public does not accept a particular view, that was no reason to deny airing the view.

> If freedom of speech is to have meaning, it cannot be predicated on the mere popularity or public acceptance of the ideas sought to be advanced. It must be extended as readily to ideas which we disapprove or abhor as to ideas which we approve. Moreover, freedom of speech can be as effectively denied by denying access to the public means of making expression effective — whether public streets, parks, meeting halls, or the radio — as by legal restraints or punishments of the speaker.

The conditions existing in the Mayflower, WHKC, and Scott cases led the FCC to specify a broadcaster's responsibilities regarding coverage of controversial issues. The fairness doctrine involved a twofold obligation for broadcasters: first, a reasonable percentage of broadcast time must be devoted to coverage of public issues; and second, the coverage must present contrasting points of view. The doctrine was set forth in In the Matter of Editorializing by Broadcast Licensees, 13 FCC 1246 (1949). For the next three decades, the FCC supported and enforced the doctrine of fairness.

The Brandywine-Main Line Radio v. Federal Communications Commission, 473 F.2d 16 (1972), case resulted in the denial of a broadcast license, based on a violation of the fairness doctrine. Brandywine Main Line Radio, a company owned by the Faith Theological Seminary and presided over by right-wing preacher Carl McIntire, applied for transfer of control of radio station WXUR to Brandywine from its current owners. Community groups opposed the application, but the FCC approved the transfer after McIntire promised to provide opposing viewpoints on controversial issues. At renewal time, citizen groups contended that WXUR had failed to provide such coverage. The renewal hearing determined that the moderator of a WXUR call-in program had encouraged and approved of the remarks of anti-Jewish callers. Furthermore, the station's programming systematically attacked celebrities of the New Left. WXUR failed to provide spokespersons to counteract its conservative, right-wing programming. WXUR became the first licensee to lose its license because of failure to comply with the fairness doctrine.

During the 1980s, as the FCC turned toward a policy of deregulation, the doctrine became less justifiable. In a document titled Fairness Report, 102 FCC2d 143 (1985), the FCC concluded that the fairness doctrine no longer served the public interest. The report noted that with the increase of available news sources, audiences were less dependent upon broadcasting as their source of information. Government intrusion in media regulation was not only unwarranted, but potentially harmful because of the political pressure which influenced coverage of public issues. Congress then engaged in a two-year inquiry into the fairness issue; the result was passage of legislation which supported the fairness concept. In 1987, President Ronald Reagan vetoed the legislation, a veto Congress was unable to override. That same year, the FCC's In Re Complaint of Syracuse Peace Council Against WVTH, 63 RR2d 542 (1987), decision rescinded all facets of the fairness doctrine except the "personal attack" and "limited access" rules. That position was upheld in Syracuse Peace Council v. Federal Communications Commission, 867 F.2d 654 (1989).

> Federal Communications Commission's determination that fairness doctrine no longer served public interest was neither arbitrary nor capricious; FCC relied heavily on findings in 1985 fairness report that doctrine operated to chill broadcaster speech on controversial issues and that recent increases in broadcasting outlets undercut need for doctrine.

The courts upheld the FCC's authority to abolish the fairness doctrine in Arkansas AFL-CIO v. Federal Communications Commission, 11 F.3d 1430 (1993). The case stemmed from a request by labor unions that the FCC declare a Little Rock television station guilty of failing to cover all sides fairly in a local referendum. The FCC claimed that the station had no obligation to cover all sides because the fairness doctrine had been repealed. The court sided with the FCC. Thus, in light of Syracuse Peace Council and Arkansas AFL-CIO, the principal focus of the fairness doctrine ceased to be enforced.

Personal-attack rule. In 1962, the FCC declared that when a broadcast amounts to a personal attack upon an individual or group, the broadcaster has an obligation to notify the target of the attack and offer the target an opportunity to respond. The rule was challenged in Red Lion Broadcasting Company v. Federal Communications Commission, 89 S.Ct. 1794 (1969). The case began when the Red Lion Broadcasting Company carried a program that included an attack by Reverend Billy James Hargis against Fred Cook, the author of a book entitled Goldwater — Extremist on the Right. Hargis cited several "shady" aspects of Cook's background, thereby hoping to discredit the book about Senator Barry Goldwater. Cook asked the radio station for an opportunity to reply to Hargis's attacks. The station, unclear as to its responsibility regarding who had to pay for the time, replied that the personal-attack rule required a licensee to make free time available only if no paid sponsorship could be located. Cook complained to the FCC, which held that the station was obligated to furnish free reply time; the public interest required that the public be given an opportunity to hear both sides of an issue, even if the time had to be paid for by the station. The station appealed. The case reached the Supreme Court. The Court, per Justice White, decided that the personal-attack rule was consistent with the First Amendment. In supporting his argument, White noted that without the rule broadcasters would have "unfettered power to make time available only to the highest bidders, to communicate only their views on public issues, people, and candidates, and to permit on the air only those with whom they agreed." The Court affirmed the constitutionality and desirability of the rule. Justice White also argued that

> ...as far as the First Amendment is concerned those who are licensed stand no better than those to whom licenses are refused.... It is the purpose of the First Amendment to preserve an uninhibited marketplace of ideas in which truth will ultimately prevail rather than to countenance monopolization of that market, whether it be the Government itself or a private licensee.... It is the right of the public to receive suitable access to social, political, aesthetic, moral, and other ideas and experiences which is crucial here. That right may not constitutionally be abridged either by Congress or by the FCC.

In Red Lion, even though the Court upheld the traditional "limitation of the spectrum" approach, its decision set the stage for a "limited access" doctrine.

Limited-access doctrine. The broad mandate of Red Lion was to allow as much access to broadcast airwaves as was consistent with the First Amendment. Accordingly, the FCC maintained that if a broadcaster followed the requirements of the fairness doctrine, that broadcaster was not obligated to provide access to all who requested air time, either by selling such air time or providing it free of charge. This doctrine of limited access was supported by the Supreme Court in Columbia Broadcasting System v. Democratic National Committee, 93 S.Ct. 2080 (1973). In 1970, the Business Executives' Move For Vietnam Peace (BEM) filed a complaint with the FCC, charging that a radio station had refused to sell air time to broadcast announcements expressing views on controversial issues. The station contended that since it presented full and fair coverage of public issues, including the Vietnam conflict, it was justified in refusing to accept editorial advertisements. In a related case, the Democratic National Committee (DNC) requested a declaratory ruling from the FCC that under the First Amendment "a broadcaster may not, as a general policy, refuse to sell time to responsible entities, such as DNC, for the solicitation of funds and for comment on public issues." DNC cited Red Lion as establishing a limited right of access of the airwaves. In dealing with both BEM and DNC, the FCC ruled that broadcasters who met their obligation to provide full and fair coverage of public issues were not required to accept editorial advertisements. The Supreme Court upheld the FCC decision.

> More profoundly, it would be anomalous for us to hold, in the name of promoting the constitutional guarantees of free expression, that the day-to-day editorial decisions of broadcast licensees are subject to the kind of restraints urged by respondents. To do so in the name of the First Amendment would be a contradiction. Journalistic discretion would in many ways be lost to the rigid limitations that the First Amendment imposes on government. Application of such standards to broadcast licensees would be antithetical to the very ideal of vigorous, challenging debate on issues of public interest. Every licensee is already held accountable for the totality of its performance of public interest obligations.

The DNC case broke the momentum of the right of access suggested in Red Lion. The Supreme Court weighed the competing claims of licensees and those who desired access and concluded that the broadcaster had a legitimate right to deny air time to the DNC and BEM. According to the Court, "in this case, the Commission has decided that on balance the undesirable effects of the right of access urged by respondents would outweigh the asserted benefits." In effect, the DNC decision emphasized that the First Amendment did not require a right of access for editorial advertising because such a right would mean an end to the editorial function in broadcast journalism.

PROCEDURAL GUIDELINES

Procedural questions comprise an important part of the licensing decision. Under what conditions is a complaining citizen group entitled to a hearing? Who has the burden of proof at an evidentiary hearing? Can a license be revoked for lack of candor? These procedural issues have received attention from the FCC and the courts.

Hearing and burden of proof

In 1955, the FCC received a complaint which charged that station WLBT had deliberately cut off a network program about racial problems. In 1957, another complaint alleged that WLBT had presented a program urging racial segregation and had refused to present the opposing viewpoint. In 1962, the FCC again received complaints that WLBT had presented only one viewpoint concerning racial integration. In 1963, the FCC requested the station to submit reports on its programs concerning racial issues. In 1964, while the FCC was investigating WLBT's programs, the station filed a license-renewal application. Enraged citizens, members of the Office of Communication of the United Church of Christ, filed a petition urging denial of WLBT's application. The group argued that WLBT had failed to serve the general public because the station did not give a fair and balanced presentation of controversial issues — especially those concerning blacks, who comprised almost 45 percent of the population within the station's service area. The FCC concluded that "serious issues" were presented as to "whether the licensee's operations have fully met the public interest standard." Nevertheless, the Commission awarded a one-year renewal in the form of a probationary grant. The conditions required WLBT to comply with the requirements of the fairness doctrine; observe strictly its representations to the Commission in this area; have discussions with community leaders, including those active in the civil rights movement, as to whether its programming is meeting the needs of its area; cease discriminatory programming; and make a detailed report regarding its efforts in meeting these conditions. On appeal, the United Church group contended that since the FCC concluded that WLBT was guilty of "discriminatory programming," the Commission should not renew the license, even for one year, without a hearing. The FCC argued that it took all the necessary steps to insure that the discriminatory practices would cease. For this reason, the Commission granted a short-term renewal in the hope that WLBT would improve. The court acknowledged the authority of the FCC, while noting the importance of "audience participation" through a hearing.

> In order to safeguard the public interest in broadcasting, therefore, we hold that some "audience participation" must be allowed in license renewal proceedings. We recognize this will create problems for the Commission but it does not necessarily follow that "hosts" of protestors must be granted standing to challenge a renewal application or that the Commission need allow the administrative process to be obstructed or over-whelmed by captious or purely obstructive protests. The Commission can avoid such results by developing appropriate regulation by statutory rulemaking.

In Office of Communication of the United Church of Christ v. Federal Communications Commission, 359 F.2d 994 (1966), the court acknowledged that the FCC holds "broad discretion" in setting rules for a hearing — including the number and type of witnesses required and the extent of "audience participation" allowed. The right to a hearing is not absolute; it is granted only after weighing the claims of the various petitioners and the nature of the complaints.

Another procedural issue concerns the burden of proof. This issue was considered in Office of Communication of the United Church of Christ v. Federal Communications Commission, 425 F.2d 543 (1969). After the probationary period, the FCC conducted a hearing and then granted a three-year renewal to WLBT. Once again, the United Church of Christ took the FCC to court. The group criticized the FCC examiner's treatment of evidence and the burden of proof. The court agreed:

> The Examiner seems to have regarded appellants as "plaintiffs" and the licensee as "defendant," with burden of proof allocated accordingly. This tack, though possibly fostered by the Commission's own action, was a grave misreading of our holding on this question. We did not intend that intervenors representing a public interest be treated as interlopers. Rather, if analogues can be useful, a "Public Intervenor" who is seeking no license or private right is, in this context, more nearly like a complaining witness who presents evidence to police or a prosecutor whose duty it is to conduct an affirmative or regulatory investigation of all the facts and to pursue his prosecutorial or regulatory function if there is probable cause to believe a violation had occurred.

The court recognized that the United Church group protested WLBT's license, not for selfish reasons, but to help determine whether the station operated in the public interest. The court noted that a procedure which favored the incumbent licensee had guided the examiner while conducting the evidentiary hearing. In effect, the examiner had disregarded substantial evidence that showed WLBT's discriminatory programming. In United Church II, the court revoked the license-renewal grant to WLBT and directed the FCC to invite applicants to apply for the license. In reversing the FCC's decision, the court indicated that the burden of proof rested with the incumbent licensee.

One year later, in Hale v. Federal Communications Commission, 425 F.2d 556 (1970), the court rejected the requirement of an evidentiary hearing, and reconsidered the burden-of-proof obligation. The case began when two citizens in Salt Lake City challenged the renewal application of station KSL-AM. The citizens claimed that the station had violated the fairness doctrine. They applied for a hearing, which the FCC refused to grant. This FCC decision limited the scope of the United Church I decision. The court of appeals affirmed the FCC's determination not to grant a hearing. The court said:

> To establish a violation of this [fairness] doctrine, appellants must

show that specific programs have dealt with controversial issues partially, and, if so, that other programs on the station have not balanced the coverage by presenting the alternative viewpoints. Appellants claim their inability to survey KSL-AM's general programming is due to the fact that the station does not publish a daily log of its programming in any newspaper. Such logs, however, are required to be kept by the licensee and could have been made available upon request.

The court, in effect, accepted the FCC's interpretation of the 1934 Federal Communications Act, that a hearing was required only when the petition raises a new issue that requires resolution by a hearing. Furthermore, in protesting renewal, the citizen group had to carry the burden of proof. According to the court, proof of a violation of the fairness doctrine must be based on specific facts.

Where complaint is made to the Commission, the Commission expects a complainant to submit specific information indicating 1) the particular station involved, 2) the particular issue of a controversial nature discussed over the air, 3) the date and time when the program was carried, 4) the basis for the claim that the station had presented only one side of the question, and 5) whether the station had afforded, or has plans to afford an opportunity for the presentation of contrasting viewpoints.

In Hale, the court established strict guidelines for meeting the burden of proof. The court made it quite difficult for citizens to obtain a hearing and to prove a violation. The Hale decision made renewal easier for the incumbent licensee.

In Stone v. Federal Communications Commission, 466 F.2d 316 (1972), the court again faced the issue of when and how a citizen group may obtain an evidentiary hearing. In 1969, 16 Washington, D.C., community leaders filed a petition to deny renewal of the television license for station WMAL-TV. The group contended that the station maintained discriminatory programming and employment policies. The FCC dismissed the petition, arguing that the group had not proven its claims. The group had failed to show that WMAL's programming exceeded the discretion afforded licensees or that WMAL used discriminatory employment practices. The court of appeals agreed with the FCC's ruling. According to the court,

...in the event, then, that a petition to deny does not make substantial and specific allegations of fact which, if true, would indicate that a grant of the application would be *prima facie* inconsistent with the public interest, the petition may be denied without hearing on the basis of a concise statement of the Commission's reasons for denial.

In Stone, the court decided that citizen groups had to clear several rigorous obstacles in order to obtain an evidentiary hearing. First, the

FCC was not required to hold a hearing when no substantial and material issues existed. Second, a hearing was not required when facts necessary to resolve an issue were not disputed or when the issue turned on inferences from facts already available to the Commission. In Stone, the citizen's group did not raise questions of such a nature as to require a hearing. According to the court, the objections the group had raised lacked the required specificity; they were largely conclusionary and not tied to specific programming considerations. The court noted that "such generalized criticisms run the risk of turning the FCC into a censorship board, a goal clearly not in the public interest." The court went on to rule that the plaintiff bears a substantial burden of specificity: "In the absence of a competing broadcast application situation, where a hearing is required, plaintiffs bear a substantial burden of specificity, a burden they have not met...." The Stone decision demonstrates that in order for a citizen's group to obtain an evidentiary hearing, it must first raise substantial questions of fact and sufficiently prove specific allegations. In Stone, as in Hale, the court established procedures favorable to the incumbent licensee.

Lack of candor

In RKO General v. Federal Communications Commission, 102 S.Ct. 1974 (1982), the court of appeals upheld a denial of license renewal based on lack of candor. The case began in 1965, when RKO petitioned to renew its license for WNAC-TV in Boston. The petition was opposed by a competing applicant on the allegation that RKO had engaged in illegal trade practices. A comparative hearing on the two applications led to a FCC finding in favor of RKO, subject to further analysis of the trade practices. Because of strategic maneuvering by RKO competitors, however, the FCC did not reopen the proceedings until 1979. The hearing revealed several cases of misconduct by RKO, including reciprocal trade practices conducted during the mid-1960's and a lack of candor during the current proceedings. The FCC decided to deny license renewal to RKO. On appeal, the court set forth two principles related to the FCC's authority in determining license renewal. First, a finding by the FCC of anticompetitive practices that are not in the public interest cannot be applied retroactively to conduct that ceased almost 15 years before. Second, a licensee's lack of candor in proceedings before the FCC constitutes a valid reason for denial of license renewal. In 1982, the Supreme Court declined to hear the RKO General case, thus allowing the lower court decision to stand.

CONCLUSION

The following principles regulate communication law regarding ELECTRONIC MEDIA:

1. The Federal Communications Act of 1934 established the Federal Communications Commission and entrusted that body with the task of regulating the broadcast media in the "public interest, convenience, and necessity." The FCC regulates the broadcast industry primarily through its power to grant, renew, and revoke licenses.

2. The FCC has refused to grant or renew licenses under certain conditions. The FCC believes that
   a. diversification of mass media ownership serves the public interest by promoting diversity of program and service viewpoints, as well as by preventing undue concentration of economic power,
   b. regulation of "indecent" as well as "obscene" expression is consistent with the public interest,
   c. lack of candor in investigative proceedings warrants denial of license.

3 The FCC has enthusiastically granted or renewed licenses under certain circumstances. The FCC is impressed by applicants that
   a. demonstrate an interest in serving the local community,
   b. provide programming of superior quality,
   c. offer a programming format that is in the public interest, though the FCC acknowledges that formats are largely influenced by economic competition among broadcasters,
   d. are merely the incumbents. In order for citizen groups to obtain an evidentiary hearing, they must raise substantial issues and sufficiently prove specific allegations.

4. During the 1980s, the FCC has adopted a policy of deregulation, as evidenced by
   a. encouragement of new satellite and multi-channel distribution systems which create a marketplace of viewing options, thus reducing the need for governmental intervention in order to protect the public interest,
   b. rescinding principal aspects of the fairness doctrine.

KEY DECISIONS

1943 — NATIONAL BROADCASTING COMPANY — upheld the FCC's authority to regulate network programming

1959 — WDAY — granted broadcasters immunity from libel based on the remarks of political candidates presented in accordance with the equal-time rule

1963 — CARTER MOUNTAIN — expanded the scope of FCC regulation into the domain of cable television

1968 — SOUTHWESTERN CABLE — affirmed the FCC's power to regulate the cable television industry

1969 — RED LION — affirmed the constitutionality and desirability of both the personal attack rule and the fairness doctrine

1973 — DEMOCRATIC NATIONAL COMMITTEE — maintained that broadcasters who met fairness doctrine requirements were not obligated to accept editorial advertisements

1978 — PACIFICA — acknowledged that the FCC may regulate "indecent" programming and recognized that the context in which the program occurs is of vital importance

1978 — NATIONAL CITIZENS COMMITTEE — upheld FCC regulations that required diversification of mass-media ownership

1981 — COLUMBIA BROADCASTING SYSTEM — noted that once a political campaign begins, broadcasters must give reasonable attention to access requests from legally-qualified candidates

1981 — WNCN — upheld FCC policy statement that maintained that the public interest is best served by promoting diversity in formats through market forces and competition among broadcasters

1984 — LEAGUE OF WOMEN VOTERS OF CALIFORNIA — overturned a law that forbade any federally-funded noncommercial educational station from "editorializing"

1987 — CENTURY COMMUNICATIONS — restricted the scope of FCC power over the cable industry

1987 — SYRACUSE PEACE COUNCIL — rescinded the fairness doctrine

1989 — SABLE — determined that circumstances which justify the restriction of "indecent" material on broadcast media are not applicable to dial-it media

1997 — TURNER — upheld constitutionality of must-carry rules

1997 — RENO — determined that circumstances which justify the restriction of "indecent" material on broadcast media are not applicable to the Internet

RECOMMENDED READING

Christensen, Shaun, "Cable Television: Competition and the First Amendment," South Dakota Law Review 37 (1992), 566-599.

Corboba, Rocio De Lourdes, "To Air or Not to Err: The Threat of Conditioned Federal Funds for Indecent Programming on Public Broadcasting," Hastings Law Journal 42 (January, 1991), 635-681.

Cronauer, Adrian, "The Fairness Doctrine: A Solution in Search of a Problem," Federal Communications Law Journal 47 (October, 1994), 51-77.

Geller, H., A. Ciamporcero, and D. Lampert, "The Cable Franchise Fee and the First Amendment," Federal Communication Law Journal 39 (May 1987), 1-25

Hafen, Jonathan O., "A Distinction Without a Difference -- The Spectrum Scarcity Rationale No Longer Justifies Content-Based Broadcast Regulation," Brigham Young University Law Review (1991), 1141-1162.

Hendricks, John Allen, "The Telecommunications Act of 1996: Its Impact on the Electronic Media of the 21st Century," Communications and the Law 21 (June, 1999), 39-53

Krattenmaker, Thomas G., "The Telecommunications Act of 1996," Federal Communications Law Journal 49 (November, 1996), 1-49.

Lampert, Donna N., "Cable Television: Does Leased Access Mean Least Access?" Federal Communications Law Journal 44 (March, 1992), 245-284.

Lipschultz, Jeremy Harris, Free Expression in the Age of the Internet: Social and Legal Boundaries Boulder, Colorado: Westview, 2000.

Lively, Donald E., "Modern Media and the First Amendment: Rediscovering Freedom of the Press," Washington Law Review 67 (July, 1992), 599-624.

Miller, Philip H., "New Technology, Old Problem: Determining the First Amendment Status of Electronic Information Services," Fordham Law Review 61 (April, 1993), 1147-1201.

Schoaff, Donna J., "*Meredith Corp v. FCC*: The Demise of the Fairness Doctrine," Kentucky Law Journal 77 (1988-89), 227-241.

Weinberg, Jonathan, "Broadcasting and Speech," California Law Review 81 (October, 1993), 1103-1206.

CHAPTER 13

ADVERTISING

The public has been bombarded in recent decades with advertising strategies and messages. During these years, the array of new products introduced to consumers has multiplied and the amount spent annually on advertising has increased several-fold. The mass media — television, radio, print, billboards, transit, mails, computers — have been employed in increasingly sophisticated ways to reach potential consumers. Concomitantly, the use of advertising techniques has produced heightened concern about fairness and honesty. This concern is not new. An inquiry into the history of advertising reveals that legislatures, consumer groups, and the courts have applied various tests and guidelines in an effort to police the claims of advertisers.

TESTS OF ADVERTISING

Over the years, the Supreme Court has examined the relationship between advertising and the First Amendment. In <u>Valentine v. Chrestensen</u>, 62 S.Ct. 920 (1942), the Court determined that "commercial speech" enjoyed less constitutional protection than other types of communication. In that case, the Court granted greater protection to editorial than to commercial forms of advertising. In later cases, the Court expanded First Amendment protection for commercial advertising.

COMMERCIAL SPEECH

In <u>Chrestensen</u>, the Supreme Court adopted the "commercial speech" doctrine. The case began when F.J. Chrestensen charged a fee to people who visited a submarine that he had moored at a pier on the

East River in New York City. When he distributed a printed commercial advertisement on city streets, police officers advised him that he was violating a law that limited handbill distribution to "information of a public protest." Chrestensen subsequently prepared a double-faced handbill — on one side a revised commercial advertisement and on the other side a protest against the city for refusing Chrestensen the use of wharfage facilities where he intended to display his submarine. No commercial advertising appeared on this side of the handbill. Nonetheless, the police informed Chrestensen that distribution of the double-faced bill was prohibited. Chrestensen brought suit. The Supreme Court noted that New York could prohibit its citizens from distributing commercial advertising on the streets. The Court recognized that Chrestensen's protest was attached to the handbill solely to evade the prohibition. If such an evasion were permitted, any merchant could advertise in the streets, merely by appending a civic appeal or moral protest to the leaflet. The law would be rendered ineffective. In voting against Chrestensen, the Court extended a preferred position to political rather than commercial expression.

The Court reaffirmed this position in Pittsburgh Press Company v. Pittsburgh Commission on Human Relations, 93 S.Ct. 2553 (1973). The National Organization for Women filed a complaint with the Pittsburgh Commission on Human Relations, claiming that the Pittsburgh Press Company was violating an ordinance by allowing employers to place classified advertisements in gender-designated columns. The Commission ordered the company to use a classification system with no reference to gender. The case reached the Supreme Court. The Court, per Justice Lewis Powell, decided that regulation was permissible because the advertisement, an example of commercial speech, was less protected by the Constitution than other forms of expression.

> In the crucial respects, the advertisements in the present record resemble the Chrestensen...advertisements. None expresses a position on whether, as a matter of social policy, certain positions ought to be filled by members of one or the other sex, nor does any of them criticize the Ordinance or the Commission's enforcement practices. Each is no more than a proposal of possible employment. The advertisements are thus classic examples of commercial speech.

The Court reaffirmed that a high level of protection is afforded the press regarding the expression of views on controversial issues. Pittsburgh Press could publish advertisements commenting on the ordinance, the enforcement practices of the Commission, or the propriety of gender preferences in employment. The Court held, however, that the Commission's order prohibiting placement of commercial ads in gender-designated columns did not violate the First Amendment rights of the newspaper.

In Board of Trustees of the State University of New York v. Fox, 109 S.Ct. 3028 (1989), the Court again upheld the "commercial speech" doctrine. A resolution of the State University of New York prohibits commercial enterprises from operating on the campus. After university police barred a company from presenting a dormitory "tupperware" party, a group of students initiated court action. The Court, per Justice Antonin Scalia, identified the transaction as "commercial speech":

> ...parties the students seek to hold propose a commercial transaction and therefore constitute commercial speech. Although they also touch upon other subjects, such as how to be financially responsible and run an efficient home, this does not render them noncommercial.

According to Scalia, in addition to regulating "commercial speech," the resolution supported substantial governmental interests — promoting an educational rather than commercial atmosphere, promoting safety and security, preventing commercial exploitation of students, and preserving residential tranquility.

In a recent case, Florida Bar v. Went For It, 115 S.Ct 2371 (1995), a case in which the Court upheld restrictions on advertising by attorneys, the Court recognized the subordinate status of commercial advertising. In that opinion, Justice Sandra Day O'Conner wrote:

> Speech by professionals obviously has many dimensions. There are circumstances in which we will accord speech by attorneys on public issues and matters of legal representation the strongest protection our Constitution has to offer.... This case, however, concerns pure commercial advertising, for which we have always reserved a lesser degree of protection under the First Amendment. Particularly because the standards and conduct of state-licensed lawyers have traditionally been subject to extensive regulation by the States, it is all the more appropriate that we limit our scrutiny of state regulations to a level commensurate with the "subordinate position" of commercial speech in the scale of First Amendment values.

COMMERCIAL INFORMATION

During the 1970s and 1980s, the Supreme Court altered the commercial-speech doctrine. The cases involved the advertising of abortions, prescription drug prices, real estate, contraceptives, lawyers' fees, and public utilities.

Content

In a series of decisions, the Supreme Court extended First Amendment protection to advertisements covering a variety of subject matters. In Bigelow v. Virginia, 95 S.Ct. 2222 (1975), the Court granted First Amendment protection to commercial messages concerning abortion. Jeffrey Bigelow, the editor of the Virginia Weekly, published an advertisement on behalf of a New York organization that assisted women in obtaining an abortion in an accredited hospital or clinic. According to Virginia law, it was a misdemeanor to circulate any publication that encouraged abortion. When Bigelow was convicted for violating the statute, he appealed. The Supreme Court ruled that because an advertisement had commercial aspects did not negate all First Amendment guarantees. In this instance, the advertisement did more than simply propose a commercial transaction. It contained factual material of "public interest." Portions of the message — especially the lines regarding the legal status of abortion law in New York — conveyed information of potential interest to a diverse public, not only to readers in need of abortions, but also to those with an interest in the abortion controversy or the development of the law. In this case, the Court claimed that "the relationship of speech to the marketplace of products or of services does not make it valueless in the marketplace of ideas."

One year later, in Virginia State Board of Pharmacy v. Virginia Citizens Consumer Council, 96 S.Ct. 1817 (1976), the Court further eroded the commercial-speech doctrine in a case involving drug-price advertising. Virginia law banned as unprofessional conduct any advertising by pharmacists of the prices on prescription drugs. The Virginia Citizens Consumer Council brought suit to have the statute declared unconstitutional. The consumer group argued that the First Amendment entitled a user of prescription drugs to receive information concerning drug prices. The Supreme Court held that commercial speech was not "wholly outside the protection of the First Amendment."

> So long as we preserve a predominantly free enterprise economy, the allocation of our resources in large measure will be made through numerous private economic decisions. It is a matter of public interest that those decisions, in the aggregate, be intelligent and well informed. To this end, the free flow of commercial information is indispensable.

Virginia could not keep "the public in ignorance of the lawful terms that competing pharmacists are offering." The Court found that any time, place, and manner restrictions on commercial speech contained in the law were exceeded by those provisions that singled out speech of a particular content — drug-price advertising — and sought to prevent its dissemination.

The Linmark Associates v. Township of Willingboro, 97 S.Ct. 1614 (1977), case concerned real-estate advertisements. In an attempt to stop "panic selling" by whites who feared that the community was becoming all black and that property values would decline, the Willingboro Council banned the placing of for-sale signs on all but model homes. Linmark Associates, a real-estate agency that wanted to advertise property by placing a sign on the lawn, initiated court action. The Supreme Court noted that the Willingboro statute prevented residents from obtaining information of "vital interest." The statute affected one of the most important decisions citizens had a right to make — where to live and raise their families. The Willingboro Council's concern was not with any commercial aspect of for-sale signs, but with the substance of the information communicated to the citizens.

> If dissemination of this information can be restricted, then every locality in the country can suppress any facts that reflect poorly on the locality, so long as a plausible claim can be made that disclosure would cause the recipients of the information to act irrationally.

The Court concluded that even though the law was designed to promote an important governmental objective — integrated housing — the Willingboro ordinance violated the First Amendment.

In the same year, Carey v. Population Services International, 97 S.Ct. 2010 (1977), involved the advertising of contraceptives. When Population Planning Associates advertised the mail-order sale of contraceptive devices, state officials warned PPA that the ads violated an ordinance which prohibited the sale of contraceptives to minors, and outlawed sales by nonpharmacists. The company challenged the statute in court. The Supreme Court noted that the statute sought "to suppress completely any information about the availability and price of contraceptives." The law banned "the free flow of commercial information" that reflected "substantial individual and societal interests." The State argued that the advertisements were offensive and embarrassing to many who were exposed to them, and that permitting them would legitimize sexual activity of young people. The Court, however, concluded that the fact that protected speech may be offensive to some did not justify its suppression.

Numerous cases involved advertising of lawyers' fees and services; the first was Bates v. State Bar of Arizona, 97 S.Ct. 2691 (1977). Two members of the Arizona State Bar Association placed an ad in the Arizona Republic. The ad offered "legal services at very reasonable fees" and listed fees for such services as divorces, adoptions, bankruptcies, and name changes. The Arizona State Bar Association complained that attorneys were prohibited from advertising in the media and imposed a one-week suspension on the attorneys. The lawyers appealed. The Supreme Court acknowledged that false, deceptive, or misleading advertising could be regulated, but Arizona could not prevent publication of a truthful advertisement concerning legal services.

In Ohralik v. Ohio State Bar Association, 98 S.Ct. 1912 (1978), the Court clarified the commercial-information doctrine as it applies to advertising by attorneys. The case involved lawyer Albert Ohralik, who, upon learning about an automobile accident in which a young woman had been injured, went to the hospital and offered to represent the woman in any court action. Ohralik had the woman sign a contract which provided that he would receive one-third of any recovery. Shortly thereafter, the woman terminated the agreement. Ohralik insisted that the woman had entered into a binding commitment. Even though another lawyer represented her in concluding a settlement with the insurance company, the woman paid Ohralik one-third of her recovery. The woman then filed a complaint against Ohralik with the Ohio Bar Association. After a hearing, the bar found Ohralik had violated the Ohio Code of Professional Responsibility. The case reached the Supreme Court. The Court noted that "the solicitation of business by a lawyer through direct, in-person communication with the prospective client has long been viewed as inconsistent with the profession's ideal(s)." Such behavior posed a potential harm to the prospective client. The Court upheld the bar association's ruling; Ohralik's transaction was commercial speech.

> To require a parity of constitutional protection for commercial and non-commercial speech alike could invite dilution.... Rather than subject the First Amendment to such a devitalization, we instead have afforded commercial speech a limited measure of protection, commensurate with its subordinate position in the scale of First Amendment values, while allowing modes of regulation that might be impermissible in the realm of noncommercial expression.

In Bates, the Court had extended First Amendment protection to the advertising of commercial information concerning legal fees and services; in Ohralik, however, the Court denied protection to direct personal solicitation of a potential client — such activity was commercial speech.

Formats

In several cases, beginning with In the Matter of R. M. J., 102 S.Ct. 929 (1982), the Court set forth guidelines concerning the acceptable format for advertising by attorneys. The case involved a

Missouri regulation which restricted attorney advertising to certain categories of information and to certain specified language. When a lawyer announced the opening of his private practice, he distributed advertisements that included prohibited information; the ads contained the fact that he was licensed in Missouri and Illinois, and that he was admitted to practice before the U.S. Supreme Court. The ads also contained a listing of areas of practice in words that deviated from the language prescribed by the regulation — for example, "personal injury" and "real estate" instead of "tort law" and "property law." Subsequently, the lawyer was charged with unprofessional conduct. The case reached the Supreme Court, where Justice Powell discussed the issues in the case.

> Truthful advertising related to lawful activities is entitled to the protection of the First Amendment.... Misleading advertising may be prohibited entirely. But the states may not place an absolute prohibition on certain types of potentially misleading information, e.g., a listing of areas of practice, if the information also may be presented in a way that is not deceptive.

Powell acknowledged that the potential for deception was "particularly strong in the context of advertising professional services," but he pointed out that "restrictions upon such advertising may be no broader than reasonably necessary to prevent the deception." The Missouri restrictions were overly broad.

Peel v. Attorney Registration and Disciplinary Commission of Illinois, 110 S.Ct. 2281 (1990), is a similar case. A lawyer used professional letterhead that stated his name, followed by his areas of specialty, and location of practice. Holding oneself out as a certified legal specialist violated the Illinois Code of Professional Responsibility. When the lawyer was censured, he initiated court action. The Supreme Court concluded that a lawyer has a First Amendment right to advertise his or her certification as a specialist. According to the Court: "Disclosure of information such as that on petitioner's letterhead both served the public interest and encourages the development and utilization of meritorious certification programs for attorneys."

Zauderer v. Office of Disciplinary Counsel of the Supreme Court of Ohio, 105 S.Ct. 2265 (1985), involved two reprimands by the State of Ohio against a lawyer's advertisement. First, the claim that client's "full legal fees" would be refunded if they were convicted of "drunk driving" was misleading because it failed to inform clients that they would be liable for "costs," as opposed to "legal fees." Second, the ad violated rules prohibiting the use of illustrations. The Supreme Court sustained the reprimand which applied to the omission of information regarding contingent-fee arrangements. The Court, however, rejected the ruling that was based on the use of an illustration. The Court maintained that the illustration was an accurate representation and had "no feature likely to deceive or confuse the reader."

Shapero v. Kentucky Bar Association, 108 S.Ct. 1916 (1988), involved a letter that an attorney proposed to send "to potential clients who have had a foreclosure suit filed against them." The Kentucky Bar Association prohibited the letter, citing a ban against any written solicitation of specific individuals, as opposed to the general public. The Supreme Court, in an opinion prepared by Justice William Brennan, ruled that a state may not categorically prohibit lawyers from soliciting business in this fashion.

> Like print advertising, petitioners letter — and targeted, direct-mail solicitation generally — poses much less risk of overreaching or undue influence than does in-person solicitation.... Neither mode of written communication involves the coercive force of the personal presence of a trained advocate or the pressure on the potential client for an immediate yes-or-no answer to the offer of representation.

Brennan then examined two features of the letter which the Association had termed "high pressure" and "overbearing solicitation." The first feature was the letters liberal use of underscored, upperclass letters. The second was the inclusion of assertions that state no fact but constitute "pure salesman puffery." According to Brennan,

> The pitch or style of a letter's type and its inclusion of subjective, predictions of client satisfaction might catch the recipient's attention more than would a bland statement of purely objective facts in small type. But a truthful and nondeceptive letter, no matter how big its type and how much it speculates can never "shout at the recipient" or "grasp him by the lapels" as can a lawyer engaging in face-to-face solicitation.

Brennan upheld an attorney's right to solicit business by sending truthful and nondeceptive letters to potential clients. In Shapero, as in R.M.J., Peel, and Zauderer, the Court identified acceptable formats for advertising by attorneys.

During the past few decades, the Supreme Court has extended limited First Amendment protection to commercial expression. An examination of relevant cases — Bigelow, Virginia State Board of Pharmacy, Linmark, Carey, Bates, R. M. J., Peel, Zauderer, and Shapero, — reveals that the Court distinguishes between commercial and informative communication. In these cases, the justices clarified the relationship between commercial and informative speech — namely, the Court will protect the free flow of commercial information, though it is less willing to protect purely commercial messages.

GOVERNMENTAL INTEREST

In 1980, the Supreme Court established a test for evaluating whether specific instances of commercial expression satisfy First Amendment standards. The case, Central Hudson Gas and Electric Corporation v. Public Service Commission of New York, 100 S.Ct. 2343 (1980), dealt with advertising by public utilities. The Central Hudson Gas and Electric Corporation initiated suit in court to challenge the constitutionality of a New York Public Service Commission policy statement that banned certain advertising by utilities. The statement divided advertising into two categories: promotional — advertising intended to stimulate the purchase of utility services; and informational — advertising not designed to promote sales. The Commission banned promotional but permitted informational advertising. The ban was intended as a vehicle for conserving energy. Writing for the Supreme Court, Justice Powell stressed that the First Amendment's relevance for commercial speech is based on the informational function of advertising — commercial messages that do not inform the public about lawful activity may be suppressed. Powell acknowledged that a four-stage analysis is appropriate in determining the constitutionality of such expression.

> In commercial speech cases, then, a four-part analysis has developed. At the outset, we must determine whether the expression is protected by the First Amendment. For commercial speech to come within that provision, it at least must concern lawful activity and not be misleading. Next, we ask whether the asserted governmental interest is substantial. If both inquiries yield positive answers, we must determine whether the regulation directly advances the governmental interest asserted, and whether it is not more extensive than is necessary to serve that interest.

The Court then used these four stages to analyze the expression at issue in Central Hudson Gas. Powell noted that the advertising was neither inaccurate nor did it relate to unlawful activity; the expression warranted First Amendment protection. Powell also noted that there was a direct link between New York's interest in energy conservation and the commission's ban on advertising. The Court, however, declared the ban to be "more extensive than necessary to further the State's interest in energy conservation."

> The Commission's order reaches all promotional advertising, regardless of the impact of the touted service on overall energy use. But the energy conservation rationale, as important as it is, cannot justify suppressing information about electric devices or services that would cause no net increase in total energy use. In addition, no showing has been made that a more limited restriction on the content of promotional advertising would not serve adequately the State's

interests.

The Court concluded that because the Commission's order was overbroad, the ban violated the First Amendment.

The Central Hudson test has become the guideline for evaluating commercial expression. It has been applied in numerous cases. In the examples cited below, the test has been used to protect commercial speech in some cases, while being used in others to uphold governmental interests in regulating advertising.

In Bolger v. Youngs Drug Products Corporation, 103 S.Ct. 2875 (1983), the Court applied the Central Hudson Gas test in deciding the constitutionality of a federal law that prohibited the mailing of unsolicited advertisements for contraceptives. The Court's opinion, prepared by Justice Thurgood Marshall, acknowledged that most of the mailings "fall within the core notion of commercial speech." Marshall stressed that "the mailings...are entitled to the qualified but nonetheless substantial protection accorded to commercial speech." Marshall assessed the level of protection available to the mailings under Central Hudson Gas. First, Marshall found no deception; thus, the mailings were entitled to First Amendment protection under criterion one. Second, Marshall considered whether any substantial governmental interest would be served by banning the mailings. The government argued that the ban served two interests: shielding recipients from materials that are potentially offensive, and aiding parent's efforts to control the manner in which their children become informed about birth control. The Court decided that these reasons did not justify the ban. Marshall noted that simply because "protected speech may be offensive to some does not justify its suppression." Furthermore, the government is not justified in "purging all mailboxes of unsolicited material that is entirely suitable for adults." The Court concluded that the government failed to justify its sweeping prohibition.

In Posadas De Puerto Rico Associates v. Tourism Company of Puerto Rico, 106 S.Ct. 2968 (1986), the Court applied the Central Hudson Gas test to a Puerto Rican law which legalized casino gambling in order to promote tourism, but also prohibited gambling parlors from advertising to the people of Puerto Rico. In a deeply-divided decision, the Court majority held that "the advertising restrictions pass muster under the four-prong test." First, the commercial speech concerned a lawful activity and was not misleading. Second, reducing the demand for casino gambling by Puerto Rico's residents and thus protecting their health, safety, and welfare constituted a "substantial governmental interest." Third, the restrictions "directly advance" the governmental interest. Fourth, the restrictions are no more extensive than necessary to serve the government's interest since "they do not affect advertising aimed at tourists but apply only to advertising aimed at...residents." The minority argued that the advertising restriction established prior restraint and prevented Puerto Rican residents from obtaining truthful commercial information. Nonetheless, the Court used the Central Hudson Gas four-prong test to restrict the flow of such information.

In City of Cincinnati v. Discovery Network, 113 S.Ct., 1505 (1993), the Court again applied the Central Hudson test. The case began in 1989, when the city of Cincinnati authorized two publishing companies to place 62 newsracks on public property for the purpose of distributing free magazines that consisted primarily of advertisements. In 1990, the city reversed its decision on the ground that the magazines were commercial speech whose distribution was prohibited by pre-existing ordinance. The city expressed concern for the safety and esthetics of the city streets and sidewalks. The Supreme Court found that the city's action failed to meet the third prong of Central Hudson. The city failed to show that the regulation would "directly advance" the substantial governmental interest; the Court held that removing only 62 out of 2000 newsracks was insufficient, such a paltry number of newsracks affected the public in a minimal manner.

In Edenfield v. Fane, 113 S.Ct. 1800 (1993), a certified public accountant challenged Florida's ban on the use of "direct, in-person, uninvited solicitation" to obtain new clients. Justice Andrew Kennedy prepared the decision, which involved application of the Central Hudson test. Kennedy noted that in soliciting potential clients, the CPA communicated truthful, non-deceptive information proposing a lawful commercial transaction; he thus met prong one. Regarding prong two, Kennedy noted that the government had cited substantial interests; to prevent fraud, protect privacy, and maintain CPA independence in auditing financial statements. It was concerning prong three that the Florida law failed to pass the test. The government must show that the regulation directly advances the interest involved. Yet, "this burden is not satisfied by mere speculation or conjecture; rather a governmental body seeking to sustain a restriction on commercial speech must demonstrate that its restriction will in fact alleviate them to a material degree." Such proof was lacking in this case.

In U.S. v. Edge Broadcasting Company, 113. S.Ct. 2699 (1993), the Court used the test to uphold federal legislation which assisted state efforts to control the lottery type of gambling. The case arose when a broadcasting company wanted to air lottery advertisements from its location near the border of two states, one which had a legal lottery while the other did not. Since the broadcast station was licensed to serve a community located in the non-lottery state, airing the ad would violate federal law. The broadcast station challenged the law in court. In applying Central Hudson, the Court noted that concerning prong one, the station intended to air non-misleading advertisements about a legal lottery. As to the second prong, the Court acknowledged that the government had a substantial interest in supporting the policy of nonlottery states. In terms of prong three, the policy of balancing the interests of lottery and nonlottery states was directly served by applying the restriction to all stations that serve non-lottery states. Finally, the law advanced the governmental purpose by substantially reducing lottery advertising where it could not be wholly eradicated.

The Ibanez v. Florida Department of Business and Professional Regulation, Board of Accountancy, 114 S.Ct. 2084 (1994), case involved an individual who was a CPA and a member of the Florida Bar. This individual was authorized by the Certified Financial Planner Board of Standards, a private organization, to use the designation "Certified Financial Planner." The CPA referred to these credentials in her advertising, placing CPA and CFP next to her name in her yellow pages listing and on her business cards and stationary. Notwithstanding the truthfulness of the message, the Florida Board of Accountancy reprimanded her for engaging in false, deceptive, and misleading advertising." The Board claimed that any designation using the term "certified" to refer to any certifying agency other than the Board itself "inherently misleads the public into believing that state approval and recognition exists." In other words, the Board disciplined the CPA under prong one of Central Hudson. The Supreme Court disagreed, arguing that the Board had not demonstrated with sufficient proof that any member of the public would have been misled or that any harm would result from allowing such expression to reach the public eye.

In Rubin v. Coors Brewing Company, 115 S. Ct. 1585 (1995), the brewer filed suit when the Bureau of Alcohol, Tobacco, and Firearms banned the use of labels and advertisements that described the alcohol content of beer. In applying the Central Hudson test, the Supreme Court determined that Coors intended to disclose truthful, verifiable, and nonmisleading factual information about alcohol content, thereby satisfying prong one. In terms of prong two, the government had identified a substantial governmental interest in curbing "strength wars" by brewers who might seek to compete for customers on the basis of alcohol content. The government had a significant interest in protecting the health of its citizens. In applying prong three, the Court cited the "overall irrationality of the Government's regulatory scheme." The ban failed to advance the governmental interest because of contradictory existing laws. Several state laws allowed the advertising of beer strength. Also, current federal law required the disclosure of content on labels of wines and liquor. In <u>Coors Brewing Company</u>, the ban was overturned because other existing statutes "directly undermine and counteract its effects."

In <u>Florida Bar v. Went For It</u>, 115 S.Ct. 2371 (1995), the Court upheld a restriction on advertising by attorneys. A lawyer referral service filed action against a Florida Bar rule which prohibited personal injury lawyers from sending direct-mail solicitations to victims and their relatives for 30 days following an accident. The Court applied the <u>Central Hudson</u> test and decided that the rules did not violate the First Amendment. First, the Florida Bar had a substantial interest in protecting personal injury victims and their loved ones against invasive contact by lawyers. Second, the Florida Bar offered evidence that the harms targeted by the ban were real. Third, the ban's scope was narrowly tailored to the stated objectives. Furthermore, the ban's duration was limited to a specific period, and there were other means by which injured Floridians could learn about the availability of legal representation. The Court upheld the Florida law.

In <u>44 Liquormark Inc., v. Rhode Island</u>, 116 S.Ct. 1495 (1996), the Court again applied the <u>Central Hudson</u> test. Liquor retailers initiated court action challenging Rhode Island statutes which prohibited the advertising of liquor prices, except at the place of sale. Regarding prong one of <u>Central Hudson</u>, there was no question that the advertising ban constituted a blanket prohibition against truthful, nonmisleading expression about a lawful product. Second, the Court acknowledged that the government had cited a substantial interest in promoting temperance, the reduction of alcohol consumption. However, without any substantial evidence, the Court could not accept the assertion that the ban significantly advanced the interest. Furthermore, alternative methods of regulation — increased taxation, limited purchases, educational campaigns — would not restrict expression but would be more likely to promote temperance. Rhode Island had failed to provide adequate proof to demonstrate a clear connection between the abridgement of speech and the temperance goal.

The <u>Greater New Orleans Broadcasting Association Inc v. United States</u>, 119 S.Ct. 1923 (1999), case involved a challenge to federal law which prohibited radio and television broadcasters from carrying ads for privately operated casino gambling, even if gambling was legal in the station's location. The Supreme Court applied the <u>Central Hudson</u> test. Concerning the first prong, the content of the proposed advertising was truthful and covered activity that was lawful in Louisiana. Regarding the second, the asserted government interests in reducing social costs associated with gambling and helping control gambling activity were found to be substantial. But, in terms of prongs three and four, the law failed to advance those interests because it was "so pierced by exemptions and inconsistencies that the Government cannot hope to exonerate it." Justice John Stevens pointed out that some advertising for state-run casinos and tribal casinos was permitted. The law discriminated among ads "conveying virtually identical messages." In light of these inconsistencies, the government's claim that the regulation helps states discourage casino gambling was not convincing. Chief Justice William Rehnquist, who wrote the majority opinion in Posadas, claimed that application of the law in the Greater New Orleans Broadcasting case was incompatible with the First Amendment.

The cases cited in this section exemplify the Supreme Court's tendency to use Central Hudson to evaluate commercial expression. In some instances — Bolger, Discovery Network, Fane, Ibanez, Coors Brewing Company, 44 Liquormark, Greater New Orleans Broadcasting — the test has been used to protect commercial speech. In others — Posadas, Fox, Edge, Went For It — the test has served to uphold governmental interests. The key factor in specific decisions has been the level of proof demanded by the justices to prove a "fit" between the government's substantial interest and the extent to which it is furthered by the regulation. It appears likely that the Central Hudson test will continue to be the standard for evaluating commercial messages.

REGULATION OF ADVERTISING

Toward the end of the nineteenth century, the United States experienced a decided shift in the public attitude toward business. The notion that the public benefits the most in an environment that allows free competition to function without restriction was replaced by an attitude that favored governmental regulation of certain business activities. Advertising is such an activity.

DECEPTION

Until the beginning of the twentieth century, advertising was regulated by the doctrine of *caveat emptor* — "let the buyer beware." A more restrictive policy was introduced with the passage of the Pure Food and Drug Act in 1906, and the creation of the Federal Trade Commission in 1914. During the initial years of FTC regulation, the courts protected business competitors against false and deceptive advertisements; consumer rights were secondary and at times ignored entirely. Eventually, consumer interests came under the umbrella of FTC protection.

Competitor interests

Federal Trade Commission v. Winsted Hosiery, 42 S.Ct. 384 (1922), involved deceptive labeling. The Winsted Hosiery Company labeled the cartons in which their underwear was sold as "Natural Wool," even though the product contained as little as 10 percent wool. The Federal Trade Commission ordered the company to "cease and desist" from using the labels, unless the labels listed any other material that went into the garments, or unless the labels indicated that the underwear was not made wholly of wool. The company brought suit against the FTC. The Supreme Court, per Justice Louis Brandeis, decided that the consuming public understood the labels to mean that the underwear was all wool. The labels were literally false, calculated to deceive the purchasing public. The practice constituted an unfair method of competition against manufacturers who labeled their products truthfully. The Court upheld the FTC ruling.

The Federal Trade Commission's power to regulate deception came under attack in 1931. Raladam Company, manufacturer of an "obesity cure," advertised that the preparation was safe and effective. One of the ingredients, however, impaired the health of a substantial portion of the product's users. The FTC, concluding that the advertising constituted an unfair method of competition, issued a cease-and-desist order. When the case reached the Supreme Court, the justices noted that the word "competition" in the Act required the existence of competitors and injury to the business of these competitors through deceptive methods. In Federal Trade Commission v. Raladam, 51 S.Ct. 587 (1931), the Court found no evidence that the advertisements were injurious. No competitor demonstrated what effect, if any, the misleading ads had upon his or her business. The Court ruled that the FTC could not, by assuming the existence of competition, give itself jurisdiction to issue an order. The order was set aside.

In 1935, the FTC instituted another action against Raladam. This time considerable evidence was presented which indicated that the misleading advertisements induced consumers to purchase Raladam's medicine in preference to the products of competitors. The FTC issued another cease-and-desist order, which Raladam again appealed. In Federal Trade Commission v. Raladam, 62 S.Ct. 966 (1942), the Supreme Court sided with the FTC. When the Commission found that Raladam's deceptive statements referred to the quality of its competitor's merchandise, it was authorized to infer that trade would be diverted from competitors who did not engage in such "unfair methods." In Raladam II, the Court overruled the findings in the first Raladam case.

Maybelline v. Noxell Corporation, 643 F.Supp 294 (1986), a more recent example of a court protecting competitor interests, involved deceptive advertising of mascara. A Clean Lash television commercial depicted a woman putting on a dress over her head, suggesting that her mascara would not transfer to her dress or face. The woman also dabbed around her eyes with a tissue, implying that tears would not cause the mascara to run. A voice-over claimed that "water won't budge" Clean Lash and that the product "laughs at tears." A competitor, Maybelline, initiated legal action on the ground that the advertising was deceptive and provided an unfair advantage to the manufacturer of Clean Lash. The court determined that, based on independent laboratory research, the Clean Lash claims of "non-transferability" and "waterproof" were deceptive. The court also found that Maybelline's share of the market had dropped 3% since the deceptive ads began to appear. Accordingly, the court ordered Clean Lash to discontinue all deceptive advertising.

Consumer economic interests

In 1937, the Supreme Court took a strong stand against the doctrine of *caveat emptor*. The Federal Trade Commission became aware that the Standard Education Society was using deceptive advertising to sell encyclopedias. As part of its sales promotion, the society claimed to give individuals a free set of books, and maintained that the only return desired for the gift was permission to use the individual's name as a reference for advertising purposes. The cost to the individual was $69.50 for a loose-leaf extension service; the individual was told that the regular price of the books and the extension service was between $150 and $200. These statements were false, as $69.50 was the standard price for both the encyclopedia and the lose-leaf extension. The FTC issued a cease-and-desist order. The case reached the Supreme Court. Justice Hugo Black prepared the unanimous opinion of the Court, citing some shortcomings of the rule of *caveat emptor*.

> The fact that a false statement may be obviously false to those who are trained and experienced does not change its character, nor take away its power to deceive others less experienced. There is no duty resting upon a citizen to suspect the honesty of those with whom he transacts business. Laws are made to protect the trusting as well as the suspicious. The best element of business has long since decided that honesty should govern competitive enterprises, and that the rule of caveat emptor should not be relied upon to reward fraud and deception.

False promising of free books, and deceiving unwary purchasers about the price of the books, are practices contrary to decent business standards. If the Court failed to prohibit such practices, deception in business would be elevated to the standing and dignity of truth. In Federal Trade Commission v. Standard Education Society, 58 S.Ct. 113 (1937), the Court upheld the FTC order.

A year later, Congress amended the Federal Trade Commission Act to include the following: "Unfair methods of competition in commerce, and unfair or deceptive acts or practices in commerce are declared unlawful." Congress also prohibited "false advertisements" designed "to induce purchase of food, drugs, devices or cosmetics." This legislation, known as the Wheeler-Lea Amendments, signaled the demise of the doctrine of caveat emptor.

The Federal Trade Commission v. Colgate-Palmolive, 85 S.Ct. 1035 (1965), case involved deceptive demonstration on television. Colgate-Palmolive Company presented a commercial for Rapid Shave aerosol shaving cream. The commercial showed a professional football player whom the announcer described as having "a beard as tough as sandpaper...a beard that needs Palmolive Rapid Shave... supermoisturized for the fastest, smoothest shave possible." The Rapid Shave lather was then spread on what appeared to be sandpaper and a hand appeared with a razor and shaved a clear path through the gritty surface. "To prove Rapid Shave's supermoisturizing power," the announcer concluded, "we put it right from the can onto this tough dry sandpaper. It was apply — soak — and off in a stroke." Research conducted by the FTC showed that sandpaper could not be shaved immediately following application of Rapid Shave, but required a soaking period of approximately 80 minutes. In the commercial, the substance resembling sandpaper was actually plexiglass, to which sand had been applied. In support of a cease-and-desist order against Colgate-Palmolive, the FTC argued that the limitations of the television medium may challenge "the creative ingenuity and resourcefulness of copy writers; but surely they could not constitute lawful justification for resort to falsehoods and deception of the public." The FTC stressed that if a company did not "choose to advertise truthfully, they could, and should discontinue advertising." The Supreme Court upheld the FTC's order. The Court determined that the commercial contained three misrepresentations to the public: that sandpaper could be shaved by Rapid Shave, that an experiment had been conducted that verified this claim, and that the viewer was actually viewing this experiment. According to the Court, the Federal Trade Commission Act prohibited the misrepresentation of any fact that constituted a *material* factor in a purchaser's decision to buy. The Court concluded:

If...it becomes impossible or impractical to show simulated

demonstrations on television in a truthful manner, this indicates that television is not a medium that lends itself to this type of commercial.... If the inherent limitations of a method do not permit its use in the way a seller desires, the seller cannot by material misrepresentation compensate for those limitations.

The fact that the FTC faces numerous procedural and enforcement problems in regulating deceptive advertising is illustrated by the United States v. J. B. Williams, 498 F.2d 414 (1974), case. In 1959, the Federal Trade Commission determined that advertisements that promoted Geritol for the relief of iron-deficiency anemia were deceptive. The FTC issued a complaint in 1962, and a cease-and-desist order in 1964. J. B. Williams, the producer of Geritol, appealed. In 1967, the court of appeals upheld the FTC order. The court noted that

...the evidence is clear that Geritol is of no benefit in the treatment of tiredness except in those cases where tiredness has been caused by a deficiency of the ingredients contained in Geritol. The fact that the great majority of people who experience tiredness symptoms do not suffer from any deficiency of the ingredients in Geritol is a "material fact" under the meaning of that term as used in Section 15 of the Federal Trade Commission Act and Petitioners' failure to reveal this fact in this day when the consumer is influenced by mass advertising utilizing highly developed arts of persuasion, renders it difficult for the typical consumer to know whether the product will in fact meet his needs unless he is told what the product will or will not do.

When Geritol's commercials did not comply with the order, the FTC turned the case over to the Department of Justice, which in 1970, filed a $1 million suit against the company and its advertising agency. In 1973, Geritol and its agency were fined $812,000. In 1974, a court of appeals dismissed the fine and sent the case back to district court for a jury trial. Finally, in 1976, the FTC won a $280,000 judgment against the company. During those 17 years since the case began, millions of dollars had been spent on television commercials for Geritol, and the company had been able to solidify its control of the tonic market. Clearly, enforcement can be a significant problem for the FTC.

Consumer safety interests

In two cases decided a year apart, the courts provided inconsistent interpretation of advertising that threatened to harm citizens. Both cases involved murder. In the first case, John Wayne Hearn shot and killed Sandra Black at the behest of her husband, who contracted Hearn through a classified Advertisement that Hearn ran in Solder of Fortune Magazine. The ad read: "EX-MARINES — 67-69 'Nam Vets, Ex-DI, weapons specialist — jungle warfare, pilot, M.E., high risk assignments, U.S. or overseas." Hearns was apprehended, convicted of the murder, and sentenced to life imprisonment. Shortly thereafter, Sandra Black's son sued the magazine for wrongful death on the theory that it negligently published the ad. The jury awarded $1.9 million in compensatory and $7.5 million in punitive damages. In Eimann v. Soldier of Fortune Magazine, 880 F.2d 830 (1989), the court of appeals overturned the verdict.

> Given the pervasiveness of advertising in our society and the important role it plays, we decline to impose on publishers the obligation to reject all ambiguous advertisements for products or services that might pose a threat of harm.

In a similar case, Shawn Trevor Doutre killed Richard Braun by firing two rounds from an automatic pistol into the back of his head. Doutre had been hired by Braun's business associate through a personal ad which appeared in Soldier of Fortune Magazine. The ad read: "GUN FOR HIRE: 37-year old professional mercenary desires jobs. Vietnam Veteran. Discreet and very private. Body guard, courier, and other special skills. All jobs considered." Braun's sons filed a wrongful death claim against the magazine, after which the magazine filed a motion for summary judgment. In Braun v. Soldier of Fortune Magazine, 749 F. Supp 1083 (1990), the district court held that the publisher had a duty to withhold an advertisement when the likelihood and gravity of the possible harm from an ad implied that the advertiser was available to commit murder. The court noted:

> Nor is the wording of the ad so facially innocuous that, absent knowledge that the advertiser was soliciting murder contracts, the risk of murder was unforeseeable as a matter of law. Rather, the court believes that the language of this advertisement is such that, even though couched in terms not explicitly offering criminal services, the publisher could recognize the offer of criminal activity as readily as its readers obviously did.

The court returned the case for a jury trial. At the point of this writing, it is unclear as to what level of accountability publishers will be held when they publish ambiguous ads that pose potential harm to individuals.

CORRECTIVE ADVERTISING

During the 1970s, the FTC required corrective advertising in several instances of deception. Sometimes, merely stopping an ad is insufficient. When a deceptive advertising campaign has been effective over a long period of time, the effect of misleading information remains in the public's mind even after the ad is discontinued. In such instances, the FTC may impose corrective disclosures. Some examples are In re ITT Continental Baking Company, 79 FTC 248 (1971), and In re Ocean Spray Cranberries, 80 FTC 975 (1972).

In 1971, the FTC issued a corrective advertising order concerning Profile bread, a product of the Continental Baking Company. Profile had been promoted as lower in calories than ordinary bread, and of significant value for use in weight-control diets. The ads implied that eating two slices of Profile bread before lunch and dinner would result in a loss of body weight, without any rigorous adherence to a reduced calorie diet. These advertising claims were not true. After an investigation, the FTC ordered that the company cease and desist from making false advertising claims. The FTC also required that corrective advertisements constitute 25 percent of the advertising for Profile bread during the following year.

One year later, the FTC ordered corrective advertising for Ocean Spray cranberry juice. In its advertising, Ocean Spray claimed that their cranberry juice was more nutritious and had more "food energy" than orange or tomato juices. The FTC determined that Ocean Spray's claims were deceptive, so the Commission issued a cease-and-desist order. In addition, the Commission ordered that corrective advertising constitute 25 percent of the promotion for Ocean Spray cranberry-juice cocktail during the ensuing year. In Ocean Spray and Continental, the FTC ordered corrective advertising in an attempt to curb the impact deceptive advertising had on the consumer.

In Warner-Lambert v. Federal Trade Commission, 562 F.2d 749 (1977), the corrective-advertising practice was challenged. Warner-Lambert Company asked the court to determine whether the Federal Trade Commission had authority to order corrective advertising for Listerine antiseptic mouthwash. According to FTC research, Listerine's advertising claim that the mouthwash cured colds and sore throats was false. The FTC ordered corrective advertising. Warner-Lambert argued that corrective advertising exceeded the FTC's statutory power. The company claimed that the Federal Trade Commission Act authorized the Commission to issue cease-and-desist orders, and did not mention any other remedies. The FTC claimed that, in this case, corrective advertising was "absolutely necessary," because "a hundred years of false cold claims have built up a large reservoir of erroneous consumer belief which would persist, unless corrected, long after petitioner ceased making the claims." The court agreed:

> Listerine has built up over a period of many years a widespread reputation. When it was ascertained that that reputation no longer applied to the product, it was necessary to take action to correct it....
> It is the accumulated impact of past advertising that necessitates disclosure in future advertising. To allow consumers to continue to buy the product on the strength of the impression built up by prior

advertising — an impression which is now known to be false — would be unfair and deceptive.

In <u>Warner-Lambert</u>, the court decided that the FTC has authority to order corrective advertising in appropriate cases.

MANDATORY ADVERTISING

A recent Supreme Court decision approved of a form of mandatory advertising. The case involved various California tree fruit growers who challenged the validity of orders issued by the Secretary of Agriculture under the Agricultural Marketing Agreement Act of 1937. Congress had passed the Act to establish orderly agricultural-commodity marketing conditions and fair prices. The policy, which is exempted from antitrust laws, displaces competition in favor of collective action in the markets regulated. The specific orders at issue in this case required growers to share the cost of generic advertising of certain fruits. In <u>Glickman v. Wileman Brothers & Elliott</u>, 117 S.Ct. 2130 (1997), the Court upheld the orders. Justice Stevens identified three characteristics which distinguished the orders from other laws which the justices had found to abridge speech. First, the marketing orders imposed no restraint on any freedom to communicate any message. Second, the orders did not compel anyone to engage in any specific expression. Third, the orders did not require anyone to endorse or to finance any political or ideological views. Justice Stevens concluded:

> Appropriate respect for Congress' power to regulate interstate commerce provides abundant support for the marketing orders' constitutionality. Generic advertising is intended to stimulate consumer demand for an agricultural product in a regulated market. That purpose is legitimate and consistent with the regulatory goals of the overall statutory scheme. The mere fact that one or more producers do not wish to foster generic advertising of their product is not a sufficient reason for judges to override the judgment of the majority of market participants, bureaucrats, and legislators that such programs are beneficial.

ACCESS

During the 1970s and 1980s, two media access questions faced the Supreme Court: May a communication medium deny access to a particular advertiser, while at the same time accepting ads from other advertisers? Under what conditions does an individual have the right to counteradvertise?

Right of refusal

The issue of right of refusal applies to various media in different ways. Print media are subject to different standards than broadcast media. Private media are subject to different standards than public media. Commercial messages are subject to different standards than noncommercial messages.

The print media involve private enterprise and are entitled to conduct business with whom they choose. For example, in Resident Participation of Denver v. Love, 322 F.Supp. 1100 (1971), the court decided that a general circulation newspaper could not be forced to publish controversial ads. Chicago Joint Board, Amalgamated Clothing Workers of America v. Chicago Tribune Company, 435 F.2d 470 (1970), upheld a newspapers right to refuse publication of a labor union's editorial advertisement; the union's right to free speech did not give it the right to make use of printing presses without the publisher's consent. The broadcast media enjoy a limited right of refusal. In Columbia Broadcasting System v. Democratic National Committee, 93 S.Ct. 2080 (1973), the Supreme Court noted that a broadcaster's degree of freedom is somewhat less extensive than that of a newspaper publisher, yet, broadcast media are not "common carriers" or "public utilities" required to accept all advertisements.

Non-private media, such as government-owned transit systems, print publications, or broadcast stations, cannot absolutely refuse to publish advertising. In Wirta v. Alameda-Contra Costa Transit District, 434 P.2d 982 (1967), the court noted:

> We conclude that defendants, having opened a forum for the expression of ideas by providing facilities for advertisements on its buses, cannot for reasons of administrative convenience decline to accept advertising expressing opinions and beliefs within the ambit of First Amendment protection.

Clearly, public media enjoy less right of refusal than private media.

In 1974, the Supreme Court grappled with the question of whether the rapid transit medium can reject a political advertisement, while at the same time accepting other ads. In Lehman v. Shaker Heights, 94 S.Ct. 2714 (1974), the Court held that the medium is not bound to accept the advertising of all who apply for it. Harry Lehman, a candidate for the office of state representative, wanted to advertise his candidacy on the Shaker Heights rapid transit system. He was informed that although space was available, political advertising was not permitted. Lehman sued, arguing that the transit displays constituted a public forum protected by the First Amendment. In a sharply-divided opinion, the Supreme Court majority noted:

> Here, we have no open spaces, no meeting hall, park, street corner, or

other public thoroughfare. Instead, the city is engaged in commerce. It must provide rapid, convenient, pleasant, and inexpensive service to the commuters of Shaker Heights. The car card space, although incidental to the provision of public transportation, is a part of the commercial venture. In much the same way that a newspaper or periodical, or even a radio or television station, need not accept every proffer of advertising from the general public, a city transit system has discretion to develop and make reasonable choices concerning the type of advertising that may be displayed in its vehicles.

Justice Harry Blackmun's majority opinion stressed that "revenue earned from long-term commercial advertising could be jeopardized by a requirement that short-term candidacy or issue-oriented advertisements be displayed." Blackmun was joined in the opinion by Chief Justice Warren Burger and Justices Byron White and William Rehnquist. Justice William Douglas supplied the fifth vote on the ground that a political candidate had no right to force his message on a "captive audience" of commuters — the customer's privacy rights should shield him or her from exposure to all advertising. The dissenting justices viewed the city's actions as unconstitutional; Shaker Heights had opened up advertising space on its buses as a "public forum" and should not be able to prefer commercial advertising to the exclusion of political advertising. The majority, however, upheld the right of transit media to select which types of advertising they will display. In Lehman, a unique decision, the Court provided greater protection for commercial than for noncommercial messages.

In Metromedia v. San Diego, 101 S.Ct. 2882 (1981), the Supreme Court weighed the constitutionality of an ordinance that afforded greater protection to commercial than to noncommercial outdoor billboard advertising. The San Diego statute permitted on-site commercial advertising — a sign promoting goods or services available on the property where the sign is located — but forbade other commercial and much noncommercial advertising. The stated goals of the statute were to promote traffic safety and to improve the appearance of the city. Several outdoor advertising companies initiated court action to halt enforcement of the law. The Court acknowledged that San Diego could favor one kind of commercial advertising over another, but the city could not favor commercial over noncommercial messages.

> The city does not explain how or why noncommercial billboards located in places where commercial billboards are permitted would be more threatening to safe driving or would detract more from the beauty of the city. Insofar as the city tolerates billboards at all, it cannot choose to limit their content to commercial messages; the city may not conclude that the communication of commercial information concerning goods and services connected with a particular site is of

greater value than the communication of noncommercial messages. Furthermore, the city could not favor one kind of noncommercial advertising over another. The Court stressed that although San Diego could distinguish between the relative value of different categories of commercial speech, the city "does not have the same range of choice in the area of noncommercial speech." Concerning noncommercial expression, the city may not choose the appropriate subjects for public debate: To do so would "allow that government control over the search for political truth." In Metromedia, the Supreme Court reaffirmed the long-established principle that noncommercial speech enjoys greater First Amendment protection than commercial speech.

Counteradvertising

In 1968, the courts applied the fairness doctrine to advertising. The case began when John Banzhaf asked WCBS-TV in New York for free reply time for antismokers to respond to the prosmoking views implicit in cigarette commercials. WCBS rejected Banzhaf's request. The station claimed that it had broadcast several programs about the smoking-health controversy. In addition, WCBS had aired American Cancer Society public-service announcements free of charge. The station was confident that its "coverage of the health ramifications of smoking has been fully consistent with the fairness doctrine." When Banzhaf complained to the FCC, the Commission decided that reply time should be provided. The Court of Appeals, District of Columbia, affirmed the Commission's order on three grounds: the fairness doctrine, the public-interest standard, and the First Amendment. In terms of the fairness doctrine, cigarette smoking's effect on health was viewed as a controversial public issue. The Commission's ruling aimed to provide fair and balanced coverage of this issue. With respect to the public-interest standard, a dialogue between cigarette advertisers whose ads comprised a sizable portion of all broadcast revenues, and opponents of cigarette smoking with no such financial clout, appeared to be in the public interest. Concerning the First Amendment, the court ruled that compulsory reply time was permissible when it served as a "countervailing" force where meaningful broadcast debate would otherwise be impossible.

> Where, as here, one party to a debate has a financial clout and a compelling economic interest in the presentation of one side unmatched by its opponent, and where the public stake in the argument is no less than life itself — we think the purpose of rugged debate is served, not hindered by an attempt to redress the balance.

In Banzhaf v. Federal Communications Commission, 405 F.2d 1082 (1968), the court upheld the FCC ruling that required stations that carry cigarette advertising to devote a significant amount of broadcast time to airing the case against cigarette smoking.

A few years later, Congress banned cigarette commercials from the airwaves completely. The Public Health Cigarette Smoking Act stipulated that after January 1, 1971, it was illegal to advertise cigarettes on broadcast media. Capital Broadcasting Company sued, alleging that the ban prohibited the "dissemination of information with respect to a lawfully sold product" in violation of the First Amendment, and that it violated due process because print media were not prohibited from publishing cigarette ads. Only electronic media were restricted, and such a distinction was "arbitrary and invidious." The court rejected both allegations. First, the statute restricted only the airing of commercial messages — it did not prohibit disseminating information about cigarettes. Second, Congress could regulate one medium at a time if there were a rational reason for such regulation. The court noted that "...substantial evidence showed that the most persuasive advertising was being conducted on radio and television, and that these broadcasts were particularly effective in reaching a very large audience of young people." In Capital Broadcasting Company v. Kleindienst, 92 S.Ct. 1289 (1972), the court decided that the unique characteristics of broadcast communication made it especially subject to regulation in the public interest.

During the early 1970s, the courts considered other attempts to apply the fairness doctrine to advertising. In Green v. Federal Communications Commission, 447 F.2d 323 (1971), the court turned down an effort by peace groups that wished to respond to military recruitment advertising. According to the court, broadcast stations were justified in interpreting such ads as involving only the issue of military manpower recruitment by voluntary means. That was not a "controversial issue of public importance." The draft issue and the Vietnam War question [the focus of the peace groups] had been "ventilated in extenso for years on [probably] every television and radio station in the land." According to the court, "no individual member of the public had the right of access to the air." The Green case rejected the right to counteradvertise.

In Friends of the Earth v. Federal Communications Commission, 449 F.2d 1164 (1971), the court considered an environmental protection group's effort to reply to automobile ads. The group claimed that the companies contributed significantly to air pollution, and that the broadcast media had not met their fairness-doctrine responsibility of informing the public of the other side of the antipollution controversy. The Federal Communication Commissions acknowledged that automobile air pollution contributed to many deaths each year, but that was true of numerous other products. According to the Commission, cigarettes (the product counteradvertised in Banzhaf) were distinguishable from such products; government officials had urged the public to quit smoking, but they did not urge discontinuance of the use of automobiles. The Commission refused to extend the Banzhaf ruling "generally to the field of product advertising." The court of appeals disagreed with the FCC; the judges claimed that Friends of the Earth was indistinguishable from Banzhaf in the reach of the fairness doctrine. The case was remanded to the FCC for reconsideration. The Friends of the Earth decision gave impetus to the right to counteradvertise.

The movement soon lost momentum, however, because of two court decisions. In 1973, the Supreme Court ruled in Columbia Broadcasting System v. Democratic National Committee, 93 S.Ct. 2080 (1973), that a medium that provided full and fair coverage of public issues was not obligated to accept any editorial advertisements. The case involved the efforts of a peace group and of a national political party to gain access to the broadcast media in order to expound their views on controversial issues. In this case, the Supreme Court agreed with the FCC that providing access to the marketplace of "ideas and experiences" would not be served "by a system so heavily weighted in favor of the financially affluent, or those with access to wealth." If broadcasters were required to accept editorial advertisements, the ideas of the wealthy could well prevail because they had the financial capability to purchase time more frequently. As a result, the time a station "allotted for editorial advertising could be monopolized by those of one political persuasion." The ultimate effect might be the

> erosion of the journalistic discretion of broadcasters in the coverage of public issues, and a transfer of control over the treatment of public issues from the licensees who are accountable for broadcast performance to private individuals who are not. The public interest would no longer be "paramount" but, rather, subordinate to private whim, especially since...a broadcaster would be largely precluded from rejecting editorial advertisements that dealt with matters trivial or insignificant or already fairly covered by the broadcaster.

Though the DNC decision dealt with editorial advertising, it also thwarted attempts to apply the fairness doctrine to areas of product advertising.

The movement was further stifled by the National Citizens Committee for Broadcasting v. Federal Communications Commission, 567 F.2d 1095 (1977), decision, which provided judicial support for the FCC's 1974 Fairness Report, a document that denied application of the fairness doctrine to broadcast communications promoting the sale of commercial products. According to the court of appeals:

> The Fairness Report concludes that the fairness doctrine should not

be applied to broadcast advertisements promoting the sale of a commercial product. This decision was made with a conscious awareness that it represents a marked shift from previous FCC policy. That previous policy, which was developed in a series of ad hoc decisions by the Commission and the courts, was never subject to precise articulation or definition, leading to uncertainty and difficulties in achieving full and fair enforcement. While we are under no illusion that the new policy...will solve all or perhaps even most of the implementation problems encountered heretofore, we believe that we are without warrant to deny the Commission the opportunity to attempt a new resolution of those difficulties.

The Supreme Court refused to review the National Citizens for Broadcasting case, thereby affirming that the public does not enjoy a general right to counteradvertise.

CONCLUSION

The following principles regulate communication law regarding ADVERTISING:

1. The Supreme Court protects the free flow of "commercial information" though it is less willing to protect "purely commercial" messages.

2. The principal regulatory agency for advertising is the Federal Trade Commission which monitors advertisements in an effort to protect the consumer from deceptive messages.

3. The FTC may employ several actions in an effort to regulate deceptive advertising: letter of compliance, consent order, cease and desist decree, corrective advertising.

4. Generally, there is no right of access to media for the purpose of advertising or counteradvertising.

KEY DECISIONS

1937 — STANDARD EDUCATION SOCIETY — took a strong stand against the doctrine of "*caveat emptor*"

1942 — CHRESTENSEN — determined that purely "commercial speech" enjoyed less constitutional protection than other forms of communication

1965 — COLGATE PALMOLIVE — decided that simulated
         demonstrations in television advertising must be done in
         a truthful manner

1972 — CAPITAL BROADCASTING COMPANY — decided
         that the unique characteristics of broadcast media make
         them especially subject to regulation in the public interest

1973 — DEMOCRATIC NATIONAL COMMITTEE — ruled
         that a medium that provides full and fair coverage of
         public issues is not obligated to accept any editorial
         advertisements

1974 — LEHMAN — upheld the right of transit media to select
         which types of advertising they will display

1975 — BIGELOW — eroded the "commercial speech" doctrine;
         the free flow of "commercial information" is
         constitutionally protected

1978 — NATIONAL CITIZENS FOR BROADCASTING —
         upheld FCC order that denied application of the fairness
         doctrine to broadcast communications that promote the
         sale of products

1978 — WARNER-LAMBERT — decided that the FTC has
         authority to order corrective advertising

1980 — CENTRAL HUDSON GAS — established four-stage
         analysis for determining the constitutionality of
         commercial expression

1981 — METROMEDIA — determined that while a law may
         favor one kind of commercial advertising over another, it
         may not favor commercial over noncommercial messages,
         nor may it favor one kind of noncommercial advertising
         over another

1986 — POSADAS — restricted the flow of "commercial
         information"

1997 — GLICKMAN — approved of mandatory generic
         advertising to guarantee orderly and fair marketing

RECOMMENDED READING

DiLullo, S. A., "The Present Status of Commercial Speech: Looking for a Clear Definition," Dickinson Law Review 90 (Summer, 1986), 705-730.

Hemmer, Joseph J. Jr., "Commercial Speech: Assessing the Function and Durability of the *Central Hudson* Test," Free Speech Yearbook 34 (1996), 112-130.

Konrad, Helen McGee, "Eliminating Distinctions Between Commercial and Political Speech: Replacing Regulation with Government Counterspeech," Washington and Lee Law Review 47 (Fall, 1990), 1129-1157.

Kozinzki, Alex, and Stuart Banner, "Who's Afraid of Commercial Speech?" Virginia Law Review 76 (May, 1990), 627-653.

Lively, Donald E, "The Supreme Court and Commercial Speech: New Words with an Old Message," Minnesota Law Review 72 (1987), 289-310.

Nutt, Mary B., "Trends in First Amendment Protection of Commercial Speech," Vanderbilt Law Review 41 (1988), 173-206.

Preston, Ivan L., "The Compatibility of Advertising Regulation and the First Amendment," Journal of Advertising 9 (1980), 12-15, 45.

Scammon, Debra L., and Richard J. Semenik, "Corrective Advertising: Evolution of the Legal Theory and Application of the Remedy," Journal of Advertising 11 (No. 1, 1982), 10-19.

Scharlott, Bradford W., "The First Amendment Protection of Advertising in the Mass Media," Communications and the Law 2 (Summer, 1980), 43-58.

Schiro, Richard, "Commercial Speech: The Demise of a Chimera," Supreme Court Review (1976), 45-98.

Siegel, Paul, "Smart Shopping as Patriotism: Avoidance, Denial, and Advertising," Communications and the Law 12 (June, 1990), 37-58.

Stern, Nat, "In Defense of the Imprecise Definition of Commercial Speech," Maryland Law Review 58 (1999), 55-149.

CHAPTER 14

EPILOG

The preceding chapters verify that the First Amendment has often been the focus of Supreme Court case law. This area of study has also received attention from philosophers and academicians who defined the nature, scope, and function of the First Amendment. This chapter identifies several of those theories and offers a personal critique.

THEORETICAL PERSPECTIVES

Throughout history, scholars have approached freedom-of-expression issues from a variety of philosophical bases. The resulting theories provide meaningful insight into the essence of the First Amendment. The most influential theories include: marketplace of ideas, social exchange, social utility, moral sensibilities, political expediency, self-government, expression/action dichotomy, worthy tradition, media access, and communication context.

MARKETPLACE OF IDEAS

During the early decades of the seventeenth century, censorship was practiced extensively by the Star Chamber in England. That body, operating with Parliament's approval, exercised considerable power over the licensing of printed material. In 1644, against this background, John Milton published a call for unlicensed printing. In Areopagitica, he introduced the rationale behind the marketplace of ideas theory.

> And though all the winds of doctrine were let loose to play upon the earth, so Truth be in the field, we do injuriously by licensing and prohibiting to misdoubt her strength. Let her and Falsehood

grapple; who ever knew Truth put to the worse in a free and open encounter?[1]

Almost three centuries later, the theory was supported and clarified by Justice Oliver Wendell Holmes in <u>Abrams v. United States</u>, 40 S.Ct. 17 (1919).

> But when men have realized that time has upset many fighting faiths, they may come to believe even more than they believe the very foundations of their own conduct that the ultimate good desired is better reached by free trade in ideas — that the best test of truth is the power of the thought to get itself accepted in the competition of the market, and that truth is the only ground upon which their wishes safely can be carried out. That at any rate is the theory of our Constitution.

The marketplace of ideas notion holds that the First Amendment was designed to allow ideas to enter the marketplace freely, where the public can pick and choose from among contrasting views. Out of such competition, truth hopefully will emerge and win out over error. Proponents of this theory argue that the First Amendment rests on the assumption that the widest possible dissemination of information from diverse sources is essential to the welfare of society. And, it is the purpose and function of the First Amendment to preserve an uninhibited marketplace of ideas in which truth will ultimately prevail.

SOCIAL EXCHANGE

Nineteenth-century philosopher John Stuart Mill described a related concept of free expression; he stressed the importance of social exchange. According to Mill, citizens can trade false ideas for true ones only if they can hear the true ones. An open exchange of ideas guarantees that both false and true ideas are expressed.

> If all mankind minus one were of one opinion, and only one person were of the contrary opinion, mankind would be no more justified in silencing that one person, than he, if he had the power, would be justified in silencing mankind.... But the peculiar evil of silencing the expression of an opinion is, that it is robbing the human race: posterity as well as the existing generation; those who dissent from the opinion, still more than those who hold it. If the opinion is right, they are deprived of the opportunity of exchanging error for truth; if wrong, they lose, what is almost as great a benefit, the clearer perception and livelier impression of truth, produced by its collision with error.[2]

Social exchange theory recognizes the importance of providing the public with a variety of political, moral, and aesthetic ideas. Fundamental to this end is a free flow of information. Proponents of the theory argue that the First Amendment must provide a national commitment to the principle that debate on public issues should be uninhibited, robust, and wide open.

SOCIAL UTILITY

In 1941, Zechariah Chafee, Jr., Langdell Professor of Law at Harvard University, set forth a social utility view of the First Amendment. Chafee recognized two types of expression — that which serves the individual interest and that which serves the social interest. Of the two, expression related to the social interest is by far the most important. Such expression should be restrained only when the public safety is imperiled. Chafee viewed the First Amendment as functioning to balance the societal interest in public expression against the societal interest in public order. For Chafee, the balance clearly fell on the side of public expression.

> The true meaning of freedom of speech seems to be this. One of the most important purposes of society and government is the discovery and spread of truth on subjects of general concern.... Nevertheless, there are other purposes of government, such as order, the training of the young, protection against external aggression. Unlimited discussion sometimes interferes with these purposes, which must then be balanced against freedom of speech, but freedom of speech ought to weigh very heavily in the scale. The First Amendment gives binding force to this principle of political wisdom.[3]

According to Chafee, it is useless to define the First Amendment in terms of rights. Instead, the facts of the situation play heavily in each case. For example, in times of war, the dissenter asserts a constitutional right to be heard, while the government asserts a constitutional right to wage war. The deadlock must be resolved. Chafee recommends a process of balancing the competing social interests.

> The true boundary line of the First Amendment can be fixed only when Congress and the courts realize that the principle on which speech is classified as lawful or unlawful involves the balancing against each other of two very important social interests, in public safety and in the search for truth. Every reasonable attempt should be made to maintain both interests unimpaired, and the great interest in free speech should be sacrificed only when the interest in public safety is really imperiled, and not...when it is barely conceivable that it may be slightly affected.[4]

For example, in wartime, expression should be unrestricted "unless it is clearly liable to cause direct and dangerous interference with the conduct of the war." Chafee thus suggests the point at which the social utility theory places the boundary line for freedom of expression — it is established close to the point where expression gives rise to unlawful acts.

MORAL SENSIBILITIES

Walter Berns, Professor of Political Science at Louisiana State University, held that it was the duty of the courts to render moral decisions while interpreting the First Amendment. To Berns, a major fault of adjudication rested with the tendency to view freedom in general, and free expression in particular, as unassailable foundations of American government. As a result, justices "refuse to distinguish between the inherent worth of the ideas expressed." The result is detrimental.

> So long as the judge holds that freedom of speech, press, and religion are basic or matters in which government cannot concern itself, there is no room for a consideration of the dignity and value of the particular speech, press or religion. Prudence is excluded; justice difficult to obtain; and decency irrelevant. Instead, "the character of the *right* involved" determines the standards governing the case.[5]

Berns suggested an alternate criterion to freedom, that being virtue. Berns argued that the principal duty of government should be the formation of character, and moral education is the means of achieving that duty. The judicial system should contribute to moral education by evaluating expression in terms of its virtue. Berns conceded that the proscription of non-virtuous speech might include the abridgement of some virtuous speech, but the court would be in a position to prohibit the former and permit the latter "if it developed principles that recognize the difference between virtue and vice." Overall, the question of virtue should provide the focal point for court interpretation.

POLITICAL EXPEDIENCY

Leonard W. Levy, Andrew W. Mellon Professor of Humanities and Chairman of the Graduate Faculty of History at Claremont Graduate School, contended that states' rights constituted the motivating force behind adoption of the First Amendment. He argued that the drafters, in choosing the words "Congress shall make no law" were focusing on the term "Congress" rather than placing emphasis on the words "no law." The founding fathers sought to restrain Congress, but not necessarily the state legislatures, nor the other branches of the federal government. The intent of the framers had little to do with protecting free expression, other than providing protection against prior restraints. In 1960, Levy described this theory as follows:

> I find that libertarian theory from the time of Milton to the

ratification of the First Amendment substantially accepted the right of the state to suppress seditious libel.... The evidence drawn particularly from the period 1776 to 1791 indicates that the generation that framed the first state declarations of rights and the First Amendment was hardly as libertarian as we have traditionally assumed. They did not intend to give free rein to criticism of the government that might be deemed seditious libel, although the concept of seditious libel was — and still is — the principal basis of muzzling political dissent. There is even reason to believe that the Bill of Rights was more the chance product of political expediency on all sides than of principled commitment to personal liberties. A broad libertarian theory of freedom of speech and the press did not emerge in the United States until the Jeffersonians, when a minority party, were forced to defend themselves against the Federalist Sedition Act of 1798.[6]

Twenty-five years later, Levy modified his position slightly. He acknowledged that the colonial press actually enjoyed considerable freedom and the framers of the First Amendment intended to protect publication from criminal liability even after it appeared in print, not just from the perils of prior restraint. Nonetheless, Levy stuck to his original conclusion that the framers did not adopt libertarian views until debate took place in Congress over enactment of the alien and sedition laws. Accordingly, Levy viewed the First Amendment as a "lucky political accident."[7]

SELF-GOVERNMENT

Alexander Meiklejohn, Professor of Philosophy at the University of Wisconsin, recognized two types of expression: public and private. Both types are entitled to different levels of protection. Public expression enhances self-government and is entitled to absolute protection. According to Meiklejohn, the First Amendment's principal function is to provide citizens with the opportunity to discuss society's problems. Only then are citizens exposed to the information that is necessary to make the informed judgments on which self-government depends. Meiklejohn identified four categories of public expression:

Education, in all its phases, is the attempt to so inform and cultivate the mind and will of a citizen that he shall have the wisdom, the independence, and, therefore, the dignity of a governing citizen. Freedom of education is...a basic postulate in the planning of a free society.

The achievements of philosophy and the sciences in creating knowledge and understanding of men and their world must be made available, without abridgement, to every citizen.

Literature and the arts must be protected by the First Amendment. They lead the way toward sensitive and informed appreciation and

> response to the values out of which the riches of the general welfare
> are created.
> Public discussions of public issues, together with the spreading of
> information and opinion bearing on those issues, must have a
> freedom unabridged by our agents.[8]

Private expression, on the other hand, such as the advertisement of
vendors selling a product, is not within the scope of the First
Amendment, and can be regulated. Meiklejohn recognized two types of
expression (public and private), but he maintained that their
constitutional status differed radically.

EXPRESSION/ACTION DICHOTOMY

Thomas Emerson, Lines Professor Emeritus of Law at Yale
University, enunciated a theory that is based on the distinction between
expression and action. Emerson believed that the First Amendment
should help maintain four social values: assuring individual self-
fulfillment, attaining the truth, securing participation in decision
making, and providing balance between stability and change.[9]
According to Emerson, these social values can be realized only if
expression receives full protection under the First Amendment.
Emerson's theory distinguishes between expression and action.

> The central idea of a system of expression is that a fundamental
> distinction must be drawn between conduct which consists of
> "expression" and conduct which consists of "action."
> "Expression" must be freely allowed and encouraged. "Action" can
> be controlled, subject to other constitutional requirements, but not
> by controlling expression.[10]

Emerson demanded that expression be safeguarded against curtailments
at all points, even when expression conflicts with social interests that
the government is charged with protecting. The government may
protect such interests — for example, public safety and order —
through suppressing action, but not by regulating expression.

WORTHY TRADITION

Harry Kalven, Jr., Professor of Law at the University of Chicago,
viewed freedom of expression as more than a theory; it is a tradition,
and, in fact, the worthiest tradition in American law. Kalven noted the
numerous on-going arguments which center around First Amendment
issues. He realized that the Supreme Court "has not fashioned a
single, general theory which would explain all of its decisions; rather,
it has floated different principles for different problems." Kalven treated
First Amendment controversies not only as inevitable, but also as
desirable — they provide evidence of the vitality of the tradition and

serve as a means of furthering that vitality.

> Altogether apart from resolution of the point at issue, such
> controversies serve a range of functions. By dramatizing the
> tradition, they serve as vehicles for its transmission. They often
> provide extended occasions for that "counterspeech" which classic
> First Amendment doctrine prescribes as the appropriate remedy for
> evil speech short of outright incitement to criminal action....
> Perhaps most important, they are occasions for renewing our
> understanding of the norm, for articulating it anew.[11]

Kalven envisioned tradition-as-argument; he saw the Supreme Court at
the center of the debate, and passionately identified with the Court as
that institution from which evolved new First Amendment doctrine.

MEDIA ACCESS

Jerome Barron, Professor of Law at George Washington University,
introduced a media access theory of the First Amendment. Barron
claimed that inequality exists among the members of society in terms
of their power to communicate ideas. Changes in the communications
industry, especially the technological development and growth of media
coupled with the rise of media oligopoly, have altered the
"equilibrium" in the market place of ideas. The commercial nature of
the mass media industry makes it difficult to give full expression to a
wide spectrum of public opinion. Barron argued that when commercial
considerations lead the media to suppress ideas, the function of the
First Amendment is thwarted.

> The "marketplace of ideas" has rested on the assumption that
> protecting the right of expression is equivalent to providing for it.
> But changes in the communications industry have destroyed the
> equilibrium in that marketplace.... A realistic view of the first
> amendment requires recognition that a right of expression is
> somewhat thin if it can be exercised only at the sufferance of the
> managers of mass communication.[12]

Barron favored interpreting the First Amendment in terms of the rights
of the public, rather than the rights of media owners and operators. He
called for a right-of-access statute that would forbid the mass media
from arbitrarily denying space in print media or time on broadcast
media. Such legislation would guarantee an effective forum for the
expression of divergent opinions. This type of governmental regulation
of media would promote vigorous debate and expression at a level
consistent with the meaning of the First Amendment.

COMMUNICATION CONTEXT

Franklyn Haiman, Professor of Communication Studies at

Northwestern University, offered a communication context theory of the First Amendment. Haiman rejected the notion that there are specific categories of expression, which, by definition, are always unlawful. Instead, he argued that the particular context in which expression occurs provides the basis for limitation or freedom. Haiman identified four contexts and offered a basic principle that applies in each context:

> Communication About Other People — Unless the harm done by an act of communication is direct, immediate, irreparable, and of a serious material nature, the remedy in a free society should be "more speech." The law is an inappropriate tool for dealing with expression which produces mental distress or whose targets are the beliefs and values of an audience.
>
> Communication To Other People — Unless deprived of free choice by deception, physical coercion, or an impairment of normal capacities, individuals in a free society are responsible for their own behavior. They are not objects which can be triggered into action by symbolic stimuli but human beings who decide how they will respond to the communication they see and hear.
>
> Communication And Social Order — So long as there is a free marketplace of ideas, where the widest possible range of information and alternatives is available, individuals will be the best judges of their own interests. The law is properly used to enrich and expand the communications marketplace and to insure that it remains an open system.
>
> Government Involvement in the Communication Marketplace — Government in a free society is the servant of the people and its power should not be used to inhibit, distort, or dominate public discourse. There must be a compelling justification whenever the government requires unwilling communication of its people or withholds information in its possession from them.[13]

In the vast majority of instances, Haiman upheld the side of freedom. Haiman concluded that the implementation of these principles requires "a strong and vigilant citizenry." Safeguarding the function of the First Amendment rests, to no small degree, in the hands of the citizens.

OVERVIEW

The theories discussed in this section, though derived from varied assumptions, tend to recognize five basic principles:

1. The First Amendment guarantee of free expression is essential for the preservation of U.S. society.
2. A liberal interpretation of the First Amendment, one that favors free expression over competing concerns, is in the best interests of society.
3. The First Amendment should provide for robust debate — the free exchange of varied views.

4. Public expression (social interests) enjoys more freedom than private expression (individual interests).
5. Government regulation of the First Amendment may suppress action, but not expression.

SOCIAL RESPONSIBILITY — A PERSONAL PERSPECTIVE

The First Amendment, and the extent to which that standard protects freedom of expression in the United States, has been the subject of extensive discussion and debate. Two somewhat contradictory approaches have emerged as the principal foci of academic and judicial thought.

The first approach views freedom of expression as a right that is guaranteed by the First Amendment, a right that is absolute and which should not be subjected to any form of regulation. This approach, the philosophical stance of civil libertarians, holds that the best solution to evil or harmful speech is more speech. The approach receives support from academic and philosophical theories presented earlier in this epilog. For example, the "marketplace of ideas" concept assumes that truth will emerge from the widest possible dissemination of information. The "social exchange" theory favors an open exchange of both true and false ideas so that truth will emerge victorious in its collision with falsehood. The "expression/action dichotomy" notion acknowledges that while action may be regulated, expression must be freely allowed and encouraged. The "worthy tradition" idea holds that counterspeech is the suitable remedy for evil speech. The "communication context" theory also supports "more speech" as the preferred remedy for most harms that result from communicative acts.

This approach also receives endorsement from respected Supreme Court jurists. Justice Hugo Black held that "the Federal Government is without any power whatever under the Constitution to put any type of burden on speech and expression of ideas of any kind" (Ginzburg). He also claimed: "Both the history and language of the First Amendment support the view that the press must be left free to publish news, whatever the source, without censorship, injunctions, or prior restraints" (New York Times). Justice William Douglas agreed, arguing that "the First Amendment allows all ideas to be expressed whether orthodox, popular, offbeat, or repulsive." Under the U.S. Constitution, "all regulation of control of expression is barred" (Ginzburg).

The second approach views free expression as a right that must be practiced responsibly in a multicultural society where individuals shape personal esteem, form relationships, and make politco-economic decisions on the basis of communicative behavior. The "social responsibility" approach holds that while more speech is a desirable solution for harmful speech, regulation may be essential in some instances. For the most part, this has been the historical performance of federal adjudication. Supreme Court opinions reveal that freedom of expression is not absolutely free. Various justices have applied limiting judicial tests to the right of expression. In Gitlow, Justice Edward Sanford espoused the "bad tendency" test, a standard that conferred low priority to freedom of expression. According to Sanford, any expression that had a tendency to lead to substantial evil should be "nipped in the bud." Justice Oliver Wendell Holmes introduced the "clear and present danger" test in Schenck, noting that a government may punish expression "that produces or is intending to produce a clear and imminent danger that it will bring about forthwith certain substantive evils." Holmes cited a classic example: "The most stringent protection of free speech would not protect a man in falsely shouting fire in a theatre and causing a panic." The "balancing" test, fashioned by Justice Fred Vinson in Douds, recognizes that when other rights conflict with the right to free expression — for example, the right to a fair trial, right to privacy, right to peace and order — the competing rights should be balanced to determine which has priority. Another standard, the "preferred position" test, places expression in a position of prominence but acknowledges that free speech is not absolutely free. In Kovacs, Justice Stanley Reed noted:

> The preferred position of freedom of speech in a society that cherishes liberty for all does not require legislators to be insensible to claims by citizens to comfort and convenience. To enforce freedom of speech in disregard of the rights of others would be harsh and arbitrary in itself.

The opinions of Justices Sanford, Holmes, Vinson, and Reed recognize that while individuals are entitled to the right of free expression, failure to use that right responsibly may lead to restriction of the freedom to communicate.

In addition, Court decisions have identified specific forms of expression that are subject to regulation. In Konigsberg, Justice John Harlan acknowledged that "certain forms of speech, or speech in certain contexts, has been considered outside the scope of constitutional protection." In Chaplinsky, Justice Frank Murphy identified "certain well-defined and narrowly limited classes of speech, the prevention and punishment of which has never been thought to raise any Constitutional problem." He cited as examples "the lewd and obscene, the profane, the libelous, and the insulting or fighting words." In Roth, Justice William Brennan affirmed that libel and obscenity fall "outside the protection intended for speech and press." In Chrestensen,

Justice Owen Roberts limited the protection awarded to "commercial speech." The Brandenburg *per curiam* held that speech may be restricted when "such advocacy is directed to inciting or producing imminent lawless action and is likely to incite or produce such action." In Ferber, Justice Byron White approved "the regulation of pornographic depictions of children." And, in Beauharnais, Justice Felix Frankfurter affirmed the punishment of "criminal group libel." The conclusion to be drawn from this survey of judicial opinions is that expression which falls within specific categories — obscenity, defamation, fighting words, commercial speech, advocacy of criminality, child pornography, group libel — enjoys less protection than other forms of expression.

The Supreme Court has consistently supported a two-tiered approach to expression. Tier one includes worthless expression, that which has little, if any, social value. It consists of the forms of expression cited above. Tier two consists of worthwhile expression, that which has social value. This category includes such communication as gathering and disseminating news, education of the citizenry, political debate of controversial issues, public assembly and peaceful protest, petition related to a redress of grievances, and utilization of airwaves in the public interest. Communicative behavior that falls within the second tier receives greater protection because it is perceived to be of greater value, more socially responsible expression.

It seems clear that First Amendment protection of free expression is the fundamental bedrock to the democratic form of government that is cherished in the United States. Nonetheless, with that right comes responsibility. I agree with libertarian scholars who claim that the best and preferred remedy for bad speech is more speech. Society should provide educational programs as well as public forums devoted to increased understanding of the nature, scope, and function of expression in a free society. Communities, campuses, workplaces, and other societal environments should encourage an atmosphere of free and open discussion between different viewpoints and different cultures.

Yet, it seems naive to think that the right to more communication will resolve all bad speech. More expression may, in fact, exacerbate the situation. The right to more speech may function as motivation for additional bad speech. The remedy of more speech seems counter productive when it provokes further abuse because the communicator, whether an individual or institution, is in a position of authority over the victim/s. Some individuals, without fear of sanction, may choose to repeatedly demean, defame, or denigrate a hapless victim, who must remain subjected to such abuse. Some individuals, faced with no restriction, may continue to advocate the violent overthrow of the government, or persist in urging colleagues to engage in criminal behavior. Some individuals may feel no compunction to cease distribution of obscene literature or deceptive advertisements. Or, an uncontrolled government may invade an individual's privacy, lie to the public, censor news, and/or refuse to release vital data to the public. In all such instances, regulations which compel responsible expression may be both useful and desirable.

NOTES

1. Milton, John <u>Areopagitica,</u> ed. by Edward Arber. London: English Reprints, 1868, p. 74.

2. Mill, John Stuart, <u>On Liberty,</u> ed. by David Spitz. New York: Norton, 1975.

3. Chafee, Zechariah, Jr., <u>Free Speech in the United States</u> Cambridge: Harvard University Press, 1941, p. 31.

4. <u>Ibid.</u>, p. 35.

5. Berns, Walter, <u>Freedom, Virtue, and the First Amendment</u> Baton Rouge: Louisiana State University, 1957, pp. 249-250.

6. Levy, Leonard W., <u>Legacy of Suppression: Freedom of Speech and Press in Early American History</u> Cambridge: Harvard University Press, 1960, pp. vii-viii.

7. Levy, Leonard W., <u>Emergence Of A Free Press</u> New York: Oxford University Press, 1985, p. xii.

8. Meiklejohn, Alexander, "The First Amendment is an Absolute," <u>Supreme Court Review</u> (1961). 256-57. See also <u>Free Speech and Its Relation to Self Government</u>. New York: Harper and Brothers, 1948; and <u>Political Freedom: The Constitutional Powers of the People</u>. New York: Harper, 1960.

9. Emerson, Thomas I., <u>Toward a General Theory of the First Amendment</u>. New York: Vintage Books, 1966, pp. 3-15.

10. Emerson, Thomas I., <u>The System of Freedom of Expression</u>. New York: Vintage Books, 1970. P. 17. See also "The Affirmative Side of the First Amendment," <u>Georgia Law Review</u> 15 (1981), 795-849.

11. Kalven, Harry, Jr., <u>A Worthy Tradition: Freedom of Speech in America</u> New York: Harper and Row, 1988, p. xxi. See also "Tradition in Law," in <u>The Great Ideas Today</u> ed. by R. Hutchins and M. Adler, Chicago: Encyclopedia Britannica, 1974, pp. 21-34.

12. Barron, Jerome A., "Access to the Press — A New First Amendment Right," <u>Harvard Law Review</u> 80 (June, 1967), 1647-48. See also <u>Freedom of the Press for Whom? The Right of Access to Mass Media</u>. Bloomington: Indiana University Press, 1973.

13. Haiman, Franklyn S., <u>Speech and Law in a Free Society</u>. Chicago: University of Chicago Press, 1981, pp. 425-26.

INDEX OF CASES

Forsyth County, Georgia v. The Nationalist Movement, 64
Fortnightly Corporation v. United Artists Television, 248, 249, 259
Fortune; Molpus v., 79
Fort Wayne Books v. Indiana, 113
44 Liquormark, Inc., v. Rhode Island, 380, 381
Fox v. Board of Trustees of the State University of New York, 370, 381
Franklin Computer Corporation; Apple Computer v., 253
Franklin Mint v. National Wildlife Art Exchange, 237
Fraser; Bethel School District v., 90, 93-94, 99
Freedman v. Maryland, 110, 111, 120, 126
Freedom Newspapers, Inc.; McNamara v., 211-212
Freeman; Burson v., 153
Frena; Playboy Enterprises v., 254
Friede; Commonwealth v., 102
Friede; People v., 102
Friends of the Earth v. Federal Communications Commission, 392-393
Frisby v. Schultz, 61
Frohwerk v. United States, 20
Fujishima v. Board of Education, 92-93
FW/PBS v. City of Dallas, 111

G
Galella v. Onassis, 199-200
Gannett v. DePasquale, 284
Garrison v. Louisiana, 174-175, 176
Geanakos; Keefe v., 82, 83
Georgia; Jenkins v., 108
Georgia; Stanley v., 118, 120, 121, 127
Georgia; Wood v., 309, 310
Gernsback; Thompson v., 243
Gertz v. Welch, 4, 182-183, 184, 185, 197
Gibson v. Florida Legislative Investigation Committee, 46-47
Gilleo; City of Ladue v., 156-157, 160
Ginsberg v. New York, 83, 117, 118
Ginzburg v. United States, 15, 116, 126, 405
Ginzburg; Goldwater v., 168
Gitlow v. New York, 2, 11-12, 20-21, 24, 43, 406
Givhan v. Western Line Consolidated School District, 86, 87, 99
Glen Theatre, Inc.; Barnes v., 124
Glickman v. Wileman Brothers & Elliott, 388, 395
Glines; Brown v., 141-142
Globe Newspaper Company v. Superior Court for the County of Norfolk, 285, 286
Globe Publishing Company; Gobin v., 166
Gobin v. Globe Publishing Company, 166
Gobitis; Minersville School District v., 74
Goguen; Smith v., 37
Goldstein v. California, 250
Goldwater v. Ginzburg, 168
Gooding v. Wilson, 27
Goodson; Wood v., 310
Goodwill Stations, 351
Goss v. Lopez, 90, 96-97, 99
Grace; United States v., 152